The Filth of Progress

The publisher gratefully acknowledges the generous support of the Director's Circle of the University of California Press Foundation, whose members are:

Lloyd Cotsen
Richard E. Damm & Sara Duryea Damm
John & Jo De Luca
Harriett & Richard Gold
Gary & Cary Hart
Fred M. Levin & Nancy Livingston / The Shenson Fdn
David Littlejohn
James & Carlin Naify
Margaret L. Pillsbury
Lucinda Reinold
Marc & Rowena Singer
Larry & Rosalie Vanderhoef
John & Priscilla Walton

The Filth of Progress

IMMIGRANTS, AMERICANS, AND THE BUILDING OF
CANALS AND RAILROADS IN THE WEST

Ryan Dearinger

UNIVERSITY OF CALIFORNIA PRESS

University of California Press, one of the most distinguished university presses in the United States, enriches lives around the world by advancing scholarship in the humanities, social sciences, and natural sciences. Its activities are supported by the UC Press Foundation and by philanthropic contributions from individuals and institutions. For more information, visit www.ucpress.edu.

University of California Press
Oakland, California

Library of Congress Cataloging-in-Publication Data

Dearinger, Ryan, 1979- author.
 The filth of progress : immigrants, Americans, and the building of canals and railroads in the West / Ryan Dearinger.—First edition.
    pages   cm
 Includes bibliographical references and index.
    ISBN 978–0–520–28459–3 (cloth : alk. paper)—ISBN 0–520–28459–3 (cloth : alk. paper)—ISBN 978–0–520–28460–9 (pbk. : alk. paper)—ISBN 0–520–28460–7 (pbk. : alk. paper)—ISBN 978–0–520–96037–4 (ebook)—ISBN 0–520–96037–8 (ebook)
    1. Canal construction workers—United States—History.   2. Railroad construction workers—United States—History.   3. Foreign workers—United States—History.   4. Canals—United States—History.
5. Railroads—United States—History.   I. Title.
    HD8039.C2582U62 2016
    331.6′20978—dc23   2015011849

25 24 23 22 21 20 19 18 17 16
10 9 8 7 6 5 4 3 2 1

For Jessica, Taylor, and Ryder

In loving memory of Jason Douglas Gritten (1979–2015)

CONTENTS

ILLUSTRATIONS

FIGURES

MAPS

TABLE

ACKNOWLEDGMENTS

So often we overlook the work and significance of those who are not in professional jobs, of those who are not in the so-called big jobs. But let me say to you tonight, that whenever you are engaged in work that serves humanity and is for the building of humanity, it has dignity and it has worth. One day our society must come to see this.

DR. MARTIN LUTHER KING JR.
Memphis, Tennessee, March 18, 1968

This book has been many years in the making, and its publication gives me the opportunity to thank the folks who inspired and shaped it. My ideas and arguments have developed over a decade-long journey in libraries, archives, classrooms, and offices, as well as in stimulating discussions with teachers, colleagues, and students. In terms of the research and writing, the road was long, rugged, and often seemed impassable. Because of the book's elusive subject matter, I was prepared for a difficult voyage. Yet I struggled far more than I ever envisioned, had fits and starts, and agonized over every idea and then over every paragraph, sentence, and word. Histories, like canals and railroads, require knowledge, toil, and perseverance. Humans have to create them, refine them, bring them to life, and then evaluate them. They do not magically appear, nor are they self-evident or without problems. A colleague once told me that writing in history is not poetry but carpentry; it demands the strain of both mind and muscle and the sweat of brow. Crafting this book has reminded me that whether the work is mental or physical, reliant on picks and shovels or pens and keyboards, all labor has dignity and worth.

It is difficult to find the words to express my thanks to the teachers, professors, librarians, archivists, colleagues, friends, and family members who made this project possible. Nonetheless, the best place to start is Fort Vancouver High School in Vancouver, Washington. I want to express my gratitude to the fellow Trappers who influenced my life in meaningful ways. My classmates and I were fortunate indeed to grow up in a time and at a place where a challenging liberal arts education was among society's greatest virtues and responsibilities.

My training as a historian began fifteen years ago at George Fox University in Newberg, Oregon. There, Kerry Irish, Ralph Beebe, Mark Weinert, and David Peterson Del Mar introduced me to U.S. history, the nineteenth century in particular, and to the problematic history of violence in America. I am grateful to them for sending me down those trails, and for being such fine teachers. Another mentor, Mark David Hall, first encouraged me to apply to graduate school, and I cannot thank him enough for his guidance. I also owe more than I can say to Pat Bailey, Mike Thompson, Luke Wolf, and my classmates and teammates at George Fox.

At Purdue University in West Lafayette, Indiana, where I pursued my master's degree, I worked with a number of wonderful people. My adviser, Michael A. Morrison, stuck his neck out and somehow found a way to secure funding for a student with much ambition but little practice. His faith in me strengthened my fortitude immeasurably. Mike still ranks as the best classroom teacher I have encountered, and his ability to bring nineteenth-century political history to life has inspired my own efforts. Frank Lambert, a remarkable scholar and teacher, sharpened my grasp of historiography and my writing and analytical skills with the same talent and precision that helped him boom footballs as a punter for the Pittsburgh Steelers. Nancy Gabin introduced me to the fields of labor history and gender studies, exercised tremendous patience with my earliest conference papers and journal articles, and taught me more than I ever imagined about history and academia. John Lauritz Larson deserves special mention. I am unsure whether to thank or blame him for encouraging me to pursue this project, but John played a greater role in my development as a young historian than he would ever admit. It was in his research seminar where we first wrestled with the idea of crafting a history of the immigrants who toiled in the mud and muck to build America, with the paradox of progress, and with Indiana's ill-fated Wabash & Erie Canal. His guidance, joyful criticism, and encouragement convinced me that I was, to use the words he scribbled on my final seminar draft, "on to something with legs." I only hope to have proved him right. At Purdue I was also surrounded by fellow graduate students who nurtured and challenged me. Andrew Busch, Carson Cunningham, Ryan Anderson, Jim Buss, Scott Randolph, Renee Searfoss, Alex Demonte, Carla Hostetler, Erin Kempker, and others supported and improved this project in some way and helped cultivate a wonderful graduate community. I'll never forget our memorable postclass meetings at Chumley's across the Wabash River in Lafayette, a place we closed down with regularity.

At the University of Utah, where this project grew in scope and significance, I was surrounded by people who believed in my ability to carry it out. I offer thanks to my fellow travelers in the graduate program, especially Benny Harris, James Seaman, Jon Moyer, Michael Van Wagenen, Mark Christensen, Alan Morrell, and J.B. Haws. Two special Utes, Annie Hanshew and Murry Warhank, are in a class by themselves. Choosing the PhD program there was one of my wisest academic decisions, and my doctoral committee merits endless praise and thanks for steering an ambitious project over a long haul. Eric Hinderaker, who served as department chair for most of my time at Utah, is among the most amazing scholars, teachers, and human beings I have ever known. From the moment I entered old Carlson Hall until the day I departed the sparkling new Tanner Building and earned my doctorate, Eric was there to support me, and his generosity was limitless. Rebecca Horn expanded my horizons by training me in Latin American history and situating my research in a comparative context. I totally lucked out when the department hired two rising stars in western history, Matt Basso and Paul Reeve, as I began my dissertation research. They proceeded to deplete the department's stock of pens while marking up every draft I produced. Their work on race, ethnicity, and gender in the West has been an inspiration for my own. During the past decade, my graduate adviser, Robert Alan Goldberg, has had a tremendous impact on me and on this study. Bob pushed me to stretch my capabilities, inspired me with his infectious personality, and strengthened this project beyond what I thought was possible. More than any other person, Bob helped me realize the goal of becoming a historian. I will never forget our years together at Utah, and while I am grateful to have him as a friend, he will always be my teacher.

Researching and writing this book demanded more time, energy, patience, and support than I ever anticipated. It also required luck. Without generous funding from multiple sources, this project would have died on the vine. I want to thank the graduate schools and history departments at Purdue

University and the University of Utah, the Marriner S. Eccles Graduate Fellowship Committee, the Tanner Humanities Center at Utah, the American Heritage Center at the University of Wyoming, the Western History Association, the American Historical Association, the Newberry Library, the Charles Redd Center for Western Studies, and Eastern Oregon University for the monetary support that allowed me to travel, research, and write. I am also grateful for the support of the EOU Foundation, which generously picked up the tab for the maps and illustrations that grace the pages of this volume.

Archival materials are far more accessible today than they were when I began this project, and the lion's share of my research straddled the eclipse of the print age by the digital era. Microfilms, rare documents, original manuscripts, those little white reading room gloves, and plenty of dust figured prominently in this study. Online historical newspaper projects and other digital collections, equipped with full-text searching, came too late for this historian, who spent an inordinate amount of time parked at a microfilm machine. When Stanford University unveiled its impressive (and ongoing) digital archive devoted to Chinese railroad workers in North America, I combed through the documents with a degree of bitterness (I had located nearly all of them in their original form) before I came to my senses and agreed that research is made more democratic, and scholarship more relevant, through the judicious use of technology. Still, I can rest assured knowing that, like the workers this book examines, I did it the hard way. My sincerest gratitude goes out to archivists, librarians, and staff at Purdue's HSSE Library; the Indiana State Library; the Indiana Historical Society; the Illinois State Archives; the Library of Congress; the Chicago Historical Society; the Newberry Library; the Beinecke Rare Book and Manuscript Library at Yale University; the Denver Public Library; the Colorado Historical Society; Coe Library and the American Heritage Center at the University of Wyoming; the Wyoming State Archives; the Stanford University Libraries; the Bancroft Library, University of California Libraries, and the Phoebe A. Hearst Museum of Anthropology at Berkeley; the California State Library; the California State Railroad Museum and Library; the Oakland Museum of California; the Chinese Historical Society of America in San Francisco; the Utah State Historical Society; the Archives of the Church of Jesus Christ of Latter-day Saints; the Merill-Cazier Library at Utah State University; the Marriott Library at the University of Utah; the Washington State University Libraries in Pullman; and the Becker

Collection at Boston College. I am also indebted to Jeffery McDonald, the tireless interlibrary loan specialist at Eastern Oregon University, and to the Pierce Library staff, for enduring the largest ongoing book order in the history of the university.

Constructive criticism from the wider scholarly community enhanced this project at every turn. Early on, I made the decision to present the chapters of this book at conferences and seminars—still the most reliable venues for critical discourse—rather than unveil them as journal articles. Panelists, commentators, and audience members at annual meetings of the American Historical Association, the Western History Association, and the Pacific Coast Branch of the AHA made invaluable suggestions that strengthened my research and arguments. I offer particular thanks to Nayan Shah, Thomas Andrews, Mark Fiege, Monica Rico, Matt Basso, Richard Orsi, Annie Hanshew, Katy Fry, and Brian Leech. I am similarly indebted to Rick Ewig at the American Heritage Center and Bob Goldberg at the Tanner Humanities Center for inviting me to present this project in its earliest, and roughest, form. Portions of two chapters survived the scrutiny of scholars at a 2011 seminar on immigration in the Far West sponsored by the Charles Redd Center for Western Studies. Thanks go to Brian Q. Cannon and Jessie Embry for organizing the seminar and to Michelle Charest, Mindi Sitterud-McCluskey, Phylis Martinelli, Brenden Rensink, Matt Basso, and the other participants who offered valuable tips and made me rethink explanations.

I always imagined publishing this book with the University of California Press, and now that I have, I cannot imagine working with anyone else. I am forever indebted to my editor, Niels Hooper, for turning my dream into a reality and for pushing me to refine my arguments, marshal better evidence, enliven the story, and reconsider my audience. Kim Hogeland, Bradley Depew, and Francisco Reinking deserve thanks for steering this project in a creative direction, answering endless emails and questions, and exercising the utmost patience. Susan Silver, a master copyeditor, polished the rough edges of this book, exorcised every grammatical and stylistic mistake, and made me look good. Niels assembled an all-star lineup of external reviewers, for whom I am incredibly grateful. Katherine Benton-Cohen and two anonymous reviewers read through several iterations of the manuscript and pulled no punches, challenging me to clarify my thinking and enhance my analysis while saving me from all sorts of embarrassing errors and omissions. Katie deserves extra special thanks, because she really let me have it, and much of the rethinking and rewriting came as a result of her trenchant critique of the original manuscript. Several tries later I finally got it right, and the book is infinitely better due to her many suggestions. As always, the buck stops here; any remaining mistakes or misinterpretations are my fault alone.

As much as I enjoyed my time in Indiana and Utah, the Pacific Northwest has always been my home. I am forever indebted to Greg Monahan and Rebecca Hartman, who helped bring me back to my native soil, and to my wonderful students and colleagues at Eastern Oregon University, who have helped make the tranquil, mountainous small college town of La Grande my home. I have had the pleasure of teaching so many excellent students, several of whom are now fine teachers, as I worked on *The Filth of Progress,* and the book is better because of what I have learned from them. A heavy teaching schedule over the past several years made it difficult to finish this project, but my students have kept me on my toes, interrogated my interpretations, and reminded me that history is contested terrain. Whether they have known it or not, students like Deneil Hill, Andrew Yoder, Jeff Ranstrom, Maggie Byrd, Aislinn Becktold, Suzanna Keithley, Brook Smith, Kaely Cox, Dominic Clay, Kyle Swartz, Robby Perry, and Cassie Jeffries have been my discussants in grappling with the problems of class, race, gender, labor, capitalism, immigration, and progress in the American West. Students and faculty are the lifeblood of EOU, and since 2009 I have been a proud member of a history department that has shaped this place in meaningful ways. For teaching me, challenging me, inspiring me, and making me laugh until it hurts, my gratitude goes out to Greg Monahan, Rebecca Hartman, Nicole Howard, Phil Travis, and Matt Schauer. Thank you for creating an intellectual community and an egalitarian culture I have yet to see replicated in any department, anywhere.

For years upon years my family has paved a right-of-way with hard work, integrity, compassion, and humor. My parents, Dan and Glenda Dearinger, veteran educators, brought history to life for me at an early age, nurtured my ceaseless curiosity, and sacrificed so that I could receive the best education possible. They have given me love, guidance, and support extending from the corridors of Fort Vancouver to the plains of Indiana and to the mountains of Utah and back. My in-laws, Courtney Dearinger; John, Debbie, Joel, and Ashley Nelson; and Julie and Nic Iannarone, have enriched my life in countless ways. My twin brother and best friend, Bryan Dearinger, has supported me emotionally and financially, joined me on research trips around the country, and has inspired me daily. Following his lead for so many years has made me a better human being, and one day I'll catch up with him so that we can work on the same campus, forever teaching those kids. The youngest generation, Calvin, Theo, Jaxon, and Brooklyn, have made my heart leap with joy.

The subject matter of this book brought me to countless historical dots on the map as a scholar. But many of the dots in the Midwest, Mountain West, and Far West mark places both familiar and special to me on a personal level. Chicago, which the Illinois & Michigan Canal transformed from a small frontier town into the nation's fastest-growing city, is among the most memorable of those places. My paternal grandfather (Asa Dearinger) and grandmother (Celia Dearinger) met in that city and shared a love of life, laughter, and history that has infected my family ever since. A 2007 summer research fellowship at the Newberry Library allowed me to reestablish my connection to the city my grandma Celia (or "Hornut," as generations called her) held especially dear. As she neared the end of her long and colorful life, grandma and I exchanged letters and phone calls during my stay at the Newberry, just blocks from Adams Street, where she grew up. That our family has long shared a respect for the dignity of labor and an appreciation for storytelling made my research in Chicago even more meaningful. I will never forget those days at the Newberry, on the city streets where my grandma came of age, knowing how proud she was of me, the grandson of a hairdresser and her husband "Ace," a barber who, in search of new opportunities, rode the rails west to Washington, where he worked as a longshoreman and later as a janitor. Similar love and guidance from my maternal grandparents, Harvey and Martha Schweigert, made me the beneficiary of the very best that family can offer. When we lost Papa Harv in the summer of 2009, I was nearing the completion of my doctoral dissertation. A World War II veteran who worked at Portland's Ameron Pipe and Construction for forty-three years, I often thought he invented hard work, and his helpfulness and loyalty never ceased to amaze me. I marched on with his memory near to my heart, and I am truly blessed to have one remaining grandparent, Gram, in the top spot as I have established my career and helped raise a wonderful family—just like she did. Thank you Hornut, Asa, Harvey, and Martha for charting tracks for all of us to follow. What a ride!

My canine editor in chief and I contemplated several of this book's most significant ideas during long walks together in Utah, many of them near the Great Salt Lake opposite of Promontory Summit, where in May 1869 the nation celebrated the meeting of the Union Pacific and Central Pacific railroads. Sadly, Haley did not survive to see this book completed, though she tried with all of her heart and might. Her successor, Trapper, has soldiered on, but even he would admit that the top position remains unfilled.

My wife, Jessica; daughter, Taylor; and son, Ryder, deserve the greatest thanks. Taylor was born during the early stages of this project, and I remember rocking her while reading and thinking late into the night. Today she reads to me and has grown into a spirited and talented second grader. Ryder, her tenderhearted and equally clever younger brother, has been an endless source of joy. Jess is the true talent of our family, an accomplished interior designer who is our rock, inspires us all, and keeps this absent-minded historian on track. The love of my life, she has contributed and sacrificed more than anyone else over the past decade. Her love, strength, and patience have known no limits. With deepest gratitude, infinite love, and laughter to last a lifetime, I have reserved for them a page of their own.

Ackerman Hall
La Grande, Oregon

ONE

———————

"Bind the Republic Together"

CANALS, RAILROADS, AND THE PARADOX OF
AMERICAN PROGRESS

Let us bind the Republic together with a perfect system of roads
and canals. . . . Let us conquer space.

JOHN C. CALHOUN, 1817

THE STORY OF CANALS AND railroads, westward expansion, and national
progress holds an enduring place in the pageant of American history. In
many respects, canals and railroads were the ultimate technologies and symbols of nineteenth-century America. The building of these early "internal
improvements" promised the triumph of U.S. labor and manhood over wilderness, distance, and time.[1] Nothing better symbolized this march toward
the future than the jubilant May 1869 Golden Spike celebration at
Promontory Summit, Utah, which marked the joining of the Central Pacific
and Union Pacific railroads. While this event honored one of America's
greatest technological achievements, numerous lesser-known celebrations
both preceded and followed the triumphant transcontinental ceremony. As
early as the 1825 completion of the Erie Canal, Americans envisioned internal
improvements as the key to progress and distinctiveness. When subsequent
canals, turnpikes, and railroads reified these dreams of progress, Americans
interpreted such improvements as the inevitable "blessings of liberty" writ
large.[2] Canal and railroad company officials, politicians, religious leaders,
and journalists were even bolder in their predictions of continued progress.
More than merely enhancing the wealth and reputation of the nation, they
argued, internal improvement projects would "bind the republic together,"
eliminate sectional differences, transform America into a powerful continental empire, and raise up God's kingdom on earth.[3]

Nineteenth-century Americans of every background considered the process of western expansion as one of the country's foundational experiences, as

instrumental as the American Revolution in shaping a national identity and charting a course for the future. Transportation projects simultaneously accelerated and validated such expansion, helping naturalize it as uniquely American. Thus, canals and railroads made the West a moving epicenter of progress; the cloud of dust, ripple of a current, puff of steam, and the transit of goods and people became its most visible manifestations.

In America's historical imagination, toil and triumph against nature and overwhelming odds characterizes such achievements as the Erie Canal and the transcontinental railroad. America's debt to the perceived architects of these technological marvels was great. Triumph transformed canal and railroad entrepreneurs into visionaries whose work brought the nation bountiful riches and did the Lord's bidding. Celebrated for their spirit and perseverance in "building" the nation's infrastructure, they found respect for looking to tomorrow and creating a future. Mountains named in their honor and statues raised in towns were fitting tributes to their patriotic efforts. For generations, most indexes of American history supported and reinforced this narrative of progress.

Yet, if this is the historical memory, it is conveniently stunted. What of those whose bodies strained and broke under the load of such glories? What of those men beyond the din and fanfare who appear only in old photographs with faces blurred and indistinguishable? In their lives and deaths in the mud, muck, and mountains is another history of American achievement. These barely visible and forgotten, ordinary men, "unskilled" immigrants from Ireland and China, Mormons, and native-born American workingmen rank, as well, as the creators of national growth and progress. Their experiences and voices, along with those of the privileged and well connected, are the subjects of this study. I examine the rise of western canals and railroads to national prominence through the menial labor of countless men, largely hidden from view because they left virtually no paper trail, who strung together livelihoods at the economic fringes of society. These men both endured and shaped the dark underbelly of progress. This book examines the contest for control of American progress and history as distilled from the competing narratives of canal and railroad construction workers and those fortunate enough to avoid this fate.

The idea of progress was imperative to Americans in the expansion-minded nineteenth century. Yet the right stuff of labor had to be consistent with the national imagination. Early nineteenth-century supporters of internal improvements praised a labor force composed of virtuous, American-born small farmers who worked overtime to build canals and railroads during lulls in the agricultural cycle. But such part-time digging and tracklaying had proven insufficient for projects that sought to promote the "general utility." Moreover, no one wanted to imagine a class of independent American men relegated to the status of ditchdiggers. For those deemed closest to God because of their nearness to his fertile soil, the brutish labor of digging ditches and laying track could only deny farmers both their independent status and holy calling. Early nineteenth-century American values suggested that republican "free men" were beholden to no one, and only independent adult white males who produced for themselves and their kin qualified for political manhood.[4]

The fact that northern and western states gradually relaxed property qualifications for suffrage by the time the Erie Canal was under construction did not diminish an earlier conception of citizenship, standing, and even personhood that distanced menial laborers, and particularly immigrants, from the American ideal, regardless of the work in which they were engaged. Scholarship on nineteenth-century political theories, namely classical liberalism and republicanism, has exposed the hypocrisy inherent in laws regulating citizenship at the state and national level. Just as universal manhood suffrage replaced property ownership as the litmus test for voting rights, forms of second-class citizenship emerged, denying personal liberties and opportunities for political participation on the basis of race, ethnicity, religion, and gender. States went so far as to insert the word "white" into statutes governing voting rights. At the same time, forms of civic inequality and national identity took shape from the deep-seated belief that America was by rights a white, Protestant country and that true American citizens were native-born men with Anglo-Saxon ancestors.[5]

Of course, one's occupation could only contribute to his social dislocation. Wielding pickaxes and shovels to clear swamps, dig ditches, move rocks, and build roadways was the work of the desperate "laboring poor," not of free and independent American men. Even worse, canal digging, in particular, had always been associated with unfree labor. Southern canals relied almost exclusively on slave labor, and as early as 1817 New York sanctioned the use of convict labor to haul stones on the Erie Canal.[6] Race and labor put Irish immigrants in a double bind, and for the first half of the nineteenth century they reacted with hostility to narratives comparing them to African Americans. The Irish immigrants and enslaved and free black men who toiled under oppressive conditions on the Chesapeake & Ohio Canal in the

1820s proved that common laborers—and the capitalist system—entertained no visions of racial harmony. As one visitor to the canal noted in 1826, "The Irish and Negroes are kept separate from each other, for fear of serious consequences."[7]

The ongoing search for able-bodied men who could move earth and construct transportation networks flung American capitalists all over the country and even overseas. America needed men willing to relocate to the periphery of the nineteenth-century industrial world, to the distant and unforgiving western frontiers of canal and railroad building. This proved a formidable task. Railroad companies in the mid-nineteenth century complained endlessly about a "deficiency of hands," while also noting that they were "deluged with applicants" for the highly coveted positions of engineers, machinists, conductors, telegraph operators, and clerks. Companies found that Americans were unwilling to risk their lives and reputations for a bare subsistence, shoveling dirt in these ditches of progress. It was a miserable, dangerous, unsteady, and apparently uncivilized form of wage labor.[8]

Consider, for a moment, the titles conferred on the men who performed the most incredible feats of construction in the nineteenth century—canals, railroads, dams, bridges, and turnpikes. From the popular British term for navigation workers, in the United States a "navvy" was literally seen as a human earth-moving machine.[9] Immigrant laborers on canals ("navvies") and railroads ("gandy dancers" for track workers) were unfairly categorized by the companies as "casual" or "common" laborers. These terms were euphemisms for "unskilled" workers, which, when applied to immigrants, particularly Irish, Chinese, and Mexicans, implied that their work was the type that any strong, able-bodied man could perform.[10] On such "common workers" or "hands," the late David Montgomery noted in *The Fall of the House of Labor*, his definitive study of capitalism, labor relations, and workers' control, that "these men had no name, except perhaps the colloquial *ditchdigger*. What does the lack of a suitable name tell us about the place of such laborers in America?" As Montgomery argued, America's name for these common laborers "reminds us that wherever they worked, they were strangers. Sedentary Americans knew songs and legends about them, but shunned personal encounter" except when they had to "defend their communities against the alien invasion."[11]

Still, progress demanded such hard labor to secure the place of the native born. The rapid physical and economic growth of the United States in the nineteenth century eventually unleashed an unbridled form of early capitalism. American employers turned to immigrants as cheap labor to plow fields, construct canals and railroads, dig mines, and operate machinery in the country's emerging factories. This was the "free labor" that slavery's apologists such as George Fitzhugh and James Henry Hammond frequently condemned. Much like the Atlantic coast states had done in the colonial era, western states and territories in the nineteenth century made every effort to entice immigrant workers to their ditches, tracks, towns, and fields. Without these newcomers from Europe and Asia, the nation's vast riches could not have been exploited as quickly and cheaply. Leonard Dinnerstein and David M. Reimers note that these immigrants' "strong backs and steadfast enterprise were necessary to turn American dreams into American accomplishments."[12] This quotation, while true in part, reads awkward. It also makes for a rather problematic history. Canal and railroad construction offers one of the most significant examples of this labor trend, yet just how "American" were these accomplishments if the workers producing them were considered anything but?

To succeed, America had to rely on the most "un-American" kinds of men—far from respectable citizens—to build the transportation networks so vital to the nation. The following chapters interrogate the problem of progress, its inner workings and outward appearance, from the 1820s forward. Though western residents embraced plans to bring canal and railroads to their localities, they treated the approaching diggers and tracklayers as unwelcome invaders, unworthy of citizenship. To confront the reality that "uncivilized" workers were physically bringing progress to the West, local communities sought, in earnest, ways to celebrate and redefine the very nature of canal and railroad progress. If transient laborers interpreted their efforts and struggles as self-sacrificing and manly, community members pointed discouragingly to their reckless behavior in shanty towns and construction camps as evidence of their unfitness for citizenship. According to native-born citizens, canals and railroads indeed marked a triumph and were solely attributable to the independent, civilized, entrepreneurial, hardworking, and masculine character of *Americans*. Opinion makers spun this dominant narrative, identifying destitute, transient, and immigrant laborers as necessary but uncivilized, unmanly, drunken, violent, and unproductive. In the process, and in denial, true Americans, great and small, laid claim to national progress while distancing foreign-born and working-class men from the fruits of their labor.[13]

In exploring workers' encounters with race and ethnicity, masculinity, and progress in the American West, I am particularly interested in questions of identity, power, and nation in the context of the massive transportation projects that advanced America's continental empire. Heretofore a rather elusive scholarly quest, it nonetheless highlights how workers' understood themselves and their work over space and time and how elite and ordinary Americans understood and described this diverse array of workers and the canals and railroads they built. Beginning with the nineteenth-century arrival of Irish immigrants to America, both before and after the Great Famine, and continuing well into in the latter decades of 1800s with waves of Chinese and Mormon workers, the racial discrimination and class, religious, and cultural prejudice aimed at these groups were fierce and pervasive. Scholars have charted this history in considerable detail, particularly in relation to individual culture groups in America. But an emphasis on canal and railroad construction, the definitive symbols of American expansion and progress, as well as a focus on moving frontiers, adds significant elements to these histories. Frankly, we know too little about how labor and progress *worked* from the perspective of those laboring in the ditch and on the track.

This book is as much about immigrant and native-born construction workers as it is about the very idea of American progress, particularly as it relates to western history. But the problem of *creating* progress cannot be separated from the problem of *defining* it, and the building of canals and railroads in the American West provides a lens through which to analyze both aspects of this dilemma. At its core was the challenge of physically creating and expanding an American empire through transportation projects that promised to conquer distance and time, link towns and distant hinterlands, increase the flow of goods and people, create new markets and consumers, and facilitate economic development on state, regional, and national levels.

This physical task of creating progress thus sounds straightforward, but the reality was quite messy—even in the West, that place of boundless freedom and unlimited opportunities. First and foremost, American progress was built on the backs of people deemed second-class citizens at best. Its dark underbelly was punctuated by grueling labor, low wages, suffering, and survival. Not only was canal digging and railroad building physically demanding, but these occupations were inherently dangerous and violent. Pain and misery, while ubiquitous in this type of labor, are thorny historical subjects due to their disturbing character and the way they elude the historical record. Workers moved earth but were also subject to its unrelenting forces. They were exposed to cycles of blistering hot and bone-chilling cold weather as they toiled in knee-deep muck, braved water-borne illnesses, chipped away at solid granite, and endured hard rock blasts and cave-ins. Anyone who has experienced the stickiness of the Great Lakes region in summer, the temperature extremes in Utah and Wyoming, and the snows of the Sierra Nevada understands well the challenges these workers faced.

Workers also faced the constant pressure of their section bosses to finish the job—in an occupation where blunt force, rapidity, and technology didn't always harmonize. Railroads, in particular, were praised as a novel technology that would annihilate the space and civilize the wilderness of the West, but they too often annihilated the men building them instead. In the late nineteenth century a man was more likely to die working on the railroad than by any other cause.[14] In this sense, railroads carried a far more lethal character than guns in the American West. One railroad historian has recently highlighted "the irony that the tools of civilization were themselves instruments of acute suffering."[15] In 1889 President Benjamin Harrison critiqued the Iron Horse's civilizing influences in his first message to Congress, when he compared the violence of railroad work with that of war. "It is a reproach to our civilization," Harrison argued, "that any class of American workmen should, in the pursuit of a necessary and useful vocation, be subjected to a peril of life and limb as great as that of a soldier in time of war."[16] This book reckons with the violence and pain that permeated the lives of transportation workers, whether endured or inflicted, using their experiences to reconsider canal and railroad progress as a realm of trauma and not merely one of triumph.[17]

Nevertheless, Americans interpreted and celebrated progress—as a cultural construct—in ways that removed both the strain of muscle and the stain of exploitation. Canals and railroads ostensibly united the North and South; the East and West; and, more important, people from diverse backgrounds. In addition to valuable goods, they helped spread cherished institutions and ideals—freedom, democracy, and capitalism among them. Finally, they were unprecedented technological achievements that turned American dreams into a reality that allegedly benefited everyone. Common transportation workers were routinely overlooked and bypassed on this thoroughfare of national progress.

Thus, for the workers who reaped few benefits and were not considered American at all, progress was double trouble. Its consequences were physical as well as intellectual. Its relationship to American expansion, empire, and the public good provoked significant questions and concerns. Who toiled and struggled; who commanded and prospered? Who was honored, and how were they remembered? Like the daily struggle for control on the railroad and canal, the contest for control of history and memory was genuine and hard-fought. What proponents of canals, railroads, and expansion saw as inevitable, perpetual progress that embodied American greatness, others (whose gritty fingerprints marked these accomplishments) confronted—and complicated—in their daily exploits. The process of progress, of building and celebrating, of remembering and distancing, required hard work. From any angle or perspective, it makes for an uncomfortable history.

The American West figures centrally in this history of progress and the men who helped build, define, and commemorate it. To mold rugged frontier regions into a functioning continental empire was no easy feat, and such a massive undertaking was sure to elicit admiration around the world. With so many ethnic and religious groups, social classes, and cultures in the West, the idea of working together to build a transportation empire was too powerful of an impression for cultural and political commentators to resist. Timing was everything. Just as canals and railroads promised to unite the continent and cement America's empire, postwar migration and expansion to the West helped popularize the notion that the western frontier was a symbol of independence and an incubator of democracy. Readers familiar with Frederick Jackson Turner's thesis no doubt understand the power of this frontier narrative.[18] The building of these internal improvements accelerated a new peopling of immigrants and emigrants (from Europe, China, and all parts of the United States) on a wageworkers' frontier notable for its sheer diversity.[19] These groups of workers, whose brains and brawn built transportation networks, would test the limits of racial democracy in the American West, that hallowed place of ostensibly endless possibilities, a proving ground for national progress, and, for some, even a site of Americanization.

This book explores an untold history of American progress. It examines moving frontiers of unskilled construction labor on canals and railroads in the American West from the 1820s to the 1870s.[20] Investigating western, labor, ethnic, gender, and environmental histories, it situates the experiences of an assortment of "others" alongside dominant narratives of nineteenth-century progress. In doing so, it salvages the largely overlooked stories of suffering and survival that facilitated U.S. imperial expansion. This book presents a comparative dimension, long missing, in which Irish workers are considered with the Chinese, Mormons, and native-born American citizens who helped build transportation networks in the nineteenth century. It therefore marks a significant methodological departure from previous scholarship. My comparative case studies of Irish laborers on canals and railroads in the U.S. Midwest and Irish, Chinese, and Mormon workers on the transcontinental railroad in the Mountain West and Far West reveal that canals and railroads were not *ends* of progress but moving spaces of conflict and contestation. In contention, I argue, were immigrant and native-born construction workers on one hand and groups of elite and ordinary citizens on the other, who clashed over the meaning of work, progress, manhood, and citizenship. Navigating geographic and cultural boundaries, I argue that the building of massive transportation projects entailed a reconstruction of these cherished yet unresolved ideals. Transient immigrant construction workers found ways—on the job, in construction camps, in recreation, protest, and violence—to redefine their role in American progress and refashion their inherited notions of work, manhood, and citizenship. American citizens, however, used canals, railroads, and the wilderness they ostensibly conquered to rehash notions of civilization, to reconstruct boundaries of citizenship and manhood, and to distance the work of unskilled immigrants while praising the industrial progress they helped create.

With its focus on work, masculinity, and citizenship in the nineteenth-century U.S. West, this book critiques inherited and recycled notions of American progress and civilization. Using the lenses of gender, class, race, and ethnicity, this study moves immigrant workers to the foreground of national progress, assesses their cultural conceptions of work and manhood, and charts the evolution of these imported notions in the American West as workers confronted local class and ethnic fault lines. Citizens and immigrant workers were more often viewed as adversaries than as counterparts in the creation of canal and railroad progress, and each group built what I call "communities of contestation" through which to interpret their experiences. Though canals and railroads were central to the American experiment in technological, cultural, economic, and geographic expansion, an uncomfortable reality sullied the building of these projects. Their builders, many citizens argued, were among America's most uncivilized, even savage, persons. To help unearth the struggles of immigrant canal and railroad workers, this book juxtaposes their experiences with narratives that distanced them from America's frontiers of progress. Thus, it moves beyond the trenches of immigrant labor to address the labor of popular writers, illustrators, and cultural commentators who performed the important work of celebrating American progress.

Generations of historical scholarship on canals and railroads has revealed much about their design, promotion, construction, management, economic and political impact, and legacies.[21] Still, there is an alternative yet equally relevant story to tell that involves work, progress, and difference. Few studies of canals and railroads have examined how the contributions of unskilled workers were often interpreted through class, racial, ethnic, and gender stereotypes and how these contributions were likewise distanced by journalistic coverage and celebrations that praised everyone but the actual builders.[22] Today's Americans continue to celebrate progress in myriad ways without really considering the invisible labor that physically creates it. An obsession with the end result or product, rather than the process, has continued to dominate American thinking and politics whether the questions pertain to capitalism, new labor markets, immigration, or low-wage work that serves the public good. Critiquing the process is a risky proposition, for it disrupts the idea of American exceptionalism. Through an examination of internal improvements, this book thus historicizes, in some ways, the ongoing cultural debate over American progress, labor, immigration, ethnicity, and national belonging.

This book draws on a very small but significant body of literature that offers insights into workers' lives; emphasizes the dirt, grime, and subordination of unskilled construction workers; and critiques America's early transportation revolution.[23] Peter Way's *Common Labour* merits special mention. In the only book-length study of canal labor in America, Way focuses on the eastern United States and Canada, portraying the world of transient canal diggers as one of proletarianization and exploitation. While he emphasizes how unskilled workers used this alienation to foster a sense of community, Way nonetheless concludes that canallers were relatively powerless. Their resistance (by fight or flight) was generally futile, and throughout the canal era they were "unable fundamentally to alter their condition."[24] *Common Labour* articulates a less romantic paradigm of working-class consciousness than studies of skilled workers, white male craftsmen, and the urban laboring classes have revealed.[25] Indeed, Way's portrait of America's lumpen proletariat is a somber one, framed in Marxian categories of capitalist oppression and alienation. But to suggest that common and brutish work made construction workers powerless unduly pacifies these men and silences their role in—and perceptions of—national progress.[26]

While recent studies have shifted scholarly emphasis from transportation and business history to labor and social history, problems and opportunities abound. With few exceptions, much of this scholarship relies on a conventional framework in which the work of a single canal or railroad company is documented from start to finish. Ironically, it was precisely this concentration on the end result—the completed canal or railroad—that first led company officials, and then historians, to praise high-ranking employees and forget the contributions of common workers. Moreover, no western version of this story has been attempted. A focus on western expansion, an incorporation of canals *and* railroads, and an emphasis on multiple groups of immigrant and native-born construction workers helps us rethink the centrality of the West and its diverse cast of actors to the story of American industrial development. Likewise, just as canal and railroad promoters pointed to the unifying features of transportation projects, my successive frontiers framework suggests that regional diversity and historical contingencies—the "many Wests" approach—still merits analysis continental in scope.[27]

In deviating from organizational schemes based solely on transportation networks or isolated groups of workers, the comparative frontiers framework this book uses is one that spans distance, culture, and time. For this reason, Irish workers appear over time and place in each part of the book. As early as the creation of the Erie Canal, Irish workers were the mainstay of internal improvement projects, but their role and image has been subjected more to popular stereotypes than to critical analysis. The most influential studies of Irish immigrants focus on citizenship, politics, political culture, and whiteness. No book-length studies are devoted to unskilled Irish workers, especially transportation workers in the U.S. West.[28] In examining the role of Irish construction workers in the West and using a comparative lens through which to explore their interactions with and experiences alongside Mormon, Chinese, and native-born American workers, this book reinterprets the history of America's indispensable "others."[29]

This book builds on recent literature that explores how working-class men constructed masculinity and confronted challenges to their manhood. In revealing how languages of manhood and notions of manliness shaped class perceptions and work experiences, scholars have demonstrated the importance of gender and identity in America's transition to industrial capitalism in the nineteenth century. But there are some problems with this literature on men's history, and while readers should not anticipate a definitive rebuttal in this book, my hope is that its subject and scope will generate new questions and interpretations.

Most gendered analyses of industrial development focus on the deskilling of urban craftsmen and their separation from the traditional workplace and concomitant loss of control over production. These changes, along with the expansion of immigrant groups into the workplace and political arena and challenges to the structure of patriarchy, precipitated a so-called crisis in masculinity.[30] In the case of workers, this crisis was actually fourfold and involved the issues of work, class, gender, and race. Skilled male workers in various trades responded to social and technological transformations by refashioning the meanings of manhood. They crafted a collective identity of "worker" that was thoroughly raced and gendered. Most important, they organized to defend their manly identities.[31] Equating manliness with "respectability" and in opposition to femininity, blackness, and common laborers, skilled white workers in nineteenth-century America articulated an idealized notion of working-class manhood that required continual demonstration and validation and thus remained unresolved.[32]

Historians have not yet reconciled the problem of overtheorizing the languages and usages of masculinity in their subjects, particularly when they fall outside of the turn-of-the-century critiques of modernity and overcivilization familiar to anyone interested in Teddy Roosevelt's reinvention. Gail Bederman, who understands that period better than most, argues that gender is not only socially constructed but an "ongoing project," a historical and ideological process through which "individuals are positioned and position themselves as men or women."[33] She modifies the idea of a "crisis" in masculinity with what she and other gender historians interpret as an "obsession" with masculine authority on the part of middle-class men.[34] Men continually remade themselves, in the process co-opting the once-disparaged physicality and savagery of lower-class men (including nonwhites) and blending it with the white manliness valued by the rest of society for its restraint and self-mastery. For middle-class men, masculinity alone could not distinguish "bodies, identities, and power," but when reformulated with attention to race and the discourse of civilization, *manliness* held the potential to shore up and advance white dominance in all facets of American life—public and private, civil and political.[35] Such a discourse is relevant to the study of masculinity, particularly when considering that the most visible and prolific writers or voices on the topics of labor, immigration, and American progress identified with the middle class and its views.[36]

Yet where do unskilled workers, particularly immigrants, fit in this narrative of masculine formation, this history of men and male identity? Influential works on masculinity that identify the aforementioned "crisis" say comparatively little about those working-class men engaged in menial wage labor and even less about immigrant men. With so much emphasis placed on the middle class, historians studying men on the margins of society, those without the leisure to document their gendered insecurities, face a rather daunting task. Did canal diggers drink to excess to numb the pain of their harsh workdays, to carouse with coworkers, or to nurse a pathological obsession with proper masculine formation? Did men become railroaders to make a living or to fend off gender anxieties and reinvent a muscular form of outdoor masculinity? Did railroad workers' success in building America's continental empire validate a deep-seated quest for imperial power or basic recognition as capable men worthy of citizenship and gainful employment?

Although scholars of labor, immigration, and masculinity have often identified the workplace as a key site for the construction of male identity, historical interpretations of the nineteenth-century American workplace unfortunately tend to exclude many workers. Labor historians have depicted this workplace as primarily urban and dominated by artisans, trade unionists, and labor politics. They have, however, rightly critiqued "free labor" as an ideological construct popularized by men who were far more likely to hire labor than to perform it.[37] The challenge is to broaden this picture, incorporating native-born, immigrant, and transient workers, skilled and unskilled, and a workplace that was, quite literally, in motion on remote frontiers of the American West. Few studies have exceeded Gunther Peck's *Reinventing Free Labor* in this regard. Peck argues that immigrant workers' notions of manhood in the American West were unstable due to the transitory nature of their labor, the demands of their bosses (notably immigrant padrones), their ties to Europe, and familial expectations. Peck interprets the process of masculine identity formation in the West as "manhood on the move."[38] Locating workers' understandings of manhood and solidarity in mobility itself, he departs from studies of immigration and migration that highlight the importance of established ethnic enclaves.[39]

But to build on the concept of the wageworkers' frontier and explore the meanings of labor and manhood, it is imperative to address the evolution of worker masculinity over space and time. For Peck, "manhood on the move" related less to workers' notions of progress in contention with American elites than to their memory of ancestral homelands and resistance to the undue control exercised by their immigrant padrones. This book differs from Peck's transnational approach, for new ideas of manhood developed in the Midwest, Mountain West, and Far West, where masculine identity was not simply internal to class and ethnicity but actively contested by different class, ethnic, and religious groups. On these frontiers of progress, construction laborers grafted new identities to old as they struggled to brand both manhood and progress. Moreover, workers' claims to masculinity were contested not only by their counterparts and employers but by the public at large. Throughout this period American citizens as well as immigrants used transportation projects and the wilderness that they ostensibly conquered to reconstruct boundaries of citizenship and manhood and lay claim to history in the making. Beyond men in motion, these were communities in contestation.

The following chapters explore the moving frontier of canals and railroads and consider this contest for authority. The Irish, Mormons, Chinese, and native-born Americans defended their manhood and their stories of progress against ostensible superiors: company officials, political and religious leaders, newspaper editors, and all who had a connection to—or an investment in—a conjured public image of internal improvements and western progress. The first half of this study introduces the paradox of progress on canals and railroads in the nineteenth-century American West and examines Irish laborers on three competing yet historically neglected projects: the Wabash & Erie Canal in Indiana, the Illinois & Michigan Canal, and the Illinois Central Railroad. The second half focuses on the experiences of Utah's Mormons who helped complete the transcontinental railroad in 1869 and on the Union Pacific's and Central Pacific's Irish and Chinese construction workers in the Mountain West and in California. Across time and space America's moving transportation frontier featured a clash of cultures that defined a nation, an elite, and multitudes of unskilled workers.

This conversation over progress and manhood is not always discernible. Loud are the voices of the articulate and the propertied. Their forums, such as speeches, editorials, and sermons, are open to view. The ordinary workers, however, leave fainter tracks. Like their images in old photographs, their words are often indistinct. Yet we can glean their thoughts from a diverse collection of sources. When workers spoke loudly in protests and strikes, we can hear them and gauge the reactions of employers and community members. Canal and railroad companies have records that offer clues about the workers' lives, but they are rarely complete and too often biased. More fruitful are letters and memoirs that help to unearth the lives of construction laborers. Newspapers figure prominently in this project, for it was through them that individuals—workers and otherwise—discussed the importance of canal and railroad labor and the meanings of progress, citizenship, and manhood. Workers' petitions, though rare, are especially rich sources that document laborers' efforts to challenge their employers, protect their economic interests, and defend their value to society. Equally revealing are the writings of priests and missionaries who occasionally ministered to and pacified transient construction laborers. Yet religious figures, much like political and community leaders, more commonly deprecated the role of canal diggers and railroad builders. Their thoughts, along with the perceptions of contemporary journalists, travelers, and artists, reveal the inherent tensions that dominated frontiers of transportation labor. Miscellaneous sources such as workers' songs, notes on canal and railroad celebrations, and town and county histories help bridge the gap between the vocal and the silent, the visible and the disregarded.

After the completion of artificial waterways and the driving of final railroad spikes, dignitaries, tourists, journalists, and illustrators crafted narratives that reimagined the indispensable yet unskilled laborers as cultural curiosities, unmanly and reckless slaves of industry, or as mere accessories to uniquely American triumphs over nature. Far from a Turnerian frontier where immigrants became Americanized, frontiers of transportation labor witnessed the separation of unskilled transients and immigrants from this ideal, despite their engagement in work central to national development and Americanness. Workers fought back, laying claim to a rightful place in the success of America. In the contest of words and images, charge and countercharge, emerged conflicting narratives of labor, manhood, citizenship, and progress. If one dominated the American imagination, it does not deny identities that sustained the vulnerable and the subordinated in their daily struggles. It is to these frontiers of progress, these conflicting cultures of work and manhood, triumph and pain, which we now turn.

TWO

———

"A Wretched and Miserable Condition"

IRISH DITCHDIGGERS, THE TRIUMPH OF PROGRESS,
AND THE CONTEST OF CANAL COMMUNITIES IN
THE HOOSIER STATE

> The Irish are, by the great majority of Americans, considered
> as an oppressed and injured people ... who arrive poor, and ...
> tainted by the vices of poverty, which, in some of the states, have
> created a prejudice against them. But, considered collectively,
> they constitute a highly useful part of the American commu-
> nity, and contribute, by their honest industry, to increase the
> wealth of the country. They perform the hardest labors at the
> lowest wages given, and are satisfied and happy to provide for
> themselves and their children the bare necessities of life. But it is
> even their being contented with little, and their less heeding the
> future, which renders their actions and motives less acceptable
> to the Americans.
>
> FRANCIS J. GRUND, 1837

THUS BEGAN FRANCIS GRUND'S DISCUSSION of American "prejudices
against the Irish," in his account *The Americans in Their Moral, Social, and
Political Relations.* Competing on the same ideological battleground as
Alexis de Tocqueville, Frances Trollope, and countless other observers of
antebellum America, Grund was convinced, after ten years' residence, of the
righteousness of America's democratic experiment. This led the German-
born writer to defend his "grossly misrepresented" compatriots with an "honest desire to correct prejudices" and provide "more just conceptions of
American worth." Grund contrasted Americans, who loved their country
"not *as it is,* but *as it will be made* by their enterprise and industry," with the
Irish, who, by habit, were pleased to acquire merely "what is necessary for the
present." Because the Irish, he argued, were "content" to be hired en masse
to dig canals and construct railroads, "they neglect[ed] the more useful

cultivation of the soil, which would, at once, make them independent and respectable"—in short, more American.[1]

While Grund was quick to differentiate ditchdiggers from virtuous, freedom-loving farmers, his account boasted of a nation "heartily in favor of internal improvements," which "relied entirely on the ingenuity of *American* workmen."[2] Like many of his contemporaries, Grund masterfully distanced actual work from its end results, for nowhere in his lengthy celebration of American progress did he acknowledge the contribution of the Irish construction laborers who literally performed the groundwork. Struggling for a living wage and basic job security, the Irish were written out of his triumphant story and countless others like it. Similar to the hundreds of thousands of immigrant laborers who, throughout the nineteenth century, toiled in the name of progress for the land of liberty, Irish "hands" ran up against dominant narratives of progress, civilization, and American manhood. They were ignored as agents of change and conjured up instead images of a faceless, violent, uncivilized army of laborers.

Whether their days were spent draining land, grubbing, mucking, or digging ditches, unskilled canal construction laborers, as early as the heyday of the canal era in the 1830s, endured brutal working conditions, punishing state and company policies, and hostile community reactions that demarcated their experiences from those of the free laborers so romanticized in American history. This chapter examines the conflicting cultures of progress—American told and Irish made—as they evolved on the Wabash & Erie Canal in Indiana. America's longest canal, and by most accounts an abysmal failure, the building of the Wabash & Erie typified Indiana's reckless approach to internal improvements. It also coincided with the arrival of Irish immigrants, whose presence threatened Hoosier visions of civilized development and altered American images of worker masculinity.[3]

The problem of progress on the Indiana frontier begs inquiry beyond traditional economic history. Thus, charting Indiana's communities of contestation entails neither a retelling of the state's transportation history nor a company history of the Wabash & Erie. Much more than a story of debt, delusion, and despair, the Indiana canal experience underscores the human cost of public works. At its core was the dilemma of building an American nation on the backs of the poor, unskilled, and exploited. A history both physical and intellectual, the Wabash & Erie Canal raises significant questions about those who toiled and survived and those who directed and profited. At stake were daily contests over power on the canal line as well as contests over the representation, narrative, and memory of the canal. These contests were fierce and their legacies enduring.

A host of canal cultures existed on the Indiana frontier. The historical challenge is to unearth the struggles of the immigrant and native-born workers who were the bone and sinew of progress. Yet their story was only one of many. Also considered are the Hoosier politicians and businessmen whose inexhaustible search for state, national, and private funds for their grandiose transportation projects was tied to both personal and political fortunes. These men cast long shadows that hid other actors. Company officials and their contractors promoted the canal, recruited armies of workers, and directed daily construction operations. Their understanding of progress was rooted in the genius of unbridled capitalism and divorced from the lives of their workers. Although missionaries and reformers were fewer in number, their voices were equally important, as they sought to pacify the transportation frontier and convert the souls of its heathen residents. Newspaper editors, journalists, and travelers played parts as eyewitnesses, entering their interpretations of progress and its builders into the historical record. Whether they were supporters or critics, their opinions shaped Hoosiers' and Americans' opinions of the canal and its creators.

This chapter explores this cast of characters and the interplay among them. Their interactions and competing narratives complicate our understanding of American progress—its contributors, its underworld, and its legacy. The story begins in frontier Indiana, along the canal route. It considers how and why the distancing of laborers became essential to progress, examines the ways in which workers' resisted, and reveals how, in the process, construction laborers and their ostensible superiors chiseled out their own definitions of progress and manhood.

The canal fever that engulfed the nation following the success of New York's Erie Canal infected the Hoosier State to extremes (see map 1). What began as George Washington's idea to connect Lake Erie through the short portage between the Maumee and Wabash Rivers eventually became the longest American canal, extending 468 miles from Lake Erie at Toledo, Ohio, to Evansville in southern Indiana (see map 2). Its completion entailed the cession of more than three million acres of Miami and Potawatomi Indian lands in the Wabash Valley, rampant corruption and legislative folly, and large-scale deficit spending to appease an impatient citizenry whose adherence to the spirit of improvement had revealed the unintended consequences of republicanism.[4]

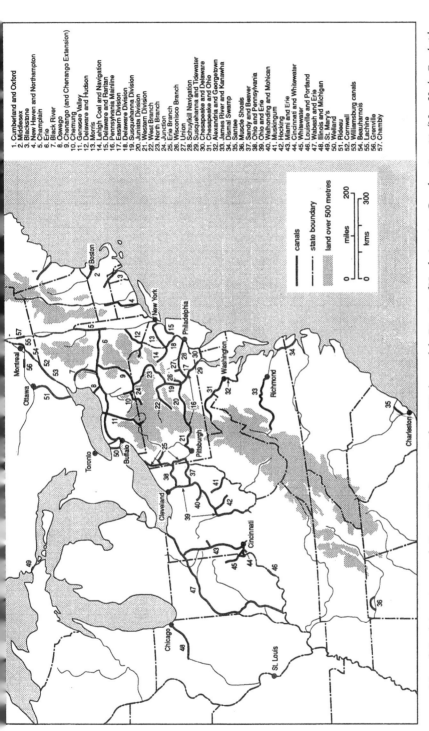

1. Cumberland and Oxford
2. Middlesex
3. Blackstone
4. New Haven and Northampton
5. Champlain
6. Erie
7. Black River
8. Oswego
9. Chenango (and Chenango Extension)
10. Chemung
11. Genesee Valley
12. Delaware and Hudson
13. Morris
14. Lehigh Coal and Navigation
15. Delaware and Raritan
16. Pennsylvania Mainline
17. Eastern Division
18. Delaware Division
19. Susquehanna Division
20. Juniata Division
21. Western Division
22. West Branch
23. North Branch
24. Junction
25. Erie Branch
26. Wisconisco Branch
27. Union
28. Schuylkill Navigation
29. Susquehanna and Tidewater
30. Chesapeake and Delaware
31. Chesapeake and Ohio
32. Alexandria and Georgetown
33. James River and Kanawha
34. Dismal Swamp
35. Santee
36. Muscle Shoals
37. Sandy and Beaver
38. Ohio and Pennsylvania
39. Ohio and Erie
40. Walhonding and Mohican
41. Muskingum
42. Hocking
43. Miami and Erie
44. Cincinnati and Whitewater
45. Whitewater
46. Louisville and Portland
47. Wabash and Erie
48. Illinois and Michigan
49. St. Mary's
50. Welland
51. Rideau
52. Cornwall
53. Williamsburg canals
54. Beauharnois
55. Lachine
56. Grenville
57. Chambly

canals
state boundary
land over 500 metres

0   200
miles
0   300
kms

MAP 1. Map of North American canals. Peter Way, *Common Labour: Workers and the Digging of North American Canals, 1780–1860* (New York: Cambridge University Press, 1993), xvii. Reproduced by permission from Cambridge University Press.

SOURCES: Carter Goodrich, ed. *Canals and American Economic Development.* New York: Columbia University Press, 1961, pp. 184–8; Donald Creighton. *The Empire of the St. Lawrence.* Orig. ed. 1937. Toronto: MacMillan Co. of Canada, 1956, pp. 420; Madeline Sadler Waggoner. *The Long Haul West: The Great Canal Era 1817–1850.* New York: Putnam, 1958, back cover.

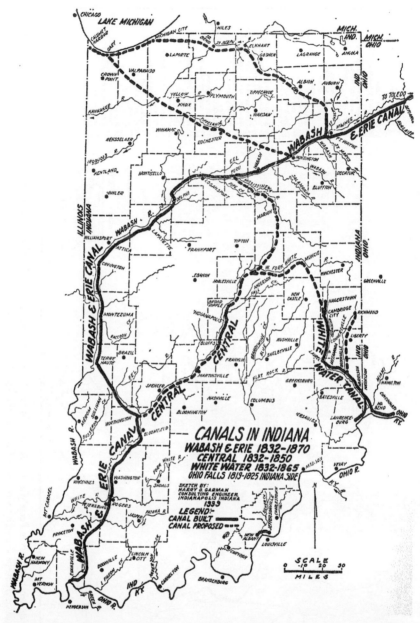

MAP 2. Map of Indiana canals. Harry O. Garman, "Whitewater Canal, Cambridge City to the Ohio River," in *Yearbook of the Society of Indiana Pioneers* (Indianapolis: Society of Indiana Pioneers, 1944), 23. Reproduced by permission from the Society of Indiana Pioneers.

Following nearly a decade of legislative debate over the implementation of a "general system" of improvements, the Mammoth Internal Improvement Act of 1836 passed the Indiana legislature, bolstered by federal land grants, state and private loans, and a new ad valorem property tax. The act created a board of internal improvement and authorized its commissioners to survey and construct eight turnpike, canal, and railroad projects at an estimated cost of $10 million.[5] The Wabash & Erie Canal was the centerpiece of the act. This "scarcely believable" system, "conceived in madness and nourished by delusion," to quote two prominent canal historians, resulted in financial disaster for Indiana.[6] Construction on all projects, except for a section of the Wabash & Erie, was suspended in 1839, and the state defaulted on its bond payments from 1841 to 1846. After disbanding the board of internal improvement in 1842, the state assembly invited private companies to complete the abandoned projects. Indiana went bankrupt in 1850, three years before the canal's completion, did not clear itself of debt until 1903, and amended its constitution in 1851 to prohibit borrowing money except to pay the interest on the state debt, suppress rebellions, and repel invasions. The Wabash & Erie did enjoy profitable periods, but floods, damaged locks and aqueducts, vandalism, and railroads (built along the canal route) hastened its closure in 1874.[7]

For Indiana and its citizens, the early success of the Wabash & Erie Canal initiated an orgy of celebration. Fort Wayne held a massive public celebration on July 4, 1835, to honor both American independence and the commencement of navigation along the first thirty-two miles of the canal. One observer felt it important to remind everyone that the country, "through which canal boats are now passing, was purchased of the Indians only eight or nine years ago." Such an "instance of rapid improvement," he argued, "is nowhere else to be found," and "the credit is due ... to the enterprise of the state of Indiana." The hundreds of "citizens" in attendance, he noted, applauded one another on this remarkable accomplishment, doing so "in a spirited and becoming manner."[8]

Judge Hugh McCulloch, an esteemed Hoosier, president of the Bank of Indiana, and the future U.S. treasury secretary, was invited to deliver the keynote address at the Fort Wayne celebration. After multiple toasts, huzzahs, and gun salutes, McCulloch proudly declared that the successful completion of the Summit section of the canal offered ample evidence that "the better genius of the state [had] triumphed." He expressed an "earnest appreciation" for the "citizens of Indiana" and praised "with gratitude and respect" the "services of the Canal's supporters." Yet, for McCulloch, highest accolades were due to the commissioners, surveyors, and engineers of the Wabash & Erie. "The work, as far as it has been completed," he noted, "reflects high honor upon those under whose management it has thus far progressed." As the Wabash & Erie connected Indiana's distant frontiers, McCulloch argued, it promised to "destroy local prejudice and to unite our whole country in the bands of national attachment." Hoosiers and foreigners, citizens and noncitizens, would, he insisted, "become more familiar with each other, [and] the peculiarities which distinguish them will become less and less perceptible." Moreover, this "noble enterprise" would elevate Indiana to a "dizzy height of glory and power."[9]

For the Irish laborers building the canal, there was little to celebrate. Six days after the July Fourth festival in Fort Wayne, canallers at Lagro, less than forty miles from the celebration, threatened to kill one another. Since the previous fall Irish diggers on alternate sections of the canal, divided into groups known as "Corkonians" and "Fardowns," each endeavoring to dominate the available work in the region, had exchanged taunts and warnings and engaged in intermittent attacks. During this time, according to canal commissioner David Burr, these canallers had "manifested their ill will to each other by merciless beatings on such of each party as chanced to fall in the power of the other." From the fourth to the tenth of July, Burr noted, "the alarms were constant and aggravated by the threats and outrages of the worthless" workers, as both sides, now numbering more than six hundred, prepared for a "general battle" on the tenth.[10] According to the residents of Lagro and neighboring communities, newspaper editors, canal company officials, and even the governor, these canallers were "belligerent" and "least worthy," a group of "deluded ruffians" who sought to "trample on the laws of the State with impunity" in their "predetermined" violence aimed at a "total suspension of the work on the canal."[11] One Hoosier editor warned that even "our own citizens" have not "at all times been safe from the attacks of these ruffians" and pleaded for state assistance to "suppress the disturbances" and "protect the citizens from the dangers to which they would be exposed, if the parties should come into contact" in open warfare.[12]

Yet, in their conversations with Commissioner Burr, the Irish canallers and their families told a much different story. Indiana's canal frontier, a place where they "wished to work and remain peaceable," had succumbed to "mutual fears" and "threats of burnings and murder." Driven out of their shanties, the Irish workers were "forced . . . to fight in order to protect themselves" and their livelihoods.[13] Far from the unifying, "noble enterprise" that

Judge McCulloch described, Lagro's transient Irish canal community experienced the worst of an underworld of progress.

Digging canals was painfully hard labor, aggressive by nature. More than the mere brute force of shoveling ditches, construction involved many skills that make the designation "unskilled" misleading. Canals were cut through miles of diverse terrain, ranging from low-lying marshes to rock-studded territory, while maintaining a controllable descent in altitude. Workers built reservoirs, burrowed tunnels, arched aqueducts over wide rivers, and erected masonry locks with watertight wooden gates. The channel or "prism" of the canal required precise specifications. If the soil was sandy or porous, teams of men and oxen resorted to pressing mixtures of impermeable clay, known as "puddle," to reinforce its sloping sides and bottom. This was the filth of progress; yet in the muck lay complex tasks, demanding both brains and brawn.[14]

"Grubbing" the land—clearing brush, trees, rocks, and other impediments from the width of the canal plus twenty feet on either side—preceded actual excavation: the cutting, digging, and removal of earth. An early report publicized by the commissioners of the Wabash & Erie Canal stipulated that wherever "the natural [earth] surface is above the canal" and "where the line requires excavation," all "trees, saplings, bushes, stumps, and roots shall be grubbed . . . dug up . . . and removed . . . to [a distance of] at least sixty feet wide." In cases where the earth was below the surface of the water in the canal, "a muck or public ditch shall be dug under the centre of each bank, of the depth and width . . . directed, in order to guard effectively against leakage."[15] Instructions such as these appeared in newspapers and broadsides throughout the region, always making reference to "sufficient digging . . . and construction" in an "industrious" or "workmanlike" manner.[16] Emphasis, however, was continually placed on the strict behavior demanded of the worker, not on the physically dangerous nature of the work.

In excavation, workers used shovels, pickaxes, wheelbarrows, and scrapers and ploughs pulled by oxen or horses to move the earth, digging through the loosest soil to the hardest rock. John TenBrook Campbell, a common laborer on the Wabash & Erie in Parke County, recalled,

> The dirt was removed in carts and wheelbarrows. Each teamster led two horses, one at a time, from the shovel pit to the dump, or tow path. . . . The boss would throw his weight on the back end of the cartbed when it would tip down and shoot the dirt out backward and down the embankment. The drives [sic] (or leader, more properly) would lead the horse and cart back to

the shovel pit and turn and back the cart to the pit and lead the other horse and cart to the bank. While one horse was being led to the bank or towpath, six to eight shovelers would be filling the other cart.[17]

If tree stumps posed a particular problem during the task of grubbing, rocks were a nuisance during both grubbing and excavation, requiring the arduous use of axes and picks. In many cases workers blasted them using rock chisels, sledgehammers, and powder. In wet areas excavation was especially difficult, as canallers waded in waist-high water, shoveling slimy muck while sharing the swamp with leeches and swarms of malarial mosquitoes. Though contractors regularly paid higher wages for water (and rock) excavation, it was often a challenge to convince men to stay on the works when the wet season arrived in Indiana. The "Song of the Canal," popular among New York's Erie canallers who shoveled in the Montezuma marshes at Cayuga Lake, may have served a similar role on the Wabash & Erie in these conditions:

We are digging the ditch through the mire;
Through the mud and the slime and the mire, by heck!
And the mud is our principal hire;
Up our pants, in our shirts, down our neck, by heck![18]

Canal construction was also associated with Asiatic cholera, which plagued the United States from 1832 to 1834 and again from 1848 to 1854. Dublin-born Matthew Carey, newspaper editor and activist in Philadelphia, estimated that over 50 percent of America's Irish canallers were infected with an illness or disease due to their dangerous working environments.[19] Appearing in Indiana in 1832, cholera was so immediately devastating that Governor Noah Noble proclaimed a day of fasting and prayer. Attributed not only to artificial waterways but to places polluted with garbage, sewage, manure, and unhealthy drinking water, cholera elicited a moralistic response from citizens, medical experts, and reformers, who viewed it as divine punishment against sin, intemperance, and uncivilized behavior. In doing so, reformers distanced this disease from the physical danger of construction labor on internal improvements and instead suggested that it was the scourge of poor transients and immigrants.[20] In an 1832 editorial that was reprinted throughout the region, Dr. Daniel Drake, a prominent midwestern physician, counseled residents on the precautionary measures to take against the spreading pestilence. Drake's first preventative, "that no one should get drunk," was a rather curious one, but no doubt confirmed the popular belief that cholera was a canal-borne (or canaller) disease. Echoing such a belief, the doctor then suggested that persons "avoid the rain and night air, keep [their] rooms dry ... lodge warm, and dress, as much as possible, in woolens."[21] Based on the doctor's detailed report, and perhaps its implicit message, canallers had little hope of combating the illness.

While the dangers of canal building, labor shortages, and the slow pace of construction indicated the harsh realities of progress, Indiana nonetheless celebrated its reckless pursuit of improvements with patriotic, republican zeal. Canal celebrations on Washington's Birthday, Independence Day, and "Jackson Day" (commemorating the Bank War) were launched before the work had progressed or Irish shanty towns thrown together. For Hoosiers who viewed the canal as inevitable, such details were irrelevant; celebrations, on the other hand, inspired citizens and garnered national attention. The first, a groundbreaking ceremony complete with military regalia and marching band, commenced at the Saint Joseph feeder line in Fort Wayne on February 22, 1832, to the roars and huzzahs of eager spectators. The ceremony and the night parade that followed, marked by street bonfires, candles flickering in windows, and a massive canal boat float "symbolizing the unanimous sentiment of the north," was largely metaphoric and nearly belated.[22] The inaugural shovelful of dirt was scraped only eight days prior to the expiration of a five-year limit set by the federal government. Without signed contracts or an adequate labor force (the latter discouraged by a rumored outbreak of cholera in the Wabash Valley), "canal fever" was less figurative, and the panic was real for anxious Hoosiers.[23] The editor of the *Lawrenceburg Palladium* cautioned against a citizenry overly anxious for and entitled to internal improvements and argued that bright visions of future prosperity would grow dim when burdensome taxes were considered. Frontier Indiana, he argued, "too young and altogether too weak in her resources to compete with New York," had taken this "improvement mania" to extremes.[24]

Indiana thus faced challenges—natural and material—markedly different from its eastern counterparts, such as available capital and incentives to encourage ready hands to labor in a distant and unsettled frontier. These obstacles underscored the urgent need for a workable redefinition of progress, including both its agents and limits. Though Hoosiers saluted, serenaded, and toasted "the dawning of future happiness and prosperity" and this great "march of Improvement," as one editor described it, the image of the project as the innovative work of a free people belied the reality of the canal scheme.[25]

As was the case on other American canals, early laborers on the Wabash & Erie Canal were local farmers. Farmers were accustomed to the type of work required for initial construction, such as draining and clearing land. But this work was seasonal and presented an opportunity to earn additional income only during slack periods in the agricultural cycle. Canal contractors noted that even when native-born laborers were put to work, they had an "alarming habit" of disappearing during harvest time, which often coincided with the peak period of canal construction.[26] In May 1843 William Lalor, a farmer in Lima, Indiana, wrote to his father in Tinakill, Queen's County, Ireland, that, out of necessity, he was renting out his farm on shares. Unable to make ends meet, Lalor's financial distress led him to contemplate the unthinkable: "I suppose for the purpose of earning clothes &c I shall have to go (greatly against my will) to work on some canal or rail road amongst the wicked, ignorant, profligate, dregs of Society."[27]

Moreover, for independent Hoosiers, ditch digging was degrading work. Manual wage labor held the potential and, more important, the perception of burdening one's native endowment and position in the incipient class structure of the antebellum Midwest. As historians such as Jonathan Glickstein and Eric Foner contend, the ambiguous antebellum ideology of "free labor" celebrated the "small producer," a republican set of values that drew on economic independence and the exceptionalist notion of America as a nation of "self-made men." Clearly, canal digging, as contractual, transient, and undignified labor, was the antithesis of an ideology that exalted the ability of "enterprising" Americans to achieve economic independence. Contract labor on canals, in fact, more closely resembled chattel slavery and the state of the "economically subjugated and depressed" workers of Europe. The problem, however, was that the tenets of free labor also identified personal enterprise as beneficial—even essential—to the generic American "common good."[28] This belief was central to supporters of the Wabash & Erie, and labor recruiters recycled it when they espoused the virtues of canal digging, crafting an image of canal labor as a temporary stage—a ladder of mobility—in the quest for permanent settlement and personal independence.

Prior to the Irish, German immigrants, including a nucleus of twenty-three German Lutheran families organized by Pennsylvania-born merchant Henry Rudisill, settled in the Fort Wayne area in the late 1820s and 1830s. Upon his arrival in 1829, Rudisill wrote with pleasure that Fort Wayne's citizens "appear to be very attentive and obliging to Strangers." Many were attracted by the fertile, heavily wooded soil in the region, and the then comparatively easy route from New York City to the Erie Canal and eventually into Fort Wayne. Day laborers, such as John Siebold, a German Lutheran, came to Fort Wayne with the intention of becoming independent farmers, and the canal promised not only a more viable all-water route for future German immigrants but the reassurance that they could market their goods. Thus, for German farmers, merchants, and craftsmen, Fort Wayne held the promise of a sound economic future in a hospitable community. Of those who engaged in canal construction, most fell under the category of "skilled" workers, including carpenters and stonemasons who erected canal structures such as locks and aqueducts, often in the form of supplementary, subcontract work.[29]

In March 1833 the commissioners of the Wabash & Erie, then including David Burr, Samuel Lewis, and John Scott, drafted at their Fort Wayne office a "Notice to Contractors" that was reprinted in the Indianapolis *Indiana Journal* and in newspapers across the state. The notice requested bids for "25 or 30 sections of the Middle Division of the Wabash & Erie Canal," consisting of about fifteen total miles, to take place "in the counties of Allen and Huntington" and continuing as "far westwardly as the junction of Little river with the Wabash." The commissioners noted that along with the nineteen miles of the canal currently under contract, the new sections would "give employ to 1000 or 1500 men for about two years, in liberal cash wages." This advertisement was typical in that the commissioners used the availability of land and wholesome local conditions as an incentive for canal work, while at the same time exaggerating the opportunity for permanent settlement: "As the country is healthy . . . [and] new lands of a good quality immediately on the canal route are offered for sale . . . an excellent opportunity is offered for enterprise and industry, which must be an object to settlers, labourers, and canal contractors."[30]

While theoretically the responsibility of contractors, labor recruitment was often undertaken by canal commissioners and agents if workers had to be recruited from great distances. Agents for the Wabash & Erie Canal followed the example of the Chesapeake & Ohio Canal Company in the 1820s, which advertised for "workmen" in Irish newspapers, promising "meat three times a day [and] plenty of bread and vegetables, with a reasonable allowance of liquor, and eight, ten, or twelve dollars a month for wages."[31] Similar "Labor Wanted" advertisements were reprinted in local, national, and international newspapers. In 1833 Wabash & Erie officials sent one labor agent to Buffalo to recruit German and Irish immigrants and another across the interior of the state. Wabash & Erie contractors and labor agents, keeping in line with the "spirit of progress," counteracted the designs of Irish "combinations" and secret societies elsewhere by advertising for workers in numbers that far exceeded needs to guarantee an adequate turn out and depress wages.[32] Through this process workers became no more than "hands," preparing the ground for industrial production. An August 1832 advertisement published throughout Indiana offered jobs to seven hundred laborers and promised "very liberal wages, in *Cash,* and good accommodations."[33] That same month a notice in the Indianapolis *Indiana Journal,* posted by contractors "Murray and Vermilya," was more specific concerning wages and endeavored to paint a tranquil picture of canal work in the Hoosier State:

Cash for Canal Hands

We wish to employ laborers on the Wabash and Erie Canal, 12 miles west of Fort Wayne. The situation is healthy and dry. We will play $10 per month for sober and industrious men.[34]

The scarcity of labor enticed contractors to lure one another's employees from one job to another, and the tactics of companies in neighboring Illinois, such as the Illinois & Michigan Canal (which began construction in 1836) and the Illinois Central Railroad (1850), were of little help to scrambling Wabash & Erie agents. The Illinois & Michigan Canal issued a circular calling for ten thousand laborers at the opening of construction, promising high wages and investment opportunities in the "healthful climate of Northern Illinois," despite the fact that the canal never intended to employ over three thousand and that a cholera outbreak had ravaged the state's labor supply.[35] The Illinois Central, guaranteeing two to three years' work for ten thousand men, used wholesome imagery (however dishonest) that rivaled that of its labor-hungry neighbors:

COME ALONG STRANGERS. . . . Come forward and assist in the laying of this mighty track . . . [and receive the] bountiful monthly dispensations of the contractors. . . . [And] when the road is finished, purchase a farm, marry a wife, and dwell contented under . . . [your] own vine and fig tree.[36]

Similarly, an 1837 advertisement for Indiana's Central Canal, an Indianapolis-bound branch of the Wabash & Erie, called for two thousand workers and offered twenty dollars a month, promising "fare and lodgings . . . of the most comfortable character."[37] This particular ad not only assured permanent settlement "with the avails of a few months labor" but tried to convince workers that wage guarantees were included in every contract, noting that the commissioner "reserve[d] the right to see that every laborer receives his just dues." Linking canal labor to "honest industry" and civilized behavior, the resident canal engineer vowed that "no man need lose one dollar of his wages" (presumably at the hands of a domineering contractor) so long as he "pursues a proper course." In ads such as this, canal commissioners and engineers went beyond promises of steady employment and crafted an image of canal labor as a ladder of mobility. This explains the frequency of per-acre land prices, which, at first glance, seem rather misplaced in advertisements for canal digging—perhaps the most dangerous, degrading, and low-paying job on the American frontier. Yet according to the canal company, "no section of country" possessed "greater inducements to the industrious laborer than the state of Indiana." For company elites the "proper course" for "industrious" ditch-diggers was a linear one that involved a public-spirited duty, civilized masculinity, and, in return, the almost certain opportunity to purchase land and build a "permanent home in this flourishing and rapidly growing state."[38] In other words, the chance to toil on the Wabash & Erie Canal was an act of benevolence on the part of company officials, an invitation to Americanness or independence for those unskilled immigrants and transients desperately in search of a better life. Building the canal was the opening act in the settlement of a new Western frontier, and in time temporary canal diggers would metamorphose, as if by magic, into permanent and respectable farmers.

In an 1837 report the board of internal improvement submitted to the Indiana General Assembly information on the "average rate of wages for common laborers exclusive of boarding," with housing being provided, albeit erratically, on some sections of the Wabash & Erie. Canallers received a monthly average of twenty-one dollars, an exceedingly high wage that reflected ruthless competition for labor. In his general remarks to the assembly Chief Engineer Jesse Williams noted that

> for the first nine or twelve months after contracts were made, laborers were scarce, and their wages soon became unusually high.—Not only was the progress of the work retarded ... but ... many of the contractors abandoned their jobs, which were subsequently let out at higher rates, increasing in proportion the cost of the improvements.

Williams, however, remained optimistic and informed the assembly of reports that large numbers of Irish workers, as well as Germans, had arrived in Indiana within the past six months. The employment of these immigrants, he noted, was expected to lower wages to "ordinary rates."[39]

The response to the opportunities America presented was a mass migration of men and women. Between the years 1815 and 1845 close to a million Irish immigrants came to North America, and another 1.8 million arrived in the decade following the Great Famine of 1845. According to immigration historian Kerby Miller, while almost half of the Irish who came to America between 1825 and 1832 were from Protestant Ulster, those who emigrated after were primarily poor laborers and tenants from Ireland's southern Catholic counties. Nearly four hundred thousand immigrants arrived between 1828 and 1837. Contemporaries observed that of those who arrived during America's cholera years (1831–32), many were "of the most useless description" or "mere beggars." In 1836 only 3 percent of those who disembarked in New York were characterized as artisans or professionals, and two-thirds were single men in their early twenties. These mid to late 1830s immigrants possessed "no capital but their manual labor" and were "without acquired skill of any kind." Moreover, post-Famine immigrants were even less skilled, more destitute, and desperate for immediate employment upon their arrival.[40]

Canal construction in the antebellum period suffered from continual labor shortages, due primarily to the sheer number of ongoing state and private projects that required thousands of able-bodied men. While early accounts of canals such as the Erie and the Ohio & Erie point to native-born, local residents as a majority of the construction workforce, by the mid-1820s European immigrants far outnumbered them. Various eyewitness reports mention English, Scottish, Welsh, and German immigrants at work on canals. Compared to the Irish, though, their numbers were rather limited because these groups typically arrived in families and counted more skilled artisans and professional men in their ranks. Transportation and labor historians contend that by the 1830s the bulk of North America's canal diggers were Irish, who, in contrast to other European immigrants, were primarily single, male, unskilled, and transient. In 1830 Charles F. Mercer, president of the Chesapeake & Ohio Canal, noted that among his common laborers, "the greater part of them are transient foreigners; sometimes on the Pennsylvania Canals; sometimes on the Baltimore & Ohio Railroad; sometimes at work on our canal."[41] Irish diggers on the Chesapeake & Ohio Canal whose passage was paid by the canal company signed contracts prior to leaving Europe and were thus reduced to the status of indentured servants—with the exception that they were guaranteed neither a fixed term of labor nor "freedom dues" upon fulfilling their contracts. Historian Seth Rockman has revealed the Chesapeake & Ohio's reliance on this antiquated labor system—despite its failings—as late as 1829, when the company imported five hundred bound laborers from Britain. After an unbearable voyage to America, these men found canal work just as debilitating and absconded—hundreds of them. Two who were recaptured filed a habeas corpus petition in federal court, stating that they "could not make themselves slaves." Immigrant canallers protested their treatment as commodities as the vestiges of indentured servitude persisted alongside the rapid proliferation of wage labor.[42]

As historian Carol Sheriff observes, inhabitants of Lockport, New York, remembered "hundreds" of Irish immigrants arriving as early as the 1820s. Among them, according to resident Mary Ann Archibald, were scores of "wild Irish working upon the Canal."[43] Though active overseas recruitment was limited in scope, consisting of contacts with American consuls at Belfast, Cork, and Dublin, pools of Irish workers were, in fact, directed to various American canals by organizations such as the Union Emigrant Society and the Irish Emigrant Association. Irish immigrants who arrived at eastern ports utilized advertisements in periodicals, including the *New York Truth Teller,* to find canal work, while others used kinship connections to inform friends and relatives of opportunities.[44]

Whether they were Corkonians (from southern Ireland), Ulstermen (from northern Ireland), or Fardowners (from north-central Ireland), strong regional, cultural, and religious identities shaped the experiences and perceptions of the Irish immigrants who built America's canals. Despite the fact that many early Irish immigrants were Protestants, native-born citizens imagined all Irish as Catholic—a religious group that became a target for nativists who feared its hierarchical organization, allegedly superstitious beliefs, and ties to political corruption.[45] Moreover, despite the prevalence of internecine conflicts on canals initiated prior to the Wabash & Erie, Hoosiers, like other American citizens, tended to portray Irish canal diggers as a monolithic group.

The number of Irish canal workers coming to the Hoosier State during the construction of the W&E in the 1830s and 1840s was substantial, if unknown, for neither the state nor contractors kept detailed records of their employees. But based on 1840 and 1850 state census returns, the number of Irish-born settlers tripled, and in many cases quadrupled, in counties along the route of the Wabash & Erie. Even considering the notable absence of transient workers in census reports, returns for 1850 reveal 1,766 Irish-born residents in northern Indiana, 47 percent of whom were between the ages of twenty and thirty-nine.

Various state and private sources indicate that more than 200 Irishmen were hired in the spring of 1832; that approximately 1,000 immigrants were at work near Fort Wayne in the summer of 1833; and that in 1834 and 1835 there were close to 2,000 immigrant workers on the canal between Fort Wayne and Huntington, thus marking the early period of construction.[46]

Canal contractors at first regarded Irishmen as unqualified and unemployable as skilled workers. Fort Wayne's German settlers may have endured a similar journey to the Hoosier State as their Irish counterparts, and a few, in fact, enjoyed equivalent (skilled) occupations on the canal, but the similarities ended there. The Wabash & Erie commissioners and labor agents had much different designs for Irish immigrants, and the state and its citizenry had much different perceptions of their role in canal building. As a result, Irish canallers shared neither the socioeconomic trajectory of most German settlers, nor the sentiments echoed by Henry Rudisill when he spoke of Hoosiers as "very attentive and obliging to Strangers."[47]

In his *American Notes for General Circulation,* Charles Dickens noted that without Irish laborers, "It would be hard to keep your model republics going . . . for who else would dig, delve, and drudge . . . and make canals and railroads, and execute great lines of internal improvement!" This need was evident but balanced by a repulsion of the new immigrants. Even after his conversion to Catholicism, American-born intellectual Orestes Brownson noted in a letter to James McMaster that "it is an undeniable fact that the Irish Catholics, and I speak only of them, bring here a civilization far below that which they find here. The great body of them are but one or two removes from the state of barbarians." Similarly, James Silk Buckingham, traveling through the midwestern frontier in the early 1840s, was disgusted at the conditions of the "colony of Irish laborers" engaged in canal labor in neighboring Illinois:

> A more repulsive scene we had not for a long time beheld. The number of persons congregated here were about 200, including men, women, and children, and these were crowded together in 14 or 15 log-huts temporarily erected for their shelter. . . . Whiskey and tobacco seemed the chief delight of the men; and of the women and children, no language could give an adequate idea of their filthy condition, in garments and person.[48]

Many commentators who wrote about canal life focused on its "rough" living, away from the more "civilized" centers of development. J. Gould, who wrote articles for the *New England Farmer* about his travels in the West, observed that "the influx of adventurers and foreigners attracted hither by the public works in vicinity, has exerted a deleterious influence upon the morals of the people, gambling and dissipation being too common, and petty theft scarcely rebuked."[49] Local residents often perceived the Irish as subhuman, willing to live in poverty and engage in disgusting work. The editor of the *Maumee City Express,* while traveling along the Wabash & Erie Canal in 1838, more directly projected Indianness onto the canallers' lifestyles and even their bodies. He noted that the canal passed through "a fine but uncultured country, with few inhabitants except the Irish abergoins *[sic]* that labor upon the canal." Equating the "uncultured" Irish canallers with the region's Indians [aborigines], the editor next described the shanty villages along the canal line, where apparently canallers and their progeny had fully crossed over the frontier line of civilization, located as they were on "the edge of the woods . . . [where] scores of naked, tow headed urchins play all sorts of antics by the way-side."[50]

Similarly, when Indiana received its first visit from a missionary affiliated with the Western Seamen's Friend Society, he was frustrated in his attempts to rectify the behavior of the uncivilized canallers who were then laboring to bring civilized progress to the West.[51] Arriving in the late 1840s, the missionary noted that "there is more out-breaking wickedness here than on any other thoroughfare of equal magnitude," a consequence, he argued, of the fact that "not one boat in ten had either a Bible or testament on board." Though the Friend Society focused its attention on the canal's boatmen and not its ditch-diggers, the missionary, after four months on the canal, was unhappy with its apparently godless atmosphere. He noted that "profane swearing, drinking, and card playing are allowed and indulged in to any extent on board." The men were simply incorrigible and reminded him "of the old Erie ten years ago . . . [with] men swearing just to hear themselves swear."[52]

The image of Irish transportation workers as uncivilized savages or animals was not unique to the Indiana frontier, for in 1859, when Irish workers in Jersey City barricaded the railroad track they had completed in protest of denied wages, elites denounced them as "*animals* . . . [a] mongrel mass of ignorance and crime and superstition," who were "utterly unfit for . . . the common courtesies and decencies of civilized life."[53]

Other writers, such as Rev. John O'Hanlon, criticized the accounts of local elites and travelers. O'Hanlon challenged both the republican image of America as a righteous land of "free labor" and the tendency of labor agents to lure workers with tales of progress and prosperity. In his *Irish Emigrant's*

Guide for the United States, O'Hanlon wrote sourly that Irish immigrants, while informed that beyond the Atlantic lies "the Land of Liberty, the Model Republic," soon learn that

> the Utopia of the imagination, is not the United States of our experience. By substituting fancy for judgment, romantic hopes are first formed to be afterwards destroyed.—Thus it often happens that the Irish emigrant who imagines he has escaped from the misery and oppression of his own misgoverned Island when he abandoned it, from pauperism and its attendant ills, finds a thousand difficulties stare him in the face [in America].[54]

In addition to authors of emigrant guides, Irish canallers occasionally found allies among newspaper editors and popular intellectuals of the period. Lamenting the conditions facing new immigrants working on canals, Ralph Waldo Emerson noted, "the poor Irishman, the wheelbarrow is his country," implying that Irish notions of belonging in America were rooted in hard manual labor.[55] While the popular transcendentalist and abolitionist Unitarian minister Theodore Parker claimed that Irish immigrants were "the worst people in Europe to make colonists of," the editor of the *Boston Pilot,* the official newspaper of the Archdiocese of Boston, disagreed and instead denounced the meager opportunities for Irish immigrants in America. He implored the Irish to avoid canal work, stating that it was "the ruin of thousands of our poor people," who were treated "like slaves" on massive transportation projects.[56]

Irish canal workers did not passively accept their reputation as un-American barbarians or their popular image as wage slaves. Behind the idealistic overtures of canal officials, diatribes on the squalid conditions of canal life, and prejudiced images of uncultured, drunken, and animalistic Irish diggers lay another story. Although less noticeable than canal celebrations and colorful narratives of American progress, this story is perhaps more telling. In bits and pieces, it points to the ways in which canallers struggled to liberate themselves from both the reality of exploitation and their image as uncivilized outsiders. The Irish canal story incorporates religion, networking, politics, alcohol, violence, and war, but from a much different perspective. In their encounters with missionaries, bosses, citizens, and coworkers, Irish canallers struggled to control their jobs and reputations, construct a masculine identity, and defend their niche on the transportation frontier.

In terms of organized religion, Catholic canallers were no less spiritually devoted than native- or foreign-born Protestants. Although in the early

1830s, only one-fifth of Indiana's Catholic population had regular contact with a priest, the writings of these frontier religious leaders suggest the desire of workers to wield their shovels and pickaxes in the creation of chapels along the canal route. For many, the visit of a priest was the most satisfying respite from their daily toil. Workers were known to prepare a *scalán,* or improvised sanctuary, a vestige of and tribute to the eighteenth-century penal code days when their forefathers celebrated Mass in secret under the direction of priests. Father Stephen Badin, a French-born missionary and the first Catholic priest ordained in the United States, was closely attuned to the difficulties facing the Wabash & Erie's Irish workers and enlisted their help in building a chapel at Fort Wayne. Thereafter, canallers helped build churches in Peru, Logansport, Lagro, Huntington, and other towns along the canal line.[57]

Despite the efforts of his Irish canallers, who literally worked overtime in building their places of worship along the ditch, Father Badin was disappointed in his flock. In a letter to John Baptist Purcell, the Cork County, Ireland-born bishop of Cincinnati, Badin described the condition of his congregation: "I will not expatiate on the character of our Catholics. It is known that the lower class of the Irish, such as work on canals &c. is too fond of drinking ... that there are very few of the devout sex [women], and few children among them."[58]

Still, Badin remained optimistic. He disclosed that "prevailing sickness & mortality, [and] the absence of a pastor & poverty" had prevented the establishment of church affairs for the Irish. Having observed both the transient nature of canal work and the dire condition of the Irish, he recommended that "no time should be lost in ... the erection of chapels along the canal line, because as soon as the work is done in one section of the country, the Catholic hands move to another section, and the prospect of such erections diminishes or vanishes." Badin felt that at least two priests should ride every week along "a line of 80 miles: They should be active, pious, learned and disinterested, courageous & mortified." Along the Wabash & Erie, he warned, "The character of our Cath[olics] ... has been so little respectable in general, that they rather confirm Protest[ant] prejudices than are available to any conversion."[59] In spite of such challenges, Badin recognized in his parishioners a desire for respectability and community. It was they who mustered what little energy they had after a day of ditchdigging to help build places of worship.

For some clergymen and missionaries, moralistic diatribes on canallers' "uncivilized" behavior were tempered with harsh critiques of management, decrying the unjust labor arrangements and exploitative conditions on the canal line. Invariably, contractors who cheated and mistreated their workers drew the wrath of religious leaders. Father John McDermott, a Catholic priest on the Wabash & Erie, complained to its trustees about a contractor who absconded "without paying his just debts," thereby "defrauding the poor men" in his employ. McDermott himself witnessed the "important work" the Irish canallers had completed, and the laborers complained to him that they had rightfully "earned hard, what was coming to them." McDermott argued that due to an inequitable labor system, the canal diggers had been degraded to "a wretched and miserable condition . . . without food, without raiment, without shelter, without those common necessaries, the absence of which will press heavily upon them during this cold and inclement season." Speaking on behalf of the men, he stated that they now counted on the canal's trustees "to see that they will be treated with kindness and I will add from myself, with justice."[60] In this way, canallers used religious leaders as a medium through which to voice their grievances, expose the unlawful behavior of irresponsible contractors, demand more respectful treatment from the company, and secure better conditions on the canal line.

Reactions to the aggressive and fraudulent attempts of company officials and contractors to lure canal diggers are similarly revealing. Canallers' familiarity with sickness, overbearing contractors, transiency, and late or denied payments taught them to distrust milk-and-honey stories of ideal wages and environments. Neither did they interpret such offers of employment as direct passageways to prosperity and citizenship. According to canal company reports and travelers' accounts, a firsthand information network developed among floating groups of Irish canallers, its purpose being to advise workers of actual conditions of employment on various canals. Such networks also countered the claims of canal companies, such as the Wabash & Erie, which guaranteed excellent wages, conditions, and settlement opportunities and which implied in annual reports that Irish workers routinely recruited friends and relatives to relocate to Indiana.[61]

Workers recognized the very cruel and unjust aspects of canal capitalism. Canal officials expressed alarm, privately, that Irish immigrants were fed up with poor conditions on canals and had written letters back East informing their friends of "the most false and discouraging accounts of frauds practiced upon the laborers here, the sickness of the country, etc., etc."[62] Peter Way has used these networks of firsthand accounts to demonstrate the collective action of workers, who sometimes turned their mobility into a bargaining tool. Moreover, friendly newspapers were also known to serve job-seeking canallers by spreading information about working conditions. Various pseudo-agents or "canal jobbers" ostensibly in the employ of the Wabash & Erie Canal circulated false reports, like the following in 1842, which infuriated the editor of the *Fort Wayne Sentinel,* who reported,

> A number of stone-cutters, chiefly Irish, and many with their families, have arrived here the past week, from New York on their way to work on the canal.... They were engaged by G. M. Nash ... who advertised in the [New York] papers and by bills posted ... that he was authorized by Messrs. Moorehead & Co. of Lafayette to engage them in work on the canal. Nash got $6.50 from each and gave them passage to Toledo. From Toledo, Moorehead and Co. would give them passage to Lafayette, where their fares would be returned. The Company denies all knowledge of Nash and needs no stone-cutters since the locks are made of wood. These families are to be pitied. Induced by high wages, now [they have] ... no money and no jobs.[63]

In the same year, the editor of the *Freeman's Journal* in New York targeted Indiana contractors and phony canal jobbers. Warning Irish canallers and notifying readers of changes in the newspapers' policy of printing labor notices, the editor remarked,

> We have received through the post a copy of a placard advertising for laborers on a state work in Indiana. We cannot consent to give insertion to anything of this kind, without receiving an assurance from some respectable friend in the vicinity,—as for instance, the Catholic clergyman,—that no deception is intended to be practiced. Much as we should be pleased to publish any information that would enable the hundreds of poor immigrants that land daily on our shores to find employment, we have known too many instances when such statements were put out merely as "decoy ducks" by heartless and unprincipled contractors, not to take the utmost caution necessary before giving them an implied sanction, by insertion in this journal.[64]

The English traveler and novelist Frederick Marryat connected with this information network in 1839 when he visited an impoverished group of Irish immigrants building a new lock on the Erie Canal outside of Troy, New York. Marryat was astonished at their shanties, noting that they looked "more like dog-kennels than the habitations of men." In one particular fourteen-by-ten-foot shanty lived an Irishman, his wife and children, and "seven boys as he called them, young men from twenty to thirty," who boarded with the family. The immigrants "complained bitterly of the times," noted Marryat, and since their wages were not equal to "2 shillings 6 pence of our money per day," they found it impossible to make a living. When

Marryat asked the group why they did not travel to Ohio and Indiana where canal wages were reportedly as high as $2 a day, they informed him that "such were the price *[sic]* quoted, to induce people to go, but that they never could find it when they arrived." Even on canals actively employing workers, "the clearing of new lands was attended with ague and fever." If the canallers became sick, "there was no one to help them to rise again."[65] Information sharing was a form of mutual aid and a survival mechanism that also bolstered class and ethnic solidarity. It helped canallers navigate a harsh environment and negotiate in an unforgiving economy.

Though Marryat was at first surprised by the collaboration and wherewithal of these Irish workers, the experience convinced him that the immigrants, though desperate for work, could be scrupulous in weighing the merits of canal opportunities. Such evidence contradicts the claims of many contemporary observers, such as Francis Grund, who insisted that Irish immigrants "perform[ed] the hardest labors at the lowest wages given" on canals and railroads because they were "contented" with the mere "bare necessities of life." Moreover, shrewdness on the part of Irish immigrants seeking employment in the canal network discredits Grund's contention that Americans deplored the Irish for their willingness to "settle" with canal labor and "neglect the more useful cultivation of soil," which would immediately render them "independent and respectable."[66] For many Irish workers, seeking out steady and decent-paying canal jobs was in fact an attempt to earn a sense of respectability and independence in an immigrant-dominated field of employment. The popular nineteenth-century ballad "Paddy on the Canal" spoke to such a sense of pride, masculine courage, and expertise in the craft of canal building:

> When I came to this wonderful rampire *[sic]*, it filled me with the greatest surprise,
> To see such a great undertaking, on the like I never opened my eye.
> To see a full thousand brave fellows at work among mountains so tall,
> To dig through the vallies *[sic]* so level, through rocks for to cut a canal.
> I learned for to be very handy, to use both the shovel and spade,
> I learnt the whole art of canalling, I think it an excellent trade.
> I learnt to be very handy, although I was not very tall,
> I could handle the sprig of shallelah *[sic]*, with the best man on the canal.[67]

Of course, one of most powerful statements Irish canallers made was to refuse a contractor's offer of employment, which happened on several occasions in Indiana, especially during outbreaks of cholera on the canal line.

During a particularly devastating appearance of the illness, a frustrated contractor on the Wabash & Erie protested having to offer "extravigant [sic] wages" to obtain workers.[68] Aided by fellow diggers and friendly editors, information networks functioned as eyes and ears for floating groups of canallers, providing a measure of control in an unfair and uncertain labor market.

Along with the transiency, skill, determination, and pride inherent in building transportation networks, a vigorous masculine identity was a defining characteristic of canal construction communities. This sense of masculinity differed in important ways from both middle-class notions of civilized manliness and the idealized masculine republicanism of organized white workers in the early republic period.[69] For those who built canals and even those who observed the building, aggressive masculinity was considered a prerequisite for this type of labor. Because Irish canallers were denied the protection of labor unions and many of the privileges of citizenship, a sense of masculine pride was perhaps their only short-term advantage or internal reward, not unlike the "psychological wage" that David Roediger and other labor historians have analyzed.[70] At its core, canal labor was masculine labor, and although no evidence exists of a masculine crisis among Irish canallers, performing and internalizing masculinity carried both benefits and consequences. Masculinity was a source of worker camaraderie, born in the yoke of American progress. It was strengthened or contested through regional loyalties, challenged in exploitative labor arrangements, and hardened by the dangers and tragedies of canal building. It permeated the daily life of canallers.

Politics also revealed varying degrees of autonomy. Canallers' active participation in the political process was irregular in the 1820s and 1830s despite the rise of Jacksonian democracy and the concomitant growth of universal manhood suffrage, which eliminated most property and taxpaying qualifications. Nonetheless, some exclusions persisted, reflecting a desire to protect state sovereignty against outsiders, recent immigrants, the insane, paupers, criminals, and "persons under guardianship."[71] State laws rarely made ethnic distinctions, but nativists believed that since immigrants comprised a clear majority of the poor and criminal element, "neutral" exclusions would keep them off the voting roles. Indiana's canallers who were recent immigrants or transients technically did not meet the state's one-year residency requirement to vote, but selective enforcement of the requirement, along with the Democratic Party's political reliance on the Irish, suggests avenues of opportunity—however limited. Evidence also points to the exploitation of canal workers by their bosses, who registered them to vote only to stuff ballot boxes with illegal votes in favor of particular political candidates. In addition to voting fraud, Irish canal workers were sought after as bodyguards for various politicians based on their reputation as tough, intimidating men and skilled fighters. This they sometimes used to their advantage. For example, after incessant bargaining, a canal superintendent in charge of a maintenance crew on the Wabash & Erie guaranteed his workers less onerous duties on the job if they agreed to serve as bodyguards at political meetings.[72]

Irish canallers rejected both their tenuous political status as transients and their mistreatment as political pawns at the hands of employers. In 1844 a group of workers on the Wabash & Erie near Lafayette rejected contractor James Johnson's offer of employment after coworkers informed them that, in the previous (1840) election, unless his workers promised to vote Whig, Johnson "only had to point his level at an Irishman and he was dismissed from the work."[73] Such evidence reveals that Irish immigrants seized opportunities to capitalize on their status as hardy and manly canal builders to negotiate and ameliorate their conditions. It also suggests that canallers saw their role in canal building as worthy of the same rights and privileges as American-born, working-class men.

A major source of the prejudices directed toward Irish canallers centered on the use of alcohol. Labor and social historians have argued that "ardent spirits" constituted an influential prop of worker identity, and in some communities the tavern or grog shop functioned as both an independent cultural sphere and leisure institution for the ethnic working class. Irish culture reserved a special place for alcohol: as a food substitute; a panacea for aches, pains, and chills; an illegal source of income among distillers; and a facilitator of social interaction. The "shebeen," or unlicensed drinking establishment, was a location where working-class Irish men could escape their harsh daily routine. While scholars have acknowledged liquor's tendency to unite the working classes, erode the social and physical health of their communities, and reinforce notions of an aggressive masculinity, the canal ditch and shanty camp are locations that complicate historical understandings of the benefits and consequences of alcohol.[74]

For canal workers the consumption—and even the abuse—of alcohol served several interrelated purposes. Canallers drank to assert manhood, to rouse (or trick) their minds and bodies into performing dangerous work, and to deaden the physical pain and emotional suffering associated with canal building. Despite its consequences, the bottle provided an outlet for workers' community, resistance, and aggressive masculine identity. In the drink a man found insulation and also the power to assert his will.

On the Wabash & Erie the role of intoxicating liquors followed two general patterns. Workers imbibed on the job, soaking up their daily ration of hard liquor (normally whiskey), which consisted of three to four gills a day, for a total of twelve to twenty ounces. This form of drinking was an inherent part of the moving "workplace" of transportation labor. Canallers also enjoyed "ardent spirits" after hours at local grog shops and in the comfort of their shanty camps. Typically, this type of drinking reinforced solidarity among workers, though such social drinking often devolved into bingeing, which could incite taunts and fistfights—practices that, while difficult to quantify or substantiate, were recycled in accounts by native-born and foreign-born observers of the Irish shanty scene.[75]

When asked why canallers relied so heavily on their preferred intoxicant, a former Wabash & Erie jigger boss replied, "you wouldn't expect them to work on the canal if they were sober, would you?"[76] Looking back on the canal period, another traveler remarked that the very "idea of constructing a canal without whiskey would have been viewed as preposterous.... In a word, [it was] an article that possessed specific virtues at all times." This traveler continued, "Every shanty was supplied with whiskey which cooled them when it was hot, and heated them when it was cool; that was good in prosperity or adversity, in sickness and in health, before breakfast in the morning, and on retiring to rest at night."[77]

If observers made much of Irish drunkenness, sources also point to contractors routinely using "grog carriers" or "jigger bosses" and thus knowingly violating company rules in permitting whiskey on the canal line. Stoking the fires of preexisting conflicts among their workers, contractors often provided barrels of whiskey in lieu of cash, in the hope that melees would ensue, thus driving off perhaps hundreds of workers and leaving far fewer hands demanding payment.[78] David Watkins, who emigrated from Wales in 1819, later took such a job in Lagro as a "grog carrier for the laborers digging the big ditch . . . most of them Irishmen." For his services, the canallers paid Watkins seventy-five cents "in the 'blue pup' and 'white dog' [paper] currency of those days."[79] The provisioning of alcohol to workers particularly disturbed traveler Frances Trollope, who condemned the "large allowance of whiskey" that contractors furnished to lure canallers into longer hours, to help them "stand the boiling heat" and perform dangerous tasks, and to both placate workers and precipitate conflict between them.[80]

On the neighboring Illinois & Michigan Canal, canallers' reputation for hard drinking led the canal board to write contracts guaranteeing pay in ninety-day intervals, since shorter periods led to "frolics" and delayed progress. But this quarterly pay schedule became problematic for small contractors with more temporary projects who sought employees for a matter of days or weeks, and so the policy was reversed. Irish canallers collaborated in attempts to avoid "dry" employers, putting contractors in a frustrating position. On one occasion, a group of Illinois contractors noted in a letter to the board of trustees that, upon securing a large group of construction workers, the men collectively demanded "$1.25 per day or $1.00 and liquor."[81]

According to the writings of Presbyterian minister James Chute, Irish workers on the Wabash & Erie Canal were even more successful in bargaining for alcohol than their fellow diggers in Illinois. Though Chute labored tirelessly to eliminate "the use of ardent spirits on the line" and distributed temperance tracts to canal officials and workers, his first year in Indiana led him to believe "that no part of the west has been more addicted to intemperance than this region."[82] The minister eventually convinced the canal commissioners to include a provision in contracts such as the following for section 2 of the Middle Division: "The party of the first part [contractor] shall not permit any of the workmen in his employ while they are engaged in constructing this Section [Fort Wayne] to drink distilled spirits of any kind under the liability of forfeiting this contract at the option of the party of the Second part [canal commissioners].[83] Chute, however, was not convinced that the commissioners and contractors observed the rules. By the summer of 1835 the minister remained dejected at the state of affairs on the Wabash & Erie, noting that contractors "in some instances have broken over, being too much influenced by the character of their workmen."[84]

Such negotiating on the part of workers suggests that alcohol was much more than a source of degenerate and uncivilized behavior, as elites, travelers, and citizens argued. For Irish canallers, alcohol was an incentive or concession to demand. It was a bargaining chip, central to workers' pride, masculinity, and solidarity, which demonstrated their power to act effectively in—and even determine the course of—an often unfair labor arrangement. The centrality of alcohol to canal building was memorialized in the ballad "Paddy on the Canal":

I being an entire stranger, be sure I had not much to say,
The Boss came round in a hurry, says, boys, it is grog time a-day.

We all marched up in good order, he was father now unto us all,
Sure I wished myself from that moment to be working upon the canal.[85]

This humor in this ballad masks a paternalism that was also evident on the canal line, with bosses and contractors as father figures and diggers as boys. Such paternalism, in fact, could be exacerbated through the strategic use of alcohol on and off the job. It was, after all, the "Boss" who controlled the dispensations of liquor in this instance. Of course, not all Irish canallers abused "ardent spirits," and in many cases the elite company officials and businessmen who decried alcohol actually facilitated its use. Moreover, contractors often reneged on their contractual obligations by forcing workers to consent to payment in "grog and provisions."[86] The *New York Truth Teller* was persistent in warning its Irish readership of this notorious custom and, in public notices such as the following, confronted the "unmanly" character of contractors and linked payment in booze to the brutal routine of canal labor:

> The immoral contractor ... distributes among his laborers the fatal draft of ardent poison for the unmanly purpose of working his unfortunate victims beyond their natural strength, of weakening, during the delirious excitement which follows the maddening libation ... [their] reason ... at the time most sedulously selected for the settlement of accounts.[87]

Canallers' few allies in the press, recognizing the consequences of alcohol abuse, did not single out intemperate workers as unmanly or uncivilized. Instead, it was those persons with direct ties to the canal company who demonstrated unmanliness in using alcohol as a means to exploit their workers, weakening strong and respectable men who devoted life and limb to building American progress.

Although shared cultural norms and values could produce solidarity among Irish workers, canallers identified with one another more on the basis of shared regional identity, as opposed to a common national identity as "Irish." Forces at work within Irish canal communities provoked internal discord, one involving their relationship with their employers, the other stemming from Irish tradition. In many instances, such as on the Erie Canal, Chesapeake & Ohio, Illinois & Michigan, and Wabash & Erie, factional combinations typical of pre-Famine Ireland shifted overseas and were intensified on America's transportation frontiers.

Irish workers endured the struggles of canal building in America with time-honored strategies familiar to them in Ireland. The secret society, which assumed various forms in America, was an organizational model used to both mediate ethnic rivalries and combat oppressive labor conditions on canals. In pre-Famine Ireland, the self-identified poor, small farmers and rural laborers of Cork, Limerick, Killkenny, Waterford, and Tipperary Counties engaged in frequent conflicts with the rural middle class, including the large farmers, millers, shopkeepers, employers, and landlords. The most powerful expression of these conflicts was known as "Whiteboyism," outbreaks of agrarian terrorism aimed at the rural middle classes, the goal of which was to address and rectify the economic hardships of the laboring poor.[88] In pre-Famine Ireland, traditional faction fighting, of which Whiteboyism was a part, was transformed from its territorial origins to more modern, economic, and class-based conflicts. While historians such as David Grimsted have argued that Irish labor riots on American canals were solely products of "imported clan battles," recent evidence suggests that canal riots also stemmed from issues of job security in a brutal and unyielding labor market and that conflicts between regional Irish factions were in fact exacerbated on American canals.[89] Canallers working on remote transportation frontiers utilized secret societies and other organizations to threaten competitors and bosses, drive up wages, protect their meager subsistence, and assert their manhood.[90]

On the Wabash & Erie, Irish canallers were just as often targets of violence as they were its perpetrators. Indiana-born Josiah McCafferty, whom the *Indianapolis News* celebrated as a "hale and rugged . . . survivor of canal-boat days," spent most of his life near the W&E and captained a boat during the busiest days of the canal era. When a newspaper reporter asked him to discuss his exploits and experiences on the artificial river, McCafferty recalled his pride and excitement at the time of the canal's construction, noting that he "used to hide behind the trees and throw stones at the Irish laborers, who were brought here to dig it."[91] Far more than a random act of violence, casting stones at Irish workers was an outward sign of community contempt for immigrant canallers, despite the fact that they were engaged in the most important construction project in the state's history.

Hoosiers and other American citizens often interpreted violence as a negative consequence of the uncivilized canal working environment and, more particularly, as endemic to Irish work camps. Trollope lamented this inattention to the dangers facing immigrant canallers during her experience on the transportation frontier. On two separate occasions, she witnessed the casualties of canal labor, and though murder was presumed in at least one case, as the unfortunate victim "had marks of being throttled," it struck her as appalling that "no inquest was summoned; and certainly no more sensation was produced by the occurrence than if a sheep had been found in the same predicament." More often than not, noted Trollope, when an Irishman died along the canal, he was "literally thrown on one side, and a new comer takes his place."[92] In Indiana this perception of violence changed if it involved a local community member, such as when a group of Irish workers assaulted a man for telling them to be quiet. The man's brother pulled out a gun and shot at the attackers, murdering one of them.[93]

Incidents such as this convinced many Irish workers that America was far from the "best poor man's country," as some contemporaries argued. According to one irritated immigrant, the life of an Irish laborer in the mid-nineteenth century was "despicable, humiliating, [and] slavish." There existed "no love for him" and "no protection of life." The Irish immigrant worker "can be shot down, run through, kicked, cuffed, spat on—and no redress, but a response of served the damn son of an Irish b[itch] right, damn him."[94] "Had I fallen from the clouds amongst this people," declared another poor Irishman, "I could not feel more isolated, more bewildered."[95]

For exploited groups, whether as perpetrators or victims, violence has often been a sign of agency, and such was the case on the Wabash & Erie Canal. Fifteen-year-old John TenBrook Campbell, an Indiana-born orphan, worked as a farm laborer for four dollars a month when, in 1848, he took a job on the W&E for Irish boss Tom Burns, who promised him boarding and seven-dollar "canal scrip" for a "dry month" of work.[96] According to Campbell, who performed odd jobs such as tending horses and hauling fill from the excavation site to a dumping area, he was "the only Hoosier among 150 Irish" who worked for Burns. Each day at noon he was forced to "allow two Irish boys . . . to whip me for the amusement of the men." As Campbell recalled, "when I had worked four and a half weeks . . . I asked Burns if my month was up. He stormed out with boy-scaring oaths—'that time is not up yet.'" Inquiring after six weeks, and again after seven, Burns had not yet paid up, and, according to Campbell, "he drove me off without any pay at all."[97]

Campbell's unpleasant experience reveals not only the dependency of the contractor-employee relationship but also the rare opportunity for Irish canallers to assert their manhood (and their rank on the canal) in violent confrontations with native-born workers. The daily assaults on Campbell suggest several readings. The Irish "boys" targeted him as an American, a scapegoat who bore the collective guilt of his countrymen for their sins. This would help explain why the beatings took the shape of a performance, with two Irish boys attacking Campbell, whom they considered an arrogant and insolent American based on his alleged claim that he could "whip" the young assailants.[98] The workers' resentment also drew on the fault lines of class, as the young, inexperienced Campbell was offered employment in a section crew of seasoned canal men who struggled mightily to secure employment in an uncertain job market. At the very least, these violent encounters functioned as episodes of self-definition and masculine solidarity for Irish workers. Such physical abuse provided an occasion for disgruntled immigrant canallers to defend their tenuous position at the bottom of the canal-building industry before it shifted, once again, to another ditch.

Physical confrontations on the canal often turned deadly, and by reading beyond prejudiced accounts of canal violence, the character of Indiana's Irish canal communities is revealed. J. Wesley Whicker, a lawyer from Attica, Indiana, lived through the end of the canal era and wrote one of the earliest histories of the Wabash Valley, portions of which appeared in the *Attica Ledger*. The Wabash & Erie reached Attica in 1848, and Whicker discussed the difficulties facing Irish construction workers in the region and the problem of canal violence. In particular, he recalled an incident that "illustrate[s] the attitude of the people toward these imported laborers." Large gravel beds south of Attica caused problems for canal diggers, as the ditch was unable to hold an adequate amount of water. Thus, a contract to build a feeder dam at Shawnee Creek was offered to Col. James McManomy, who was also the principal contractor for the canal section from Attica to Fountain. One morning, while on the job, McManomy and his subcontractor Douglas Trott "found their Irish laborers coming late to work," and a dispute arose after McManomy "reproved them." Apparently, the tardy canallers were "still arrogant from the effects of their Sunday carousal." When one "big Irishman" assumed his position on a "gangway scaffold" erected to wheel loads of dirt, he disputed Trott's right to pass him on the narrow causeway. Despite his alleged hangover, the Irish canaller endeavored to control the wheelbarrow work on this section, even if it involved a direct challenge to his boss's authority. Without saying a word, Trott punched him in the face, knocking the man off the scaffold and to the ground. When Trott and McManomy checked on the man, they were "surprised to find that his neck was broken and that he was dead."[99]

Trott was not charged with manslaughter, and neither a coroner nor the grand jury investigated the cause of death. The Irishman's wife was employed as a cook at the shanty camp, and her reaction, seen through the eyes of

Whicker, confirmed prevailing stereotypes about Irish canal families. Although she "set up a great lamentation" upon arriving at the scene, "the burden of her grief" was focused primarily on the fact that her husband had been laid to rest "in nothing but an old dirty shirt." When McManomy offered his own clean shirt, the Irishman's wife expressed her approval of the proper burial (near the canal bank). She then "went on cooking for the workmen and doubtless acquired another husband." One can only speculate as to whether McManomy or Trott informed the woman of her husband's true cause of death, since fatal accidents were prevalent during canal construction. Moreover, Attica's Irish community had grown accustomed to the tragedies of frontier canal building, as cholera appeared on the canal in the spring of 1848, killing close to four hundred of the six hundred men, women, and children in one camp alone. Most of the dead were thrown into trenches dug near the shanty camp and "covered with a soft lime or marl."[100]

Lost in this account of the murder of an Irish canaller in Attica is the poignant reaction of the deceased's wife, herself an important member of the canal network as a cook for several hundred transient Irish workers. Though no justice in the form of a trial or punishment was meted out, her desire for a respectable burial for her husband speaks to a demand for dignity that permeated—but was denied to—Irish canal communities on the Indiana frontier. Whether or not the murdered canaller's wife learned of the circumstances surrounding his death, her insistence that supervisors properly inter her husband along the canal ditch where he toiled in the name of American progress suggests that Irish canal communities valued life and death in ways the belied their uncivilized image. Her lament forced the canal boss to recognize, at least temporarily, a worker's and fellow Irishman's humanity.

Irish immigrants' struggle for control was readily apparent in reports of Indiana's "Irish War" at Lagro in 1835. This conflict involved a contest of canal communities from within. The Lagro War was Indiana's only incidence of open warfare during the canal era, and while authorities swiftly prevented lethal violence between the combatants, contemporaries found in this unfortunate conflict ample evidence to substantiate their prejudiced views of the Irish "problem" on American canals. According to canal commissioner David Burr, who observed the hostilities at Lagro, the Irish factions involved had only recently emigrated from Williamsport, Maryland, where, while building the Chesapeake & Ohio Canal, their "bloody affrays" had traumatized the local community.[101] Yet there was more to the story than the prejudices of the authorities.

In January 1834 two contending groups of Irish canal workers had engaged in a "kind of guerilla war" on the Chesapeake & Ohio near Williamsport. These "armies" of Irish canallers included the Longfords (or Fardowns) from north-central Ireland and the Corkonians from the south.[102] The canallers from Cork had organized to protect their jobs and control the work on a section of the C&O. On January 16 Corkonians assaulted a group of Longford laborers, killing one of them. The deceased worker's comrades vowed revenge, and on January 20 two hundred Longfords attacked Corkonian canallers working a few miles south of Williamsport. On January 24 both sides armed themselves with guns, clubs, and other crude weapons in preparation for battle. Nearly seven hundred Longfords crushed an outnumbered force of three hundred Corkonians, chasing the remaining survivors through the woods. Witnesses noted "five men in the agonies of death, who had been shot through the head," as well as "several dead bodies ... in the woods, and a number wounded in every direction."[103] The bloody conflict horrified local residents, and, in addition to the arrest of thirty-five rioters by the state militia, for the first time in American history federal troops were dispatched to quell a labor dispute. Soldiers from Baltimore were stationed in Williamsport for the remainder of the winter. During a peace meeting between the rival factions and the "leading citizens of the village" at Lyle's Tavern in Williamsport, delegates from the Longfords and Corkonians signed a treaty pledging to avoid interference along the canal line and to report anyone attempting to violate the agreement.[104] The *Niles' Weekly Register* described this treaty as "somewhat of a novelty in diplomatic history," which read, in part,

Whereas great commotions and divers riotous acts have resulted from certain misunderstandings and alleged grievances, mutually urged by two parties of laborers and mechanics, engaged on the line of the Chesapeake and Ohio Canal, and natives of Ireland; the one commonly known as the Longford men, the others as the Corkonians; and whereas it has been found that these riotous acts are calculated to disturb the public peace, without being in the least degree beneficial to the parties opposed to each other, but on the contrary are productive of great injury and distress to the workmen and their families. ... Therefore, we, the undersigned, representatives of each party ... pledge ... that we will not ... interrupt ... any person engaged on the line of the canal, for or on account of a local difference or national prejudice, and that we will use our influence to destroy all these matters of difference growing out of this distinction of parties, known as Corkonians and Longfords ... and we further bind ourselves to the State of Maryland, each in the sum of twenty dollars, to keep the peace towards the citizens of the state.[105]

This deadly conflict grew out of tensions characteristic of the underworld of progress on America's canals: the endemic problem of job security, strained relationships between employers and employees, and rival factions of workers who utilized organization, violence, and intimidation to protect their livelihoods. During the winter of 1834, as the Chesapeake & Ohio Canal Company neared bankruptcy, its commissioners lobbied local banks for loans that would provide contractors with overdue funds. One contractor, in particular, released his group of canallers without pay after they had completed their work. A local newspaper editor argued that these unpaid laborers were responsible for the guerilla war in late January, as they reacted to "either the suspension of the work, or of payment" on various sections of the canal.[106] Although the company soon acknowledged its role in the war, paid the contractor, and instructed him to place announcements in local papers to track down his unpaid men, some of the dynamics of this conflict resurfaced on the Wabash & Erie.

When these canallers migrated to Indiana in September 1834, Burr was convinced that they "brought their animosities with them." Even worse, argued Governor Noah Noble, these workers, in accepting jobs on the canal, had planned on "making the Wabash country the theatre of their riotous conduct."[107] Upon their arrival, Corkonians dominated the construction along the "upper part" of a fifty-mile stretch of the canal in Wabash County, with Fardowns working alternate sections on the "lower end of the line."[108] Evidence suggests that the Corkonians initiated the violence, perhaps in retaliation of their defeat at Williamsport. As the "strongest party on the line," noted one editor, the Corkonians "embraced every opportunity of maltreating such of the Fardowns as might fall into their hands." When, in the summer of 1835, the Fardowns "received great successions to their numbers," they in turn determined to drive the Corkonians from the canal.[109] According to Burr, on July 10 "at least 700 armed and highly exasperated men," almost equally divided, "left their work and commenced a march towards the centre of the line for a general battle."[110]

An engineer had informed Burr that the Fardowns were the first group to march to the reputed field of battle. Upon arriving, Burr found the canallers "in very orderly array, well armed, and not a noisy or drunken man amongst them." The conflict, according to the Fardowns, did not involve alcohol, illness, or the dangers of canal digging but rather was based on job security and exacerbated by the regional loyalties of the workers. Both groups had hired themselves out to contractors on different parts of the line, and the goal of each was to dominate the work and ensure the wages of its people. The Fardowns convinced Burr that if given the choice, they preferred to "remain peaceable," but this was no longer an option. They were "forced to fight" or else "have their cabins burnt and their inmates slain" under the cover of darkness. Frustrated that the "civil authority" from whom they toiled "did not protect them," for weeks the Fardown workers and their families "hid out in the woods, without light or fire to betray the places where they were." Now, with increased numbers, the workers insisted that they "had no recourse left but a battle" and would rather "fight fairly in open day" than be subjected to "depredations at night." Much to his surprise, Burr found that the Corkonians "expressed the same fears of the others" and agreed to "suspend hostile operations" with the Fardowns until they learned of the terms of the joint peace agreement.[111] Far from a monolithic group of "worthless," uncivilized, drunken, and "degraded ruffians," Burr found a canal community contested from within, with genuine fears, legitimate grievances, and a determination to control their destiny along a canal that held the potential to divide their own countrymen.[112]

A local militia force ended any threat of violence. Eight "ringleaders" among the Irish factions were arrested and transported under guard to Indianapolis, the closest site with an adequate prison. When the men were released under a writ of habeas corpus, the militia members, along with Commissioner Burr and his associates, were outraged.[113] Capt. Elias Murray, in particular, thought that his service to Indiana and canal progress necessitated far more than the one dollar a day he received as leader of the military escort to Indianapolis. Even more upset by the lack of public admiration, he noted that "no reward but that of ingratitude has been meted out to the Citizens who prevented the intended Massacre."[114]

Though the threat of overt violence may have resulted in employers being closer attuned to the rights and concerns of canallers, in other instances the effect of violence and rioting was insignificant and only exacerbated the harsh working conditions on the transient frontiers of canal construction. Riotous workers were often laid off or blacklisted, such as after the Lagro War, when the W&E Canal Board instructed its contractors "to dismiss any laborer who may engage in a broil and give his name to the engineers that he may not be employed on the line." From Indiana's point of view, the Lagro War on the W&E was a chance to squash "disorderly" Irish rioters and for the state to flex its muscle and promote, in the words of Burr, "working men and not fighting men" to the benefit of the improvement scheme.[115]

Meanwhile, a dominant narrative continued, as it had throughout the canal era in Indiana, one of violence, drunkenness, and disorder—a story that had sacrificed the "fair" subsistence due to the industrious canallers and distanced them from their daily investment to the progress of internal improvements. Construction was seen as a preliminary phase to the true goal of the business, the operation of a completed canal. In this triumph, canal diggers provided mere "animal power."[116] They were rendered a faceless, commodified, dehumanized army of economic units. They were, however, much more.

According to Burr's letter to Governor Noble, excessive debts, the safety of local citizens, and the interruption of the canal construction caused by an ill-defined threat of violence overshadowed any recognition of the investment the Irish had made in this monumental project and the toll it was taking on their daily existence. In his response to Burr, Governor Noble noted that the Lagro War was an occurrence of an "unusual kind, growing out of, and threatening the progress of, the work in which the state is engaged." Unconcerned about the immediate safety of the canallers, Noble, who insisted that "the treasury of that [Wabash] county is not justly chargeable with the expense," thus ignited a healthy debate over who would assume the debts resulting from expenditures made in hopes of ensuring peace, order, and progress in the construction of the canal.[117] As such, the government was unwilling to protect or assist the Irish workers, who, as the answer to the state's crucial problems of excessive cost and an inadequate supply of labor, were essential to the success of the canal experiment. Their plight marked the paradox of progress, the underworld of improvement, and the absurdity of canal mania in Indiana.

When residents, settlers, and dignitaries described how canals had transformed their midwestern frontier—and their nation—they did so in ways that Frederick Jackson Turner rehashed in his interpretation of the "new West," where democracy and national character gained strength each time Americans touched (or conquered) a new frontier.[118] In tying the building of the Wabash & Erie Canal to the fate of the American republic and to the struggles and honors associated with white American manhood, Gen. Lewis Cass surpassed even the canal's most virulent supporters. Invited to give the oration at the July 4, 1843, canal celebration at Fort Wayne, Cass noted with pride that in the completion of the Wabash & Erie, American social and political institutions, as well as its "national character," had "never achieved a prouder triumph nor furnished a more irrefutable proof of their tendency to promote human happiness, than in this peaceful victory over the natural impediments which divided us." According to Cass, the canal, having improved a "great highway of nature" and united the Great Lakes with the Mississippi, was the "greatest of enterprises in the history of internal improvement." At the very least, he argued, the canal offered living proof that "the frontier [was] fading and falling," and in its place "a morally intelligent and industrious people are spreading themselves over the whole face of the country and making it their own."[119]

Nonetheless, General Cass's oration reveals the paradoxes that accompanied previous (and future) canal celebrations. Most glaring was his explanation of the "triumph" of labor, considering the absence of non-American workers in his narrative. Cass matter-of-factly attributed the completion of this massive work to hardy, virtuous American citizens. First, he reminded his anxious audience that the day was not one for "figures" but for "results," because "this ardor of expectation, this confidence in the result, is at the foundation of all great success." Next, Cass reduced physical labor to "the triumph of mind and the exertion of intellect." This, he argued, was the "reckless energy" behind the Wabash & Erie Canal, and it was the "energy and perseverance" of the state that led to the completion of such a "stupendous undertaking." Finally, Cass pointed to the "power of association" linking Hoosiers and Americans to the canal, a power "which binds together the past and the present and connects both with the future."[120]

General Cass's address was only one part of the "largest assemblage ever witnessed in Indiana" since the "Tippecanoe" convention of William Henry Harrison. The *Fort Wayne Weekly Sentinel* reported that an estimated ten to fifteen thousand "citizens of Indiana and Ohio" attended the celebration of the canal's completion from Lake Erie to Lafayette, a distance of 225 miles. According to the editor, "citizens cheerfully entered into the spirit of the occasion," commemorating "a work ... which ranks in importance second only to the great New York canal" and one to which Hoosiers "have looked forward for so long with such earnest solicitude and fond anticipation." Visitors from Indiana's interior "flocked in by hundreds on horseback or in wagons and vehicles of every description," while canal boats draped with American flags packed the entire length of the canal in Fort Wayne. A mile-long procession featuring four marching bands, the Toledo Guards, indigenous Miami "warriors," veterans of the Revolution and the War of 1812, engineer corps, and a host of thirty-five invited dignitaries marched from the public square to the celebratory grounds. Amazingly, despite a free dinner, the "plenteous cold collation" of twenty-three toasts, and the firing of seventy-six rounds of ammunition in corresponding salutes, "Everything was conducted with the utmost regularity and decorum . . . and nothing occurred to mar the pleasure of [the] celebration."[121]

Toasts and gun salutes honored the Fourth of July, military branches and veterans, the president (John Tyler) and deceased former president (William Henry Harrison), Congress, the Union, statesmen, and distinguished guests. Predictably, the canal's common laborers, its literal builders, were ignored, just as they were in 1835 at Fort Wayne's first canal celebration. Instead, the ninth of thirteen "regular toasts" granted "just gratitude and honor" to Congress for its 1827 land grant and to Ohio and Indiana "for their energy and enterprise in consummating the great work."[122]

Following the regular and "volunteer" toasts, the organizers read aloud letters of congratulations from the twenty-three invited guests who could not attend the celebration. John Johnston of Piqua, Ohio, who had previously served on the canal board of Ohio, honored the "bona fide taxpaying citizens of Indiana and Ohio," who "by their public spirit and patriotism in the completion of the Wabash & Erie Canal . . . have reflected imperishable honor on themselves and their posterity." Martin Van Buren praised these same "worthy and enterprising" citizens in completing "an undertaking for which they have so long, so sedulously, and so perseveringly labored." Samuel Ruggles, a New York canal commissioner, thanked the western politicians, whom he considered "valued fellow laborers in the broad field of internal improvement," and honored the Wabash & Erie as "a signal triumph of intelligence, patriotism, and honest enterprise." William C. Bouck, governor of New York who spent twenty years as a member of the Erie Canal Commission, predicted that the W&E would replicate the success of the Erie, which transformed western New York, "as if by magic from agricultural despondency to a high state of prosperity." In this respect, John McLean, U.S. Supreme Court justice, concurred, writing that "along the line of this great work, flourishing villages and towns will rise as if by magic."[123]

Bestowing honor upon states and their citizens was undoubtedly a common feature of canal-era celebrations, but even a cursory analysis of these jovial gatherings reveals their carefully constructed purpose. The repeated omission of both immigrant and transient common laborers and the displacing of these individuals with statesmen, engineers, and "worthy" citizens suggests a reimagining or reclaiming of history that mirrored celebrations of the early American republic. When Americans of various social, ethnic, and political backgrounds feted (in print or in parades, demonstrations, and public speeches) the Declaration of Independence, the Second Treaty of Paris, the ratification of the Constitution, and other significant events, they projected not only consensus but dissent. In other words, celebrations, particularly during the nineteenth century, surpassed mere romantic associations with the past and became planned, politicized "struggles for recognition" and rites of nationhood.[124]

Indiana's Irish canallers played no role in canal celebrations, despite the fact that their labor was central to the rites of nationhood that statesmen and citizens commemorated. Nonetheless, when these canal diggers refused to bend their backs, when they engaged in violence, protested conditions, refused work, jostled to protect their jobs, and drifted to different canal sections in search of better opportunities, were they not drawing on—even creating—their own "struggles for recognition"? Lost in the haze of the canal ditch were the outward signs of their struggle, their quest for power, fair treatment, job security, and recognition as canal men who sweat and bled and died while building American progress.

For most historians, the failure of the Wabash & Erie Canal highlights the fundamental controversies over internal improvements: public versus private enterprise, consolidated governmental power versus local autonomy, and "particular interests" versus the "general welfare," along with the bane of public debt.[125] Judge David Kilgore, who voted for the 1836 Mammoth Bill while a state legislator, noted in 1851, with lingering puzzlement and regret, that those who voted for the bill may not have fully grasped its ramifications, seeing as "it never entered into the minds . . . that all the public works should be carried on simultaneously." Hoosier citizens, he suggested, were as guilty as its politicians, for the "very fact that those surveys were made . . . made the people lose their mental balance; every neighborhood became so intoxicated with the idea that a railroad or canal was to pass near it, that the people became mad, as it were, and were unable to judge."[126] The consequences of Indiana's internal improvement plan, and particularly the reactions to it, should come as no surprise. Politicians, dignitaries, canal promoters, agents, and the general populace saw the canal through a lens of inevitability—as a public work that would somehow magically appear.

Upon closer examination, Indiana's canal experience highlights the interconnectedness of construction labor, identity, and progress in an era laden with strident, masculine, patriotic rhetoric and in a region emblematic of the American democratic experiment in westward expansion and development. The canal marked a crucial episode in antebellum and frontier history, but it advanced the American experiment in democratic and technological perfection at the expense of the central contributors to this endeavor. Irish canallers were left to endure a rugged underworld of progress, where construction labor was distanced from and overshadowed by the greatness of the completed canal. Moreover, on frontiers such as Indiana's, where progress necessitated large quantities of immigrant labor, nationalistic rhetoric was needed to obscure the participation and physical exploitation of these foreign-born wageworkers and to perpetuate notions of a democratic American masculinity. Workers on the Wabash & Erie exposed this rhetoric as inherently contradictory in their daily struggles. While digging the canal, these armies of transportation laborers adhered faithfully and fervently to the commonsense core of an American and frontier ethos that valued manly independence, uninhibited self-expression, and hard work.

On the Wabash & Erie, as in similar construction sites across the American frontier, competing definitions of progress were at work. While Hoosier leaders and citizens felt entitled to improvements, no matter how they were achieved, Irish canallers felt that they were worthy of an honest and respectable subsistence—fair play involving decent wages and job security—that was earned, not merely assumed. Rank exploitation in a free society, in this case, was made easier through a popular portrayal of the canal diggers as violent, unproductive, and uncivilized. Marginalized from mainstream society, their person was manipulated, distanced, and dehumanized. Through the silencing of their story, the stain of exploitation was made invisible.

Although Irish canal diggers lacked the support of labor unions and political outlets for their grievances, their toil in the mud and muck, amid diseases, dangers, and community hostility, helped ensure American progress. Against great odds, these workers were determined not to become perpetual victims of an unfair labor market. To this end, Irish canallers protested their conditions; refused uncertain opportunities on various canal sections; drove off Hoosier and even fellow Irish coworkers; drank to assert themselves while building, challenging, and severing community ties; and clashed with competitors to protect their jobs, wages, manhood, and dignity. Beyond digging ditches, these men labored to defend their role or niche on the canal frontier—their piece of progress and history—however fleeting it was.

Hoosiers, like their neighbors in Illinois and elsewhere, learned from experience that internal improvements were not the work of private parties pursuing their own good. Instead, the success of these massive projects relied on armies of laborers marshaled by commanders of some sort. Once sections of the canal were completed, celebrations, newspapers, letters, and speeches praised the construction, often in the most colorful democratic rhetoric, as an innovative feat symbolic of all that was good about national growth and progress. Though inseparable from this process, the Irish canallers were written out of a project—a history—that had been intimately their own. Paradoxically, then, the immigrant laborers whose efforts produced progress and whose lives personified new variants of western manhood on this wage-workers' frontier lost out to narratives that privileged nationalistic results and histories that recycled imaginary heroes, feats, enemies, and traditions. Yet, in reality, beneath the improvement mania was the need for a communal workforce to set the rest of "the people" free of time and space constraints, just as slaves freed masters.

THREE

"Abuse of the Labour and Lives of Men"

IRISH CONSTRUCTION WORKERS AND THE
VIOLENCE OF PROGRESS ON THE ILLINOIS
TRANSPORTATION FRONTIER

> The progress of the internal improvements, a year or two in
> advance of what they would have been without this [Irish] labor,
> will be a poor compensation, offset by the corruption of man-
> ners, the forfeiture of freedom, and the transfer of power to those
> who know not how to use it wisely. There are things of value in
> this world besides mere physical aggrandizement. These foreign-
> ers came here to benefit themselves, not from any love of us or
> our country.
>
> JESSE CHICKERING, 1848

ON APRIL 16, 1848, THE PASSENGER packet *General Fry,* named for
canal commissioner Jacob Fry, made the thirty-mile trip from Lockport to
Chicago, thus opening navigation on the long-awaited Illinois & Michigan
Canal. Although the cumbersome canal boat weighed more than 150 tons
and was towed into Chicago by a propeller boat, the editor of the *Chicago
Weekly Journal,* echoing the sentiments of Illinoisans, noted that its arrival
signaled the most "eventful period in the history of our city, of the State, and
of the West . . . the wedding of the Father of Rivers to our inland seas." Earlier
that day, thousands of citizens, including Mayor James H. Woodworth, and
a "committee of reception . . . carriages, ladies on horseback, and horsemen"
assembled at "Lock No. 1" and were instantly fascinated by the "splendid
machinery for pumping water into the canal . . . with such clock-like regularity." The anxious throng then gathered to welcome the incoming vessel,
"crowded to her utmost, with ladies and gentlemen from the interior."
Participants exchanged cheers, toasts, and congratulations, with several
"bands striking up enlivening airs"; then Mayor Woodworth, Commissioner
Fry, grain merchant Charles Walker, and other dignitaries addressed the

crowd.[1] Another local editor, summing up these speeches, declared with pride that "the finishing of the canal was a glorious triumph" and that Illinoisans "may be justly proud . . . that we have met successfully all the difficulties incident [sic] to its completion," including "the ceaseless hostilities of enemies."[2]

Among the "enemies" this editor singled out were the same Irish immigrants whose backbreaking labor created the canal. Although by the time of Chicago's 1848 celebration, these workers were but a dim memory, their fingerprints on the canal's progress, and on similar patriotic celebrations, were indelible. Twelve years earlier, on July 4, 1836, the steamboat *Chicago* brought tourists and dignitaries up the Chicago River from Lake Michigan to Bridgeport to celebrate Independence Day and the official groundbreaking of the Illinois & Michigan Canal. Newly appointed Canal Commissioner William B. Archer turned the first ceremonial shovelful of dirt. After several rousing speeches, a reading of the Declaration of Independence, toasts, huzzahs, and gun salutes, the steamboat prepared for its return trip to Chicago. As the boat departed, a collection of Irish canallers stationed in a quarry on the riverbank threw a rough festival of their own. At once the "irate" workmen violently hurled rocks at the ladies and gentlemen aboard the vessel, prompting the captain to make an emergency landing. Close to fifty passengers ran ashore, armed with bludgeons, and bloodied the "heroes of the Emerald Isle," apprehending twelve of the canallers for arrest.[3]

At the outset, exclusion from the pomp and pageantry of progress did not sit well with the Irish diggers whose brains and brawn literally produced the canal. While the Irish were encouraged to produce such a symbol of progress, they were not to celebrate or enjoy its inevitable fruits. This history was not theirs to receive. Though likely an attempt to mock the canal diggers, the label of "heroes" perhaps pointed to the indignant pride that motivated the canallers to respond violently to this elite celebration, as it excluded them from a nation they sweat, bled, and died to build. Prohibited by social, economic, and cultural barriers from participating in the celebration, workers attacked the very symbol of these barriers: white citizens celebrating progress. This was but one of several forms of violence that shaped the experience of Irish transportation workers in the Land of Lincoln.

Breaking ground in 1836 after years of fits and starts, legislative battles, and financial struggles, the Illinois & Michigan Canal was the state's first large-scale transportation project.[4] It was separated into three divisions, the Summit from Chicago to Lockport, the Middle from Lockport to Seneca, and the

Western from Seneca to LaSalle. Completed in 1848 at a total cost of $6,170,266, the Illinois & Michigan linked Illinoisans to the Great Lakes and the Mississippi River, the preeminent routes of American commerce and transportation. The Illinois Internal Improvement Act of 1837 resembled Indiana's Mammoth Internal Improvement Act, as it projected a massive network of transportation projects, including the Illinois & Michigan Canal, to traverse the state. Opponents would later refer to it as the "General Insanity Bill." As historian Ray Allen Billington argued, the Illinois bill surpassed even Indiana's in "utter impracticality," requiring nearly $10,500,000 (and eventually $15,000,000) from a state with only four hundred thousand inhabitants.[5] Observers who boasted that this "gigantic" canal project would "startle citizens of the east" celebrated the I&M as a testament to company officials and dignitaries, for "any judicious person, in examining the nature and extent of this great State, would say they evince great energy and sagacity."[6] Though the Illinois Central Railroad would soon eclipse the Illinois & Michigan Canal, the latter's role in the growth and prosperity of Chicago from 1848 to 1860 was substantial.

The first federal land grant railroad, the Illinois Central, after four years of construction (1852–56) was the longest railroad in the world, at more than seven hundred miles in length. Its main line extended from Cairo, at the southern tip of the state, to Galena, in its northwest corner, while a branch line ran from Centralia to Chicago, giving the railroad a unique "Y" shape that traversed the state. Upon its completion the ICRR provided Chicago with a route to New Orleans by way of a railroad-operated steamboat line between Cairo and New Orleans.[7] As the ICRR expanded into Iowa, South Dakota, Wisconsin, Kentucky, Tennessee, Mississippi, Alabama, and Louisiana in the postbellum period, the railroad's sponsors praised it as the "Main Line of Mid-America."[8] Yet before the Illinois & Michigan Canal and the Illinois Central Railroad created such triumphant progress, they both had to be built through sparsely settled lands far removed from the central arteries of national commerce. Moreover, both faced a vexing labor problem.

Plagued by manpower shortages throughout their construction periods, the I&M and the ICRR looked abroad for able-bodied workers. Seeking to lure Irish immigrants from neighboring construction projects in Indiana, Ohio, New York, and Pennsylvania, the Illinois & Michigan employed agents, such as Lorenzo Sanger, to "proceed to any place within the United States to provide . . . any number of affluent Labourers not exceeding one

Thousand in number for the Use of the contractors."[9] Through emigration societies such as the Irish Emigrant Association and the Union Emigrant Society in New York, as well as through individual contractors in the East and in Canada, hordes of Irish workers answered their call.[10] In Illinois they were promised that monthly compensations would be "bountiful," and "when the road is finished" workers would be able to "purchase a farm, marry a wife, and dwell contented under . . . [their] own vine and fig tree."[11] Thus, the Illinois Central Railroad also tapped into—and courted—this floating market of transient construction workers.

Their position as a floating proletariat at the very bottom of the working class did not prohibit Irish immigrants from cultivating a power on their canal or railroad lines; in their temporary construction camps; in their religious activities; and in fights, strikes, riots, and open warfare. A violence of progress, a pain and suffering that Irish canallers endured, often inflicted, and yet were determined to contest, characterized their role in bringing internal improvements to the Illinois frontier. An examination of living and working conditions and their response to them in flight, bargaining, alcohol, religion, politics, violence, and protest will unearth the experiences of Illinois's Irish construction workers. Although the harsh world of construction labor held the capacity and power to squeeze the life out of its immigrant workers, they also made this world their own. What follows is the history of those laborers who built the Illinois & Michigan Canal, often referred to as the "Erie Canal of the West," along with comparative evidence pertaining to Irish workers on the Illinois Central Railroad.[12]

The Prairie State, like its eastern neighbors, was infected with a severe case of canal and railroad fever. The Illinois & Michigan Canal was the final canal of the 1815–60 period in which state governments spent $121 million and private companies $74 million in support of artificial waterways. Initiated in 1836 and weathering a host of economic storms, by 1848 the backbreaking labor of the Irish immigrant workforce that created the ninety-seven mile canal had finally ceased. This new waterway linked Lake Michigan to the Illinois River and thus the Great Lakes with the Mississippi and the Gulf of Mexico. Its impact on the landscape of Illinois was dramatic, as the canal altered the direction of commerce from Saint Louis northwest to Chicago and transformed the latter from a muddy outpost to a preeminent national commerce hub and metropolis. Its population grew from 1,200 at the outset of construction in 1836 to 74,000 after six years of the canal's operation. Thus, by 1854 Chicago's population had increased over 400 percent. On an

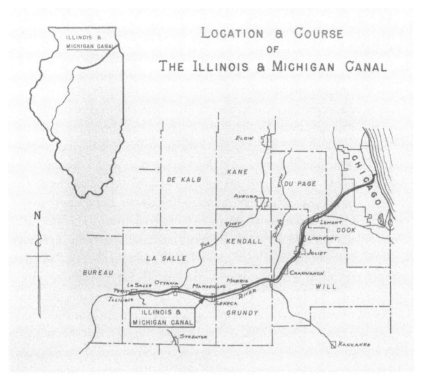

MAP 3. Location and course of the Illinois & Michigan Canal. Courtesy of the Illinois State Archives, Springfield.

annual basis in the mid-1850s, the Windy City shipped north and south more than twenty million bushels of wheat and corn by boat. As towns emerged along the canal, settlement, agriculture, and manufacturing followed.[13]

As the last of America's artificial waterways, the Illinois & Michigan Canal shared several similarities with neighboring projects in Indiana and Ohio (see map 3). Like the Wabash & Erie Canal, the Illinois & Michigan was built through so-called wilderness regions in the northern part of the state. On both of these frontier projects, transient workers "lived a rough life away from civilized centers" of the country.[14] Due to the dearth of timber along the Illinois & Michigan canal line, officials, from the outset, proscribed the use of wood in the construction of workers' shanties.[15] According to newspaper sources, some canallers defied this prohibition because of their squalid living conditions. The *Boston Pilot*, a prominent Catholic newspaper, noted that workers on the I&M were "lodged to the number of fifty in a single log cabin!"[16] A Chicago newspaper correspondent characterized these shanties as coming in "all sizes, shapes, and materials, sod and straw; shingled or boarded sheds being in great demand." Nonetheless, the reporter noted that "some of these habitations, if they can be dignified with a title, are wretched looking tenements."[17]

Although contractors typically provided shanties for workers, at times the state or canal company built the dwellings for contractors to purchase, with the latter often deducting accommodations or food costs from workers' wages. For example, in 1838 construction workers were paid sixteen to twenty dollars a month, with contractors subtracting provisions and shelter from that amount. In 1845, after years of intermittent work and the outright suspension of construction, workers earned fourteen dollars a month including board or twenty-two dollars without board. According to company reports, not only were contractors who submitted the "lowest possible bids" generally awarded jobs, many were so strapped that they did not even directly furnish their men with equipment.[18] Canallers reportedly paid the canal company a ninety-four-cent deposit for shovels, which were returned to the workers when labor was completed.[19] Moreover, evidence suggests that the struggling Irish workers, forced to buy other necessities (often on credit) from suppliers and businessmen closely connected to the canal company, purchased only one shoe at a time.[20]

English author and traveler James Silk Buckingham's perception of Illinois's Irish canal builders was typical of travelers' accounts of the canal scene. He was repulsed by the "dirtiness and disorder" of a shanty town he visited in 1840 on the Western Division near Utica, Illinois. According to Buckingham, "The number of persons congregated here were about 200, including men, women & children, and these were crowded together in 14 or 15 log-huts, temporarily erected for their shelter. . . . And a more repulsive scene we had not for a long time beheld."[21]

Yet the dwellings of Illinois's Irish canallers were not the only problem for Buckingham, who argued that the ditchdiggers were "not merely ignorant and poor—which might be their misfortune rather than their fault—but they are drunken, dirty, indolent, and riotous." As a result, these transient, uncivilized builders of progress became "the objects of dislike and fear to all in whose neighborhood they congregate in large numbers":

> It required only a little industry to preserve both in a state of cleanliness, for water was . . . close at hand, and soap abundant and cheaper than in England.

It is not to be wondered that Americans conceive a very low estimate of the Irish people generally, when they have such unfavorable specimens of the nation, as these almost constantly before their eyes.[22]

Buckingham clearly demonstrated a misunderstanding of canal labor in Illinois, for the water in which workers waded was a breeding ground for infectious diseases. There was, however, hope for the "industrious" Irish immigrant. Buckingham's travels along the Illinois transportation frontier convinced him that with decent wages (he noted that poverty was a poor excuse as workers earned "a dollar a day for their labor") "the remedy is within their own reach to be clean, sober and industrious," for this "is surely within the power of every man."[23] Yet low, uncertain wages and the financial problems of Illinois contradicted the writer's views, as did the unyielding nature of canal digging and the oppressive labor relationship between contractor and canaller. One anonymous digger, disgusted with the brutal pace of work, complained that construction bosses only "gave you twenty-one minutes to eat / . . . scream, threaten, and shout at you / While forcing you back to work."[24]

It is hard to quantify canallers' standard of living based on wages, for canal construction was an irregular system of labor, subject not only to state and local economic conditions but to the whims of canal companies and contractors. It was a system associated with slave, servant, and convict labor in its early years, and even in the 1830s and 1840s wage-earning canallers were paid in "kind" through the provisioning of food, whiskey, and lodging. Furthermore, workers were often denied payment by unscrupulous contractors. A reporter for the *Boston Pilot* summed up the relationship between canal contractors and unskilled immigrant workers by arguing that the overarching goal of these employers boiled down to "how much money can I screw out of these men?"[25]

In the wake of the nation's 1837 economic panic, states such as Illinois and Indiana that had relied on loans to fund construction faced spiraling debts and irate creditors and were compelled to curtail or suspend projects. Unskilled canallers bore the brunt of this unfortunate situation. On the Illinois & Michigan Canal monthly wages fell precipitously, from a high of twenty-six dollars in 1836 to twenty in 1837, and then plummeted to sixteen by 1843. Worse, many canal workers were simply dismissed, left to fend for themselves in a frontier environment replete with sickness, unemployment, and disappointment.[26]

The Western Division of the Illinois & Michigan in 1838–39 demonstrated the vagaries of the canal labor market in the antebellum period. The I&M's workforce fluctuated considerably every three months, swelling during the summer and fall and shrinking in the winter months. In March 1838 the canal commissioners counted 350 men at work on the Western Division. This number increased to 595 by June 1 and to 960 in September and declined to 445 by December. The following year witnessed a similar trend, with 475 men at work in February, 886 at the end of May, 824 in late August, and 676 by the end of November.[27] An I&M engineer pointed to climate as a cause of transiency, noting that the "migratory character of the men is … a main cause of this variation, as many of them go to the south at the setting in of the winter, to return in the spring." Based on the ebb and flow of labor, the Illinois & Michigan Canal Company continually sent contractors north to Canada in hope of luring a steady stream of workers, mainly Irish immigrants.[28]

The unfavorable state economic climate that coincided with the initiation of construction was an immediate source of complaint on the part of canal officials and contractors. With the State Bank of Illinois unable to make its bond payments, the state resorted to remunerating contractors in treasury notes, or "scrip," that made its way into the hands of those workers who were not paid in kind. Construction was suspended in 1837 as the canal company, like Indiana's, sunk into default. In May 1839 acting commissioner Jacob Thornton noted in a letter to Gov. Thomas Carlin that "no money at the disposal of the Board [of Commissioners] could be applied to the payment of contractors," many of whom were ruined by the financial woes of the state.[29] According to the canal commissioners, those contractors who received "scrip" or "certificates of indebtedness" from the canal board "could not divide it among [their] numerous creditors, embracing [their] laborers, mechanics, farmers, drovers and merchants."[30] By 1840 there was no end to the financial panic, as "each day increased the general anxiety produced by the uncertainty of payments and consequent dangers of [canal] suspension," and "the contractors and their creditors became seriously alarmed."[31]

Although normally mentioned as mere sidelights in the canal board's reports, the I&M's unskilled Irish laborers, depicted simply as "vulnerable workers" in these writings, utilized their own wits to weather the economic storm. Canal officials wrote that these "laborers, apprehensive of losing their wages, if they continued to work without security, grew restive." Moreover, many "threatened to leave the country."[32]

Flight was a means of resistance and control for Irish canallers, as were firsthand information networks, particularly in this prelabor union period. Whether they were cheated by contractors, were casualties of a suspension of canal work, fell ill, or were angry with the oppressive conditions on the line, canal workers often left projects for better opportunities on the moving frontier of transportation labor. In July 1846 Illinois & Michigan Canal secretary Robert Stuart informed trustee William Swift that workers were abandoning various sections of the canal, noting that "a good many went off in disgust, from being cheated out of their wages." In the same month, Chief Engineer William Gooding, in a letter to Swift, bemoaned this tendency among workers. In Gooding's opinion, disgruntled canal workers had damaged the company's reputation by informing their friends and relatives of the poor conditions on the canal. The dilemma of contractors denying wages to canallers, he noted, "has been raised abroad," and in addition to "driv[ing] many men from the line" has also "prevented others from coming [to Illinois]"[33]

Geographic mobility and the threat of flight on the part of canal workers, though not always the product of unfair company practices or dishonest contractors, plagued Illinois & Michigan canal officials throughout the construction period. Despite the brutal nature of canal labor on the Illinois frontier, evidence points to Irish canallers threatening to desert to hasten payment from contractors. As Gooding noted, wage guarantees resulted in workers' willingness to remain on the canal, for as soon as "payment was made a better feeling seems to exist amongst the laborers." Moreover, he predicted that "one or two more payments promptly made, as they unquestionably will be hereafter, will set everything right" with the workers.[34]

To set things right, the Illinois & Michigan Canal Company sought financial help from abroad, and reemerged with a new board of canal trustees.[35] However, coinciding with the reopening of construction in November 1845 was a devastating outbreak of illness, once again leading to a suspension of work. Hampered by a five-month delay between their original work estimates and payments by the canal company, contractors complained to the commissioners that they were unable to pay and retain enough workers. Commissioners, in turn, blamed the contractors, for, "instead of getting gold or silver or good Eastern bank paper, they get the worst paper which can be made to circulate." Given that irresponsible contractors "will take *any thing* that they can pay out," argued Gooding, "the [canal] community is suffering by the present system." Stuart worried that this failure to provide wages "would inevitably cause a rebellion" of the disgruntled laborers "and perhaps an abandonment of the work."[36]

His fears proved accurate. In the midst of denied wages and a wet summer in 1846, officials noted that "hundreds of laborers were [left] unemployed upon the line until their means of support were wholly exhausted and they left the work discouraged and disaffected."[37]

Repeated delays in progress convinced the canal company that outside contractors were a source of its problems, and in the spring of 1847 contracts on the several divisions were transferred to state superintendents. Company opinion was that cutting out these middlemen would hasten—and enable direct supervision of—the work. Thus, as the canal neared completion, Gooding impatiently asked George Green, a supervising engineer for the Western Division, to remind a group of state contractors on Lock 14 in LaSalle that "no time is to be lost about the gates of the said Lock and . . . [they] must work fast." Additionally, he was to inform a bridge supervisor on sections 148 and 154 "that *every thing* depends upon his finishing his work just as soon as practicable." As for Green himself, Gooding provided the following motivation: "In fact I desire you to push every thing and if you are a good boy and do well perhaps there will be [no] reduction of your pay. Seriously I think that you will find enough to do to occupy all your time. . . . I say again *push, push!*"[38]

Irish laborers not only disapproved of this temporary regime change; they defied it. In 1847, when these new state contractors tried to manipulate their rejuvenated labor source and extend the average work day to fifteen hours, Irish canallers went on strike, sending a formal petition to the state canal trustee. Despite the recycled narratives of Irish drinking, fighting, and behaving immorally, the real canal violence, according to the strikers, was the oppression they endured on a daily basis while building this symbol of American progress. These fed-up workers argued that their bosses were guilty of the "abuse of the Labour and lives of men."[39] As a result, Illinois citizens, politicians, farmers, and businessmen who impatiently awaited their Erie of the West were saddled with yet another delay, a two-week work stoppage courtesy of the immigrant "enemies" without whom there was no hope of a completed canal. The patriotic celebrations would have to wait.

In some ways, then, the actions and reactions of the I&M's Irish canallers mirrored those of free and unfree workers *outside* of the industrial trades throughout North America—from southern plantations to Atlantic coast farms and even as far as Hawaii's sugarcane fields. Literature on workers' control has long emphasized "voting with one's feet" as a survival mechanism and bargaining chip, with industrial factory workers serving as a classic example. Strategies aimed at slowing down or obstructing work, destroying production, and evading the surveillance of bosses were common throughout the American West during the contract era.[40]

Canals, and particularly railroads, helped facilitate these strategies by way of movement. They transported wageworkers to opportunities across the American West and delivered them, if needed, from evil and oppression to different farms, mines, ditches, and frontiers. Mark Wyman's recent study of hoboes in the West underscores the human consequences of boom-and-bust economies that, like canals and railroads, came to rely on immigrants and transients. Indeed, hoboes and employers both banked on mobility: the former equating it with survival; the latter depending on floating groups of transients to squeeze profits from the earth.[41]

At times even overshadowing wage conflicts on the Illinois & Michigan, however, was the violence of sickness on the swampy, humid Illinois frontier. Travelers, commentators, canal officials, and physicians were particularly troubled by the reoccurrence of illnesses on the canal line and found outbreaks peculiar to the Irish. In 1838, the same year that "Billious complaints & Chills & Fever Ague" was reported on Indiana's Whitewater Canal, with "Deaths occur[ing] frequently among the workmen . . . and some of the work [being] wholly ceased on account of sickness," the Illinois & Michigan was beset with sickness.[42] Well into December, over a hundred workers on the Western Division who survived the "sickly" summer and had not abandoned the construction site were restricted to their cramped shanties as malaria wreaked havoc along the canal.[43] One observer of canallers' shanties on the I&M concluded that the spread of illness should come as no surprise "amongst people living in such apologies for dwellings."[44] Dr. Daniel Drake, a well-known physician and medical writer, traveled along the Illinois & Michigan Canal corridor in 1844 to survey local physicians in several canal communities about the nature of malaria and the conditions of those afflicted. One doctor, who had lived for eight years in LaSalle County, informed Drake that in the towns of Peru and LaSalle, "he had seen epidemics of autumnal fever in only two years and then chiefly in immigrants from the north [Canada] and in Irish laborers on the canal." From another group of physicians with experience in Ottawa, Illinois, Drake learned that "autumnal fever is common in this locality," and that it was the "Irish laborers on the Canal" who "suffered greatly."[45]

Once again in 1846 disease devastated the men, and with contractors complaining that only one in five workers was fit to perform his duties, company officials feared that sickness would slow progress and drive up wages. Stuart noted in the fall of 1846 that for at least two months, "more than three quarters of the officers and men on the line have been prostrated" by illness. Based on the financial consequences of illness, especially related to construction deadlines, the I&M Board of Commissioners recommended the building of a hospital on the Western Division, arguing that previous canal companies had demonstrated "their utility in the construction of public works."[46] But while company records credit canal commissioners with the hospital proposal, other sources indicate that as early as December 1838 Irish canal diggers in LaSalle broached this to Ward Burnett, an Illinois & Michigan engineer. Stating that they were in desperate need of medical care for both sickness and "accidents at the quarries, and others," the canallers promised to offer a portion of their wages to help build a hospital in the region. Burnett, in fact, noted that these were the same workers who participated in a deadly 1838 riot on the canal.[47] Apparently these Irish rioters were neither as primitive nor as savage as their critics claimed.

Cholera, a disease caused by drinking water contaminated by human waste, ravaged American populations from the 1830s to the 1870s and was particularly prevalent among canal and river communities in the Midwest. Once entering the body, a toxin damaged the stomach and intestinal walls, leading to diarrhea, vomiting, and extreme dehydration. The illness attacked swiftly and could include a variety of symptoms, including skin discoloration, sunken countenance, cramps and spasms, and kidney failure.[48] Irish immigrants were reputed to have carried the disease to North America and in a June 1832 letter, Charles F. Mercer, president of the Chesapeake & Ohio Canal, described the consequences of the illness in his appeal for a hospital: "If the Board but imagine the panic produced by a mans [sic] turning black and dying in twenty four hours in the very room where his comrades are to sleep and dine . . . they will readily conceive the utility of separating the sick, dying and dead from the living."[49]

Though it did appear on the I&M, cholera was more of a concern for the Irish construction communities on the Illinois Central Railroad in the early 1850s, killing 130 workers in two days at Peru in 1852 and claiming 150 victims in Galena in August 1854.[50] At LaSalle in the summer of 1852, an outbreak infected 30 Irish workers, nearly 20 of whom died within hours of developing symptoms.[51] The summer of 1854 brought more violent deaths, as an Irish construction camp lost 70 to 80 men, half while on the job and the other half as "they fled in terror from the work camp into town."[52] Illinois Central president William P. Burrall referred to the summer 1854 outbreak as "real malignant cholera, killing in 3 to 8 hours."[53] Roswell B. Mason, chief engineer of the ICRR, reported that "sickness of the most violent character on many parts of the line" was by far the greatest obstacle the railroad company encountered in its march to progress.[54] According to the local press, however, Irish construction workers were not random casualties of such "violent" sickness, for it seemed to pursue them on canal and railroad frontiers. Following the deadly outbreak in Peru, the task of reporters for the *Bloomington Intelligencer* was to inform the areas native-born "citizens" that they were not among the scourge's targets:

> We regret to learn ... that the cholera has again made its appearance among the laborers on the railroad and public works in the neighborhood of Peru.... Sixteen deaths had occurred, nine at Peru and seven at LaSalle. None of the citizens had been attacked, and no great alarm was felt of the disease spreading to any great extent.[55]

Malaria, commonly referred to as "autumnal fever" or "the ague," was more prevalent on the canal line, owing to swampy conditions and the stagnant, mosquito-infested water in which canal diggers often waded.[56] Normally infected by the bite of a female anopheline mosquito, workers suffered a range of symptoms, from fevers, chills, and nausea to anemia-related issues, coma, and, in severe cases, death.[57]

Unfortunately, what some observers perceived as a tragedy, others contested as evidence of the unwillingness of Irish immigrants to seek the more independent and respectable trade of farming. Elmer Baldwin, a former judge and state politician from Farm Ridge, Illinois, arrived in the region in 1835 and noted that "there was more sickness and more deaths in proportion to the population, in 1838, than in any year since the settlement of the country." Great "fears were expressed" at towns along the canal in LaSalle County, as "nearly all were sick, and many died." However, in response to an eastern newspaper correspondent who observed a cemetery near the canal in LaSalle with "300 graves that had never been rained on," Baldwin criticized such "exaggerated and fearful stories" and qualified the correspondent's report:

> That might have been true, but the cemetery belonged to the Catholics ... and thousands of men were at work on the canal, and they nearly all came to La Salle for burial.... [But] when the land around a residence had become thoroughly cultivated, the inmates ceased to have the ague, the tilled soil readily absorbed the rainfall, and no doubt the deleterious gases of the

atmosphere; but whatever the cause, the annual sickness so annoying for many years gradually disappeared as the country became improved.[58]

Baldwin, like other native-born commentators, interpreted malaria as a byproduct of both the canal-building environment and the consequences of Irish workers' reluctance to choose farming over canalling. He suggested that independent farmers were protected from the disease by their efforts to till and "improve" the soil. The virtues of civilization had apparently immunized American farmers from "the ague," a sickness, that, according to observers, disproportionately infected—and was spread by—Irish immigrants on the canal frontier. Irish actor Tyrone Power lamented the "sweeping pestilence" that produced "enormous mortality" among Irish canallers, quickened by the crowded and unsanitary conditions in "the solitary log-hut." Though Power blamed contractors for showing no "consideration . . . to their condition" and argued that the men were "worse lodged than the cattle of the field," local editors and commentators saw disease as a consequence of the decision to "settle" with canal labor.[59] After all, it was Irish canal and railroad construction workers, who, as Francis Grund argued, "neglect[ed] the more useful cultivation of the soil, which would, at once, make them independent and respectable."[60]

According to Father John Blasius Raho, a Vincentian priest in LaSalle County, widespread illness had indeed hampered canal construction on the Illinois & Michigan and devastated its Irish workers. "The diseases," he noted, "are horrible and so many die that there is hardly any time to give Extreme Unction to everybody. We run night and day to assist the sick. For three weeks the temperature was excessive, up to 110 F, and this for a few days in a row." Nonetheless, Raho argued that the sickness had little to do with ideals of yeoman independence and was more a result of the low morals and violent exploits of the Irish canallers. Though he pitied the transient Irish immigrants who "die[d] like dogs among the dirt and mud," Raho could not contain his anger. He concluded that the sickness was a form of divine punishment for the actions of the Corkonians and Fardowns in a bloody riot at LaSalle earlier that year. Accordingly, he noted, "It almost seems that the Lord wants to punish the workers of the canal for getting drunk all the time, their riots, their fights and homicides."[61] He elaborated in a letter to a colleague:

> The season here has been very sickly, and we have been very busy in visiting the sick and burying the dead, and would to God, that His holy justice

was appeased. Still the people are afflicted with dangerous diseases. Day and night we both [Raho and Aloysius Parodi] have been laboring, in order to afford the help of our religion to the poor sick. I do not know how long it will last. The will of God be done. Amen. It is said that the ... parish priest of Chicago, from the altar pronounced upon them (the rioters and scandal givers) the malediction of God. If it is so I see the effects of it. They die ... without having time to prepare themselves for the other world. All the sickness, I may say, is among them. We are tired.[62]

Indeed, the Western Division was hit particularly hard by this 1838 outbreak of malaria. One visitor stated that "of 1500 laboring men employed on the Illinois and Michigan Canal, 1000 died, during this past year." As a result of their "laboring from day to day in low lands amid stagnant water," this commentator surmised that "human life has proved to be very short." Rather than blame the Irish, he noted that "diseases incident to the climate, fever and ague and bilious weather" contributed to the frequency of illness and death along the canal; but importantly, so did "over-exertion" on the part of the ailing Irish workers.[63] Performing physically exhausting and often fatally dangerous work from sunup to sundown, as long as sixteen hours a day on some sections of the Illinois & Michigan, canallers were pushed beyond their limits on a routine basis. Tyrone Power, whose travel narrative detailed the toils of his countrymen on American canals, noted that they were "excluded from all the advantages of civilization ... [and] at the mercy of a hard contractor, who wrings his profits from their blood."[64]

Even members of the elite could not deny the humanity of the Irish workers who, in their arduous labor, succumbed to deadly diseases. Yet disease was a source of contestation, as sick and dying canallers had both defenders and adversaries. For some, illness was a product of the environment, an "autumnal fever" prevalent in the swampy soil and the mosquito-infested waters in which canallers plied their craft. Others, citing expert physicians who discovered malaria "chiefly ... in Irish laborers on the canal," insisted that the immigrants were in fact carriers of the ague.[65] Sympathetic observers pointed to workers' filthy and cramped dwellings as a determining factor, thus implicating company officials, whereas detractors suggested that disease was a consequence of the Irish immigrants' abhorrent lifestyles. Religious leaders often grieved for the poor souls who "died like dogs" in the mud, but they just as frequently interpreted outbreaks of illness as divine vengeance on canallers' reckless, violent, and intemperate ways. For Irish workers, debates over the proximate causes and consequences of disease were overshadowed by the painful reality that sickness, injury, and death were an inescapable feature of canal building. Such dangers, however, heightened their sense of masculine courage and stimulated efforts to improve working conditions on the canal.

The dangers of overexertion were no different on the Illinois Central Railroad. President Burrall noted that in southern Illinois, "when summer comes drouth [sic] prevails and the weather is intensely hot." The weather, he claimed, "ranged from 101 to 105 in the shade every day we were there," and amid severe drought "the men have no water to drink except what is hauled by teams from 3 to 10 miles." The rainy season, however, was just as difficult for construction workers. Burrall called Vandalia the "most abominable place to work":

> A large force has been started there three or four times, and as many times driven off by high water. During the winter months some 400 or 500 men were there and ... they were so completely flooded that every shanty had 3 or 4 feet of water on its floor, and it became necessary to build flat boats to bring the men off, which occupied 2 days, and two were drowned.... It is impossible to conceive the difficulties attending the execution of the work in the southern part of the state.[66]

The reality of overexertion as a cause of illness, injury, and death merits more analysis than the comments of observers of the canal scene provide. The arduous labor required of canal construction workers stimulated an ardent masculinity unequaled in most other occupations. This keen sense of masculine courage was intensified in light of squalid, dangerous, and oppressive conditions. Canal building, an occupation that native-born citizens shunned, was transformed into a niche by immigrants, who felt they, alone, were man enough to perform it. Bolstered by masculine pride and camaraderie in their all-male construction gangs, the exploits that observers condemned as "recklessness" Irish canallers honored as manly and daring. They even flaunted their relative control over dangerous circumstances at work. Traveler and dietician Thomas Low Nichols, shocked at the hazard of rock blasting on the canal line, noted that Irish laborers "were so reckless of life" that once the signal for a blast was given, "instead of running to their shelter provided for them, they would just hold their shovels over their heads to keep off the shower of small stones, and be crushed every now and then by a big one."[67]

What, exactly, did Nichols's view that canallers were "reckless of life" reveal about such endeavors? His interpretation compares favorably to that of Francis Grund, who argued that Irish canallers performed such drudgery because they were "contented with little" and neglected more honorable, stable occupations.[68] Both interpretations are problematic when considering the opportunities available to these men and the rough nature of their work. Histories of western miners have suggested alternate definitions of masculinity based on danger and risk. Certainly mining labor and construction labor compare unfavorably insofar as flat construction wages and wages for tonnage (and portions of a company's profits) are concerned, but their physical similarities are lost on no one. Gunther Peck has argued that immigrant and native-born miners in the nineteenth century based their own definitions of danger, chance, and masculinity in the everyday challenges of wage labor. The same could be said of construction workers. Dangerous work meant a day's wages, solidified a man's reputation, and exposed him to broken bones, extreme heat, muck and mire, frostbite, illnesses, and even death. Considering that companies seldom compensated workers for lost wages or positions, the financial consequences of work-related hazards were overwhelming and well known. Yet these men risked their lives and livelihoods anyway. The western frontier undoubtedly shaped their experiences and approaches. As a physical place in need of development, the frontier offered a livelihood to those willing to shape it with their toil, a shared fate that built group identity and fostered class relations in the process. As an idea or metaphor permeated with myths about freedom, mobility, white manhood, and risk, the western frontier exerted a powerful influence on those who improved it and those who documented internal improvements.[69] Performing dangerous work, Irish canallers confronted challenges and even relished the opportunity to throw caution to the wind. It came with the territory and was seemingly expected of them.

One of Cook County's first historians, Alfred T. Andreas, described these masculine qualities in a rare firsthand account of an injury suffered by an Irish canal worker while building the Illinois & Michigan near Lockport in 1838. The canaller, whom Andreas characterized as having an "excellent physique," suffered a major fracture to his thigh, rendering him unable to move, let alone work. Nonetheless, he left the construction site and hobbled to Chicago in excruciating pain, "where he found himself unable to walk further." Lacking money, the man was admitted to the city's poorhouse, where his injury worsened, "the limb becoming excessively oedematous [sic]." A group of doctors performed an amputation of his leg, with one completing the operation while another "controlled the femoral artery ... with his thumbs." After a month the man's resiliency astonished the physicians as his wound had healed considerably. Before long, however, "a secondary haemorrage *[sic]* occurred," opening a massive portion of the original wound, and "the patient died almost immediately."[70] This canaller had given life and limb to a project his countrymen had made their own. Even in death he exhibited the same daring, uninhibited fighting spirit that, while it often appalled native-born citizens, sustained Irish workers on the transportation frontier.

Employed on projects that demanded brutal and even life-threatening work, Irish construction laborers sought other outlets, in addition to their labor power, protests, and threat of flight, to help them cope with the struggles of canal building. Workers turned to both alcohol and religion to mitigate the physical and emotional burdens of building American progress and to exercise authority over their lives and livelihoods. Though, for some, these outlets revealed workers' desperation, for others it symbolized their power.

Alcohol, despite attempts to restrict its use, was a fixture of canal life and functioned as a source of power on the part of beleaguered canallers. Irish workers purchased alcohol from local businessmen or demanded it from their bosses as a condition of their labor agreement.[71] Illinois & Michigan contractors such as Philo Lindley, William Byrne, and Isaac Hardy opened "supply stores" along the canal line where Irish canallers could purchase alcohol and other provisions. Lindley's was the first of its kind in LaSalle, and he "kept this store mainly to supply the necessities of his [canal] men, and such of his fellow settlers, then few, as chose to patronize him."[72] Moreover, on the Illinois Central Railroad, contractors who had prohibited alcohol among their workers were thwarted so often that they reportedly begged local businessmen and citizens to discontinue selling "spirits" to the workmen.[73]

On the Illinois & Michigan Canal, evidence points to Irish canallers seizing opportunities to obtain alcohol on and off the job. Particularly in "sickly seasons" when malaria, typhus, dysentery, and other illnesses ravaged the canal line, workers demanded whiskey, shrewdly mentioning its medicinal qualities, before entering the swampy ditch to construct the canal's foundation. Various contractors, despite company policy, acquiesced to these demands and factored a daily "gill" (four ounces) of whiskey into canallers' wages.[74] Contractors who risked their contracts by offering alcohol to their hands did so in light of several advantages, including company fears about labor shortages and the fact that whiskey retained workers, tempered the burden of securing real wages for them, and diminished the threat of a strike. Upon interviewing the superintendent of labor at Ottawa, the English traveler James Silk Buckingham learned that while company officials' mandated a "dry" working environment, they soon recognized that "they could get no Irish workers with such a stipulation."[75]

In August 1846 contractor William Perce and his partner, John Clifford, complained to the Illinois & Michigan trustees that workers had pressured them to either raise their wages to "$1.25 per day" or else guarantee "$1.00 and liquor."[76] The trustees, equally frustrated, responded that while strict policies were in place to restrict the use of "ardent spirits," workers reacted by moving from "dry" contractors to "wet" ones who disregarded the rules. The ditch-diggers' penchant for imbibing even provoked discussions of a change in company pay schedules. Requests from contractors in the spring of 1847 to switch to a quarterly pay system were based on their experience that more frequent payments delayed the canal's progress, as workers "have a frolic" when payday arrives, wasting crucial time during the peak season of construction activity.[77]

This determination to drink repeatedly frustrated company-implemented prohibition and confirmed popular opinions of the Irish as uncivilized drunks. Still, it demonstrated the power of these "heroes of the Emerald Isle" to retain cultural customs and exhibit a rugged masculinity, drunk with independence from the rigors of canal labor. On several occasions, in fact, crossing paths with antagonistic observers roused canallers into outward—perhaps premeditated—displays of drunkenness that bordered on the comical. For example, when journalist Anne Royall encountered a large group of Irish canal workers in transit to another ditch via stagecoach, she was overwhelmed by the seemingly uncivilized presence of these builders of progress. She complained that the canallers were "eternally getting in and out, and suffocating you with the stench of drunkenness. They are, for the most part, covered with mud, where they have rolled when drunk, and never think of buying a little trunk, or light valisse [sic], to carry their clothes from place to place, but always have a wad of something tied up in a black greasy old pocket handkerchief, and crowd you, and grease you, and stench you to death."[78]

In many cases, commentators' observations and tired expressions confirmed what anxious Americans believed, that the "wild Irish" were inherently fond of drinking and fighting.[79] In Illinois the mere presence of the canal Irish had transformed once-peaceful villages into dens of "Sodom," with doggeries and "everlasting groceries," places "where whiskey and Irish were plenty."[80] Similarly, with the arrival of Irish construction workers on the Illinois Central Railroad in the mid-1850s, towns such as Vandalia became, according to one editor, "blessed with the presence of several doggeries, where rot gut is dealt out with impunity to those whose appetites are stronger by fearful odds than their judgments."[81]

Cultural commentators saw brawling and boozing as inherited traits and subjectively ascribed these violent and immoral practices to the Irish as a way of earmarking their undesirability as a *race*. They wanted readers to understand just how embedded these problems were in Irish culture. Henry Giles, in articles for the Boston serial the *Christian Examiner* in the antebellum period, argued that immigrant behavior triggered negative assessments, for "the vicious Irishman always attracts attention ... [and] is soon felt in a community of order as a disturbing character."[82]

Historians Dale Knobel and Matthew Frye Jacobson point to the 1840s as a period when American commentators' depictions of "Irish character" became increasingly derogatory and racialized.[83] Anti-Irish contemporaries coined the terms "Irishism" and "Celtism" to describe the cultural depravity and degradation that was ostensibly habitual to Irish immigrants and their kin.[84] Though visibly white in the social category of color, Irish immigrants were depicted as nonwhite in the nation's dominant racial social system.[85] This system produced structural racism and discrimination—even against immigrants who appeared and were often counted as undoubtedly white vis-à-vis their color. In such a systemic racial hierarchy, argues Eduardo Bonilla-Silva, the race in the superior position "tends to receive greater economic remuneration and access to better occupations and/or prospects in the labor market, occupies a primary position in the political system," and "has a license to draw physical (segregation) as well as social (racial etiquette) boundaries between itself and other races." What is more, this superior race collects and even monopolizes what W.E.B. Du Bois termed a "public and psychological wage" with which skilled white workers were compensated when they received a low wage.[86] What historian David Roediger calls the "pleasures of whiteness," which portended an elevated status—through real and imagined privileges—helped mask exploitative class relationships.[87] Menial canal labor, as well as management, denied unskilled Irish immigrants such privileges.

On the antebellum frontier seemingly innate racial deficiencies were amplified in popular publications such as *Harper's Weekly*, and a "fixed" set of inherited traits became associated with pejorative physical descriptions of the Irish as "brutish," "low-browed," and "simian."[88] Thus, not color but racial difference was central to narratives of Irish immigrant behavior and helped distinguish native-born "Anglo-Saxons" from immigrant "Celts."[89] Anti-Irish commentators' and particularly artists' attempts to package these immigrants as visibly darker, seemingly ridiculous to today's readers, had more to do with perceived racial, not color, inferiority.

On the Illinois & Michigan Canal the drinking, disease-carrying, browbeaten, violent, and rough-edged Irish canallers were most definitely seen as a race apart. At the same time, these builders of progress were also Irish Americans in the making, transferring their culture and traditions to a new environment. Although contemporaries objected to their taste for hard drinking (among the other moral depravities of their "race"), Irish canallers valued alcohol as a critical component of their transplanted culture and masculinity. In the bottle workers sought and performed self-identification as rough, daring, and formidable Irish workingmen.

In pressuring their bosses to provide or tolerate alcohol, Irish canallers were not exhibiting uncivilized behavior but in fact astuteness that neither contemporaries nor historians understood. Though labor historians have pointed to the integrative and disintegrative effects of alcohol on canal and railroad construction communities, most have cited the problems it created along the canal line, in recurrent shanty brawls, episodes of domestic violence, and faction fighting between rival workers, despite evidence that some of this violence (such as Indiana's Lagro War) did not involve alcohol. Even fewer scholars examining gender and masculinity among wageworkers have factored notions of shrewdness (as opposed to brawn and violence) into discussions of masculine identity, and particularly not in relation to transient immigrant construction workers.[90] While the potential consequences of alcohol abuse undoubtedly loomed large, evidence from the Illinois transportation frontier suggests that Irish workers drank to combat illness, to endure the physical risks of construction, to escape the brutal and repetitive regime of canalling, and to bolster a rough masculine identity. More important, alcohol was one aspect of workers' experience over which they possessed a considerable amount of control.

As expected, some of the most acerbic critiques of Irish workers' drinking habits came from spiritual leaders, who, next to contractors, were most familiar with the daily grind of these men. Priests and missionaries, however, played a much more proactive role than their diatribes on Irish depravity suggest. A careful analysis of religious sources reveals that Irish construction workers were far from unthinking pack animals trailing the righteous lead of their spiritual advisors. Irish canallers understood that religion provided an outlet to build community and enabled them to find a sense of control over their transient existence. At the same time, religious leaders and commentators found in the plight of Irish construction workers everything that was wrong with American progress. What they witnessed, in fact, was an underworld of progress.

Although determining the religious affiliation of the Irish canal workers on the Illinois & Michigan is fraught with difficulties, canal officials, contractors, journalists, and spiritual leaders routinely commented that most were Catholics. In a December 1837 letter to Bishop Joseph Rosati in Saint Louis, William Byrne, an Irish contractor on the Western Division, expressed his own and his workers' desire for spiritual advisers, noting that the Irish canallers currently at work as well as those being recruited were Catholics.[91] One year later a colleague informed Rosati that approximately two thousand Irish Catholics were engaged in canal construction in Illinois.[92] When describing the potential canal "congregation" at Peru, Byrne elaborated on the character of his countrymen and confessed, "I regret to add, tho. with strong and national attachment to the Catholic religion, yet ignorant of its divine precepts—with this devotion to religion is combined all the ardent feelings and propensities of their early education and country—I speak of the Irish Catholics, as there are few else."[93]

Byrne noted that some of these men were experienced canal diggers, having worked on the Erie and other eastern canals. Others had only recently arrived from Ireland, including immigrants who traveled to Illinois from Canada, where they had helped build the Rideau and Welland Canals. They were, he observed, industrious men in search of decent jobs and a sense of freedom that was relatively unfamiliar in their native land. Nonetheless, what disturbed Byrne was the extent to which some of these workers carried sectional rivalries from Ireland with them to Illinois, as well as their penchant for drinking and brawling. He complained that his Irish diggers were "mostly of the lower order . . . often divided by and contending with party spirit and causes that sever, disgrace and ruin their unhappy country. The silent sneer and intemperate expression and manner of a few bigoted and unthinking Protestants, with whom they are sometimes obliged to mingle, causes or rather keeps alive an irritability or temper anything but Christian."[94]

Notwithstanding Byrne's assessment of his poor countrymen, the Irish canallers on the Western Division initiated this call for priests along the line, pressuring contractors to carry out their request. Thus, Vincentian Fathers John Blasius Raho and Aloysius Parodi, though attuned to the narratives of the immigrants' degenerate behavior, did not undertake their civilizing mission at the behest of company officials or contractors. Their appearance was largely due to the efforts of this "lower order" of Irish construction workers, who grasped the chance to foster a sense of normality within their struggling community. The luring of these men of the cloth to the Illinois canal frontier confirms both agency and respectability on the part of the Irish workers, who, in requesting the priests, were staking their claim to the freedom of organized worship, a right that denoted citizenship and civic belonging. Byrne was confident that within the span of a few months, he could collect $1,000 "from the contractors, superintendents, and labourers of the work and those interested in the prosperity of the place." This money was spent to construct a church at Peru for the incoming priests, built, of course, by the Irish canal workers.[95]

The arrival of Raho and Parodi at their headquarters at LaSalle (Peru's neighboring town) in March 1838 was cause for a rare celebration—rare in that it included the town's Irish canallers. Led by contractor William Byrne, a procession featuring a small band of "flutes, fifes, and drums" and "whole-souled cheers from Irish hearts" greeted the priests, with the canallers taking up the rear, "carrying lighted torches."[96] According to the priests, the LaSalle mission was an immediate success. Rev. Thomas A. Shaw, in his *Story of the LaSalle Mission,* noted that, unlike those "unreasonable and niggardly missions" in the nineteenth century that perished due to lack of community and financial support, the Irish of Illinois "set a high value on the services of the Holy Faith." Father Shaw recounted a sense of responsibility, pride, and dignity on the part of the Irish canallers, who pledged their hard-earned wages toward the construction of a church:

> Father Raho on his days of collecting along the canal, at the boarding houses or shanties, had comparatively an easy time to obtain what [money] he sought. The smile that greeted him from the housewife or boarding mistress, or men assured him: "Your Reverence is welcome," and the shake of the hand followed.

Utilizing an information network prevalent among canallers, Irish laborers in Ottawa, twenty miles east of Peru, soon learned of Raho's and Parodi's positive influence on the canal, as this news was "noised abroad" by the workers. The "pressing demands . . . of [these] poor people" convinced the priests to come to Ottawa. There the canal workers arranged for Mass in the town courthouse until they had time to build a church.[97]

At LaSalle workers supplemented their financial contributions to the construction of a church with sweat and toil. Such honorable devotion was not lost on their priests, particularly after the Irish canallers painfully recounted how they had previously been duped by their former contractor, A. H. Bangs. After promising them a church, Bangs fled the country "carrying away $9000.00, the hard-earnings of the poor canallers he had employed; and therefore, the contributions promised by these good people." When the "enraged" workers finally tracked down Bangs, they "inflicted the punishment of tarring and feathering the swindler." However, now blessed with the leadership of Raho and Parodi, the immigrants generously performed the "felling, hauling, and hewing ... thatching and plastering" to build their place of worship—their symbol of cultural and spiritual progress—on the canal.[98]

Despite the mission's early progress, the daily struggles, dangers, and privations of canal building alarmed the priests. The Irish canallers at LaSalle "lived from hand to mouth ... depending on the work of the canal which might come to suspend for want of appropriations."[99] Sickness claimed the lives of hundreds, and during the first few months the priests' energies were devoted to burying these poor men, who died like pack animals "among the dirt and mud."[100] Even the first marriage ceremony Father Raho performed on the canal frontier served the righteous as an example of unrefined behavior, for this Irish Catholic couple "had concluded to change their mode of living and enter into the normal condition of mankind." Following vows and pronouncements, the canal village burst into bedlam. To Raho, the canallers appeared no more cultured than the Kaskaskia; it was "as if the spirits of the departed warriors ... had besieged the place, yelling their wild war whoop, and uttering their discordant jargon, accompanied with sounds horrid and unearthly."[101] Though both groups were considered nonwhite, noncitizens, and savages, the writings of these missionaries suggest that Irish canallers were even more depraved than Indians, with Raho stating on one occasion (similar to Father Stephen Badin in Indiana) that he preferred to "be among the Indians."[102]

Raho was quite discouraged that not all the immigrants shared the same zeal for spiritual progress, and on occasion he singled out various groups of canallers for their sinfulness. "Thank God," Raho noted, "the people living in LaSalle are quieter, drink less and come to Church. Unfortunately the same can't be said of the people living along the [canal] line, two or three miles north of here. They are extremely depraved and untouched by the grace of God."[103]

His colleague Parodi echoed these complaints. Though the Irish canallers "declared themselves Catholic," he argued that they were "worse than infidel[s] and care only about money and liquor." Parodi was disgusted with the apparent immorality of the workers, which was attributable, he argued, to the fact that "almost every house in the place sold liquors and kept gambling establishments etc., etc." The Irish canallers, Parodi suggested, were the chief source of debauchery: "the inhabitants profain [sic] beyond conception and the place was full of [Irish] canal hands and others on the Sabbath quarreling and a general field fight was no uncommon thing. It was a virtual Sodom."[104]

On the canal's Summit Division, at Lockport, northeast of Morris, a Protestant missionary for the American Home Missionary Society articulated similar thoughts on the decadence of these Irish laborers. Minister Jeremiah Porter noted that the Irish Catholic canallers were simply a "bad sight. They fight and swear, and drink and murder. Truly madness is in their hearts while they live."[105] Porter's reaction may have stemmed from canallers' rejection of the Bibles he offered them, for some of his Protestant colleagues expressed a grudging respect for Irish Catholics, who reportedly donated their meager financial resources to support their church and its missionaries. In a letter to the society's executive committee, one missionary argued, "Could we make Protestants equally ready to give for the support of their institutions, we should no longer need the aid of your society."[106] According to the resident priests at LaSalle, Ottawa, and Peru along the line of the Illinois & Michigan, some of the most generous supporters were in fact poor Irish canallers. Father Parodi noted that the workmen regularly gave a day's worth of hard-earned wages when he solicited funds for church construction at LaSalle.[107]

Financial and physical support for missions, however, did not fully convince Raho and Parodi that their parishioners were on the right path. On the issues of drinking, violence, and rioting, the priests complained that the canallers acted as rebels, divorced from the tenets of their faith. Religion, though it promised stability and community, could just as often produce divisions between priests and their flock. Spiritual leaders such as Raho and Parodi felt that such contestation on the part of workers reinforced the cultural depravity of the unassimilable Irish. Experience, however, taught Irish canallers that a brutal and unfair labor system was a more accurate cause of strife and sin. Workers exercised a powerful mobility between the overlapping worlds of progress: the world of faith and community, and the underworld of rough

labor, sickness, and violence. Preoccupied with a concern for their own preservation and their masculine reputations, they had neither the leisure nor the
energy to reflect on the contradictions of these worlds.

Irish violence and rioting on the canal, particularly when aimed at countrymen, struck religious leaders as perplexing and appalling. To be sure, Raho
and Parodi witnessed much violence during their first year in LaSalle County,
and it was in these conflicts that the priests were exposed to what they considered the worst elements of Irish canal labor. The latter described these
internal conflicts as occurring "without any reason ... [but] national passion," yet, for Irish canallers, the violence was strategic and justified.[108] Such
violence led both priests to regret their decision to come to the Illinois transportation frontier.

Genuine fears and difficulties aside, citizens, political leaders, and newspapers heaped praised on Raho and Parodi as peacekeepers and civilizers.
Not only did the priests boost morale on the part of these downtrodden,
foreign workers; they cared for the workers in seasons of illness, provided a
model for manners and temperance, and were so respected that they even
gained a measure of success in dissuading hostile workers from combat. "The
Rev. Mr. Raho and Rev. Mr. Parodi," wrote the *Ottawa Free Trader,* "deserved
... great credit for their efficient efforts to better the condition and correct
the habits of the laborers in this section of the country." Similarly, the
Catholic Telegraph, the official paper of the Archdiocese of Cincinnati,
claimed that the "Irish priesthood," due to its role in quelling violence on the
works, merited appreciation from anyone "interested in the progress of internal improvements." According to the editor, "hundreds of [Irish] laborers in
a state of great excitement" could be pacified instantly once those "whose
sacerdotal character, they had been taught to respect, stood before them."[109]

Additional evidence points not only to the loyalty of Irish canallers to
their priests but to the influence they had over some of these civilizers.
Timothy O'Meara, an Irish Catholic priest who ministered in Chicago and
on the Summit Division of the Illinois & Michigan Canal, was apparently a
favorite among the workers. Though his tenure was brief (1837–38), O'Meara
was known to mingle freely with the canallers, prior to his sudden removal
by Rev. William Gabriel Bruté.[110] James Silk Buckingham, who was visiting
Chicago at the time, dug deeper and learned that O'Meara had embezzled
church funds and had committed various other frauds. Moreover, he had
"defied all his exclesiastical [sic] superiors" and, due to his time spent with
the Irish workers, "had been for some time habitually intemperate."[111]

After first endeavoring to replace O'Meara, Bruté traveled to Chicago to excommunicate the priest. According to Buckingham, the Irish workers vehemently protested this decision and declared that they were prepared to "clear the church if any attempt were made to excommunicate their favorite." In response, Bruté swiftly "calm[ed] them into submission" by threatening the canallers with excommunication if they "offered the slightest resistance" to the banishment of O'Meara, who turned over the usurped funds and left the area immediately.[112] Regardless of the outcome, it seems that these immigrants had baptized Father O'Meara in the manly lifestyle of canalling and made him their comrade.

Catholic newspaper editors and church representatives on both the regional and national levels had discouraged Irish immigrants from seeking employment on canals and early railroads. Yet, while they were mortified when rival Corkonian and Fardown groups engaged in pitched battles such as on the Illinois & Michigan in 1838, they were sensitive to the suggestion that labor violence and moral disorder was unique to the Irish.[113] Cincinnati's *Catholic Telegraph* challenged the efforts of anti-Irish and anti-Catholic commentators who crafted uncouth and immoral behavior as a customary trait of the canal Irish. "The enemies of our religion," argued the editor, "are ever harping upon the supposed immorality of Irish emigrants to this country" and

> the disaffection occasionally manifested by laborers on works of internal improvement, is triumphantly mentioned as an unanswerable argument of depravity, disgraceful alike to themselves, their country, and their religion. But why should this inference be drawn against Irishmen alone, as if they were the only peace-breakers in the country? Look at the riots continually occurring within the bosoms of our most polished cities, and in spite of a well organized police ... [and] efficient military force, and then put the question, whether it is strange that individuals amongst several thousand men, huddled together without a restraining hand, should sometimes infringe the laws of perfect harmony?[114]

Canal riots, although appalling to officials, citizens, and spiritual leaders such as Raho and Parodi, were justified according to other witnesses. Thus, the *Telegraph* editor argued that these riots were not only "grossly exaggerated" to justify the claims of bigoted commentators and citizens but an honorable, masculine, and democratic expression of the workers, who, trapped in an inequitable and oppressive labor system, sought to achieve a degree of control over their lives and livelihoods. Agreeing with traveler Thomas

Nichols that Irish ditchdiggers were a "source of wealth and strength," the editor stressed that "the actual conduct of Irishmen, thus disadvantageously situated, reflects honor on both themselves and their religion."[115]

Although priests, contractors, company officials, and other commentators noted that drinking and fighting were among the time-honored Irish characteristics that workers' transplanted to canal and railroad frontiers, evidence also points to Irish canallers' creative adaptation to new opportunities in America. Politics provides a useful example, for some Irish canallers wielded considerable voting power. Still, nativist political commentators often focused on the susceptibility of immigrants to political manipulation when arguing against—and distancing—Irish participation in American political and civic life.[116] While political manipulation sometimes entailed the coercion of canallers, it also held the power of agency.

Anti-immigrant groups demeaned the manner of Irish involvement in the political process, viewing the Irish tendency to create voting blocs as a product of "clannishness."[117] Yet clannishness meant cohesiveness and power. The frequency of nativist and Whig diatribes on the fraudulent voting practices of transient Irish canallers in the 1830s and 1840s, as well as justifications for why the Irish were unfit for citizenship, implied a tangible level of political agency on the part of canal workers. Moreover, historians suggest that, in nineteenth-century America, claims to political power both reflected, and grew from, a claim to manhood and civilization.[118] When they engaged in politics, Irish canallers asserted their authority as men and their influence as worthy and manly builders of progress.

Yet the political agency of Illinois's Irish canallers threatened those who distrusted and feared the workers' Catholic beliefs and connections. Rev. Nahum Gould of the American Home Missionary Society expressed such fears of the Irish Catholic laborers on the canal line in Rockwell, Illinois. "Some of our people," Gould noted, "are . . . alarmed at the Catholic population, while others consider them but transient inhabitants." Gould, however, offered an even more pessimistic outlook for Rockwell's citizens. He was "pretty certain that some of them are becoming permanent residents," and, alas, "it is expected that ere long they will erect a chapel."[119] While the Catholic church provided a positive community reference point for transplanted Irish canallers, anti-Catholic commentators who sought to deny the immigrants' contribution to national progress argued that their religion was hostile to the very foundations of American republicanism.[120] Even worse, argued nativists, Irish Catholic immigrants were part of a "Papist conspiracy to bring down Democratic institutions."[121] Nativist John P. Sanderson argued that even recently naturalized Irish Catholics were unworthy of political participation, for they had not honed the set of nationalistic attitudes, traditions, habits, and civic rituals central to Americanism:

> Race, kin and kindred, training and education, devotion to country, knowledge of its institutions, history, trials, progress and achievements, an aggregation of men that have a country and love it, feel that they have nationality and place a value upon it, have ancestral graves and ancestral toils to look and dwell upon, an ancestral spirit to be inspired with ... examples to imitate ... an inheritance to glory in ... [and] a present blessing to be enjoyed—all these are requisite to make an American.[122]

Such exclusive nationalistic criteria, however, did not deter Irish canallers from seeking political influence. On various divisions of the Illinois & Michigan Canal, transient Irish workers vastly outnumbered the local population, and there is some evidence that canallers took advantage of a state law that required only six months of residency to earn suffrage.[123] When the votes of Irish canal workers contributed to Democratic Party victories, Illinois's Whig newspapers saw this as an affront to native-born citizens and the democratic process. In 1839 the editor of the *Chicago American* grumbled that the voting power of the canal Irish was "equal to one half the whole vote of the county."[124] One year later, when Democratic presidential candidate Martin Van Buren won Illinois in his 1840 defeat at the hands of the Whig William Henry Harrison, pro-Harrison forces, confident the Prairie State would go for "Old Tippecanoe" based on its proximity to his native Indiana and Ohio, erupted in protest. A Chicago editor complained that the true voice of Illinoisans had been silenced by the "enormous illegal [Irish] vote on the canal line." The Irish canallers, argued the *Chicago American,* had fraudulently conspired with the Democratic Party. Critical pro–Van Buren enclaves "of about 900 [people] in the small precincts of Athens and Romeo in Cook county," when visited after election day, revealed that only "300 [Irish] laborers could be found by the engineer on all the jobs around."[125] Similarly, an early historian of Will County contended that the Irish in Lockport voted at least twenty times each in the 1840 election to secure the state for Van Buren.[126] For Whigs, this must have been a bitter defeat. Their party, after all, saw the "American System" of internal improvements, first proposed nationally by Henry Clay, as the path to power, of which canals and railroads were a centerpiece.

Based on their agency as a formidable voting bloc, Irish canal workers found themselves in the crosshairs of fierce political debates in Illinois. Propped up by Jacksonian Democrats as evidence of the potency of "common man" politics and decried by Whigs as dangerous foreign influences, debates over their voting habits raised Irish canallers onto local and national stages in ways that their actual role in building American progress did not. The *Chicago American,* shocked at the "immense locofoco majorities given by laborers on the Canal in the counties of Cook, Will, and LaSalle," interpreted the actions of canallers and Democrats as the opening bell of a "contest" in which the Whigs would eventually triumph. As the editor noted, "Whenever the contest passes away from the Canal, and enters the farming regions of the state . . . then and there the black and piratical flag of locofocoism is struck to the dust and the glorious banner of Whig principles waving in an atmosphere of intelligence and virtue, sweeps on 'conquering and to conquer.'"[127]

Democrats countered this prediction in the *Ottawa Free Trader,* where they exposed the hypocrisy of the Whigs. According to Democrats, Whigs, while supporting longer residency requirements on a national level under the pretext that "foreigners have no right under the Constitution to approach the ballot-boxes," actively pursued the immigrant vote on Illinois's canal corridor come election time. The pro-Democratic *Free Trader* suggested that Whig attempts to scare Irish canal workers into voting their way in 1840 backfired, for the party had offended and underestimated the intelligence of the workmen. Whigs, the editor argued,

> mounted their tin carts, bag and baggage and traversed the canal from one section to another, crying at the pitch of their voice, their eyes literally squeezed from their sockets, "the canal is in danger." . . . Every effort that ingenuity could devise, was resorted to, to raise a false issue on the canal line and if possible to induce the laborers to support their candidate. But they signally failed in the 1840 election.[128]

Evidence suggests that, far from being manipulated in these elections, Irish canallers utilized the new political campaigning tactics of the antebellum period to their advantage. In particular, they were adept at bartering their votes for various benefits and favors. Protestant ministers criticized not only the voting power of Irish canal workers but also the methods by which their votes were gathered. Rev. Nahum Gould complained that the "Sabbath was desecrated" in order for politicians to exploit the Irish canal vote, "when harangues were made and whiskey dealt out" in unlimited quantities to secure votes from workers who had not yet met the residency requirement.[129] Though they did not personally document this bartering, there is little doubt that success in acquiring both alcohol and suffrage—simultaneously— buoyed the confidence of the Irish and demonstrated the compatibility of their practices with modern electoral politics.

On the local level Irish canallers used their voting clout to elect Patrick Kelley as Grundy County recorder in 1846. An early history of the county, in reference to Kelley's victory, noted that "the canal vote was by no means an uncertain or doubtful element in elections of county officers," and on several occasions a cohesive group of canallers "licked the platter clean." Though evidence suggests this voting strength on the part of Illinois's Irish canallers was as temporary as their existence on the canal frontier, it did not diminish the power these immigrants, on occasion, marshalled to the benefit of their lives and communities.[130]

Although nativism did not take hold in Illinois to the extent it did else-where in the country, due mostly to the lack of an entrenched (Anglo-Saxon and Protestant) elite as well as to the strength of the Democratic Party, it targeted the uncultured exploits of Irish canal and railroad workers to justify exclusionary political and civic practices. By the mid-1840s a common refrain crafted Irish construction workers as hostile to nationalism and progress for their willingness to work for meager wages. Not only did Irish workers take jobs away from native-born citizens; their presence destabilized the regular wages of American-born workmen, who were often depicted as "old settlers," signifying their gradual (and idealistic) rise from free laborers to independent employers or farmers. As one commentator noted in the aptly titled newspaper the *Native American*, "Our laboring men, native and naturalized, are met at every turn and every avenue of employment, with recently imported work-men from the low wages countries of the old world. Our public improvements, railroads, and canals are thronged with foreigners. They fill our large cities, reduce the wages of labor, and increase the hardships of the old settler."[131]

Ideas about Irish ethnicity dovetailed with broader American discussions of national culture in the antebellum period. Yet, as Dale Knobel argues, while physical, cultural, and even biological distinctions were thought to exist between presumed Anglo-Saxons (who were inheritors of American nationality and citizenship) and "Celts" (who could attain legal citizenship but were distanced figuratively from American national identity), these dis-tinctions were obscure and ill-defined.[132] Thus, anti-Irish groups relied on "extrinsic" features of race, including immigrant conduct and appearance. The written, "verbal image" of Irish immigrants as "low-browed," "choleric," "dark," and "brutish" institutionalized popular prejudices and became a useful indicator of Irish cultural difference, according to many native-born citizens.[133] "Obviously Irish Catholics were white," notes historian Nell Irvin Painter, "but as Celts, the poor Irish could also be judged racially different enough to be oppressed, ugly enough to be compared to apes, and poor enough to be paired with black people."[134] A distinction between race and color is again important here, even as we sift through the work of anti-Irish commentators. Irish immigrants could and did benefit from their color status as whites, just as they suffered for their supposed racial undesirability as Irish.[135]

As was the case in many regions undertaking internal improvements, Irish canallers, despite negative portrayals, counted important allies among both local and national newspaper editors. The work of Patrick Donohue, an Irish immigrant and editor of the *Boston Pilot*, was reprinted in papers throughout the East and Midwest, particularly in states where canal and railroad construction had generated (or recycled) popular opposition to Irish wageworkers. Following the completion of the Illinois & Michigan Canal and the rise of Chicago as an influential shipping and manufacturing hub, Donohue's columns crafted a favorable picture of Irish construction workers as indispensable to America's transportation networks and its economic development in general. Generations of Irish immigrants, he argued, had given their lives and labor to build up a powerful nation:

> Irishmen were called in to dig the deep foundations of huge factories, to blast the rocks, to build the dams; and when the great structures arose, the children of Irishmen were called in to tend the spindles of the furnace. The Irish were absolutely necessary to the manufacturing success of the new world. Without them the railroads would be uncut, the canals undug, the factories unbuilt.[136]

Combating nativist attacks on the uncivilized culture of Irish immigrants and the corruption involved in securing the Irish vote, Donohue reminded readers that no other immigrant group could "half stand up to the Irish," who were more manly, loyal, and industrious than most Americans, as evidenced by the fact that nearly three-fourths of the "great mechanical works of America had been done by their iron muscles."[137] Donohue's comments bring to mind the violent actions of the Irish canallers at the 1836 groundbreaking ceremony for the Illinois & Michigan Canal. In assaulting the social barriers (and persons) that excluded their formal participation in and contributions to American progress, Irish workers were mocked as the "heroes of the Emerald Isle" by the editor of the *Chicago American*. In reality, along with pride in their native land, these builders were bearers of American progress. The *New York Freeman's Journal* elaborated on this theme amid Whig and nativist calls for immigration restrictions in the mid-1840s. For the "great public works of our cities, our canals, railroads, and indeed every enterprise of physical power," the editor argued, America was indebted to the Irish immigrants, who were among its creators. He continued, "seeing what yet remains to be accomplished before this continent can have fulfilled its destiny, the interruption of immigration would be an actual decree against improvement—a ban on civilization,—a fiat for the perpetual existence of wilderness, and for the everlasting establishment of savage life."[138]

Whether opponents of nativism acknowledged the worthiness of Irish immigrant workers or merely thought of them as a necessary ingredient in America's formula for capitalist development, they emerged as a voice for the Irish laborers on public works. Their arguments reserved a place for the Irish as central to manifest destiny, economic growth, and efforts to settle America. In a very real sense, then, the culturally deficient Irish were the physical agents of civilization. This counters the views of historians who limit the gendered, class, and political power of civilization primarily to more fortunate Americans and their attempts to subjugate and assimilate inferior peoples, monopolize political authority, or masculinize the image of the middle and upper classes. Moreover, arguing that skill imparts power, labor historians have often charted a diffusion of masculine ideals from skilled workers, who used control within the workplace, independence in the community, and political activism to combine against capital, launching successful resistance movements on the basis of a flourishing working-class culture. This narrative of empowerment underestimates both the disintegrative effects of industrial capitalism and the ways it obstructed class and gender ideals. The sometimes-powerful role of these "lower orders" of immigrant wageworkers in attaining political power and crafting their own variants of masculinity thus challenges many interpretations of masculine and political formation among nineteenth-century workers. Canallers eked out a subsistence, carved out their identity by the shovelful, and improved their lot in society whenever opportunity knocked. Their development as workers and men was as uneven and unpredictable as it was painful.[139]

In an 1848 pamphlet, *Immigration into the United States,* political economist Jesse Chickering argued that Irish immigrants were *not* essential to the construction of American canals and railroads, which, he argued, would have been built regardless of the surge in immigration during the antebellum period. The hurried pace of canal "progress," he noted, came at the hands of Irish immigrants, whose "forfeiture of freedom" and "corruption of manners" would threaten the virtuous American republic. Chickering pointed to what he and other American citizens saw as the grave consequences of Irish labor on transportation projects, jobs that he interpreted as benevolent (albeit unwarranted) gifts to immigrants on behalf of states, canal and railroad companies, and their contractors. Arguing that "these foreigners came here to benefit themselves" and "not from any love of us or our country," Chickering bemoaned what he called a "transfer of power to those who know not how to use it wisely," for the Irish cared mostly about "physical aggrandizement."[140]

Underestimating both the disdain that native-born citizens held for canal construction labor and the concerted efforts of companies such as the Illinois & Michigan to recruit Irish immigrants as cheap workers, Chickering placed blame on the shoulders of the Irish and the contractors who employed them for the hurried pace in which canals and railroads were constructed. His condemnation of Irish workers' "forfeiture of freedom" and their unwise use of "power" is significant for a couple of reasons. The association of construction labor with "freedom" contradicts reality, as both workers and impartial observers of transportation labor agreed that it was often in practice little better than slavery. At the same time, Chickering conceded, and is noticeably disturbed by, the broad "transfer of power" to these immigrant workers. Though it is unclear whether he implied a nascent political power or an authority resulting from their influence on transportation projects, this anti-Irish commentator clearly acknowledged a level of sociopolitical clout emanating from the "foreign labor" that built America's canals and railroads. Nativists, it seems, were not imagining when they denounced the political power of Irish canallers. Their opposition reflected strength and influence on the part of the downtrodden.

Events on the canal line confirmed this notion, but no form of agency was more potent than violence and protest. The violence, riots, and strikes of construction workers in Illinois upset the lofty prediction that canals and railroads would "bind the republic together."[141] The public's image of such conflicts, however, was sensationalized in the antebellum period, and, as a result, labor historians face the thorny problem of unpacking these incidents to reveal an unheard cry in the actions of manly yet poor and despised immigrant workers. Such information is central to understanding the inner workings of American progress.

Reacting to antebellum outbreaks of Irish labor violence, a writer for the anti-immigrant Saint Louis *Native American* commented, "Who are the political, street, canal, and railroad rioters? Foreigners! Men who are always ready and prepared to enter into any fray, whose object may be to resist the authorities."[142] Though intended as criticism, this commentator revealed a propensity on the part of Illinois's immigrant construction workers, who refused to bend their backs under an oppressive labor system and resisted in hopes of bettering their lives on canal and railroad frontiers. For canallers, violence was a form of contestation that could strengthen a canal community as well as tear it asunder.

In June 1838 Father John Blasius Raho wrote from LaSalle to Bishop Joseph Rosati in Saint Louis about a tragedy, "a moral conflagration."[143] The Illinois & Michigan Canal had turned red from the blood of Irishmen. Being away from the construction for a short period, Raho learned upon his return that "there was a riot among the Irish workers." According to Raho, the "Corkmen did not want the workers from northern Ireland (that they call Fardowns) to work on the canal." Previously, noted Raho, conflict between the Irish canallers had involved only an exchange of insults and threats. Thus, early clashes on the Illinois & Michigan mirrored the Lagro War on the Wabash & Erie Canal in 1835, for Raho claimed that "a few people were beaten but thank God nobody was killed." But subsequently, it appeared to Raho that "the Corkmen [were] the worse of the two [groups]," as "they want to be the only ones to work on the canal and therefore try to force the Fardowns to give up and leave."[144]

In the first town history of LaSalle, Elmer Baldwin, a former judge and state legislator, insisted that the conflict between the Corkonians and Fardowners in the summer of 1838 was no surprise to local residents. He noted that "the large number of laborers on the canal, all transient persons, generally without families," were not only "more numerous ... than the citizens of the county" but had been a "source of uneasiness" since the beginning of construction. Along with LaSalle Mission sources, county histories provide additional details surrounding this wave of summer violence, as it was ignored in company reports.[145]

The first skirmish took place in the vicinity of Marseilles on June 11, in which a group of Corkonians defeated its Fardown rivals. One commentator painfully recalled that, "At ... the head of the canal, the fire had broken out ... [and] unchecked, it swept along, fed by the fuel of hate, wrecking many a home, until it reached its maximum between Ottawa and LaSalle."[146] The Corkonians, seeking to dominate work on the canal, "pressed rapidly westward," where sympathetic members of their "clan" joined ranks, brutally attacking Fardowns on the journey. In the words of Baldwin, "woe to the poor Fardown who fell in their way."[147] Corkonians were indeed ruthless in their persecution of the numerically inferior Fardowns, for, according to Raho, "they [the Corkmen] ravage and destroy their cabins and harm them in any way they can." Frustrated by this violence, the priest attempted to settle the conflict by inviting both groups for Mass; in his view, the only solution was to "sp[ea]k to them inspired by God." Most of the clashing workers resisted this gesture, and Raho noted that "to convince them to come I had to go and pick them up one by one."[148]

Apparently "under the influence," the Corkonians undertook an eight-mile "rampage" in which they attacked Fardowners and destroyed their property, joining two hundred other Corkonians under the leadership of Edward Sweeney on the canal line at Ottawa.[149] Seizing a ferry boat at Ottawa, where the Corkonians promised to "clean out" rival canallers upon their return, they crossed the Fox River into LaSalle. This augmented faction then traveled nearly twenty miles to the western end of the line at Peru, forcibly ejecting all Fardowners from the canal and burning their shanties, before turning east toward Ottawa again. Meanwhile, Sheriff Alson Woodruff sent word to his deputy, Zimri Lewis, at Peru, to assemble a party and secure whatever arms were available to resist the Corkmen. Joining this group was contractor William Byrne, whose Fardown employees had earlier been driven off of the canal.[150] En route to Buffalo Rock, near present-day Naplate, Illinois, this enraged group of Fardowners was prohibited by authorities from burning and pillaging the Corkonians' shanties. At the battlefield, despite Sheriff Woodruff's orders to surrender their arms, the Corkonians attacked, and both groups exchanged a series of "charges," until the authorities (aided by Byrne's Fardowners), gained the upper hand. Several Corkmen jumped into the Illinois River, where they were hunted down and executed, while others were summarily arrested; no fewer than sixty men were captured and jailed in Ottawa. Between ten and fifteen Corkonians died in this conflict, as did two members of Woodruff's volunteers. It was one of the bloodiest canal conflicts in American history, made bloodier by the presence of an Illinois militia.

Father Aloysius Parodi, whose mission field included several towns in LaSalle County, was an eyewitness to a portion of this bloody scene. His letter to Bishop Joseph Rosati in Saint Louis, dated June 13, 1838, expresses his fear as he observed the conflict:

Yesterday afternoon at five about two hundred Irishmen passed through LaSalle armed with guns and sharp sticks. Without any reason they went down to Peru insulting the people of the adverse province. Many were beaten so badly that they were bleeding heavily. At night they camped about a mile away from our house, almost all of them were under the influence of liquor. . . . They were resolved to burn all the houses along the Line that belong to people of the hated province without any reason. The following morning they were chased by almost 1000 citizens headed by Mr. [William Byrne]. . . . At three o'clock in the afternoon I heard that forty people were already in jail in Ottawa. . . . Now I know how national passion can carry people to these excesses.[151]

For Father John Raho, this was indeed "the darkest hour of the LaSalle Mission." Writing to a colleague, he acknowledged that the Irish Catholics in this conflict were "worse than barbarians, savages, thirsty for the blood of their countrymen." That said, he pointed out that the canallers closest to the mission's headquarters were not the source of the problem:

I do not know what to do with those of Ottawa. They beat and kill their own countrymen; they destroy houses and crops, and they pretend to send away for their lives those of the north of Ireland, called "Fardowns." I am fatigued, I am tired. Would to God I could go away from among them. . . . I would wish to be among the Indians.[152]

The canal company was silent in the face of this violence. Surely, company officers knew that their labor policies sparked the bloodshed. Chief Engineer William Gooding's 1838 annual report noted that, prior to onset of the "sickly season" in July, Irish workers were arriving in large numbers to help build the canal.[153] When Corkonians rose up to drive off their rivals, they did so knowing that a large increase of the canal's labor supply would depress wages.[154] Violence against rivals, in this case, was not a random, uncultured act ("without any reason") as Parodi argued, but a way for Corkonians to gain leverage and dominate the work at honorable wages. Without access to labor unions to protect their livelihoods, these canallers resorted to a union of fists, rocks, pickaxes, and shovels. Through violent force they expressed their aggressive canal manhood, desire for a sense of stability, and claim to a rough independence among ditchdiggers.

Beyond group violence, for canallers, violence was also a means of individual and collective agency, a weapon wielded to both protest and exercise physical control over their difficult situation. It was far from savage behavior, though at times it was unsystematic. In most cases, company and newspaper coverage described but did not analyze acts of violence between employers and employees, posing an unfortunate problem for researchers. Nonetheless, bits and pieces of such reports speak to the centrality of threats, intimidation, property destruction, and physical and lethal violence as central to canallers' experiences. Granted, this violence was a far cry from the banners, strikes, and political protests of the skilled and civilized workers that historians have identified as inheritors of a labor republicanism.[155] Although rough-hewn, the rocks, fists, shovels, strikes, and other protest weaponry of Irish canallers were more shocking to observers and victims. This was apparent in the violence that emanated from the canal line outward, to bosses and superiors, and doubly true of violence directed inward, toward fellow workers. Workers' violence defied greater odds considering their position at the bottom of the free labor system. The socioeconomic position of canal diggers was also much different from that of the subjects historians typically examine to gauge the evolution of civilized masculinity in America. Canallers' actions highlight class-based distinctions in masculine identity. Whereas "kindhearted manly chivalry" was a central component of middle-class male power in nineteenth-century America, for ditchdiggers, power had more to do with "aggressive masculine violence."[156] Not necessarily racialized or politicized, workers' violence and sense of manhood were typically less performative than middle-class and elite variants. Canal violence came with the territory and was wielded in ways that expressed dissatisfaction, pain, and anger as well as pride and callousness.

When the Illinois & Michigan Canal reduced workers' wages from twenty-six to twenty-two dollars in the summer of 1837, canallers halted work and destroyed their contractors' property and equipment. In this labor dispute an Irish canaller was shot to death while attempting to destroy a water pump, which "restored quiet along the line."[157] The following year, when Irish workers near Joliet learned that the bank notes given as wages were worth just a fraction of their face value, they battered a local contractor and destroyed his property. The contractor, James Brooks, complained to the canal commissioners that the "outrages" and "rapacity of the Irish" made it "unsafe" to continue his work. Moreover, Brooks admitted, "I have no men who can, or who dare, to take measures to preserve my property" and "restore order" on the canal.[158] His urgent appeal to the commissioners reveals that disgruntled Irish canallers not only were fierce and effective rioters but struck fear in the hearts of native-born Illinoisans.

When, in the spring of 1846, Irish canallers working near Ottawa assaulted their contractor, W. M. McDonald, it was again a dispute over wages that fueled resistance. When the workers' earnings fell "considerably short" of the amount due, the contractor was beaten and kidnapped by "the hands . . . in his employ." The laborers imprisoned their boss in a crude shanty for several days and thus left him "without any means afforded him of complying with [the workers'] demands."[159] Only the direct intervention of canal trustee Jacob Fry quelled the dispute, but the result was unfavorable to the canal company, which was desperate for laborers. General Fry, noted a local newspaper editor, "succeeded in effecting a compromise," but as a result "all the workmen engaged in the affair . . . [were] discharged from the line." In other instances Irish canallers resorted to threats of violence to protect jobs from outside competition. One commentator witnessed a gang of Irish workers stake "a warning around their work area prohibiting any 'damned Yankees' from laboring there, and threatening anyone who might consider doing so with 'power and ball' which would 'send them to hell.'"[160] Despite the oppressive nature of construction labor, canallers used violence and intimidation to dominate and gain a measure of manly respect (or elicit fear) from their ostensible superiors.

The notion that internal improvements would "bind the republic together" was also contradicted by the men in charge of managing the canal. Conflict between high-ranking Illinois & Michigan officials negatively impacted the workforce and damaged public opinion of the project. According to some historians, the acrimonious relationship between state canal trustee Charles Oakley and Chief Engineer William Gooding both triggered and dictated the strike by Irish canal workers on the Summit Division in 1847.[161] Unfortunately, this strike has largely escaped critical analysis from the workers' standpoint, even by labor historians, as eastern canals and railroads undoubtedly witnessed more significant "turn-outs" and bloodier riots. The evidence, however, suggests that the I&M's Irish canallers, in waging this strike, interpreted their role in canal progress as worthy of the same dignity and rights accorded to native-born white workingmen. Exposing the cruel conditions of canal building, they demanded an adequate share in the fruits of their grueling and indispensable labor.[162]

After state superintendents wrestled control of construction from outside contractors in the summer of 1847, sixty-one Irish workers on the critical Summit Division went on strike, sending a carefully worded petition to Oakley. In this petition, the workers outlined their cause: "That since the said work has been worked by the State Superintendants, there has been abuse of the Labour and lives of men on said works." Such a grievance, addressed to the highest echelon of the I&M company hierarchy, was a deliberate attempt to contest the oppressive practices on the canal. To pressure Oakley they utilized language common to America's immigrant wageworkers in more respected occupations and, in particular, a powerful metaphor to voice their grievances and protest their condition. They claimed treatment no better than African American slaves:

> We hope it will be taken into Consideration by You, whom we believe to [be] both Humane and Gentlemanly. Beside[s] being an independent, born American, who should abhor oppression in Any form[,] To take the matter into your own hands. So as not to have white Citizens, drove Even worse than Common Slave Negroes.

The canallers demanded changes to their working hours, stating that "from ½ Past 4 in the morning until within ¼ of 8 in the Evening is too long to be withstood at hard labour and by men who have got to stand it in A hot climate in A sickly state and for month After month." Moreover, they requested to "have such regulations Established" that would "give the men time for sleep and rest, $1.25 per day, or one dollar per day & board, with hours of work from 6 oClock AM. to 7 PM. Saving 2 hours for Breakfast and Dinner." Until these demands were met, the workers agreed to "mutually pledge ourselves one to the other to refrain from work on said Canal." Attacking the exploitative nature of the free labor system by claiming a whiteness and citizenship that merited better treatment, the Irish workers believed their role as canal-building men would win them a concession from management.[163]

They may have been up to more. Much has been made of how white wageworkers, and particularly Irish workers, fashioned identities as "not slaves" and "not Blacks" in the antebellum period. As the American working class matured in the North and drew on the legacy of personal independence, enshrined in the revolutionary period, to distinguish its wage labor from the edifice of human bondage that had proliferated in the South, image and identity became crucial components. David Roediger has argued that working-class formation and the development of white racial identity "went hand in hand for the U.S. white working class" and that in expressions of whiteness, workers responded to fears of dependency in an exploitative, flawed capitalist system.[164] Still, in light of the 1847 strike and the petition, we should resist the temptation to ascribe to these words and deeds an anxious fear of dependency. Canallers understood the significance of their work and were intimately familiar with its violent, unforgiving nature. Cognizant of decades-long labor shortages, they also knew that they had carved out an important place on the state's moving transportation frontier. Thus, they had immediate goals: white citizens engaged in the work of progress flatly deserved better. Instead of looking inward and psychoanalyzing these workers, we might learn more by examining their message. As evidenced in the language they used in the petition, the Irish canallers articulated an impressive knowledge of the politics of free labor and of labor-management relations—knowledge often assumed lacking on the part of common, unskilled workers.

The striking canallers drew on the nascent association of middle-class manliness with refinement and civility, on one hand addressing Oakley as "Humane and Gentlemanly," while on the other hand appealing to the essence of manly independence, that cornerstone of labor republicanism, in describing him as a native-born American, who, like any good Yankee man, "should abhor oppression in Any form." It stands to reason that these Irish workers understood well the power of their words and, by extension, the possessive investment in whiteness on the part of the management class. They skillfully packaged the labor republicanism argument with Illinois's captains of industry in mind. Certainly, the business and political leadership of a free state would not condone the type of rank exploitation associated with the southern plantation, and especially not in the name of progress. The Prairie State was no plantation, its workers not slaves, and its managers not masters of men.

Having read their petition, Oakley spoke with the workers and, informing Chief Engineer Gooding of their demands, suggested that a compromise be worked out to rectify their situation. Gooding, on the advice of Secretary Robert Stuart and trustee David Leavitt, rejected any such compromise. Unconcerned with the workers' struggles, Gooding was more troubled with the precedent a compromise might entail:

> All experience proves, that when wages are too high, men are not so well contented, are more likely to strike for still higher wages, or other unreasonable cause, and save no more money.... But the most serious objection to an advance is, that the principle being once conceded that a combination amongst the men to obtain what the employer is not required in justice to grant, and yields upon compulsion, induces other unreasonable exactions, and finally takes from him all power of control.[165]

Historian Catherine Tobin suggests that the strike was the result of "machinations" between Oakley and Corkonian leader Daniel Lynch, whom Oakley had preferred to install as a foreman on the Summit Division in place of a relative of Gooding. Moreover, she argues that Oakley encouraged the strike to expose the mismanagement of Gooding and company as the canal neared completion.[166] But additional evidence suggests that Oakley's ties to Lynch had nothing to do with an affinity for the Irish, as he had also attempted to replace a large group of Irish canallers with "100 to 150 Hollanders" from Buffalo, New York. David Weber, a contractor on Pennsylvania canals prior to working for the I&M, disagreed with Oakley's move, arguing that "one experienced Irish laborer will do as much of any kind of canal work as three raw Hollanders."[167] As the strike dragged on for three weeks, Oakley's enemies on the canal board suggested that the strikers had exploited him. Secretary Robert Stuart noted that "a few of the scamps here are making a tool of this poor weak man, & they will blow him up ere long, so that we will not be able to get hold of even a relick of what was once *the great negociator.*"[168]

Nonetheless, the strike failed. Gooding was unwilling to concede to the canallers' demands. This decision, he argued, was based on his conversations with "gentlemen of responsibility and experience, who had large interests at stake and who were exceedingly anxious to have the Canal completed at the earliest possible moment."[169] The conditions of poor, disgruntled, and oppressed canallers were exaggerated, he argued, for "one dollar per day was the established rate," and it was a higher wage than "either on the Michigan Railroad, or the Wabash and Erie canal in Indiana." Moreover, he insisted, "every man who has had the charge of a work must know that to accede to the demands of the work-people for one additional penny, would prove but the entering wedge for increased demands." A compromise "would have created a spirit of insubordination and exaction," which most certainly would have ended "in the most formidable evils to the work." Though their strike had failed, the Irish canallers still seized control of their difficult situation, as at least two hundred left the canal for work in Michigan and Indiana.[170] This peaceful protest of the strike's unfavorable outcome is noteworthy, for in other instances, strikes were accompanied by outbursts of violence and destruction. Such was often the case on the Prairie State's other remarkable transportation project, the Illinois Central Railroad.

The year 1853 was particularly violent for the Illinois Central Railroad. Although the native-born population of Illinois eagerly welcomed railroad progress and accepted the arrival of immigrant workers as a "necessary accompaniment," they frequently anticipated violent conflict and rallied in self-defense against foreigners whom they viewed "as a threat to the social order."[171] A writer for the state's leading newspaper, the *Chicago Tribune,* went further, suggesting that Irish immigrants were in fact "unfit for freedom . . . and cannot properly appreciate it . . . [for] their sense of equality is nothing but an intense selfishness."[172] While violent and riotous conflicts were relatively infrequent, rumors of violence on two ICRR divisions, including one in which workers near Decatur threatened to set the town ablaze, stimulated the creation of a volunteer militia company, consisting of the town's "best citizens," who promised to "prevent disturbances."[173]

In Decatur Irish construction workers on the Illinois Central entered a melee between two rival construction "gangs" on the neighboring Great Western Railroad, when contractors hired Irish and German immigrants to build alternate sections of the line. Learning that their countrymen were being attacked by Germans, the ICRR workers armed themselves with pick-axes and shovels and marched to the scene of violence, Decatur's courthouse square. Upon their arrival, however, the workers were halted by the town's much-improved "volunteers," armed with muskets and bayonets, and most returned to their shanties.[174]

The bloodiest conflict during the ICRR's early building period came amid a labor dispute in LaSalle, where nearly two thousand workers were on the job, including four hundred who performed dangerous construction labor on a critical embankment. Company officials noted that there was continually "a bad Set of men about the heavy work at LaSalle," and it was their opinion that alcohol abuse produced the "brutal and murderous" actions of Irish workers in December 1853.[175] In light of prevailing wage reductions on several ICRR divisions, contractor Albert Story cut his workers' daily earnings from $1.25 to $1.00. To be sure, some workers begrudgingly accepted this reduction, but others demanded to be paid off and released immediately to find better conditions elsewhere. Story ultimately agreed to this demand, but not quickly enough, as one worker, John Ryan, whom Story told would "be paid as soon as his turn came," reacted with a vengeance. An eyewitness reported the conflict:

> The man [Ryan] seized Story by the throat, a struggle ensued, Story snatched his revolver and leveled him with the ground. A number of Irishmen then rushed on Story, drove him from his store to his house, thence to his barn, where they most brutally knocked him down, beat his brains out, dragged him to the door, and then with large stones crushed his skull to a mummy. Consternation spread like a prairie on fire. The Irish assembled in great numbers, many of them in a fury of drunkenness.[176]

The frightened citizens of LaSalle sent word to the "Shields' Guards," an eighty-man volunteer military company from Ottawa, who, along with an angry group of LaSalleans, detained numerous Irish workers near the scene and assembled them in the frontier version of a criminal lineup while Story's foreman selected the known assailants. According to the editor of the *Alton Courier*, a "large majority" of local citizens preferred "instant jury . . . and if found guilty, instant suspension on the first tree," a type of popular justice that, as some historians argue, permeated antebellum and early modern locales where ethnic or economic tensions empowered native-born citizens to act as judge, jury, and executioner.[177] Among the thirty-two Irish detainees, eleven were tried for their involvement in the Story murder and six were convicted and sentenced to hang.[178] However, a clemency campaign quickly ensued, since the convicted men were only six among hundreds of rioters and did not play a direct role in the murder.

Newspaper coverage of the pardon campaign was permeated with prejudices typical of narratives of the violence of progress on canals and railroads in the antebellum Midwest. Despite their sometimes-fratricidal clashes, Irish workers were depicted as a monolithic group of uncivilized foreigners who were "unfit for freedom" and obstacles to the progress they labored tirelessly and dangerously to produce. The *Chicago Tribune* argued that its news files were filled with the bloody exploits of railroad workers, with "nine cases out of ten committed by 'noble Celts,' and almost invariably accompanied with circumstances of diabolical atrocity and cruelty." Moreover, the *Tribune* claimed that instead of having the workers "marched out and shot on the spot," a time-consuming clemency campaign resulted from a conspiracy of the Catholic Church and its messenger, the *Tablet*, Chicago's Roman Catholic newspaper.[179] John F. Farnsworth, defense attorney for accused Irishmen, not only rebutted such claims but suggested that the "poor Railroad Irishmen" were convicted only because the railroad company and its contractors had used their funds on behalf of the prosecution. Lost in most contemporary and historical accounts of this tragic violence are its roots as a labor dispute. All too accustomed to late, reduced, and denied wages, John Ryan decided to take a stand, and his comrades did not back down.

In the end, however, the beleaguered workers found an ally in Mason Brayman, the ICRR's solicitor, who supported a petition for executive clemency, and in July 1854 Gov. Joel Matteson commuted the rioters' sentences from death to life imprisonment.[180] Although Chief Engineer Roswell B. Mason opposed this decision, he noted in a letter to the company president that "the remark is not infrequently made at LaSalle by the Irish [workers] that the [Democratic] Governor is on their side."[181] Thus, the political power of Illinois's Irish transportation workers had again proven to be salient. Matteson's decision in favor of these rough builders of progress, however, did not sit well with anxious Illinoisans, who burned him in effigy at Chicago, Joliet, and LaSalle.[182] Railroads, like canals, did not bring progress without cultural, political, and physical contestation.

Historian Noel Ignatiev, in his oft-cited study, *How the Irish Became White*, argues that for Irish laborers in nineteenth-century America, "to become white" meant initially selling themselves "piecemeal" as opposed to being sold for life and eventually competing for jobs "in all spheres" instead of being stuck in ostensibly demeaning fields of wage labor. In addition, Irish workers "had to learn to subordinate county, religious, or national animosities ... to a new solidarity based on color."[183] By these criteria antebellum Irish canallers and railroad builders never achieved whiteness. Yet were Irish wageworkers actually seeking to "become white" in antebellum America? Were they already white, in *color* at least, upon arrival? Important evidence suggests not only that distinctions existed between race and color (though they were never absolute) but also that more immediate and attainable concerns stimulated Irish construction workers.

Canallers valued self-preservation, decent and prompt wages, fair conditions, and outlets—such as alcohol, religion, and politics—to help them endure (or escape) the brutality of canal building and retain a sense of community and manly pride. Moreover, for those workers seemingly mired in canal and railroad construction labor, did alternate avenues to manhood, power, nascent citizenship, and, by extension, whiteness, exist? Evidence from the transportation frontiers of nineteenth-century Indiana and Illinois suggests so. Canallers attacked the symbols and barriers of American progress, including celebrations and the actual projects their sweat and muscle had created. They fled oppressive labor situations for better opportunities, drank to bolster their manhood and community, and flaunted their rough masculinity on jobs that native-born citizens refused to perform. Irish workers sought to dominate the canal frontier by driving off competition, struck fear in their employers in episodes of violence and protest, and utilized their power as a voting bloc to elect favorable political candidates and obtain preferential treatment on the job. Taken as a whole, their struggles as transients at the bottom of the wage labor system challenge narratives of—and motivations for—racial formation in the nineteenth-century American West.

As was the case in Indiana, citizens' expectations for completed canals and railroads in Illinois dictated the narratives of progress that company officials crafted, despite their genuine fears. Thus, by 1844 Chief Engineer Gooding argued that, even considering the difficulties of cost, weather, sickness, and disgruntled workers, the I&M was "without question . . . an improvement of great capacity" that would overcome the many obstacles to completion.[184] Yet, as the canal neared completion, Gooding confided, rather embarrassingly, in board of trustees president William Swift that the actual cost of the Illinois & Michigan significantly exceeded his previous estimates. Much of this, Gooding complained, was the fault of earlier surveyors and canal officials, who, "notwithstanding their ability . . . did not give a correct idea of the obstacles to be overcome in the construction of the canal."[185] "So long as the canal remains unfinished," he argued, "shadows, clouds and darkness must continue to rest upon us."[186] Though Gooding was "excessively mortified" by this uncomfortable reality, he was even more concerned about how it would influence opinion of his leadership. Illinoisans, in anxious anticipation of their own version of New York's famous Erie Canal, had little patience for the delays, company mismanagement, and inoperable sections of the waterway, and even less for the "uncivilized" transient immigrants, who, despite their role in building the canal, were perceived as the "enemies" of progress.[187]

Joseph H. Buckingham, a journalist and delegate to Chicago's 1847 River and Harbor Convention, assessed the construction of the Illinois & Michigan Canal only to condemn the "Irish mud-diggers . . . in all their primitive ugliness and . . . nastiness" who built it.[188] Upon "further examination," he argued, Illinois "would have done far better to have turned the Canal into a Railroad." Though the canal was nearing completion, Buckingham argued that, due to the hurried pace of construction and the porous nature of the soil, it "will not hold water after it is filled . . . the water will *leech* through," and thus "the money is thrown away." Most Illinoisans, including some pro-railroad factions, disagreed with these sentiments, for the Illinois & Michigan Canal was their "Erie of the West."[189] Nonetheless, the reporter's statements are revealing, for, in criticizing the canal, he targeted the "Irish mud-diggers" whose backbreaking labor created the artificial waterway. Buckingham shed light on these unskilled immigrants—ignored in public celebrations—only to associate them with what he considered a failed project. This, according to him, was a more fitting legacy for the "dirty" and "primitive" canal workforce. "It will not be many years," Buckingham argued, "before a railroad will be built on that route, that [will] be worth to the public more than fifty canals."[190] This observation was accurate, even pro-phetic, as the Illinois Central Railroad initiated construction in 1852 and finished in 1856. The problem that Buckingham, Illinoisans, and advocates of progress everywhere learned was that railroad progress necessitated the same major ingredient as canal progress: the "primitive" Irish laborers whose backbreaking labor transformed American dreams into reality.

Nonetheless, this and other criticisms, including Charles Oakley's accusations against Gooding and Illinoisans' anticipation of a successful canal, were assuaged when prominent observers praised the chief engineer and his colleagues for a job well done. C. W. Culmann, a renowned Swiss engineer, toured canals and railroads on several continents in an 1850 trip and was quite impressed with the Illinois & Michigan Canal. Lauding Gooding and company, he noted that "the canal is only two years old, and is exceptionally well built[;] all engineering is heartily and expertly executed." Culmann even argued that "not a trace of slovenly, sloppy work could be found here, which is so characteristic of some *American* construction."[191] To canal officials and Illinoisans, this sounded like sweet music, as both groups had imagined the project as American-made. But Irish hands had built the canal. "Slovenly, sloppy work," Culmann noted, characterized American construction. Sure, many observers had argued that the contributions of transient Irish workers had been stained, even squandered, by their activities on and off the canal line. According to those with daily access to the canallers, even God wanted to punish them "for getting drunk all the time, their riots, their fights and homicides."[192] This "corruption of manners" on the part of the Irish construction workers made it even easier for native-born citizens to distance the work (and workers) from the end result and celebrate the project as the state's—and thus their own.[193] Still, while Cullman said nothing about Irish men, their construction work on the I&M had impressed this prominent Swiss engineer.

A century later Illinois Central president Wayne A. Johnston delivered a public address commemorating the railroad's hundredth anniversary, devoting his speech, in particular, to the "heritage" and "legacy" of the railroad. He noted with pride that the Illinois Central and its branch lines "were the pioneers, the trail-blazers" and the creators of American "growth and prosperity." Nonetheless, "recalling the problems and achievements" of the men "who have gone before us, and reviewing the progress of the great public service institution which they delivered into our hands," Johnston promised his audience that "we are fired with the determination to preserve our system of free enterprise and the American Way of Life." The railroad, he argued, "with its network of steel in fourteen states of Mid-America," is a symbol of "extraordinary and dramatic" progress "without precedent or parallel in the history of Mankind." Johnston noted that the millions of Americans who had reaped the benefits of the Illinois Central during the past century were indebted to "the leadership of a coterie of business leaders of outstanding accomplishments," for no group of "directors was ever filled with more earnest determination, confident resilience, pride of undertaking and honesty of purpose." In addition to bondholders and business leaders, the ICRR had "attracted many distinguished men to its service" based on its "prominent place . . . in the transportation world," including its political supporter and company lawyer Abraham Lincoln, former chief engineer and vice president George B. McClellan, surveyor Gen. Grenville M. Dodge, construction engineer (and later Chicago mayor) Roswell B. Mason, and many others. The work of these great men, Johnston argued, had made the ICRR *the Main Line of Mid-America*."[194]

Not surprisingly, the Irish immigrants who sweat, bled, battled, and died while building these projects were ignored in such celebratory accounts. As in other commemorations of canal and railroad progress, these construction workers were, at best, a necessary evil; they were transient Irish immigrant means to a more civilized and triumphant American end. Yet, day after day, Irish canal diggers and railroad builders had exposed America's frontiers of progress as frontiers of paradox.

In their transient experiences, though harsh, dangerous, and painful, Irish workers found opportunity, manhood, and even a measure of power. Without the means to create labor unions, and with scarcely any company advocates to improve their working and living conditions, Irish construction workers struggled to endure the brutal nature of canalling and railroading. Nonetheless, they used geographic mobility to flee oppressive and unhealthy situations and secure better opportunities on neighboring projects; petitioned company officials for pay increases and guarantees, reduced hours, and various benefits; drank alcohol to stimulate and celebrate their rough variants of masculinity; used their influence as a voting bloc to retain the favor of contractors and local politicians while increasing their own masculine sense of self-worth and nascent citizenship; and recruited religious leaders to the canal and railroad line in hope of enriching and revitalizing their communities.

Amid their struggles Irish canallers encountered some voices of support, but these champions were few. While several observers blamed company officials and contractors for workers' squalid living conditions and punishing work routines, others pointed to the Irish as the source of their own despair. And, of course, such critics generally had agendas of their own. Many commentators argued that Irish immigrants floated to construction sites without reputations as skilled workers, nor with the economic, social, and political power of independent Americans. Thus, they chose transportation labor precisely because they lacked these qualities. Religious leaders empathized with canallers' hardships and praised their contributions in wages and sweat to build churches that provided a haven from the underworld of progress.

Nonetheless, the persistence of this immoral underworld soured priests' and missionaries' perceptions of their flock, and they ultimately argued that death and disease functioned as divine retribution on canallers' drinking, brawling, and rioting. Company officials who rose to support Irish workers were criticized as "tools," while sympathetic politicians were decried as corrupt by nativists who considered Irish immigrants unworthy of civic responsibility and political power.[195] Elite support for Irish canallers was thus fleeting and posed several difficulties. After all, these immigrants accepted meager wages and filthy work, carried diseases, binged on whiskey, attacked contractors, threatened to kill one another, were unfit for citizenship, and exhibited inherited traits that threatened American progress. For elites, it was more convenient to laud canal construction and focus public attention on the fruits of a completed canal, tolerating Irish workers only as a temporary solution. It meant little that the immigrants who ostensibly posed a danger to the advocates and beneficiaries of progress were in fact the creators of progress. Violence, in particular, drew the scorn of a host of commentators who viewed it as unacceptable and damaging to the public image of internal improvements.

Yet the underworld of canal and railroad progress held deeper meanings than the narratives of random, innate, and savage ethnic violence portended. Irish construction communities recognized that contestation— whether in attacks on dignitaries or in battles with employers, local residents, and rival Irish construction camps—possessed the power of agency, masculinity, and survival. Violent attacks on and the forcible removal of rival workers decreased labor competition and improved their negotiating position. The use of violent force against dishonest and oppressive contractors demonstrated a bloody protest of canal and railroad working conditions and a desire for respect and leverage along the line. By extension, then, violence held the promise of endurance and power in an unfair, dangerous, and oppressive field of labor.

In contesting the problems and paradoxes of progress on the Illinois frontier, Irish immigrants sought recognition as a potent, valuable, and respected force of canal and railroad builders. Rejecting their fate as casualties of progress, Irish workers demanded a livelihood equal to "white Citizens" and superior to that of "Common Slave Negroes." Their language was real and their intentions concrete. These men used whatever means at their disposal to ensure that their role in building America's infrastructure, despite its difficulties, would not be stereotyped or ignored. Beyond the prejudiced images and public opposition was agency, however fleeting, and power, however dangerous or divisive. In the end, the so-called wild Irish built internal improvements that satisfied Americans' wildest dreams of progress.

FOUR

———

"Hell (and Heaven) on Wheels"

MORMONS, IMMIGRANTS, AND THE
RECONSTRUCTION OF AMERICAN PROGRESS AND
MASCULINITY ON THE TRANSCONTINENTAL
RAILROAD

Though [some Americans] may never see its rails, or ride on its
trains, they will feel its influence, and be more content and richer
in their lives. It puts the great sections of the Nation into sympathy and unity; it marries the Atlantic and the Pacific; it destroys
disunion ... [and] brings into harmony the heretofore jarring
discords of a Continent of separated peoples; it determines the
future of America, as the first nation of the world, in commerce,
in government, in intellectual and moral supremacy. Who shall
say that any price was too great to pay for these results?

SAMUEL BOWLES, 1869

IN 1869 MASSACHUSETTS NEWSPAPER EDITOR Samuel Bowles pub-
lished *Our New West,* which included a record of his travels along the right-
of-way of the transcontinental railroad. For Bowles, "the story of this great
enterprise" was impossible to tell without heaping praise on "the many leaders of men and of capital, under whose auspices the work ... was initiated and
constructed."[1] Though it was fashionable at that time to envision dignitaries
as solely responsible for building the railroad, America's collective memory
of the first transcontinental railroad has changed little since its completion
in 1869. Bowles thus credited the men for whom statues, libraries, and uni-
versities have been dedicated: President Leland Stanford, Vice President
Collis Huntington, and Superintendent of Construction Charles Crocker of
the Central Pacific Railroad; and their counterparts, Oliver Ames, Thomas
Durant, and Grenville Dodge of the Union Pacific Railroad.

Nevertheless, Bowles observed that "further down the list" were the "men
who perhaps contributed more to the rapid completion and real labor" of the

railroad than its illustrious coterie of leaders. These men, he argued, were the deputy-superintendents, engineers, and even the contractors, who completed a work that "called for the highest executive talent and the most indomitable energy to be found among the American people." This was a singularly American achievement, Bowles argued, for "no people other than ours,— daring in conception, rapid in acquirement, bold in execution, beyond any other nation,—could have ... done it." "The Pacific Railroad," he maintained, was a "triumph ... not only without precedent, but even without comprehension by another people."[2]

In May 1869, when the Central Pacific Railroad, built primarily by Chinese immigrants, and the Union Pacific Railroad, constructed largely by Irish immigrants, united in the "wedding of the rails," Americans celebrated and claimed this achievement as their own. The illustrious Golden Spike ceremony for the transcontinental railroad shrouded another glaring irony. This definitive symbol of American progress, built by immigrants and outsiders, was completed in what was then seen as the most un-American of American places, the Utah Territory. The transcontinental railroad was central to a dilemma that Elliott West calls the "Greater Reconstruction" of post–Civil War America, where unsettled questions about race, citizenship, and freedom were projected onto an expanding national map. Indeed, this postwar dilemma was a familiar one, for throughout the nineteenth century American expansion brought questions about race, culture, and nation into sharp focus. As the country's geographic and political boundaries expanded, its cultural boundaries—what it entailed to be or become an American— contracted.[3] During and after the transcontinental railroad's construction period, Americans were once again faced with a question as old as the nation itself: could a large republic tolerate a diversity of peoples brought within its borders? The answer was still no.

Members of the Church of Jesus Christ of Latter-day Saints knew this history only too well. Church founder Joseph Smith came of age in the "Burned-Over District" of western New York, his younger years bracketed by two notable events: the completion of the Erie Canal and the religious revivals associated with the emergence of the Second Great Awakening. Smith published the Book of Mormon in 1830 and established a church in Palmyra, New York, just east of Rochester, one of the many sleepy villages that the canal had transformed, as if by magic, into a "town awash in craftsmen, salesmen, laborers, speculators, lawyers, crooks, and clergyman, most of them strangers."[4] In the 1830s and 1840s Smith's quest to build an American Zion took him and his people to the heart of the continent's transportation frontier and also into the teeth of anti-Mormon discrimination and violence. The Latter-day Saints (LDS) moved from Kirtland, Ohio, to Independence, Missouri, and eventually settled in Nauvoo, Illinois, where Smith was assassinated in 1844 at the nearby Carthage Jail. When Smith's successor, Brigham Young, led the subsequent Mormon exodus west to Zion (eventually settling in the Salt Lake Valley, then part of Mexico) in 1846–47, he and his followers charted nearly the same path that the transcontinental railroad would traverse two decades later. Mormons were no strangers to canal and railroad progress, nor were they unfamiliar with its accompanying evils.

Even in the Utah Territory, an incredibly homogenous place, the construction of the transcontinental railroad accelerated a new peopling of immigrants and emigrants (from Europe, China, and all parts of the United States) on a wageworkers' frontier that began to mirror the diversity of other western locales in this period. These groups, whose brains and brawn built the railroad, would test the limits of racial democracy in the American West, that place of ostensibly endless opportunities, a proving ground for national progress, and, for some, even a site of Americanization. As some scholars have suggested, the building of the transcontinental railroad was not only among the greatest American achievements of the nineteenth century but a definitive episode in western, imperial, and transnational history.[5] The most famous of the several ceremonial "last spikes" driven into a polished laurel tie at the aforementioned 1869 celebration, California's offering, which contained eighteen ounces of pure gold, seemed to echo the idea of a nation transformed. Etched on its side were the words, "May God continue the unity of our Country as this Railroad unites the two great Oceans of the world."[6] The scene at Promontory Summit on the morning of May 10, though exaggerated in several popular accounts to include Indians and Mexicans, featured, according to one eyewitness, "men of every color, creed, and nationality."[7] As historian Mark Fiege notes in his superb chapter on the environmental history of the railroad, "The world had come to America, and America had become, in effect, the world."[8]

Mormon unskilled labor on the transcontinental railroad marked a significant change from earlier labor trends on America's massive transportation projects. It was one of the few times that large segments of a settled Anglo-American community were marshaled to assist in railroad construction. Not only did Mormons of all social classes participate in railroad building, but Mormon workers and leaders found in such labor an opportunity to surmount national prejudices against their religious practices and to discredit allegations of defiant isolationism. Railroad construction labor offered a chance to participate in a work of national importance, gain recognition and the acceptance of Americans, prove Mormon loyalty to the federal government, and secure the economic benefits of the country's most substantial project in western expansion and internal improvement.

Moreover, the Mormon contribution to the transcontinental railroad offers insights into alternate definitions of western work, progress, and manhood. Of particular interest is how Mormon workers and leaders interpreted the role of transient immigrant laborers and the march of civilization that supporters of the railroad predicted. In the story of triumph that followed the tracks of the Union Pacific and Central Pacific, Mormons advanced their cultural values, ideas about proper progress, and variants of masculinity, all in sharp contrast to the experiences of the railroad companies and their immigrant construction workers.

Competing definitions and understandings of masculinity were bound up in this struggle. Historian Gail Bederman's emphasis on the remaking of manhood as an "ongoing project" is certainly relevant here, for the link between manliness, citizenship, and civilization was a salient yet worrisome feature of Latter-day Saint life in the nineteenth century. Race, religion, self-mastery, power, and the notion of a virtuous brotherhood, each reinforced through a new iteration of civilized manliness, undoubtedly applied to Mormon railroad workers; they used these qualities to set themselves apart from the underworld of American progress so often associated with immigrant laborers. The problem with this endeavor, however, was that apparent cultural, political, and religious factors had also placed Mormons beyond the pale of civilization in the minds of most Americans. Shocking though it may sound to today's readers, in the nineteenth century countless citizens saw Mormons as neither white nor American.[9]

Another problem complicated by the Mormon experience was a prevailing "army of labor" model of capitalism that governed massive construction projects like the Union and Central Pacific railroads, wherein, as historian Richard White notes in *Railroaded,* his award-winning business history of America's transcontinental railroads, corporate officers commanded workers to take orders as soldiers. "They had no control over their work, how it was done, or when it was supposed to be performed," White writes. "They became a different kind of being; they were no longer, in workers' terms, men. Their opinions did not matter. They were to do what they were told. Conditions they would never accept in their civic or public life were to be the conditions of their working lives."[10] Because the Union Pacific Railroad agreed to contracts directly with Mormon leader Brigham Young (who was also a UPRR stockholder), his construction crews were almost exclusively composed of Latter-day Saint subcontractors, labor bosses, and workers, often from the same communities and even belonging to the same LDS wards. Such a labor arrangement led to a markedly different experience for Mormon construction crews when compared to their Union Pacific and Central Pacific counterparts.

Generations of historians have assessed the transcontinental railroad's impact on Utah and the Great Basin region. Mormon-focused research has addressed the "railroad threat" in Utah, but most of these studies concentrate on what political and economic change meant to Utahns and the Church of Jesus Christ of Latter-day Saints.[11] Despite the historical importance of the transcontinental railroad and its impact on Utah and the American West, scholars have done little to explore the contours and contestation of railroad progress. Nowhere do unskilled construction workers figure into the story. Thus, in examining Utah's transportation frontier, of special concern is how laborers understood their work; how dignitaries, writers, and local residents perceived it; and how the meaning of productive work, community, and respectable masculinity informed the Mormon response to railroad progress and civilization.[12]

This story cannot be told from the workers' perspectives alone. Immediate contact among Mormon, Irish, and Chinese laborers was rare, and unskilled construction workers were ignored in company records. The perspectives of Mormon and non-Mormon leaders, politicians, editors, travelers, and community residents cast light not only on these invisible agents of railroad progress but on the meanings of American progress, manhood, and citizenship. For Utah's Mormons, the discussion also entails competing narratives of national belonging. In the eyes of non-Mormon, native-born American citizens, the Mormons were "profligate outcasts," perhaps even more threatening than the Irish and Chinese immigrants with whom they shared the task of completing the transcontinental railroad.[13]

Mormon workers on the railroad marked a turning point in Latter-day Saint history. Whether born in the United States, the British Isles, or in Scandinavia, mid-nineteenth-century Mormon converts had to overcome a unique set of prejudices that placed them below even the most despised foreign immigrants. As historian W. Paul Reeve recently put it, "In the nineteenth century they were denigrated as not white enough."[14] In building the

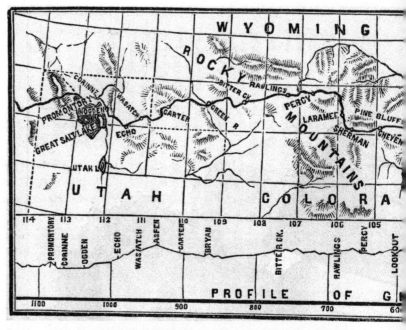

MAP 4. Map, with profile grade, of the Union Pacific Railroad. George A. Crofutt, *Crofutt's Trans-continental Tourist's Guide,* vol. 3, 2nd annual revise (New York: printed by author, 1871), 18. Courtesy of Manuscripts, Archives, and Special Collections, Washington State University Libraries, Pullman.

transcontinental, Mormons sought national belonging, acceptance as citizens, and much more. They sought not only to shape the contours of American progress but to claim the credit, benefits, and the history of such progress as their own. In Mormon hands the history of railroad progress became part of a masculine pioneer epic that both included and set them apart from American civilization.

As early as 1866 Utah and its citizens became the focal point of a tracklaying contest between the Union Pacific and Central Pacific railroads, each hoping to bring civilization to a wilderness environment that some called the American Desert (see maps 4 and 5). The 1862 Pacific Railway Act granted each company ten square miles of public land on each side of the track, authorized government bonds at the rate of $16,000 per mile of track laid in non-mountainous regions, up to $48,000 over and within the Sierra Nevada and Rocky Mountains, and up to $32,000 for track laid between the two ranges.[15]

While financing became easier, the task of constructing a transcontinental railroad remained unchanged. Common, unskilled laborers were still the

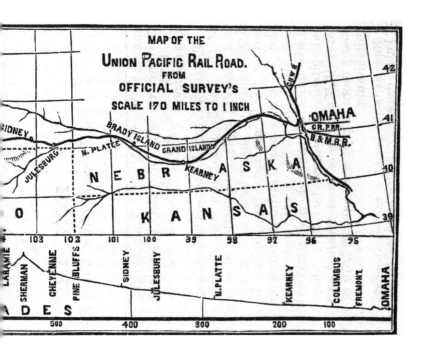

critical agents of progress. As the Central Pacific, with the help of over ten thousand Chinese laborers, built eastward from Sacramento, California, the Union Pacific, employing upward of eight thousand Irish, German, and Italian immigrants, built west from Omaha, Nebraska.[16]

The federal government's assumption that the rails would intersect at the first feasible location underestimated the power of greed. Soaking up subsidies of cash and land grants that were awarded for each mile of railroad completed, the Union Pacific and Central Pacific companies deliberately refused to meet and instead built parallel roads for several hundred miles, from eastern Nevada to southwestern Wyoming. Finally, in April 1869, just one month prior to the Golden Spike celebration, the United States Congress, in a joint resolution, selected Promontory Summit, a location north of Utah's Great Salt Lake, as the spot "at which rails shall meet and form one continuous line."[17]

Perhaps the choice of Promontory Summit was not fortuitous. Utah and the Mormons had long raised problems for Americans and the federal

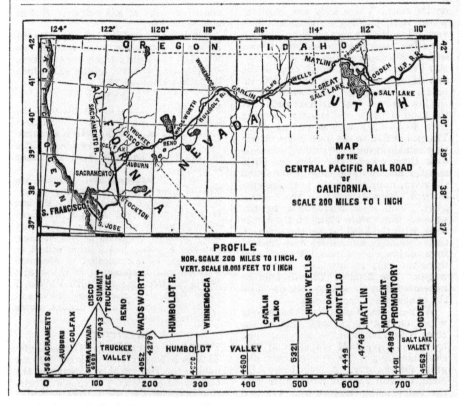

MAP 5. Map, with profile grade, of the Central Pacific Railroad. George A. Crofutt, *Crofutt's Trans-continental Tourist's Guide,* vol. 3, 2nd annual revise (New York: printed by author, 1871), 185. Courtesy of Manuscripts, Archives, and Special Collections, Washington State University Libraries, Pullman.

government. Americans considered Mormons, many of whom were native-born, incapable of citizenship and without character. Like the early Irish and the Chinese, the Mormons could not claim the rewards of their deeds. They were uncivilized "others," the antithesis of American progress, beyond the American pale.

While many supporters of the transcontinental railroad predicted that it would "civilize" the Mormons by forcing them out of isolation and into the expanding world of goods, peoples, and ideas, others praised the choice of Promontory (as opposed to Salt Lake City) for establishing yet another partition that excluded Mormon outlanders from the immediate benefits of this celebrated project—despite promises that the railroad would unite the nation's inhabitants. To exclude Utah's Mormons from America's continental empire, railroad proponents in and outside of Congress proposed removing them from its map. As historian Patricia Nelson Limerick argues, "Conquest basically involved the drawing of lines on a map . . . and the subsequent giving of meaning and power to those lines." The American West featured "an ongoing competition for legitimacy," a contest not limited to property or resources but one for "cultural dominance" that remained unresolved.[18] The contest to build, claim, and celebrate the railroad mirrored this process.

Mormonism was reviled by a majority of nineteenth-century Americans, who viewed it as an unorthodox and authoritarian religious movement, hostile to conventional values and traditions. Not only did its religious peculiarities draw the ire of critics, but Mormons' aggressive proselytizing posed a threat to mainstream American churches.[19] Moreover, like Roman Catholicism, Mormonism was perceived as an un-American and antidemocratic religion whose members were under the dominion of an autocratic leader, Brigham Young, who dictated how believers should live, act, and vote in the secular world. Critics, such as Methodist minister Daniel P. Kidder, argued that even writing on the "low and groveling" subject of Mormonism "elevated [it] . . . to a rank it never deserved," for it was a "delusion" that inflicted "spiritual blindness and misery . . . upon its successive victims."[20] Other commentators, such as Rev. Robert W. Beers, claimed that among patriotic American citizens, Mormonism was "acknowledged to be the Great Modern Abomination, the most pernicious heresy of this century."[21] Preaching a "doctrine of exclusivity" while in self-isolation from American society, Utah's Mormons combined their spiritual mission with communalistic economic practices. This provoked critics, who deemed Mormonism a mysterious cult determined to accumulate illegitimate authority, preventing non-Mormons from fulfilling the American dream of individual and democratic self-improvement.[22] According to dissenting Mormon journalist T. B. H. Stenhouse, the church was thoroughly anti-American and endeavored to "overthrow all stable governments, in order to make way for the advancement and growth of the Mormon Kingdom."[23]

Most abominable in the eyes of Americans was the Mormon practice of polygamy. With the proliferation of plural marriage, Mormonism threatened to subvert the custom of monogamy that Americans viewed as an essential bulwark against immorality and the primary tradition for the control of sexuality. Popular, political, and even religious precepts held American men responsible for guiding their energies toward financial success and respectable masculinity.[24] Those who argued that Mormons posed a danger to American democracy and manhood pointed to polygamy as evidence of a weakness of character, for it undermined nineteenth-century standards that valued the control of masculine passions as much as it did control of households.[25] Polygamy reinforced the notion that Mormonism was an authoritarian and cultish religion established by "lustful" men who sought unrestrained illicit sexual relationships with young women.[26]

While distancing Mormons from respectable manhood and mainstream American values, polygamy also racialized them as a "peculiar people."[27] Brigham Young's sexual prowess (over sixty wives) was seen as a threat to civilized masculinity, and Americans transferred the allegedly aggressive sexuality of blacks and Indians to Mormons.[28] Anti-Mormon commentators argued that practices such as polygamy had turned "the civilized world against them" and "classed [them] with Pariahs and lepers."[29] Popular American journalists and illustrators coupled Mormons with seemingly savage Indians, brutish African Americans, drunken Irish men, and heathen Chinese immigrants in periodicals such as *Harper's Weekly* and *The Wasp*.[30] Mormonism, an evil "Viper on the Hearth," was a menace to American progress, manhood, and national identity.[31]

Mormons were ridiculed as a nonwhite and uncivilized race in an 1877 *Harper's Weekly* cartoon titled *Uncle Sam's Troublesome Bedfellows* (see figure 1). While an African American hides from his counterparts underneath the bed, from left to right are the Mormon (who is noticeably upset with his uncivilized bedfellows); the Indian (who shares rye whiskey with the Irishman); the Irish immigrant, equipped with whiskey and a shillelagh; and the Chinese immigrant, who smokes opium and is seemingly content with his role as "cheap labor." Prominently displayed on the footboard of the bed is the emblem of the Union, which doubled as the logo of the Union Pacific Railroad.

In a similarly titled cartoon published in *The Wasp* at the height of the anti-Chinese movement, Mormons have yet to shake their inferior status as racial and cultural outsiders (see figure 2). In this illustration, Uncle Sam boots the Chinese immigrant to the floor, where he joins the Mormon polygamist. The Indian pokes at Uncle Sam, while the blackface Jim Crow–stage African American smiles in approval. The Irish immigrant appears passed-out drunk. Though the Union Pacific Railroad logo is again displayed on the footboard, this scene suggests depravity and disunion.

UNCLE SAM'S TROUBLESOME BEDFELLOWS.

FIGURE I. *Uncle Sam's Troublesome Bedfellows, Harper's Weekly,* December 29, 1877. Courtesy of the Bancroft Library, University of California, Berkeley, AP2.H3, 21:952.

Harsh criticisms of Mormon practices and Brigham Young's theocratic rule over the Utah Territory had often reverberated in the halls of Congress and on the national political stage. The 1856 platform of the new Republican Party stipulated that Congress could prohibit not only slavery in the western territories but polygamy as well, for these were the "twin relics of barbarism."[32] Illinois senator Stephen Douglas, arguing that the Mormons deliberately resisted federal authority and collaborated with Indian groups in robberies and murders, declared that "the knife must be applied to this pestiferous, disgusting cancer which is gnawing into the very vitals of the body politic."[33] If military measures against the Mormons failed, he recommended that Congress dissolve the Utah Territory, for Mormons "are alien enemies

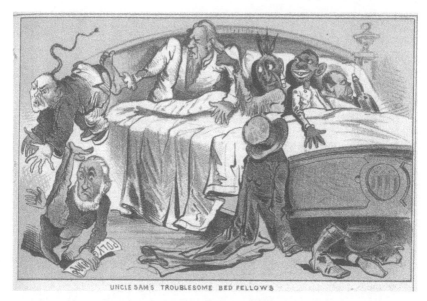

UNCLE SAM'S TROUBLESOME BED FELLOWS

FIGURE 2. *Uncle Sam's Troublesome Bed Fellows, The Wasp* (San Francisco), February 8, 1879. Courtesy of the Bancroft Library, University of California, Berkeley, "Cartoons on Current Topics," fF850.W18 vol. 3, August 1878–July 1879, no. 132:411.

and outlaws, unfit to be citizens of a territory."[34] On the issue of polygamy, Douglas thought the federal government should make every effort to cut this "loathsome ulcer" out of American society.[35] In signing the 1862 Morrill Anti-Bigamy Act, President Lincoln did just that; the act criminalized polygamy in the territories, annulled all polygamy-supporting legislation in Utah, and restricted the LDS Church's ownership of property.[36] When Mormons defied the antipolygamy law, their detractors' verbal attacks grew fiercer. In a debate with Utah's territorial delegate to Congress in 1863, New York representative Fernando Wood argued that Mormons were "profligate outcasts ... hostile to the moral and political institutions of the United States."[37]

Even the boundaries of the Utah Territory, through which the railroad would pass, became a target of anti-Mormon legislation. Taking up the cause of Stephen Douglas and others to dissolve Zion, Ohio representative James M. Ashley, chair of the U.S. House Committee on Territories and staunchly anti-Mormon, steered a bill through the House in 1866 that shifted Utah's western border fifty miles to the east, the land given to Nevada for mining interests.[38] In 1869 Ashley went further and introduced a bill designed to "blot out the Territory," reducing Utah to twenty-two thousand square miles (roughly the size of West Virginia) and thereby eliminating Mormon political power and halting the church's expansion in the Great Basin.[39] Although the bill never came to a vote, it generated popular debate on the best way to deal with the "Mormon Problem." The editor of the *San Francisco Call*, informing readers of Ashley's plan to "despoil the Mormons" by "cutting up their territory and dividing it among the neighboring powers and territories," nonetheless considered the bill "ill-advised." Political solutions such as Ashley's, the editor argued, would only "create new complications, jealousies, and disturbances." Conversely, the "Pacific Railroad" would effect a "peaceful settlement of the Mormon difficulty," based on the "impetus which will be given to inland commerce and immigration."[40] In other words, it would populate Deseret with non-Mormon people, goods, and influences.

In fact, Mormons in the Great Basin region had long promoted the construction of a national railroad through Utah Territory. As early as 1851 the territorial legislature petitioned Congress to construct a railroad to the Pacific and suggested that the tracks pass through Weber Canyon into Salt Lake City and proceed south around the Great Salt Lake to California. In 1862, as a gesture of good will toward the Union Pacific Railroad Company, Brigham Young, on behalf of his church, bought five shares of stock for $5,000 dollars and was subsequently made a director of the company. The LDS Church would eventually use the railroad for its missionary and immigration programs while it spurred the development of the territorial mining industry. Having long predicted such success, Brigham Young, as the tracks traversed what he termed the "unsettled plains and deserts" and approached Utah in 1867, argued that "the completion of this gigantic work will increase intercourse, and it is to be hoped, soften prejudices, and bind the country together."[41]

Faced with the onslaught from politicians and newspaper editors, Mormon leadership answered the railroad challenge by reframing the road as an economic civilizer while simultaneously pointing to the uncivilized nature of some of its accompanying social consequences. Mormon letters, editorials, and sermons published in the years following the initiation of Union Pacific construction in 1865 show a positive view of the railroad as an impetus to reap both converts and consumers for many of Utah's cash-starved producers. In response to allegations that railroad men and civilization threatened the church, Young wrote to overseas missionaries that "we want the railroad, [and] we are not afraid of its results" and that Mormonism "must . . . be a damned poor religion, if it cannot stand one railroad."[42]

In post–Civil War America, however, the national media refused to let Brigham Young and the editors at the church-owned *Deseret News* define westward expansion. With memories of the Utah War (1857–58) and the Mountain Meadows Massacre (1857) still fresh, and polygamy having supplanted slavery as America's evil institution, newspapers such as the *Omaha Republican* predicted that, with the coming of the Union Pacific, the "dissolution of Mormondom" was indeed "inevitable."[43] Echoing this theme, the *Providence Journal* claimed that "the cohesive power of Mormonism will soon be subjected to stern practical tests" and that "no regulations it can enact will keep out Gentile emigrants." The editor continued,

> [Mormonism's] remoteness from civilized States has, hitherto, been an effective safeguard. Brigham Young has been a supreme ruler, and any troublesome Gentiles were easily removed either by threats or force.... But the Pacific Railroad is to pass through the heart of Utah, and ... Mormonism can no longer be isolated.... Utah will soon lie open to thronging crowds of emigrants, and if Mormonism has not better elements of life than is commonly supposed, it must gradually succumb to higher civilization, or migrate to a new home.[44]

Confronting anti-Mormon sentiment, the *Deseret News* reprinted an editorial from the *Chicago Republican* titled "Mormonism Doomed," which argued that "frontier" railroad towns led by "adventurous classes" would "spring up with magical swiftness . . . and ripen into cities." The *Republican* editor reevaluated Irish immigrant traits that had been judged uncivilized east of the Mississippi River to claim them as patriotic, Christian behaviors in Utah. Armed with the accoutrements of civilization, he argued, this advance guard of "Gentiles" who feared "neither the world, the flesh, nor the devil" would "swarm into every part of Utah," set up a free press, and "open [their] batteries daily upon the iniquity of harem life."[45] Like many of his colleagues, George Q. Cannon of the *Deseret News* responded by using Chicago's village-to-metropolis model to craft a narrative of uncivilization that distanced "temporary work" and its supposed vices from the more righteous and permanent "industry" and settlement that was Utah: "Our [Mormon cooperative] system has already endured some very severe tests. We should be disappointed if we did not have to come in contact with these hostile influences and civilizing (?) agencies which he describes. Border ruffians [and] adventurers may come and go . . . [but] we shall neither tremble nor object. Our readers who are familiar with Chicago—the most notoriously corrupt city of its size in the Union—

can imagine what a change is foreshadowed by the promised introduction of such civilization!"[46]

Mormon leaders sought to diminish the railroad threat by first defining and then limiting the manner in which socioeconomic progress would unfold in Zion. It was not the railroad itself but the men who built it that posed the greatest danger. In frequent meetings at the Salt Lake tabernacle in 1867 and 1868, a narrative of "successful progress" was crafted according to the cultural values of Utah's "relatively self-sufficient . . . equalitarian, and homogenous" Mormon citizenry.[47] Church elders and editors contrasted Utah's cooperative system of work, based on agricultural production, permanent settlement, family values, sobriety, and community improvements, such as small-scale irrigation canals, with the transience, violence, drunkenness, immorality, and "pandemonium" that allegedly prevailed in railroad camps along the transcontinental route.[48] An editorial in the Mormon *Millennial Star* titled "The Great Railroad of the West," suggested that, with "God's help," "Utonians" had the "power to make Utah a most disagreeable spot for the vile and lawless rabble whose only glory is destruction and infamy." According to the writer, "the railway will no doubt bring some of that class of bipeds to our mountain State, but the same line will take them away again."[49]

Both the image and reality of such reckless progress figured prominently in Utah, where Mormons interpreted the railroad as both a threat and an opportunity. Under Brigham Young's leadership, the church responded to the railroad dilemma by transforming its School of Prophets (originally a priesthood gospel study group) into an economic organization that successfully maintained Mormon solidarity in the face of socioeconomic "revolution." In particular, the school's system of "protection" sought to minimize the influx of railroad employees and "hangers-on."[50] It was the railroad's immigrant laborers and their accompanying vices that posed a threat to the essential structure, function, and morality of the Mormon community. According to one school member, this system promised to inhibit "the swarms of scalawags that the construction of the railroad would bring" from infesting Zion.[51]

European-born converts to Mormonism echoed this perceived danger as they crossed the Atlantic and traveled by train from New York to end-of-track locations in the Wyoming Territory en route to Salt Lake City in the mid to late 1860s. After six weeks at sea on the packet ship *John Bright*, where she "was seasick before the tug boat went back . . . [and] from shore to shore," in August 1868 Liverpool native Celestial Roberts Knight's company of

Saints reached the Union Pacific's end-of-track west of Laramie, where they were excited to see "mule and horse teams" waiting to transport them to Salt Lake City. As Knight's interviewer noted, the company was immediately "counseled . . . to drive out around the railroad camps and . . . not stop day or night till they got out of the way of the camps and thus they would avoid the rough element that is generally found around the railroad camps. . . . No one was to walk."[52] Similar descriptions of non-Mormon Union Pacific camps would serve as negative reference points for the Mormon construction camps that soon dotted this landscape of progress.

The chance to contribute to American progress by building the transcontinental railroad offered Mormon men an opportunity to shift attention from their conspicuous earmarks of difference and present themselves as patriotic, entrepreneurial, and morally upright Americans. While working on the railroad, Mormons could present themselves as both American citizens and men of character. This work helped facilitate the construction of a Mormon American manhood that redefined the very meaning of railroad labor and progress. At the same time, Mormons would build their holy community, securing it politically and economically. This effort left the power of the church's leadership untouched in all matters temporal and spiritual.

Still, the opening of Zion for "great national work" was no easy decision. The Mormon response, in fact, was similar to reactions in nineteenth-century communities where the presence of immigrant improvement labor ostensibly threatened social, religious, and familial stability. Utah's Saints marked outside railroad labor in general as foreign and savage, and railroad laborers in particular as a violent, heathenish, and repugnant army. George Reynolds, a church official and member of the School of Prophets, confided to a missionary friend in England that he feared "what the result would be to our cities and settlements of 5,000 or 6,000 Irish . . . and other laborers crowding through our peaceful vales."[53] Mormons exacerbated this perceived sense of difference by arguing that immigrant laborers were "idle" and "unproductive." *Deseret News* editor Cannon often mocked anti-Mormon editorials by borrowing their titles, such as "The Coming Railroad," for his own pieces, in which he argued that mere "hard work" did not transform men and allow them to inherit the Promised Land and claim citizenship. It was the greater good of the work and the honorable behavior of the worker that did.[54]

Religion and community would thus act as bulwarks against the "other," as Mormons demonstrated the dual process of building and protecting, community endeavors that were both inward- and outward-looking. Mormon leaders and followers not only critiqued but redefined railroad "civilization," portraying railroad construction workers as "dreaded rowdies," "gamblers," "patrons of drinking saloons," and "idlers" who, "too lazy to earn their own living," were "bound to have it, if they have to steal it." Progress, according to the Saints, meant "making a living by honest industry" and was limited to "peaceable, virtuous, [and] law-abiding men."[55] Broadcasting themselves as respectable men, Mormons working on the railroad would teach the nation a lesson in citizenship.

While it was easy to project an otherness on the Chinese workingman, who, according to an Ogden editor, was a "copper-colored incubus" belonging to an "inferior and alien race," less frequent contact with Chinese immigrants led to a host of different interpretations.[56] Mormons reserved particular revulsion, however, for transient Irish railroad workers; the Book of Mormon even declared their Catholic Church the "mother of harlots."[57] According to David M. Emmons, the foremost historian of Irish immigrants in the West, "To understate considerably, the Irish did not find Utah congenial. They did not go there if they could help it and did not stay there any longer than they had to."[58]

In anticipation of a Mormon grading contract with the Union Pacific, Brigham Young called a special meeting in early June 1868 to address the benefits of, and Utah's role in, the transcontinental railroad. Held at Salt Lake City's recently built tabernacle, this "Mass Meeting" featured an "enthusiastic audience" of more than three thousand men, including both church dignitaries and "common" citizens.[59] The June assembly sought to demonstrate wide support for the railroad amid national accusations that the "isolationist-minded" Mormons opposed commercial and cultural intercourse with outsiders and thus feared the coming of the rails. An elected committee that included Brigham Young (president), Col. F. H. Head, Elder John Taylor, Apostle and *Deseret News* editor George Q. Cannon, and Judge Thomas Marshall spoke passionately on the subject but from different perspectives. Since Leonard Arrington, scholars of Mormon history have emphasized the committee's four resolutions on the railroad question to debunk the notion that Utah's Latter-day Saints were hostile to national internal improvements and "Gentile" influences. The resolutions, which were forwarded to the directors of the Union Pacific and Central Pacific, welcomed the railroad and "more intimate relations" with East and West. They proposed that the Central Pacific and Union Pacific intersect south of the Great Salt Lake (thus closer to the city) and demanded that such "great national work" be performed "for the people's benefit and not for private profit or personal speculation."[60]

A closer examination of this report and others, however, reveals varied nuances in Mormon visions of the railroad, "progress," transient immigrant laborers, and the meaning of productive work. Brigham Young was not only exceedingly optimistic about the railroad project but confident in the fortitude of his Saints to coexist and act as "co-laborers" with workers from both railroad companies in Utah. According to Young, "large cities" would likely follow the track routes and, rather than gold and silver, the "only capital required to build cities is bone and sinew," for "laboring men are the ones who build the cities." F. H. Head articulated the railroad in terms that would surely have pleased company officials, arguing that "the business of building railroads . . . has undergone remarkable change[s]" such that only "the highest order of statesmanship and profoundest knowledge of political economy" could meet such a task. He insisted that Union Pacific officials were interested in world commerce, not in "building up temporary shingle cities like Cheyenne." Elder Taylor made railroad building consistent with Mormon work practices. Mormon workers, he argued, "have always been the advocates of improvement." Nonetheless, Taylor curiously omitted the primary workforces on both the Union and Central Pacific—Irish and Chinese laborers, each of whom were then grading and laying track near Utah's borders. Instead, he drew a parallel to the Mormon experience and spoke of "the Englishmen, the Frenchmen, the Saxon, the Dane, and the Norwegian who are to-day with bare arm, strong muscle, and busy brain . . . piercing the hitherto supposed impenetrable cañon, filling up the valleys, leveling the hills and preparing a pathway for the 'iron horse.'"[61] According to Taylor, these men were partners in the process, as Mormonism united proud Anglo-American classes. Yet, for Mormons, religion, manhood, race and ethnicity, not social class, were the key variables.

Apostle and editor George Q. Cannon arrived late to the mass meeting but was no less enthusiastic and maintained that "we have arrived at that point in our history when the building of the railroad is a necessity." Disputing allegations that Mormons were "secretly adverse to the construction of this railroad," Cannon noted that anyone familiar with Utah's citizens "know[s] full well that whatever our peculiarities may be, we are not opposed to progress." While he conceded that Mormons "may view progress from a different stand point to many others," Cannon remarked that "upon matters of great national importance," there existed a "union of feelings." Yet

Cannon saw other important benefits that would result from Mormon labor on the transcontinental railroad. "Four years with the railroad," he predicted, would end in Utah achieving statehood in 1872 and its citizens having the chance to cast presidential ballots. More broadly, the railroad would provide a "common platform" on which Mormons could stand with their "fellow-men," who, in Cannon's experience, interpreted "Mormon" to signify "a creature from another planet," with "horns or a cloven foot" or other "distinguishing peculiarit[ies]" that were "different from other men."[62] The railroad, he suggested, would create Mormon *American* men.

For LDS Church leaders, the railroad was as much a commemoration of the past as it was about dreams of the future. Young, returning to the podium to close the mass meeting, noted that when the Mormon pioneers fled Nauvoo, "we left naked and barefoot. We left our property, and with the old, broken down horses and cows, and broken wagons that we could pick up, we commenced our journey into the wilderness." On this epic errand into the wild, Young recalled, "I do not suppose we traveled one day from the Missouri River . . . through the cañon, or . . . over the dividing ranges" without "look[ing] for a track where the rails could be laid with success, for a railroad . . . to the Pacific Ocean."[63]

Though the goal of the mass meeting was to "express popular feeling" concerning the railroad, Young and his colleagues went further and sought to link Mormon history to future progress. Such a narrative crafted pioneers as both refugees and amateur railroad surveyors. In this vein, Mormons' forced expulsion from the United States did not prevent them from becoming the ostensible vanguard of American progress. Perhaps they worked to build a different kind of progress. Thus, Mormons' westward migration, a story of courage and resilience in the face of extreme persecution, came to symbolize a masculine pioneer epic that was both quintessentially American and yet superior to any equivalent American story of triumph over adversity. The railroad enabled them to contrast their culture with that of immigrant "others" and stake a claim to whiteness, manhood, and Americanism above Irish, Chinese, and non-Mormon workingmen. Mormon leaders' different visions suggest the variety of ways in which progress was defined in the community. Yet affirmation came quickly as the church band performed numbers such as "Railroad Polka" and "Hard Times Come Again No More," and the audience shouted its huzzahs.[64]

By late spring of 1868 regularly scheduled trains were running as far west as Laramie, Wyoming. Although construction to this point had gone relatively smoothly, Union Pacific crews prepared for a more arduous stretch of building through the rugged Rocky Mountains. After extensive surveying Union Pacific superintendent Samuel P. Reed concluded that perhaps the most difficult area of construction would be through the canyons of Utah's Wasatch Mountains. This region was unlike any other on the route, for the Mormon communities of northern Utah could perform immediate grading work with construction provisioned locally. Superintendent Reed signed a contract with Brigham Young in May 1868 calling for up to five thousand Mormon workers organized into several hundred teams, to perform over 150 miles of grading, tunneling, and bridge masonry, beginning at the head of Echo Canyon through Weber Canyon and to the shores of the Great Salt Lake. This grading contract was worth $2,125,000, and the majority of the work was scheduled to be completed by November 1868.[65] According to President Young, "this contract is viewed by the brethren of understanding as a God-send."[66]

Earlier that year Apostle Wilford Woodruff had written in a letter to Franklin D. Richards that as "the great National Railroad is making rapid strides to meet in Utah, [o]ur enemies have great hopes of soon trapping us." Woodruff claimed that Zion's Gentile enemies "are looking for our destruction," and yet "they will be woefully disappointed," as Brigham Young planned to seize this opportunity to rebound from hard economic times, pay debts, and "gathe[r] means to bring out the Saints from abroad" to build up the kingdom. Woodruff informed Richards that Young was prepared "to remove the whole Church from England, Elders and all," as part of this "great exertion" to build the railroad.[67] Non-Mormon newspapers corroborate this. On July 12, 1868, the *New York Express* reported that the steamer *Minnesota* landed at the port of New York, carrying at least 531 Mormons, "a very motley group of young and old, male and female ... from the manufacturing districts of England and Wales." That same evening, the ship *John Bright* arrived, carrying another 700 Mormons, and the editor noted that "3,000 to 5,000 more are expected this season." The "able-bodied men" of these groups informed the newspaper that they were "engaged to work on the Pacific Railroad, under Brigham Young's contract."[68]

The company of returned missionary Joseph Smith Horne, which included 45 emigrants from Switzerland, Bavaria, Württemberg, and the Netherlands and 412 from the British Isles, departed on June 24, 1868, from Liverpool on the ship *Constitution* and arrived at Castle Garden in early August.[69] As Horne noted, a customary route was from the port of New York to Albany,

Rochester, Detroit, Chicago, and Omaha to Benton, Wyoming Territory, which was at that time the Union Pacific terminus. "Here," he stated, "men and teams from Utah waited our arrival, and on Sunday [August] 16th we were taken by wagons to 'Mormon Emigration Camp' 4 miles distant," prior to traveling by wagon train or on foot to Salt Lake City.[70] Foreign-born Mormon emigrants were incentivized by a cheaper passage rate if they opted to work on Union Pacific construction crews in the Intermountain West. Joining Elder Horne on the *Constitution* was thirty-one-year old John Lazenby, a Mormon convert from Hull, England, who noted that upon arriving at the head of Echo Canyon on September 14, "I bid adieu to my wife and boy and went to work for John W. Young upon the railroad, which I had agreed to do on arriving at New York for which I received a free pass from Omaha to the end of the track. I received 2 dollars per day and board. Stayed at work six weeks and then came on to Salt Lake City."[71]

European-born Mormon emigration records, though valuable and voluminous resources, are typically inward-looking and relatively silent on the subject of interethnic encounters with non-Mormons. That said, records from the late 1860s reveal a common occurrence: steamships full of both Mormon converts and Irish immigrants. The same was true of trains bound for the Union Pacific's westernmost depots, as both groups were headed west and contact was inevitable. Jens Iver Jensen, aboard the steamer *Manhattan* in the summer of 1867, documented 600 Scandinavian Saints and "also a lot of Irish people not Mormons."[72] When seventeen-year-old Emily Pickering, an English-born Mormon convert who crossed the Atlantic with more than 500 Saints on the steamship *Minnesota* the following summer, arrived in Laramie, she was startled by a group of teamsters who "surrounded the train." "I was very frightened," she noted, "thinking that we were surely captured, when they quickly explained that they were the Mormon boys . . . driving the horses for us." As the company trekked toward Utah, Pickering recalled that "the Mormon boys were working in the middle of Echo Canyon building the railroad. My husband was among them, but I was not aware of it then."[73] Though Elder Zebulon Jacobs, who was also aboard the *Minnesota,* commented that the sight of Salt Lake City from Parley's Canyon "seemed like a dream," the long journey to Zion was a harrowing one. He calculated 631 Saints aboard the steamship "in the forward steerage," most of whom kept their distance from the "mixture of all nationalities (with enough Irish to keep them lively)" who were situated "in the other part" of the vessel.[74] At sea or on land Mormon emigrants such as Pickering and Jacobs found it necessary to contrast the dangers of strangers with the honorable qualities of more familiar Saints, especially the "Mormon boys" along the railroad's right-of-way. If Saints and non-Mormon immigrants were each laboring to bring progress to the West by virtue of the iron horse, Mormon labor, by 1868, had assumed a decidedly more civilized air.

These unskilled immigrants were armies of progress of a different sort. In taking up the national task, the Saints softened public perceptions of Mormonism. Yet their mission was to build Zion, not America. An 1868 editorial in the *Millennial Star* argued that Mormon labor on the transcontinental railroad would place the "prognostications" and threats of anti-Mormon commentators "in the heap of rubbish where lie buried so many unfulfilled predictions of the overthrow of 'Mormonism.'" Wishing "God speed to the great railroad of the West," the writer hailed that in the Saints' construction of the railroad, "Zion may be built up and adorned and beautified. . . . The State of Deseret may be enriched and developed, and that the way may be prepared for the consummation of the latter-day Work!"[75]

The editors of the Mormon *Deseret News* were overjoyed with the news of Brigham Young's grading contract and celebrated it with editorials that assessed the impact of Mormon work on the transcontinental: "How such people will be disappointed when they know that our citizens expect to do all in their power this Summer to grade the road for the rails at the head of Echo Cañon and this valley! It is gratifying to think that we have such an opportunity offered to us. . . . The grading of this road . . . [will] disabus[e] the public mind respecting us and our views."[76] The grading contract would enable struggling Mormon farmers to survive recent crop failures due to grasshopper invasions and eventually return to their fields. Mormon leaders and workers considered their railroad labor a temporary yet honorable occupation and emphasized the need to continue farming to support the community and provision future railroad workers.[77] This was a case of farmers working overtime to build a railroad, but for Mormons the "public good" was a holy endeavor. A writer for the *Deseret News* reminded readers that, despite the coming of the railroad, "Latter-day Saints" must never look "to the outside world . . . for their bread." To this end, he noted that Saints' "labors on the railroad" ought "not prevent . . . [the] sow[ing] of a wide breadth of fall grain."[78]

Immediately, Brigham Young enlisted his sons, Joseph A., Brigham Jr., and John W. to subcontract the grading work to church dignitaries and ward

TABLE 1 Mormon jobs and wages on the Union Pacific Railroad

Type of labor	Payment (per cubic yard)
Earth excavation—borrowed from embankment, wasted from cuts, or hauled—not exceeding two hundred feet from cuts into embankment	$0.27
Earth excavation, hauled more than two hundred feet from cuts into embankment	$0.45
Loose rock	$1.57
Solid lime or sand rock	$2.70
Granite	$3.60
Rubble masonry in box culverts, laid in lime or cement	$5.85
Rubble masonry, laid dry	$5.40
Masonry in bridge abutments and piers, laid in lime mortar or cement; beds and joints dressed; drafts on corners, laid in courses	$13.50
Rubble masonry in bridge abutments and piers, laid dry	$7.20
Rubble masonry in bridge abutments and piers, laid in cement	$7.65

SOURCE: Based on data published in the *Deseret Evening News,* May 21 and June 9, 1868.

bishops. John Sharp and Joseph Young were awarded the largest parts of the grading contract, and they employed crews to perform grading, bridge, and trestle work and to build two tunnels of three hundred and five hundred feet in Echo and Weber Canyons.[79] A detailed list of jobs and wages for the Union Pacific contract was published twice during the spring and summer of 1868 (see table 1). The figures indicate that Mormon wages were equivalent to those of the Union Pacific's other construction employees.

Along with the challenge of determining remuneration in this pre–labor union era of transient railroad construction is the fact that Utahns received little of their promised wages and instead were given church tithing credit, travel vouchers, and railroad bonds.[80] While several thousand Mormons worked to complete the grading, tunneling, and bridge building, Union Pacific officials stalled to avoid payment. Not until October 1868, four months after Mormon crews began digging, did the Union Pacific approve the contract. The lack of basic compensation from the railroad company shaped this project from the start, highlighting the earmarks of difference and stains of exploitation in ways quite different from the experiences of non-Mormon canal and railroad builders elsewhere in the West. It resulted in a range of unique responses to, and representations of, railroad labor in this American Zion.

Historians have observed similar challenges that faced immigrant Mormon colliers from the British Isles, where the dreams associated with the building of Zion met with the realities of industrial expansion in the Intermountain West. There "a host of tragedies, broken bodies, and shattered spirits" defined the working-class experience. Laboring to build a holy community, contribute to country, and recast manhood did not come without costs. Removed from settled Mormon life while in the mines, these colliers, similar to railroad construction workers, faced arduous, seasonal work more familiar to the laboring poor than the self-sufficiency, material well-being, and egalitarianism promised by the Mormon cooperative movement. "Wounds of class cut sharply" in both material and spiritual directions; yet, importantly, railroad labor assumed an enhanced symbolism despite offering less economic security and demand than did mining.[81]

Though frustrated by the lack of payments and the daily grind of railroad construction, Mormons both inside and outside of the construction camps focused on their investment in this "great national project." Patriotic and honorable labor was the means to gain national respect and to distinguish themselves from the faceless armies of immigrant tracklayers who were fast approaching Mormon work sites in Weber and Echo Canyons. Bishops Sharp and Young (the aforementioned subcontractors) and their laborers were under strict instructions to report their progress and the conditions of camp life to local editors and church leaders. An anonymous laborer in Bishop Sharp's camp at Devil's Gate (Weber Canyon) wrote in June 1868 that his camp of 120 men witnessed no "angry or profane word[s]," always remembered their prayers, and "strictly [observed] the third commandment." Overall, he insisted that "a better set of boys I don't believe will be easily found."[82]

Two letters from Echo Canyon reiterated similar themes. In the first, Adolphus Noon, a clerk for subcontractor E. F. Sheets, mentioned that since bookkeeping was almost useless along the line, "I made up my mind to lay hold of the pick and shovel and 'clerk' with that." Even then, Noon argued that digging was "not near so formidable a job as was generally anticipated." Mocking Irish dialect, he then assured readers that the conduct of "our Mormon Boys" was praiseworthy and that although "we have no whiskey shebangs 'or sich' here yet ... just as soon as anybody sticks them down we will stick them down ... deep in the creek." The second letter, sent from Echo City by an anonymous worker, praised the cooperative system on which Mormons based their railroad camps:

The railroad is coming. Already it is estimated, one half, if not more of the track down Echo Canyon is ready for the ties and rails. . . . All classes of profession, art and avocation, almost, are represented. Here are the ministers of the gospel and the dusky collier laboring side by side. Here may be seen the Bishop on the embankment and his "diocese" filling their carts, scrapers and shovels from the neighboring cut. Here are the measurer of tapes and calicos and the homoepathic [sic] doctor in mud to their knees or knecks [sic]. . . . Here the man of literature deciphers hieroglyphics in prying into the seams of sand rock. . . . Such an illustrious corps of practical railroad makers must surely leave their mark.[83]

Advertisements for railroad construction workers in the *Deseret News* enticed able-bodied men in the Salt Lake Valley with guarantees of "the highest wages . . . in cash, [paid] monthly" and directed them to "apply immediately at the Mouth of Weber Kanyon."[84] Yet, as evidenced in the call for workers by Bishops Sharp and Young, Mormon subcontractors had a certain audience in mind. If desperate for "500 men," they also stressed that "none but Good Men need apply" (see figure 3).

Despite the grueling nature of canyon grading, trestle, and tunneling work, reports from the Mormon work camps frequently expressed complete and efficient command over tasks—and a general mastery of the environment. Moreover, letters mentioned camp oaths against swearing, brawling, gambling, and alcohol consumption. Writing from the "Head of Echo" in late July 1868, a *Deseret News* correspondent stated that "'the boys' enjoy themselves, albeit they have plenty of hard work." The proximity and conduct of Bishop E. F. Sheets's and John W. Young's construction camps, he argued, made them "the best . . . encampment[s] I have yet seen in the Cañons. Order governs, harmony reigns, and the best of feelings exist."[85] Workers, contractors, editors, and church dignitaries referred to the Mormon men grading the railroad as "boys" in contrast to the Irish and Chinese tracklayers, the "company men," who, by the fall of 1868, were working near the Saints.[86] Such language was perhaps meant to contrast wholesome and innocent manliness from the "rough" varieties commonly associated with transient immigrant workers.[87]

In practice, however, this language achieved more while still obscuring problems within the Mormon community. Mormon culture emphasized strong male patriarchs equipped with the faith, skill, and power to provide material support, anchor families and communities, and offer spiritual guidance and protection. What position did the disadvantaged Mormon rank

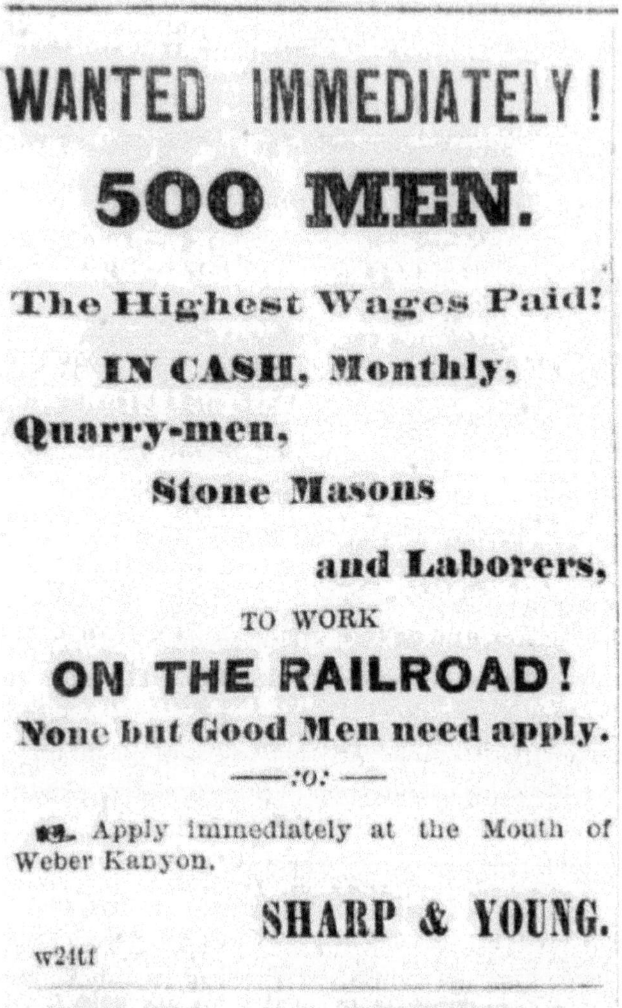

FIGURE 3. Mormon contractors Sharp and Young advertise for construction workers. *Deseret News,* September 9, 1868. Courtesy of Special Collections, J. Willard Marriott Library, University of Utah, Salt Lake City.

and file assume in such a socioreligious arrangement? On the margins of this Great Basin Kingdom, where Mormon "others" were at work building America, bishops and ward leaders personified the patriarch role as commanders of their railroad builders, to whom they extended employment preferences with the same degree of loyalty that Irish contractors and workers filled or controlled canal lines with their brethren in Indiana and Illinois.

Historians have called for further exploration of Mormon "bishop bosses" to test whether, in the process, they helped mitigate class and labor strife within Latter-day Saint communities by not only providing work for the laboring poor but in holding these men religiously accountable for peaceful working conditions.[88] Reports emanating from railroad camps, with authorship sometimes in question, must be interpreted against the grain, as they likely masked levels of subordination and exploitation common to transportation frontiers everywhere else in the country. The fact that Mormon railroaders were quick to report on the progress of the work and the conditions within the camps stands as unique (even unprecedented) in some respects but problematic in others.

In August 1868 the Central Pacific entered into contracts with Brigham Young and other Mormon leaders to grade sections of the roadbed from Ogden northwest to Monument Point. Young remarked that, for his Mormon boys, "these contracts give us many advantages, besides furnishing money for labor to those whom the grasshoppers have left but little to do, and who could not well otherwise supply themselves with food until another harvest." Additional grading was performed in the vicinity of Promontory, Utah. A second contract with Leland Stanford and the Central Pacific followed in September 1868, when Mormons were called on to grade roughly two hundred miles of roadbed from Humboldt Wells, Nevada, east into Weber Canyon. Interestingly, Stanford paid manual and "skilled" laborers fairly equal wages, three to six dollars per day, whereas wagonmen earned ten dollars a day. In light of his disappointing experience with the Union Pacific, which had failed to meet monthly payment quotas and had since decided to build its road north of the Great Salt Lake, Brigham Young required that the Central Pacific compensate Mormon laborers and contractors with a cash-down payment.[89]

In late 1868 and early 1869, when concerns about the transcontinental junction point had escalated, the Union Pacific's and Central Pacific's Mormon subcontractors and their unskilled graders worked side by side along the east slope of Promontory and often in the vicinity of Irish tracklayers. John ("Jack") Casement, the Union Pacific's chief construction supervisor (and of Irish descent), wrote to his wife in Ohio, as his largely Irish tracklaying crews entered the "wild looking country" that was Utah (see figure 4). With clear disdain, Casement noted, "Brigham Young sent me word that he would like to see us lay track . . . [and] I sent him word all he would have to do would be to come where we were at work and open His Eye. He came here

FIGURE 4. Union Pacific Railroad boarding train with Jack Casement and his Irish track-layers, ca. 1868. Casement, the Union Pacific's chief construction supervisor, is shown here with a bull whip. Photograph by Andrew J. Russell, collection 385, photo 25523. Reproduced by permission from Utah State Historical Society, Salt Lake City.

but I think so little of him and his pretensions that I did not stay to receive him."[90]

Mormon grading contracts, at one point during the transcontinental construction, brought them in the vicinity of Irish and Chinese immigrants, mainstays of the Union and Central Pacific workforces. In this context, the boys/men, sober/inebriated, peaceful/violent narratives that the Saints had crafted took on new meaning. In episodes of self-definition these encounters enabled Mormons to distinguish their manhood and interpretation of progress from those of the railroad companies and their immigrant workers.

Mormon leaders, workers, and residents championed an ordered, community-minded manhood. Contributing to this "great national project," they portrayed themselves and were perceived as peaceful and hard-working; their labor on the railroad was based on a higher moral ground than were the efforts of immigrant "company men."[91] On the other hand, the Irish and

Chinese laborers on the Union and Central Pacific were painted by Mormons as outsiders and derided as foreign-born "strangers." Undisciplined, violent, and immoral, these transitory laborers were unconcerned with the "public good."[92]

In an 1868 letter to Apostle Franklin D. Richards, Samuel Richards, anticipating "heavy rock work" and an "attack . . . upon the 'Devil's Gate'" at the mouth of Weber Canyon, discussed the plans of Mormon contractors to dominate the work: "This [work] will make a call for that portion of the community not necessarily engaged in farming labor . . . [and] will obviate the necessity of some few thousands of strangers being brought here, to mix and interfere with the settlers, of that class of men who take pleasure in making disturbance wherever they go. . . . It will show that we are interested in forwarding the great national project." "The people," Richards noted, "feel like taking off their coats and going at it."[93] In sum, Mormon workers were building a holy community, and transient immigrants were subjects of the profane world. This helps explain how and why Mormons considered railroad company men as less productive, less concerned about permanent settlement, and less civilized than their righteous boys.

When immigrant tracklaying gangs occupied former Mormon construction camps such as Echo City, Uintah, Wasatch, and Kelton, Mormon leaders and local editors characterized these landscapes as "the most wretched communities in the world" and "nests of everything vile and abominable."[94] Others, such as Corrine and Blue Creek, were "the toughest place[s] on the continent . . . morally nearest to the infernal regions of any town on the road."[95] This symbolic transformation of the landscape highlighted the uncivilized behavior of immigrants and distanced their role in building the transcontinental and contributing to western progress. Unlike Mormon boys, these company men detracted from, rather than enhanced, the civilizing venture of the Union and Central Pacific.

While railroads opened up new markets, reduced the price of freight, and offered struggling farmers a source of employment and income, Utahns soon had misgivings about the social cost to be paid for "outside world" endowments. A Mormon elder described Bear River City (just beyond Utah's northeast border) as "several hundred tents, wagons and shanties . . . erected for the sale of whiskey and for gambling and dance houses."[96] One scholar has argued that short-lived construction camps such as this one, often dubbed "Terminopolis," did not even survive long enough for "serious disorder" to occur.[97] Yet, not content with documenting only the "hell on wheels" in their midst, the *Deseret News* featured reports from church missionaries at more populated, "demoralized" frontier outposts. The writings of Mormon missionaries and journalists were in fact essential to the creation of images that dominate our understanding of the first transcontinental railroad. Bishop W. Seeley's trip to Laramie and Cheyenne, Wyoming, in late 1868 offered the following example as representative of uncivilized versions of progress:

> This town, with another on the other side of the river, has been called into creation by the building of the railway, and they are without exception the most demoralized places I ever saw. Life is of no value here. At least one man per day has been the average of murders. Women, a disgrace to the name, offer themselves openly, and, in fact, I am informed, they have printed invitations affixed to their dwellings to catch the unwary and foolish. Almost every other house is a whiskey mill, gambling hole, or a house of ill fame, and sometimes all three. This description of one city will suffice for all. . . . Such is so-called civilization!

Although per capita rates of alcoholism, violence, and "rowdyism" are unknown, many Utahns were convinced that Union and Central Pacific shantytowns were merely sites of "floating populations" of unproductive "roughs."[98] Mormon letters and editorials drew a clear line to separate the benefits of settlement from the consequences of transience. The meaning and significance of productive work differed drastically based on the men who performed it.

To position themselves as far as possible from the rough manhood that predominated among transient and immigrant work camps, Mormon men focused on the organization and the spiritual, moral, and physical health of the camps. Observers claimed that Brigham Young's subletting of contracts was a "very superior" system compared "to that usually employed for construction." A group of workers, typically from the same LDS ward, would "combine together, take their sub-contracts, and work it as partners." Unlike immigrant company men, Mormon railroaders "did not tie themselves to hours, nor did they endeavor to kill time by doing as little as possible," for the Saints "had as deep an interest in the completion of the job as the 'boss.'"[99] As a result, one witness remarked that "I have not heard of a strike on President Young's contract since the commencement of the work."[100] A Mormon railroad grader working in Echo Canyon noted that the workers "drew up and signed a cooperative agreement, and a system of rules, the strict prohibition of profane language being one of them." Demonstrating a manly control over their jobs, this worker noted that "the dirt is beginning to fly,"

FIGURE 5. Excavating in Weber Canyon, Utah Territory. The Narrows, Deep-Cut 1, Union Pacific Railroad construction, ca. 1868. Photograph by Andrew J. Russell, A-Board Historical Photograph Collection, A-2488, Special Collections and Archives, Merrill-Cazier Library, Utah State University, Logan.

and soon the Mormons' "cuts, dams, and grading" were being "repeatedly referred to by the Engineers in speaking to other companies, as fair specimens of how they want the work done."[101]

Transforming Utah's canyons with their virtuous labor, the "brethren" created railroad working environments strikingly different from those of the Union Pacific's Irish immigrants, whose "camps ... give birth to the towns along the track, which are the nests of everything vile and abominable."[102] According to an 1868 article in the *Deseret News,* when unconfirmed reports that his Mormon graders had "struck for wages" while performing "heavy work" in Weber Canyon reached Bishop Sharp, the contractor "gave his most unqualified denial." "The brethren," noted the writer, "have the best of feelings, and work with good spirits and with a desire to do all that is asked of them."[103] A surviving photograph of the "heavy work" performed by Mormon crews in Weber Canyon captures the writer's sentiment (see figure 5).

FIGURE 6. *Rocky Mountain Glee Club*, drawn from the ranks of Mormon Union Pacific Railroad workers, ca. 1868–69. Photograph by Andrew J. Russell. Courtesy of the Yale Collection of Western Americana, Beinecke Rare Book and Manuscript Library, New Haven, CT.

Further evidence suggests that the Saints carried out railroad labor for the Union and Central Pacific with even more zeal than they did in local cooperative projects, particularly since railroading in 1868 and 1869 put them in the national spotlight. The members of the Rocky Mountain Glee Club, drawn from the ranks of Mormon construction workers, dressed in coats and ties to perform for and with the men in their camps. While very little is known about the Glee Club and no record of its songs has survived, an Andrew J. Russell photograph depicts these Mormon railroad workers as the essence of masculine civility, with their boots polished and white dress shirts perfectly starched (see figure 6). These laborers were both building and refining the filthy transportation frontier. Clearly, the Glee Club was attuned to the meaning of Mormon labor on the railroad and the need to exhibit—and perform—difference from its uncivilized immigrant counterparts.

While not a member of the Rocky Mountain Glee Club, James Crane, a teamster and grader from Sugarhouse, in Salt Lake City, undoubtedly shared their sentiments. Crane; his fiancée, Alice Davis; and her brother Joseph

Davis had emigrated to the United States from Wales in 1856. They eventually settled in Iowa City and in 1859 joined the Horton D. Haight and Frederick Kesler wagon party traveling from Florence, Nebraska (present-day Omaha), to Utah along with seventy other wagons carrying 151 Saints.[104] In 1868 Crane wrote the following "ditty" to describe the Mormons' righteous railroad work. The song is noteworthy, among other reasons, for its marked difference from the songs of immigrant transportation workers that often expressed an abhorrence of wage labor in "free" America and a longing for home. The contributing writer prefaced the song, reprinted in the *Deseret News,* with his thoughts after witnessing the performance "sung with most sweetness . . . chorused by a mingling of some twenty or thirty manly voices." Observing their evening tradition at their work camp in Echo Canyon, the writer concluded that "'the boys' truly enjoy themselves, albeit they have plenty of hard work," about which they reflected on in "hymns, songs, and local effusions":

At the head of great Echo there's a railroad begun,
And the "Mormons" are cutting and grading like fun;
They say they'll stick to it, till it is complete
And friends and relations they long again to meet.

[Chorus] Hurrah! Hurrah! for the railroad's begun!
Three cheers for our contractor, his name's Brigham Young!
Hurrah! Hurrah! we'er honest and true,
For if we stick to it its *[sic]* bound to go through.

Now there's Mr. Reed, he's a gentleman true,
He knows very well what the "Mormons" can do;
He knows in their work they are lively and gay,
And just the right boy's *[sic]* to build a railway.

CHORUS.—Hurrah! Hurrah! &c.

Our camp is united, we all labor hard;
And if we work faithfully we'll get our reward;
Our leader is wise and industrious too
And all things he tells us we're willing to do.

CHORUS.—Hurrah! Hurrah! &c.

The boys in our camp are light-hearted and gay,
We work on the railroad ten hours a day;
We're thinking of good times we'll have in the fall,
Then we'll take our ladies and off to the ball.

CHORUS.—Hurrah! Hurrah! &c.

We surely must live in a very fast age;
We've traveled by ox teams, and then took the stage;
But when such conveyance is all done away
We'll travel in steam cars upon the railway.

CHORUS.—Hurrah! Hurrah! &c.

The great locomotive next season will come
To gather the Saints from their far distance home;
And bring them to Utah in peace here to stay,
While the judgments of God sweep the wicked away.

CHORUS.—Hurrah! Hurrah! &c. [105]

In another 1868 song, "The Utah Iron Horse," Mormons from Logan who performed grading and tracklaying work in Weber Canyon expressed both self-deprecating humor and self-evident racism in anticipating the impact of the transcontinental railroad. The song exulted that "the iron horse is coming, with a train in its wake," and went on:

We have isolated been; but soon we shall be seen;
Through this wide mountain region, folks can learn of our religion;

"Civilized" we shall be, many folks we shall see,
Lords and nobles, tramps and beggars, anyhow we'll see the niggers;
Saints will come, sinners too, we'll have all that we can do,
For this great Union railroad it will fetch the Devil through.[106]

Immigrant tracklaying camps, like mining camps, were allegedly littered with men whose character sharply contrasted with Mormons who labored in (and for) communities. According to historian Robert G. Athearn, Mormons feared transients and desired farmers, "handscraftmen," and persons likely to settle comfortably into already established villages.[107] Here, Mormon values resembled those of the native-born residents in eastern and midwestern canal towns during the antebellum period. But in the context of internal improvement work, a profound difference is apparent. A great majority of American farmers in the antebellum era prided their status as independent far too much to work on canals and railroads. This type of work was seen as degrading, for "gang" labor conjured up images of black slavery and was thought to strip men of their self-sufficient status by marking them as beholden to another. Such a reaction on the part of America's native-born in part necessitated the employment of large numbers of working-class immigrants throughout the nineteenth century. Mormons, while partial to an agriculturalist and permanent settlement–oriented worldview, chose to leave the comforts of home, farm, and profession to work—in gangs and under the cooperative principle—on the Union Pacific and Central Pacific railroads. They had been called to this holy work by the Prophet, another feature of cooperative labor in Zion. This fact, too, distinguished them from their non-Mormon counterparts elsewhere in the nation.[108]

In late September 1868, a broadside titled "Work and Good Wages for All" appeared in the *Deseret News*. It encouraged able-bodied and willing men to report immediately to "Weber Cañon" to complete grading for the Central Pacific, 150 miles westward from the mouth of the canyon. Writing from the construction camp, the author claimed that Mormons were "gaining a national reputation by our labor on the railroad" and in the process "disabusing the minds of hundreds of thousands who have been falsely impressed concerning us." Mormon railroad builders, he noted, had dramatically transformed the typically rough-edged environment of transportation labor: "In our grading camps there have been no drunkenness, blasphemous language, nor any of those disgraceful sights and sounds which have abounded in the grading camps farther east [in the Wyoming Territory]. We should take pride in sustaining this reputation." Moreover, the writer argued that "it would be cheaper, too, for us to build the road for nothing and make a present of it to the company, than to have our Territory cursed and our settlements polluted with the scum that infest the line east."[109] A prominent church member echoed this theme, insisting that it would be better "for the Saints to do the work for nothing . . . than to let outsiders do it, as it would cost us more to preserve our cattle and horses from thieves, and our family from insult, than to roll up our sleeves and go and do the work ourselves."[110]

Thus, daily work and experiences on the transcontinental railroad—its companies, employees, and overall mission—solidified Mormon perspectives on the benefits and dangers of progress. Faced with the threat of immigrant work camps in their midst, Mormon workers and their superiors sought to "other" themselves from the evils of progress and to "other" the Union Pacific and Central Pacific company men from the benefits of the "great national work" in which they, too, were engaged. Mormons portrayed themselves as a unique people, best able to execute the manifest work of civilizing a nation. Moreover, the "other" in their midst confirmed to Mormons the holiness of their leaders and the godliness of their mission. Mormons organized labor in a far different manner than the capitalist contract system under which other immigrants suffered. Theirs was a peoplehood superior to the nationhood promised by the railroad.

Constant references to "the East" were not only emblematic of the defensive mentality of the Saints but also indicated that Irish and not Chinese workers were more often the focus of "hell on wheels" descriptions and stories. The *Deseret News,* in fact, occasionally blamed Central Pacific officials, not their "Celestial" armies, for the uncivilized conditions on the railroad:

> We have seen it urged against the Chinese that they are bound fast in the swaddling clothes of superstition, from which they show no disposition to emancipate themselves. But who can expect them to do otherwise under the treatment they receive? Cling to their Heathenism? They would be little less than idiots not to do so under the circumstances. Men may prate to them about American civilization, free and enlightened institutions, the spirit of progress and Christianity until doomsday, but they [the Chinese] will fail to respect or attach any value to these high-sounding phrases and professions while they are treated like wild beasts.[111]

In contrast, the *Union Vedette,* Utah's first anti-Mormon newspaper, spoke admirably about Central Pacific officials who marshaled the "indomitable spirit of American enterprise" and heaped even more praise on its Chinese graders and tracklayers, whose "labor and determination" qualified them for the "herculean task" of building over the High Sierras.[112]

The *Deseret News* criticized California's politicians and citizens for being "particularly hard" on the Chinese, who "are treated like dogs. They are chased, abused, robbed and abominably maltreated . . . and even the dogs are set upon them and taught to bite them." What bothered the *News* reporter the most, however, was that the Californians who "torture this race call themselves Christians" while they "mock and denounce [the Chinese] as idolators *[sic]* and heathens." Taking the high ground, the Mormon editor argued that the "true and only correct" solution to this dilemma was to treat the Chinese workers "as human beings" and "grant them the rights of citizenship" if they "can prove themselves capable." He continued, "These Asiatics are willing to work, and work cheap at any kind of drudgery. If the Anglo-Saxon is the superior being which he affects to be, he can with safety assume the direction of this class of laborers. . . . If he treat them kindly, and pay them honestly, he will do more to convert them to his religion and ways than years of preaching with a contrary practice would do, and he need not be afraid that their degradation, vices, or barbarism will hurt him."[113]

The Mormons, busy in building the "Kingdom," did not engage in Chinese baiting. The Chinese posed no threat to the civic, political, and religious life of Utah's Mormons, and church leaders often distanced themselves from the American majority on the Chinese "problem."[114] As such, a sympathetic stance is noticeable in the columns of the *Deseret News*. Californians, the editors argued, should not worry, for the "force of circumstances" would gradually "push" Chinese workers to distant frontiers of wage labor, so long as they remained content in "work[ing] for less than a dollar" per day in various industries. At the very least, Chinese immigrants were of great value to the country as a cheap source of labor. The presence of Chinese immigrants "in large numbers in the Western States and Territories," argued the editors, "will inevitably work a great revolution in labor." Unlike the "European laborer" who "will not work for less than two or three dollars a day," the Chinese are "frugal and patient, and as industrious as a beaver." Willing to "live where one of the so-called superior race would starve," the Chinese worker could subsist on merely "a little rice," "eats meat but seldom … indulges in no dissipation," and, in general, "is simple, abstinent, and very economical."[115] Few in number, transitory, and with no desire to confront, the Chinese did little to distract Mormons from their mission.[116]

Census data is problematic because railroad construction labor was transient labor, thus presenting census enumerators with continually moving targets or none at all. As David M. Emmons notes, "building a railroad was not the same as working for one."[117] Yet numbers, proximity, and contract obligations likely influenced Mormons' sympathy for the plight of the Chinese. Immigrants from China made up only one half of 1 percent of Utah's official population in 1870, and only one Chinese immigrant was counted in the 1870 census for Salt Lake City, compared to 157 Irish immigrants in Salt Lake and 502 in the state.[118] Moreover, Mormons performed more extensive labor for the Union Pacific than for the Central Pacific and were in closer proximity to the former's Irish workers, who worked near the Mormon capital for a longer period of time—based on the UPRR's end-of-track dates for Evanston, Wyoming Territory (December 4, 1868), and Echo City, Utah Territory (January 15, 1869). But attitudes in Utah changed a decade after the completion of the railroad and amid the debates surrounding Chinese exclusion, as Utah's newspapers began to echo the sentiments of anti-Chinese westerners.[119]

During the construction period, the Union Pacific's Irish workers were an altogether different story. Local correspondents for the *Deseret News* seized on accounts that demonstrated the cultural superiority of Mormon workers in the canyons. Non-Mormon contractors Joseph Nounan, William Miller, and William L. Patterson, apparently fed up with their own "strikers," were "anxious to hire workmen from Utah." According to one report, these contractors "declared that they would discharge every man of the regular [Irish] navvies in their employment, who are always dissatisfied and give a great amount of trouble because of their intemperate and riotous habits." Miller and Patterson informed the writer that they sought "workmen from this Territory, in preference to the regular railroad hands." Summarizing this railroad work "in the Cañons," the *Deseret News* noted that the Saints, despite their "little experience" in railroading, have "satisf[ied] [the contractors] of the superiority of Utah men as workers," for "they are sober, quiet, orderly, and do their work without any trouble, giving satisfaction in performing it." Moreover, according to church leaders, strikes among Mormon workers were "not to be thought of," and the "absence of profanity, disorder, or quarrels in the camps was highly gratifying."[120] Contact with the "other" had effect, strengthening the resolve of Mormon communities and clarifying their ideas about proper manhood and productive progress.

The specter of cross-cultural interaction that railroad labor produced coincided with the thirty-eighth semi-annual LDS Church Conference in 1868. The railroad now nearing completion, a major theme of the conference centered on the potential impact of Gentile-Mormon trade in Utah. Participants voted to "withdraw the hand of fellowship from all those who persisted in the policy of sustaining our enemies" and agreed to limit economic intercourse with Gentiles to "absolute necessities."[121] Once the evils of progress were made apparent to Mormons, economic self-defense measures aimed at "the rapidly approaching dangers of outsiders, coming in with the Pacific Railroad, who are avowed enemies of Mormonism" made sense.[122] Though it did "increase intercourse," Brigham Young's earlier argument that the transcontinental railroad would "soften prejudices, and bind the country together," was realized neither by Mormons nor their avowed cultural enemies working in the Great Basin region.[123]

As camps of Irish graders and tracklayers entered Utah, the pious Mormon laborers feared the worst. In December 1868 and January 1869 Union Pacific officials replaced Mormon tunnel workers in Echo and Weber Canyons with Irish crews, "outsiders" imported from Bear River City, Wyoming, and equipped with nitroglycerin. These seasoned construction workers were meant to relieve the Mormons of their "hardest and heaviest work" in canyon tunnels.[124] According to a letter from an anonymous Mormon laborer working below the mouth of Echo Canyon, the entrance of the Irish, "direct from [a] scene of hostilities at Bear River [City]," frightened the Mormon graders. The writer discussed how, unbeknownst to him, the "Celts" had relieved Bishop Sharp's grading crew to speed up tunneling work:

> Not fully aware of such change, this evening as I passed down, everything tunnelward seemed unaccountably metamorphosed. Not one familiar face; a demented stare instead of a friendly eye, a thud-thud stalk instead of the elastic tread, and broken noses, blackened eyes and the "crayther" predominant. . . . [They claim that] they can "put her through" [the tunnel] within six weeks; which, if accomplished, will be doing more in that space of time than has been done during the past summer and fall.[125]

Mormons, whose bodies had often been racialized and dehumanized by detractors who suggested they appeared as "creatures from another planet," complete with "horns or a cloven foot," could nonetheless reciprocate in the presence of Irish immigrants.[126] As this Mormon worker noted, the Union Pacific "company's swarms of 'Ould Ireland's' sons" were unrefined, animalistic "craythers" [creatures], bruised and broken from the strain of heavy construction and as a result of their rough lifestyles. Their mere presence at "Tunnelville" had "metamorphosed" this construction environment.[127] Their pace of labor and style of living held a dangerous and foreign quality, more primitive and out of control than was common in the cultured construction communities of the Saints.

Yet, in February, the near-completed work at Echo and Weber Canyons was transferred back to the Mormon contractors to finish, and Brigham Young noted with satisfaction that "the big tunnel which the company's men took off from our hands to complete in a hurry has been proffered back again." Young seized this opportunity to contrast the two workforces. He maintained that the Irish crews, who had at least a four-to-one worker advantage over the Mormon crews, "withal, have not been doing over two-thirds as much work." Admitting that nitroglycerin's superiority over powder would allow Bishop Sharp's and Joseph Young's men to blast through the 772-foot "Tunnel 2" at the head of Echo Canyon, the Mormon leader went further, arguing that "the sobriety, steadiness and industry of our men gives us a marked advantage."[128]

Scholars have noted that throughout most of American history, masculinity has symbolized courage, physical toughness, virtue, honor, order, and the best hopes and ideals of civilized society. Some have pointed to the rough, martial, and even degenerative variants of masculinity. In this case, Mormons suggested that their immigrant and native-born counterparts on the railroad had weakened ideal manliness in their transiency, combativeness, drinking, and even in their language. Mormon workers, on the other hand, had sharpened western masculinity in their arduous yet honorable and faith-based labor in Utah's canyons. Regenerating masculinity on the wageworkers' frontier, Mormons depicted themselves as hardy, civilized, and worthy specimens of a triumphant nation. So principled and superior was their labor that they stood apart from—and above—the native-born and immigrant men whose work had come to represent the culture of American progress.[129]

When Mormons celebrated the progress of their railroad construction workers, they did so in a manner that denied the work of "uncivilized" railroad crews, in which violence, drunkenness, and disorder was thought to hinder any sense of worthy production. Historians studying internal improvements and national public works have found that canal and railroad construction laborers were often distanced by civic and community leaders, moral reformers, and politicians. In this case, however, it was Mormon workers and elites who, in their actions, writings, and communities, denigrated the contributions of their counterparts by perpetuating images of reckless, unmanly, and uncultured progress.[130] Mormons clearly exaggerated the threat of violence and the pervasiveness of alcohol abuse in an occupation that often encouraged masculine camaraderie—even its rough variants.

In completing the transcontinental railroad, Mormons were introduced to the frontier of transportation labor and the threats of "higher civilization" leveled by their detractors. Work on the railroad thrust the Saints into the national spotlight and provoked a host of responses in and outside of the Mormon community. In many ways, the progress that the Union Pacific and Central Pacific brought to Utah was no different than the social and economic developments that accompanied the Iron Horse in other locations. What was different, however, was the manner in which Mormons selectively adopted, resisted, and redefined such progress.

Relatively few Mormons actually attended the transcontinental railroad celebration at Promontory, although their work helped complete the project. Brigham Young, who declined an invitation, sent as his emissaries Bishop John Sharp, Ogden mayor Lorin Farr, and Chauncey West, who, as Young's contractors, had completed their work for both companies and had received $2 million, less than half of what was owed. Charles Savage, an official Union

Pacific photographer at the event (and a devout Mormon), commented, in reference to the railroad's Irish construction workers, that "the company [did] the country a service in sending such men back to Omaha—for their presence would be a scourge upon any community." Moreover, he noted that "at Blue River [sic] the returning demons . . . were being piled upon the cars in every stage of drunkenness. Every ranch or tent has whiskey for sale. Verily the men earn their money like horses and spend it like asses."[131]

Along with Andrew J. Russell's famous photograph of the 1869 Golden Spike ceremony (see figure 7), popular representations of the Promontory celebration published in *Frank Leslie's Illustrated Newspaper*, *Crofutt's Transcontinental Tourist's Guide*, and other periodicals manufactured a dramatic, nationalistic scene (see figures 8 and 9). Some of these carefully constructed visual commemorations incorporated Chinese, Irish, Mormon, and American construction workers—and even fictional representatives of the "warlike" Indians of the Great Plains—into the transcontinental pageant of American development. Perhaps their participation in the event was didactic: an object lesson for uncivilized "others" in the consequences of western expansion. "Progress" would soon mean territorial dispossession, Chinese exclusion, and a federal attack on Mormon authority.

Certainly the West loomed large in the imagination of countless Americans in this era of expansion, but photographs helped make this legendary place more real. In this respect, Russell's photograph of the Golden Spike ceremony was undoubtedly the most indelible in the minds of Americans. Fifteen minutes after ceremonial last spikes had been driven, under the direction of both Russell and Savage, the special trains were positioned facing each other. Accordingly, the Central Pacific's Jupiter (on the left) and the Union Pacific's No. 119 touched pilots. Chief Engineers Samuel Montague (on the left) and Grenville Dodge shook hands, champagne was distributed, and the ceremony's participants posed for what would become the most famous photograph of the nineteenth century. Meant to celebrate the nation's most remarkable feat and to document history just made, the absence of Mormon workers is puzzling but perhaps understandable considering the dispute over back wages. And the Chinese? They were pushed to the sidelines, far enough to be squeezed out of the frame. According to historian Martha Sandweiss, the Chinese were "banished from the official visual records of the scene, replaced by the wives and children of dignitaries who had come for the day." The photograph thus serves as a "celebratory and self-congratulatory" image for railroad officials and fails to narrate "in any

FIGURE 7. *East and West Shaking Hands at Laying of Last Rail.* Golden Spike ceremony, Promontory Summit, Utah Territory, May 10, 1869. Photograph by Andrew J. Russell. Courtesy of the Yale Collection of Western Americana, Beinecke Rare Book and Manuscript Library, New Haven, CT.

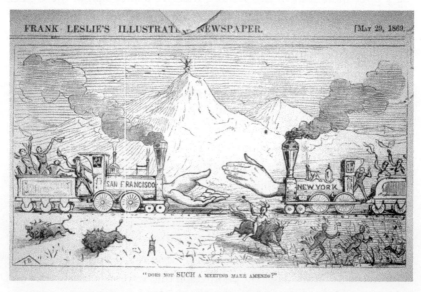

FIGURE 8. *Does Not Such a Meeting Make Amends?* Wood engraving, *Frank Leslie's Illustrated Newspaper,* May 29, 1869, 176. Courtesy of the Library of Congress, Prints and Photographs Division, LC-USZC2–747, Washington, DC.

THE EAST AND THE WEST.

THE ORIENT AND THE OCCIDENT SHAKING HANDS AFTER DRIVING THE LAST SPIKE.

FIGURE 9. *The East and the West.* Two Chinese workers appear in this illustration, on the far left near the train, marked by their silk skullcaps and a single long braid, or queue, hanging down their backs. *Crofutt's Trans-continental Tourist's Guide,* vol. 5, 4th annual revise (New York: printed by author, 1873), 118. Courtesy of the Yale Collection of Western Americana, Beinecke Rare Book and Manuscript Library, New Haven, CT.

comprehensive way the labor that allowed them this moment of triumph."[132]

Nonetheless, the Golden Spike ceremony echoed the original mission of the transcontinental railroad: to civilize a wilderness and bind a country together. Mormons, in their labor on the line, exposed the inherent contradictions of such great national work. The railroad had neither civilized nor doomed Mormons in the ways their detractors had hoped. Instead, it offered Mormon workers, leaders, and followers an opportunity to help raise the banner of American progress. In the process the Saints civilized the railroad's rough edges, transformed notions of labor masculinity in their productive work, created negative reference groups to amplify their righteous contribution, and refashioned American progress to suit the goals of their Great Basin Kingdom.

A separate celebration honoring the completion of the transcontinental railroad took place in Salt Lake City on May 10, 1869. The *Salt Lake Daily Telegraph* noted that a "large congregation assembled in the Tabernacle," and after an Ogden band played music and the chaplain offered a prayer, "Professor W. Burton" gave a stirring address. As this railroad "spans the continent," Burton noted, it "tender[s] to the world an opportunity of a better acquaintance with the people of Utah and their peculiar institutions, which will . . . correct the base calumnies that have been circulated from the pulpit and press." Gesturing panoramically to the crowd, he remarked that "land, but a few years ago was covered with sagebrush, half devoured by the crickets and the grasshoppers," had been transformed by "one of the greatest tasks ever undertaken by man." Burton then posed a rhetorical question: "Who is it that produced this mighty change? The misrepresented citizens of Utah, through the blessings of God. Jesus said that a corrupt tree could not bring forth good fruit. Then come, ye Christians of every land, and come and see and taste the fruit that the Mormon tree has borne."[133]

Though Mormon labor on the transcontinental railroad did little to divert public attention from the practice of polygamy, it kept Mormons in regional and national news that increasingly centered on the "race" to build American progress. Mormons not only endeavored to frame this news according to their cultural values but crafted themselves as both the visionaries and executors of railroad progress. Mormon dignitaries and workers contested their negative public image with manly and courageous labor on the transcontinental railroad. At the same time, they contested the character and pace of progress within the borders of Zion. Beyond laboring for recognition as Americans, Mormons worked to prove the ascendancy of their men, culture, and holy community. In reaching to heaven and manhood, they positioned themselves as superior while denying mortal and immortal rewards to their fellow workers.

For these poor, stereotyped, "profligate outcasts," the transcontinental railroad represented a heaven on wheels. Working on the railroad, in theory, held out the chance of national acceptance. Yet, in practice, it produced a renewed sense of cultural superiority. As Mormons toiled to complete the railroad, they also constructed a Mormon American identity and a Mormon masculinity by setting themselves apart from the underworld of progress and the heathen world of immigrant workers.

FIVE

"The Greatest Monument of Human Labor"

CHINESE IMMIGRANTS, THE LANDSCAPE OF PROGRESS, AND THE WORK OF BUILDING AND CELEBRATING THE TRANSCONTINENTAL RAILROAD

> There were about 4,000 men working there in the mountains, 3,000 of them Chinamen, and they all had to get out. Most . . . came to Truckee and filled up all the old buildings and sheds. . . . One old barn collapsed and killed four Chinamen. A good many were frozen to death. . . . Next morning, we saw something under a tree . . . resembling the shape of a man. We stopped and found a frozen Chinaman . . . threw him in the sleigh . . . and [then] laid him out by the side of a shed and covered him with a rice mat, the appropriate thing for the laying out of a Celestial.
>
> A. P. PARTRIDGE,
> Central Pacific Railroad

THE COLFAX EXCURSION BEGAN on May 22, 1865, at Atchison, Kansas. For the next seven weeks Speaker of the House Schuyler Colfax and his three distinguished guests toured every point of interest in the American West. Accompanying Colfax was William Bross, editor of the *Chicago Tribune;* Samuel Bowles, editor of the Massachusetts *Springfield Republican;* and Albert D. Richardson, correspondent for the *New York Times,* who chronicled the trip.[1] The highlight of their journey was an "inspection" of the Central Pacific Railroad in late August. With company president Leland Stanford as tour guide, the men chugged up to the end-of-track, a California mining camp called Illinoistown.[2] Having mentioned to his guests that four thousand men were at work in the mountains, 90 percent of them Chinese, Stanford paused to let them soak in the High Sierra scenery. To his surprise, all eyes were fixed on the Chinese workers. Richardson wrote that the Chinese were "swarming among the Sierras like flies upon a honeycomb. . . .

They were a great army laying siege to Nature in her strongest citadel." "The rugged mountains," he continued, "looked like stupendous ant-hills, swarmed with Celestials, shoveling, wheeling, carting, drilling and blasting rocks and earth while their dull, moony eyes stared out from under immense basket-hats."[3]

A week prior to their adventure in the Sierras, the excursionists had joined a group of thirty-five American businessmen and thirty Chinese "gentlemen" for another new cultural experience: dinner at the Hang Heong restaurant in San Francisco. For Bowles, navigating the exotic menu was as much of a challenge as seven weeks on the railroad. "I went to the table weak and hungry," he noted, "but I found the one universal odor and flavor soon destroyed all appetite; and I fell back resignedly on a constitutional incapacity to use the chopsticks."[4] Amid questions about the railroad, immigrant workers, and dried Chinese oysters, Bowles grew impatient. The railroad, he reminded his friends, was their priority, not the "Celestials." "The Chinese," Bowles argued, "are the poorest and most debased" creatures, "of a low type mentally and physically," who "show little capacity for improvement." Thus instigating an argument at the table, Bowles, who essentially refused his dinner at Heong's, stormed off, but not before commentating that the Chinese "can beat a raw Irishman in a hundred ways, but while he is constantly improving and advancing, they stand still in the old ruts."[5]

The Colfax excursionists revisited a fundamental American paradox as they traveled the Sierra foothills. The newest of the country's immigrants were building America's soon-to-be greatest achievement—for Americans. At the same time, the Chinese construction workers were subject to the strange and unfriendly gaze of the Americans. One party was physically making history; the other trying to interpret it, make sense of it, and claim it as its own. Such interplay is crucial to the remembering and forgetting, the praising and distancing, of Chinese workers on the Central Pacific Railroad.

Piecing together this story is crucial to understanding American progress and immigrant labor on the far western transportation frontier. But it is an exceedingly difficult and nearly impossible task to recover the voices of Chinese railroad workers, who are silent in the historical record. A partial solution is to consider Chinese construction workers on the Central Pacific Railroad from multiple and diverse perspectives and read against the grain, incorporating those of workers; employers; wealthy capitalists; newspaper editors; literary, religious, and political figures; and popular artists and illustrators.

The contestation over American progress, and the paradox of the immigrant labor that produced it, persisted in the Far West. In the case of the Chinese, waves of immigration intensified the mission of constructing, interpreting, and defending the meaning of railroad progress. The loudest voices came from those who denied workers' power and agency—the politicians, writers, commentators, and artists who crafted landscapes of progress. The Chinese were one group ensnared in yet distanced by what historians have called the "Greater Reconstruction." Many Americans wanted them erased from the continent and from the nation's history. Yet in analyzing the "Chinese problem" through railroad labor and the competing ideas of progress that emerged, this work concludes that Chinese railroad workers became a far more complex and formidable group than their opponents contended.

These workers came from Guangdong Province in the Pearl River Delta region of southeastern China. The Siyi (four counties) in rural Guangdong, among its least prosperous regions, produced 90 percent of the Chinese immigrants to California in the nineteenth century. Xinning County, home to most of these immigrants, is just over eighty miles from Guangzhou, where the Pearl River leads to the South China Sea, but a mountainous terrain isolated their farming communities from this city, its hilly, rocky soil hardly able to sustain them. Xinning produced so little rice—enough to feed the region for only half of the year—that farmers grew peanuts and sweet potatoes on the hillsides. The harsh, unforgiving landscape that impoverished entire farming communities was not the only source of worry; British economic penetration in the wake of the Opium Wars (1839–42, 1856–60) and the violence of secret brotherhood societies exacerbated already poor conditions. Siyi men often undertook seasonal migrations in and around the city of Guangzhou, where they worked as hired hands, in factories, or as street peddlers; movement to and from sites of temporary employment enabled some to encounter information networks with knowledge of and connections to work across the ocean.[6]

Whether they were peasants, experienced miners, merchants, or day laborers, the Guangdong immigrants sought a life in America free from the turmoil of their native land. Throughout the 1850s and 1860s their southern province was wrecked by poverty and war. Beginning in 1851, amid widespread social unrest and worsening famine, the Taiping Rebellion, "the world's bloodiest conflict," had, by 1864, claimed the lives of between twenty and thirty million people.[7] Hong Xiuquan, the leader of the rebellion, was a Kejia, or "visitor," whose ancestors had settled in Guangdong centuries earlier as tenants or landlords. Ethnic tensions between the Kejia and the native Bendi, though they had existed for centuries, were exacerbated during this period, as both groups frequently competed for jobs as "common" laborers, miners, charcoal sellers, and field hands for landowning families. Suffering under the economic and political instability of the Qing Dynasty and beset with overpopulation, famine, and the devastating violence of civil war, settlers in the poor Taisanese- and Cantonese-speaking regions of Guangdong Province looked abroad, to America, for a new life.[8]

Men from the Sanyi (three counties) in Guangdong on the southern and western fringes of Guangzhou who had more experience with the world of commerce and likely more connections to resources ventured abroad to work as merchants or labor contractors in America. It was the Xinning men who often became their floating proletariat in America, including in California.[9] In two great waves, first in the 1850s and then in the 1860s, these rural workers followed what became a rather well-trodden route from one of the rural Siyi to Guangzhou, where they boarded flat-bottom boats to Hong Kong, signing on for passage to San Francisco. Crammed into Pacific Mail Steamship Company vessels, they endured a harrowing two-month passage to America.

The Guangdong men were contracted either to individual merchants or to local district companies, known to the Chinese as Huiguan and to Americans as the Chinese Six Companies—the coordinating body of the six Chinese benevolent associations in San Francisco. Organized by emigrant districts and officially called the Chinese Consolidated Benevolent Companies, they located job opportunities and functioned as mutual aid societies, providing new arrivals and the most destitute residents with shelter and basic amenities. For many of the immigrants these district companies were the only familiar contact on a foreign and brutish frontier. Moreover, merchants who dominated these associations had a knack for recruiting large quantities of workers to toil in remote corners of the West. They supplied thousands of Chinese workers to the Central Pacific Railroad, advancing migrants the rate of a ticket plus interest, which the laborers contracted to repay. Once employment had been secured, the migrants' employers agreed to garnish any money owed to the Six Companies from the workers' wages. Far more profitable for the Six Companies were collateral agreements—contracts—to supply their isolated workers with clothing, food, and other essentials; this was especially true on the Central Pacific, where the Chinese, unlike white railroaders, did not receive board as part of their employment.[10]

The first wave of Chinese immigrants to California set out to discover Jinshan (English Gum Shan), "Gold Mountain," and the second, to help move mountains building the Central Pacific Railroad. This latter tide of immigration was augmented by the passage of the Burlingame Treaty of 1868, which permitted the Chinese to emigrate freely to the United States. In California, prejudice against Chinese miners was exacerbated by violence and discriminatory legislation.[11] According to an 1871 report by the U.S. commissioner of mining statistics, "Very few Chinese engaged in lode [hard rock] mining" but instead, as they had for many years, "restricted themselves to placer mining . . . working areas abandoned by whites."[12] Wage labor on railroads, however, offered a steadier form of employment, and by the late 1850s some Chinese immigrants moved from mining to railroad labor. Of the 500 graders on the San Francisco and Marysville Railroad in 1859, over 160 were Chinese immigrants, and in 1863 the San Francisco and San Jose Railroad transformed their Chinese graders into "gangs" of strikebreakers.[13] Year after year, from the California interior and abroad, the Chinese came to work on the railroad.

When these immigrants arrived, an angry, repulsed nation greeted them. According to many nineteenth-century Americans, the cultural distance that separated native-born Caucasians from Chinese immigrants was unbridgeable. It was exacerbated by unyielding physical differences. Newspapers and popular periodicals referred to the Chinese as "yellow-skinned," "almond-eyed," and "pig-tailed," or simply as the "yellow peril."[14] This racialized loathing of the Chinese crossed partisan lines. The Republican *Cincinnati Chronicle* dubbed the immigrants "dependent [and] ignorant, animal machines," while the *New York Star,* a Democratic paper, noted that the Chinese were "filthy, unnatural, and abominable."[15] Invariably cast as "John Chinaman," epithets targeted male immigrants as a faceless and homogenous mass. Anti-Chinese commentators depicted Chinese immigrant laborers as "coolies" or forced contract laborers, no better off than slaves.[16] The Chinese were considered weak, feminine, and submissive, yet also uncivilized and loathsome. Politicians such as Ohio representative William Mungen condemned them as a "poor, miserable, dwarfish race of inferior beings," who were "docile . . . effeminate, pedantic, and . . . cowardly."[17] Americans fast dehumanized the Chinese as "ants," "bees," "devouring locusts," and pests.[18] As one editor put it, "The Chinese people remain as barbarous as ever. Their pagan savageness appears to be impregnable to the mild influences of Christian civilization."[19]

It was not enough for the Chinese to be criticized as submissive and repugnant. Their degraded condition posed a danger to native-born Americans. Overseas crises, such as China's Opium Wars, transformed the opium pipe into a negative national icon of Chinese culture in the America mind. Disease was a particular concern, and American physicians argued that opium led to syphilis, consumption, scrofula, and a host of other illnesses. As Dr. Arthur B. Stout argued in an 1862 report, the introduction of the Chinese into American life created "a cancer in the biological, social, religious, and political systems."[20] Oregon senator James H. Slater was even more blunt when he warned his colleagues in Congress that cheap Chinese labor was a carrier bringing "filth and frightful and nameless diseases and contagions" to the United States.[21]

The struggling Central Pacific Railroad would soon test these prejudices. As its rival, the Union Pacific Railroad, raced across the Great Plains, soaking up public lands and generous federal subsidies on its triumphant march to Promontory, Utah, the Central Pacific was mired in the Sierra Nevada foothills, having built less than fifty miles of track during the first two years of construction. Faced with an impatient public, the loss of potential riches, and a dwindling, unsteady, and disgruntled labor force, the company made a decision that would improve its fate and change history. The desire to reach Utah and earn the equivalent land, money, and prestige that the Union Pacific had thus far monopolized led the Central Pacific to hire Chinese immigrants in an attempt to rectify its slow and unimpressive progress in the Sierras.[22] Beyond winning a railroad race, this decision would also weigh ideas about labor, race, manhood, and progress. On other frontiers of transportation labor, Irish immigrants and Mormon "others" worked hard and endured in a challenge to American notions of manhood, civilization, and even citizenship. On the Central Pacific Railroad, would labor prove Chinese manhood or would race trump the accomplishments that united a nation?

In January 1865 James Harvey Strobridge, whom Construction Superintendent Charles Crocker had recently made his labor boss, advertised for workers in newspapers and handbills at post offices throughout California. The Central Pacific needed "5,000 laborers" immediately, and promised "constant and permanent work."[23] The *Shasta Courier* noted that, of these five thousand workers, the company guaranteed it would "employ at once as many men as can be advantageously worked" on the twenty-three miles "between Newcastle and Illinoistown." The newspaper stressed that such an "opportunity affords a chance for those out of employment" to engage in a worthy enterprise for the benefit of California and the nation. Reacting to this call for workers, Lauren Upson, editor of the *Sacramento Union,* went even further, adding that "enterprising cutthroats ... can get better pay for their labor by working by the month in the mountains than by robbing Sacramentans at the alley corners."[24]

According to Crocker, these were precisely the type of men the company had employed. He complained that his force in early 1865 "never went much above 800 white laborers with the shovel and pick." These mostly Irish workers, he argued, were "unsteady" and "unreliable." "Some of them would stay a few days, and some would not go to work at all," Crocker elaborated, "some would stay until payday, get a little money, get drunk, and then clear out."[25] Meanwhile, the response to Strobridge's advertisement was discouraging, as fewer than two hundred—primarily Irish—workers showed up at Superintendent Crocker's office to join the ranks of the builders. Adding to this poor turnout, Strobridge's labor supply fluctuated heavily in early 1865, particularly after payday, when he routinely lost hundreds of men to the mines in Nevada. Workers would hire on, ride to the end of the track, and from there depart, on foot, to the Comstock Lode.[26]

In the fall of 1865 California governor Leland Stanford wrote to President Andrew Johnson and Secretary of the Interior James Harlan that "a large majority of the white laboring class on the Pacific Coast find more profitable and congenial employment in mining ... than in railroad work."[27] For many of these native-born and Irish workers, the American dream had little to do with hand carving a railroad right-of-way along the sloping foothills and through the impenetrable granite of the Sierra Nevada. Railroad building was grueling labor that paid poorly, while mining held out the opportunity of striking it rich. They wanted no part in building the nation's dream.[28]

Strobridge, though Irish himself and an experienced railroad foreman and contractor, neither softened his managerial tactics nor offered his workers special treatment on the basis of their shared cultural traits. An imposing figure who was described by one commentator as a "smart, pushing Irishman" and by another as a "wild man on the construction line," Strobridge relied on physical force and fear to manage his charges.[29] He frequently intimidated his workers to speed up the work and maintained low wages despite protests and desertions. Strobridge was also not afraid to grab a pick or shovel and mix it up with the unskilled Irish. In the summer of 1864, while his construction workers blasted away at Bloomer Cut, just beyond Newscastle, California, a piece of flying granite severely injured his right eye, forcing him to cover it with a black patch for the remainder of his life.[30] Superintendent Crocker, who praised his labor boss's work ethic, saw similarities between them. Like James Strobridge, Crocker recalled, "I knew how to manage men. I worked them in the ore-beds ... coal-pits ... and had worked myself right along with them."[31]

Yet Crocker's idea of how to "manage men" was different from that of his labor boss. Early in their partnership, mindful of the labor shortage on the railroad, Crocker disliked how poorly Strobridge treated his Irish construction workers. As he later recounted, "I ... quarreled with Strobridge when I first went in." Crocker, a physically imposing man who weighed over 250 pounds, angrily lectured his assistant: "don't talk so to the men—they are human creatures—don't talk so roughly to them." An indignant Strobridge, convinced of the superiority of his tactics in dealing with immigrant graders and tracklayers, replied, "you have *got* to do it, and *you* will come to it; you cannot talk to them as though you were talking to gentlemen, because they are not gentlemen. They are as near brutes as they can get."[32] These attitudes, when added to Irish intemperance, desertion, and demands for higher wages, led Central Pacific officials to contemplate a shift away from these common builders of progress.[33]

Certainly the existence of another supply of accessible workers made the Irish, while still undesirable in some respects, somewhat of a luxury. Yet a change in employment policies did not occur immediately. Central Pacific management considered a plan for "importing, under contract, thousands of peons from Sonora and other Mexican States," but Crocker and Strobridge balked at this idea. Mexicans were "discussed and discarded" as railroad builders, for they were reportedly "too slow and indolent to work."[34] Years later thousands of miles of tracks laid in the Southwest proved Central Pacific leadership wrong; Mexican Americans were perfectly capable of railroad work.[35]

During a wage dispute with Irish workers in late January 1865, Crocker directed his labor boss to "go over to Auburn ... and get some Chinamen and put them to work."[36] The Irish construction crews overheard, immediately ceased their protest, and pleaded with Crocker and Strobridge not to hire the Chinese. Strobridge was incensed and told Crocker, "I will not boss Chinese. ... I will not be responsible for the work done on the road by Chinese labor." Much later Strobridge admitted that he seriously doubted the company "could make a success" of the Chinese experiment and that, furthermore, he was "very much prejudiced against Chinese labor."[37] Crocker, in his 1876 testimony to a joint congressional committee on Chinese immigration, recalled that Strobridge thought that race, size, diet, and the supposed effeminacy of the Chinese prohibited them from the strenuous work of railroading. Other accounts suggest that the behavior of the Central Pacific's white workers "compelled" the company to experiment with Chinese labor and, moreover, that Crocker and Strobridge were "driven to" this position.[38]

After repeatedly rejecting Crocker's advice, Strobridge hired fifty Chinese men through one of their labor agents, to work as "dump cart" loaders. Other accounts suggest that Crocker brought in the first Chinese immigrants to "frighten" the Irish workers, who had recently instigated several strikes and protests.[39] Either way, this unskilled labor served as a test for both the Chinese and the railroad company. Strobridge paid them twenty-six dollars a month without board, compared to the thirty dollars plus board that white workers earned.[40] The Chinese impressed him, and after hiring fifty more, he began working through labor recruiters in California and China. Writing to California representative Cornelius Cole in April 1865, Judge Edwin Crocker, the Central Pacific's attorney and brother of Charles, noted that having passed Auburn, some thirty-five miles east of Sacramento, the railroad had "2000 men at work with about 300 wagons and carts . . . on some of the heaviest work in the mountains." Pleased with the progress in the Sierra foothills, Judge Crocker noted the source of the company's success: "A large part of our force are Chinese, and they prove nearly equal to white men, in the amount of labor they perform, and are far more reliable. No danger of strikes among them. We are training them to all kinds of labor, blasting, driving horses, handling rock, as well as the pick and shovel."[41]

Based on his brother Charles's and James Strobridge's experience with the diligent "Celestials," Judge Crocker was convinced that the Central Pacific had found its men. "We want a body of 2,500 trained [Chinese] laborers," he stated, for in his mind the company's success hinged on "keep[ing] them steadily at work until the road is built across the continent, or until we meet [the Union Pacific] coming from the other side."[42]

Certainly the company's fortunes hinged on keeping the Chinese "steadily at work," but Crocker's and Strobridge's rather intimidating management style deviated little throughout the construction period. Strobridge managed with an ax handle, his "persuader," in hand, while Crocker developed a reputation for behaving "like a mad bull" in his interactions with employees.[43] These were not ideal conditions for workers, and while Irishmen could escape such abuse for Virginia City's mines and other, more profitable employment, the Chinese could not. Lewis Clement, the Central Pacific's assistant chief engineer, noted that it was the "discipline of railroad work" that "high-priced" and "independent" white workers simply could not bear.[44] Yet the Chinese, who were regularly in debt to both Chinese and American merchants and encumbered with family obligations to earn and save, had to think very carefully before striking or quitting their jobs. The Chinese stayed on despite the physical dangers of the work and the ruthlessness of their "Riding bosses."[45]

Though the rails had only reached Clipper Gap, forty miles east of Sacramento, by June 1865, local newspapers cheered the sights and sounds of progress with a sense of both amazement and inevitability. The editor of the *Auburn Stars and Stripes* noted that "the boom of the powder blast is continuously heard," and "frowning embankments rise as if by magic.... High trestle bridges spring up in a week."[46] According to Chief Engineer Samuel Montague, although "some distrust was at first felt regarding the capacity of this class for the service required, [the] experiment has proved eminently successful." The Chinese, he maintained, "are faithful and industrious, and under proper supervision, soon become skillful in the performance of their duties."[47] Central Pacific president Leland Stanford, who had earlier condemned the Chinese as the "dregs of Asia," praised them in his 1865 official statement to President Johnson and the secretary of the interior. Without them, he noted, "it would be impossible to complete the western portion of this great national enterprise" within the time allotted by Congress.[48] Stanford argued that the Chinese, "as a class are quiet, peaceable, patient, industrious, and economical":

> Ready and apt to learn all the different kinds of work required in railroad building, they soon become as efficient as white laborers. More prudent ... they are contented with less wages. We find them organized into societies for mutual aid and assistance. These societies, that count their numbers by thousands, are conducted by shrewd, intelligent business men, who promptly advise their subordinates where employment can be found on the most favorable terms.[49]

The "societies" to which Stanford referred were in fact the Chinese Six Companies, the same mercantile and labor agencies through which Chinese immigrants secured passage to the Pacific Coast under the credit-ticket system.[50] Careful to distinguish this system from unfree labor, Stanford noted that "no system similar to slavery, serfdom or peonage prevails among these laborers," who were paid in coin, while their merchants were responsible for "furnish[ing] them their supplies of food."[51]

FIGURE 10. *End of Track, on Humboldt Plains,* Nevada, ca. 1865–69. Teams of Central Pacific construction workers laying track, including the Chinese. Photograph by Alfred A. Hart. Courtesy of the Library of Congress, Prints and Photographs Division, LC-DIG-stereo-1s00618, Washington, DC.

Due to a fragmentary historical record, few scholars have examined the work-gang system that predominated on the Central Pacific. Historian Manu Vimalassery has argued that the system resembled a nineteenth-century version of the pyramid scheme, as it concentrated power "in a small number at the top" while dispersing "risk and exploitation to increasing numbers below." Resting at the top of this pyramid scheme, though they did not control it, were "The Big Four," owners of the Central Pacific: President Leland Stanford, Vice President Collis Huntington, Treasurer Mark Hopkins, and construction supervisor Charles Crocker. Next came the construction bosses, men like James Strobridge, who represented the railroad company's interests along the right-of-way. Chinese merchants and labor contractors followed, operating through local networks of exchange, normally centered in the Chinatowns of San Francisco and Sacramento. They located immigrants and migrants in need of work and often carrying debt and sent these men to the end-of-track, where heavy labor awaited. According to Vimalassery, "The flow of goods and the lubricants of personal connections along these arteries formed the exoskeleton of a global community, jumping across the circuits of nations and empires."[52]

The Central Pacific put its Chinese workers to the test of becoming railroad men, and the results exceeded even the highest expectations (see figure 10). As Charles Crocker later noted, "We tried them on the light work, thinking they would not do for heavy work." But the immigrants proved him wrong. "Gradually," stated Crocker, "we found that they worked well, and as our forces spread out . . . we began to occupy more ground. . . . We put them into the softer cuts, and finally into the rock cuts." Convinced of their value, Crocker recalled, "Wherever we put them we found them good, and they worked themselves into our favor."[53] Trouble among Irish laborers only intensified this strategy, and Crocker noted that "at one time when we had a strike among our Irish brothers on masonry . . . we made masons out of the Chinamen." At the time, James Strobridge doubted this maneuver and replied angrily, "Make masons out of Chinamen!" Yet Crocker quickly dismissed his disgruntled labor boss: "Did they not build the Chinese Wall, the biggest piece of Masonry in the world?"[54]

Still, it was with more than their work habits and skills that the Chinese built a railroad. The railroad was oiled by the blood of their sacrifice. Though company officials were largely silent on such issues as Chinese deaths, reports of the Central Pacific's progress captured the risks, struggles, triumphs, and tragedies of railroad construction. Late in 1865 a group of freshly hired Chinese construction workers defied modern engineering odds in their attack on Cape Horn, a large, forbidding cliff face above Colfax, California, fifty-seven miles east of Sacramento.[55] The immigrants were lowered by ropes and chains from the top of the cliff. While suspended in midair, they not only hammered and drilled at the cliff's granite face but also tamped powder into drilled holes and lit explosives to blast the wall.[56] Robert L. Harris, in an article for *Overland Monthly,* recorded the only firsthand account of this feat. Harris, who later became chief engineer of the California Pacific Railroad, colored his brief report of the construction at Cape Horn with prejudiced references to the Chinese workers, who, he claimed, were "as thick as bees" in the vicinity of the project and whose camp "resemble[ed] a collection of dog-kennels, which, in fact, it is." Nonetheless, he noted that "the only way for the chain-men to work along these cliffs . . . was by being suspended by ropes from above, the chain-bearers signaling to those holding the ropes, up or down, forward or back." The Chinese workers, demonstrating great courage in this endeavor, often "remained suspended and swinging in the air."[57] Though they were depicted as insects and animals by this observer, the Chinese had overcome a great obstacle in physically transforming the daunting landscape at Cape Horn.

The following fall and well into the next winter, the Central Pacific's Chinese workers met perhaps their greatest challenge, when their mission to cross the rugged Sierra Nevada necessitated the boring of eleven tunnels from Cisco, California, to Lake Ridge on the eastern slope of the Sierra Nevada summit, 112 miles east of Sacramento.[58] During the previous summer, when Crocker had sent advance teams of his Chinese workers into the Sierra high country to begin excavation near the tunnels, it often took three hundred men ten days to clear and grub a single mile.[59] This was only preparatory work for the actual grading, which stymied crews for months, as the rock and soil required hand shoveling and was then carried off in successive wheelbarrows. When the winter of 1866–67 turned harsh, work in the Sierras was dreadful. The snow fell so heavily into the freshly graded cuts that it became nearly impossible to dig out. Tunnels were excavated in blizzard-like conditions, as the mountains were covered with as much as thirty feet of snow.[60] Among them, the most daunting was tunnel "Number 6" (Summit Tunnel), which, at a length of 1,659 feet, was the longest on the line, running parallel to the infamous Donner Pass.[61] The tunnel took thirteen months to build and demanded unthinkable energy and perseverance. J. O. Wilder, a surveyor's assistant working near Cisco, noted immediately upon his employment with the Central Pacific that the tunnel-bound Chinese were superior workers, even when compared to the railroads' Irish and native-born men. As Wilder stated, "The Chinese were as steady, hard-working set of men as could be found. With the exception of a few whites at the west end of Tunnel No. 6, the laboring force was entirely composed of Chinamen with white foremen."[62]

According to Wilder, nine of every ten railroad workers in the vicinity of the summit were Chinese, who, even using nitroglycerin to blast the tunnels prior to the scraping, chiseling, digging, and hauling required to clear them, advanced only at the rate of 1.18 feet per day. These Chinese workers, he noted, were "paid $30 to $35 in gold a month, finding [boarding] themselves, while the whites were paid about the same with their board thrown in."[63] The strength and endurance of the immigrants impressed the editor of the *Sacramento Union*. Despite the "very heavy" labor of "deep cuts and huge fills" in the vicinity of the summit, he noted that the "host of Celestial laborers . . . is so numerous that the mountainous obstacles are 'here today and gone tomorrow.'"[64]

Under normal circumstances, such a harsh winter would have forced railroad construction crews to withdraw. Yet, for Crocker and his associates, each week lost meant squandering hundreds of thousands of dollars in public land and federal subsidies. To the "Big Four," the construction of the Central Pacific was a race to Utah, for the company that first reached the Great Basin and the fertile Salt Lake Valley could establish an upper hand on freight and passenger traffic. To win this contest, the Central Pacific had to traverse the inhospitable High Sierra and enter civilization. Its Chinese immigrants were the critical agents and barometers of such progress. Though the construction on the Donner Pass was highlighted by the boring of the massive Summit Tunnel, here the Chinese workers also built several miles of "snow-sheds" to prevent the accumulation of snow along the mountainside and "Chinese Walls," seventy-five-foot-high hand-built retaining walls, to support the railroad grade in the deep ravines between the tunnels.[65]

It is an understatement to say that railroad workers, like the canallers before them, took great pride in their work. But what contemporaries overlooked in these matter-of-fact accounts of railroad building is that construction labor both required and imparted a profound knowledge of nature. Historians such as William Cronon, Richard White, and Thomas Andrews have grappled with the intellectual separation of work from nature and the ways this has been expressed from European-Indian encounters in the colonial period through the emergence of modern environmentalism. Cronon has critiqued the equation of wilderness with leisure, while White and Andrews challenge romantic notions of work as destructive to nature. Work in extractive industries such as logging and mining reveals the depths of workers' knowledge in what Andrews calls miners' underground "workscapes," and in the Far West the Chinese and other railroad builders honed a familiarity with soils, rocks, and place.[66] Observers documented what workers' experienced through bodily labor: that railroad construction was hard, exhausting, heavy work and that nature was hot, cold, sharp, muddy, slick, and obstinate. Nature, like work, tested men at every turn. The Chinese knew nature through labor, and if their task was to transform it, such knowledge was a powerful advantage.

Central Pacific engineer John R. Gillis, in an 1870 speech delivered before the American Society of Civil Engineers, noted that, as the track reached Cisco in November 1866, "as fast as gangs of Chinamen were released they were hurried to the Summit to be distributed among the tunnels." To avoid delays that had hampered progress the previous year, Gillis noted that "the approaches to all the tunnels were covered" with Chinese workers, who "worked day and night in three shifts of eight hours each." While this strategy saved the company time and organized its tunneling at the Sierra's summit, the work was just as dangerous. That winter Gillis recorded that "at Tunnel 10, some 15 or 20 Chinese were killed by a slide."[67] A. P. Partridge, a bridge framer on the railroad, recalled that, to the chagrin of company officials, the heavy snowfall came early in the winter of 1866–67 and drove the "Chinamen" out of the mountains. He counted three thousand Chinese among the four thousand men on the job, and the Chinese were in a most dangerous location. All who could make it to Truckee congregated in "old buildings and sheds," but an old barn structure "collapsed and killed four Chinamen." Worse, "a good many were frozen to death." The following morning Partridge and his colleagues glimpsed something under a tree "resembling the shape of a man." Finding a Chinese worker who had succumbed to the blizzard, they "threw him in the sleigh . . . and laid him out by the side of a shed and covered him with a rice mat, the appropriate thing for the laying out of a Celestial."[68]

Perhaps their numbers and not their race made the lives of Chinese immigrants seem expendable to their colleagues on the Central Pacific. Yet the ghastly scene of a frozen-to-death Chinese worker would no doubt have troubled the average passerby. Such casual accounts of railroad fatalities are as tragic as they are problematic. They succeeded in deadening sensibilities on the tragedies of railroad progress and even transformed death into an anticipated and tolerable outcome. As a result, "dead Chinamen" become a natural consequence of American progress, no different than boring a tunnel or felling a tree.

Christmas Day in 1866 brought more casualties on the Central Pacific, as "the snow fell to such a depth" that a "gang of Chinamen . . . were covered up by a snow slide and four or five died before they could be exhumed."[69] Chinese fatalities never overshadowed American progress, but even company officials could not ignore the human consequences of this race to Utah. Years later, while testifying before the Pacific Railway Commission, James Strobridge recounted the frustrating winters in the High Sierra. "The snow slides carried away our camps," he stated, "and we lost a good many men in those slides; many of them we did not find until the next season when the snow melted."[70] But snow was not the only problem. When construction teams eventually crossed the Nevada state line and pushed east toward the Humboldt Sink, a smallpox outbreak wreaked havoc on the crews. In a letter to Central Pacific vice president Collis Huntington, Charles Crocker complained that "small-pox completely demoralized our track laying force and they could not have laid much more iron if they had it." Strobridge, he noted, "sick with a very bad cold," was "afraid it was the smallpox as the symptoms were very similar." Meanwhile, Crocker claimed that the Central Pacific's men were "running scared out of their senses."[71] Yet, said Crocker, "If we found that we were in a hurry for a job of work, it was better to put on the Chinese at once."[72]

Of the Central Pacific's twelve to fifteen thousand Chinese workers, perhaps hundreds, and possibly more, died during the initial five-year construction period. A January 1870 report in the *Elko Independent* noted that six railroad cars between Elko and Toano, Nevada, were being "loaded with dead Celestials for transportation to the Flowery Kingdom," as "the Chinese [Six] [C]ompanies" typically paid the Central Pacific "ten dollars for carrying to San Francisco each dead Chinaman." Six railroad cars, "stuffed with this kind of freight, will be a good day's work," noted the writer, who protested that while "the remains of females are left to rot in shallow graves . . . every defunct male is carefully preserved" for shipment back to "the Occident."[73] Reading beyond the writers' scathing views on alleged Chinese burial practices, the image of six railroad cars filled with bones is a shocking one. Importantly, the newspaper did not indicate the nature of these deaths, but in June of the same year the *Sacramento Reporter,* in a brief report titled "Bones in Transit," referred to the "accumulated bones" of "perhaps 1,200 Chinamen," weighing twenty thousand pounds, which arrived in Sacramento via the Central Pacific. Noting that nearly all the bones were "the remains of employees of the company who were engaged in building the road," the *Reporter* cited the religious customs of the "Celestial Empire," which stipulated that "wherever possible, the bones of its subjects shall be interred upon its own soil."[74] A third report from the *Sacramento Union,* dated the same day, listed a much lower number of bones, from "about fifty defunct Chinamen who died from disease or were killed by accident while working on the line of the Central Pacific Railroad."[75]

These conflicting reports highlight the appalling conditions of frontier railroad labor, the dignity of Chinese workers, and the potency of their cultural traditions in an unfamiliar environment. Likely buried under deep snow in the Sierra Nevada, the Chinese workers' bones were the ghastly reminder of both the brutality of railroad progress and the devotion of its central contributors. In paying for and demanding the shipment of these skeletons for a proper interment, California's Chinese labor agents bestowed to their living, dead, and dying countrymen a humanity denied to them by their American critics.

Company officials realized early on that cheap and effective labor in the form of Chinese immigrants was a golden ticket to national triumph and personal fortune. Other supporters of Chinese railroad laborers were religious figures who championed the purity of their contributions. Protestant minister A. W. Loomis suggested that the Chinese were not only more valuable laborers than whites but also morally superior. Loomis engaged in lengthy conversations with Central Pacific management about the merits of the "Celestials" whom the railroad company had employed on the line. The Chinese, he noted, "have no storytelling," no guards or "sentinel set" to look out for "the boss" while their "companions" engage in intemperate behavior. "Not having acquired a taste for whiskey," Loomis reasoned, the Guangdong immigrants "have few fights, and no 'blue Mondays.'" Though already convinced that the immigrants' work on the railroad was exceptional, Loomis noted that an "Overseer" informed him that he could "drill more rock and move more dirt with Chinamen than with an equal number of the men who claim this kind of occupation as their specialty."[76] Similarly, in the fall of 1867, as company officials worried that the Sierra snows might prevent the completion of a continuous line from the Summit down to Truckee, California, Leland Stanford complained that "it is very trying to see such important results missed for the want of a few more men."[77] Although Stanford and Vice President Collis Huntington had faith in Charles Crocker, who, they agreed, "could do more than any other man in America," Huntington was convinced that "it would be all the better for us and the state if there should a half million [Chinese] come over in 1868."[78]

Another defender of Chinese immigrants was popular literary figure Samuel Clemens, or Mark Twain. According to Clemens, the Chinese in the Far West were a "harmless race when white men either let them alone or treat them no worse than dogs." Though sarcastic and prone to stereotyping, Clemens, pointing to the upright character of these immigrants in spite of white hostility, suggested that their work ethic and attitude were superior to most native-born Americans. The Chinese, he noted,

> are almost entirely harmless ... for they seldom think of resenting the vilest insults or the cruelest injuries. They are quiet, peaceable, tractable, free from drunkenness, and they are as industrious as the day is long. A disorderly Chinaman is rare, and a lazy one does not exist. So long as a Chinaman has strength to use his hands he needs no support from anybody; white men often complain of want of work, but a Chinaman offers no such complaint; he always manages to find something to do.[79]

Sympathetic western journalists who were astonished with the construction progress of the Central Pacific against insurmountable odds increasingly sought to learn more about their Chinese workers. Clemens made note of "several great companies or organizations" in California to which the Chinese workers belonged, the largest of which being the See Yup Company and the Ning Yeong Company. The latter, he stated, maintained a temple and a "numerous priesthood" in San Francisco. A writer for the *Sacramento Daily Union,* as well as Clemens, was permitted access to the Six Companies' records, which revealed that "more than one-fourth" of California's Chinese workers were "employed at this time on the Pacific Railroad, and other public improvements."[80] These firms divided among themselves the state's Chinese workers, registered a number of members, supervised labor contracts, provisioned workers, and importantly, as Clemens noted, "ship[ped] their bodies home when they die[d]."[81] Thus, as the Central Pacific weighed Chinese immigrants' masculinity in the grueling labor of American progress, the Six Companies were charged with dignifying those who had born its ultimate sacrifice.

If some American opinion makers were transformed by railroad progress, so too were the Chinese. Arduous labor in the Sierras provoked Chinese workers into a most American act. Or was it a Chinese act, which, as some scholars have suggested, drew on transplanted traditions of workplace activism?[82] After the brutally long winter in 1866–67 in the Sierra Nevada, Chinese workers staked their claim and initiated a massive strike, throwing down their picks and shovels and returning to their camps. After repeated attempts to bully them back to work, James Strobridge telegraphed construction supervisor Charles Crocker. The Chinese workers were unsatisfied with their raise to thirty-five dollars a month, he noted, and they demanded forty dollars and their days shortened from eleven hours to ten. They had timed their strike perfectly, as local mining companies were actively recruiting them and promising less difficult—and better paying—work.[83] Company lawyer Edwin Crocker, in a letter to Vice President Collis Huntington, expressed his and his colleagues' frustrations, complaining that "*we* have proved their value as laborers & everybody is trying Chinese & now we can't get them.... Our force is not increasing."[84] Of those Irish workers engaged in construction, Crocker noted that "they wouldn't work within a hundred rods of [the Chinese]."[85] It was June, the snows had still not left the Sierra summit, and the Central Pacific was experiencing a labor shortage. Edwin Crocker confessed, "This strike of the chinamen is the hardest blow we have had here." Upon receiving news of the strike, Treasurer Mark Hopkins feared that "if they are successful in this demand, then they *control* & their demands will be increased." Crocker agreed with Hopkins, but added that "the truth is ... they are getting smart."[86] The CPRR's cheap labor force was becoming more difficult to exploit, and concerns over their strike (and demands) spread not only through the company's management but throughout California and the West.

Charles Crocker confronted a group of "leading chinamen" and informed them he would choose to stop work rather than pay a cent over thirty-five dollars. After similar threats failed, the "Big Four" panicked at the repercussions of the once "placid" Chinese agitating for workers' rights. Their solution involved a man named Yates, who was in Washington promoting an idea that would utilize the Freedmen's Bureau and enlist African Americans to, in Edwin Crocker's words, "inundate this state & Nevada with laborers" and drive down wages. Yates shared his idea with Stanford, who found it intriguing and asked his associates to consider the plan. By this time the striking workers' demands had increased to forty-five dollars per month. Hopkins, agreeing with Crocker and Stanford, noted that "a Negro labor force would tend to keep the Chinese steady, as the Chinese have kept the Irishmen quiet."[87] The Yates plan never materialized, but Charles Crocker had another solution. He prohibited Chinese labor agents from supplying their workers with goods and provisions—and it proved brutally effective. The most famished strikers agreed to return to work, but the steadfast vowed violence against them. Crocker stepped in to protect any workers who crossed the picket line, promising that "his men would shoot down any man that attempted to do the laborers any injury." He even had "the sheriff and posse come up to see that there was no fighting."[88]

If the threat of starvation and lethal violence effectively terminated the strike, the installment of new Chinese work gangs eliminated any reoccurrence. A few weeks later Edwin Crocker wrote that "there is a rush of Chinamen on the work. . . . Most of the fresh arrivals from China go straight up to the work. It is all life and animation on the line."[89] In the meantime, brother Charles brimmed with pride as he addressed a large gathering of white workers and dignitaries at a Fourth of July celebration. Crocker recalled his encounter with the striking Chinese, turned it into an object lesson, and embellished, "Says I—John, Chinaman no make laws for me; I make laws for Chinamen. You sell for $35 a month, me buy; you sell for $40 a month and eight hours a day, me no buy."[90]

Despite being transplanted to a new and unfamiliar transportation frontier, the shrewd Central Pacific construction workers knew enough about American labor practices to try and exploit a scarcity of workers on the line. Though their strike did not succeed, it demonstrated their wherewithal, tenacity, and ability to defend their rights and claim dignity as builders of American progress. Still, the light at the end of the railroad tunnel was dim for Chinese workers, as moving up the pay or skill ladder was rarely an option for these "cheap" and "unskilled" laborers.

Nevertheless, Chinese immigrants, according to company officials, were perfectly suited for strenuous railroad labor in the rugged Sierras, where the Central Pacific would spend nearly four years engaged in continuous construction. But if the Chinese were remarkably efficient railroad builders, they also looked, talked, behaved, and spent their leisure time much differently than other railroad workers. Contemporaries noted that they were a strange, divisive, and "mongrel" people.[91] Moreover, their claims to manhood were bitterly contested by workers and capitalists alike.

For Americans and Europeans, both of whom carried ideological baggage—lined with ideas of race, class, and gender—as they trekked westward before and after the Civil War, the Chinese became a common foe, an "indispensable enemy" who would unite whites for generations.[92] Cultural commentators depicted California's Chinese immigrants as "sojourners," temporary migrants who came to America only to accumulate enough earnings to return to their native soil.[93] An editorial in the *San Francisco Real Estate Circular* spoke to this notion. According to the writer, comparisons between Irish and German immigration and the Chinese sojourners were "absurd," for "the former make their homes here, buy farms and homesteads, are of the same general race, and [are] buried here after death," whereas the Chinese "come for a season only . . . do not settle or make homes, and not one in fifty of them is married." (The Irish, in particular, had seemingly come a long way since their days on the canal.) Moreover, the writer noted that the Chinese "women are all suffering slaves and prostitutes, for which possession murderous feuds and high-handed cruelty are constantly occurring." Conceding that they "give their labor" to California, the writer complained that, due to their clannishness, Chinese immigrants purchased goods only from their own merchants and were thus a drain on the economy. As for their labor, critics pointed to the Chinese weakness for accepting the lowest wages and accused them of engaging in "coolie" contract labor, rendering them no better than temporary "Asiatic slaves" who drove down white workingmen's wages.[94] Historian Richard White argues that "whites created the coolie long before any Chinese worker hoisted a rail or lifted a sledgehammer on the railroad." Playing up this most threatening subcategory of contract labor following the Civil War, critics of Chinese immigration submerged "what the Chinese were—free immigrant labor . . . beneath the invented and imagined coolie."[95] Still, California's Chinese assumed a peculiar space. They were alien yet necessary, simultaneously reviled by the state's citizens and preferred by its prominent railroad capitalists.

California representative Aaron A. Sargent appealed to his colleagues in the U.S. House of Representatives that the Chinese in his home state were "swarming millions of men, alien . . . to our blood and our language [and] . . . faith . . . liv[ing] upon a lower plane in the filthiest, meanest hovels, in unutterable stench."[96] Although the legal exclusion of this "dwarfish race of inferior beings" was several years away, Chinese workers on the Central Pacific provoked labor leaders to sound the tocsin for all white workers. In early 1869 Chicago's *Workingman's Advocate* characterized the crisis in this way:

> We warn workingmen that a new and dangerous foe looms up in the far west. Already our brothers of the Pacific have to meet it, and just as soon as the Pacific Railroad is completed . . . these Chinamen will begin to swarm through the rocky mountains like devouring locusts and spread out over the country this side. Men who can work for a dollar a day . . . are a dangerous element in our country. We must not sleep until the foe is upon us, but commence to fight him now. . . . In the name of the workingmen of our common country, we demand that our government forbid another Chinaman to set foot upon our shores.[97]

If railroad labor assessed the immigrants' manhood, anti-Chinese sentiments proved difficult to change despite the progress of building. Rather than becoming Americans through hard labor, their toil betrayed them and extended their distance from other workers. When Central Pacific crews pushed past Auburn, California, a visitor to the construction site commented to a crew of Irish workers that thirty-five dollars "is pretty good wages," to which one of them replied, "Yes, but begad if it wasn't for them damned nagurs we get $50 and not do half the work."[98] Of course the "damned nagurs," in this case, were the Chinese, whose very presence thwarted Irish workers' quest for higher wages, as cheap labor blunted any efforts to win concessions from employers. Degraded workers were viewed as tools of their bosses and thus scarcely counted as men.

Food and drink were also symbolic of labor's divide, and one observer equated food, low wages, and primitive living conditions to un-Americanness. The Chinese, he argued, "being . . . well fed on a handful of rice, a little refuse pork, and desiccated fish, costing but a few cents a day, [and] lodged in a pigsty, they become affluent, according to their standard, on wages that would beggar an American."[99] Whereas the Central Pacific's Irish construction workers drank whiskey and unboiled, disease-ridden water while on the job,

FIGURE 11. *Chinese Camp, Brown's Station,* Nevada, ca. 1866–69. Photograph by Alfred A. Hart. Courtesy of the Library of Congress, Prints and Photographs Division, LC-DIG-stereo-1s00615, Washington, DC.

the Chinese hands preferred lukewarm tea after it had cooled from boiling pots. In the eyes of the Irish laborers, such a practice contradicted their view that masculine authority was closely related to alcohol consumption.[100] In addition, Irish workers interpreted the Chinese custom of hot baths after work as strikingly effeminate, for the "Chinamen" soaped themselves "like a woman," in "flower water," and emerged from the tub "smelling of perfume."[101] White workers' vision of themselves depended on those they loathed, and in these observations the Chinese appeared weak and without the virility required of railroaders. Yet the same behaviors Irish workers interpreted as cheap, delicate, and feminine, Chinese workers surely understood as hygienic, respectable, and sophisticated. Photographic evidence of Chinese construction camps reveal a semblance of orderliness on this chaotic and unforgiving railroad frontier (see figure 11). For the Central Pacific's Chinese "army of the High Sierra," becoming railroad men did not necessitate the mimicking of Anglo-American conventions of manhood. More than brute force, sweat, and risk, railroad labor required both physical and mental dexterity, strategy, discipline, and endurance.

Nonetheless, the days leading up to the Golden Spike ceremony offered an instance of the "yellow peril" to America. Rival Chinese work crews clashed, in what the *San Francisco Bulletin* reported on May 6, 1869, was a "Chinese Tong War." This "battle between two rival companies of Chinamen ... laborers of the See Yup and Teng Wo Companies" included "several hundred" combatants. The workers, noted the *Bulletin,* had been "idle at [Camp] Victory" in Rozel, Utah, for a number of days leading up to the skirmish. Apparently, this "row" had occurred after fifteen dollars due to one of the companies went unpaid. According to the editor, "After the usual braggadocio, both parties sailed in ... armed with every conceivable weapon. Spades were handled and crowbars, spikes, picks and infernal machines were hurled between the rank *[sic]* of the contestants. Several shots were fired and everything betokened the outbreak of a riot." Suddenly, labor boss James Strobridge, along with several of his Irish workers, rushed into the "melee" and, after receiving the help of "leading 'Chinamen' who were more peaceably disposed," restored order. One "Chinaman" was shot in this conflict, and, according to the *Bulletin,* "If this man dies, another encounter will certainly follow and much bloodshed will doubtless ensue."[102]

Despite the relative lack of violence among the Central Pacific's Chinese workers throughout the construction period, this conflict offered Californians a counterpoint to the American triumph that was to take place two days later. Framing the brawl as a "Tong War," the *Bulletin* conjured up images of reckless gangs and secret societies that engaged in illegal gambling and opium trades, most common in San Francisco's Chinatown. Whereas, for whites, such activity might evince a masculine solidarity, when associated with Chinese immigrants, it revealed an immoral and unmanly otherness.

Since it had been announced that the "last spike" would be driven on May 8, cities and communities throughout the country celebrated the transcontinental railroad prior to its official completion. In downtown Sacramento, Judge Crocker, the first to suggest the employment of Chinese workers and whose brother Charles had supervised the Central Pacific's construction, mounted a platform to address a massive and excited audience. Champagne glass in hand, Crocker offered a toast to "the greatest monument of human labor," which had rescued a railroad company and glorified a nation. He then sounded a discordant note in the otherwise harmonious celebration: "I wish to call to your minds that the early completion of this railroad we have built has been in large measure due to that poor, despised class of laborers called the Chinese—to the fidelity and industry they have shown."[103]

On the same day, at a rally in San Francisco, the featured speaker sounded a more popular note in commemorating the great highway of nations. According to Judge Nathaniel Bennett, toasts on this triumphant day were due to the efforts of native-born Californians. It was they who were

FIGURE 12. *Chinese Laying Last Rail*, Promontory Summit, Utah Territory, May 1869. The photograph shows an unknown Chinese worker in the middle of the frame (in baggy dress, straddling the ties, with a rail-laying tool), and another on the near left (in similar clothing, standing in between the ties). Photograph by Andrew Russell, H69.459.2426. Collection of the Oakland Museum of California.

"composed of the right materials, [and] derived from the proper origins." He continued, "In the veins of our people flows the commingled blood of the four greatest nationalities of modern days. The impetuous daring and dash of the French, the philosophical and sturdy spirit of the German, the unflinching solidity of the English, and the light-hearted impetuosity of the Irish, have all contributed each its appropriate share."[104]

Bennett ignored the Chinese, who remained invisible as they were to most Americans except when their uncivilized qualities merited condemnation. Thus, even before the last rail was laid and spike driven, Bennett recrafted this triumphant achievement along the lines of a superior race and culture. After all, he noted, "A people deducing its origins from such races, and condensing their best traits into its national life, is capable of any achievement."[105] His audience vigorously applauded this sentiment, regardless of the fact that being "capable of any achievement" and actually carrying it out were two different things.

At Promontory the men closest to the Chinese laborers knew better. Most of the Central Pacific's Chinese workers had been released from their duties in April as the rails neared Promontory, but those who remained witnessed a history they helped create. A surviving photograph depicts the Chinese performing last-minute work prior to the Golden Spike ceremony (see figure 12).

A reporter for the *San Francisco Newsletter* who witnessed the ceremony at Promontory recounted an occurrence that, while extraordinary, validated the manly and respectable efforts of the Central Pacific's Chinese workers. He noted that "J. H. Strobridge, when the work was all over, invited the Chinese who had been brought over from Victory [construction camp] . . . to dine at his boarding car." When the workers entered, "all the guests and officers . . . cheered them as the chosen representatives of the race which have greatly helped to build the road." It was, according to the *Newsletter*, "a tribute they well deserved and which evidently gave them much pleasure."[106] Some historians contend that this is the primary reason why the Chinese workers at Promontory do not appear in most of the postceremony Last Spike photographs taken by Andrew J. Russell and Charles Savage. In private, they celebrated the culmination of over four years of backbreaking labor, perhaps recalling how they dug a roadbed, blasted through solid rock, moved mountains, fastened ties, and laid track at such an amazing pace. These immigrant workers, though they did not look, speak, eat, or spend their leisure time in ways recognizable to their ostensible superiors, had earned respect as an army of courageous, industrious, and resilient men. The praise and honor of their bosses meant more than inclusion in a staged, hazy, and nationalistic photograph. Still, their absence at the celebration would render them invisible not only then, but to coming generations of Americans.

Following the ceremony in Utah and similar celebrations in cities and towns across the country, American opinion makers warned the nation's citizens that the Chinese threat had not yet disappeared. If Judge Bennett and other statesmen were content with simply ignoring the Chinese and their contribution to railroad progress, popular publications preferred to use fear in awakening Americans to the dangers the railroad had introduced. Artist W. L. Palin promptly reminded the country of the potential consequences of Chinese immigrants' success in building the transcontinental railroad in an 1869 illustration in *Harper's Weekly* (see figure 13). In *Pacific Railroad Complete* two licentious Chinese railroad workers confirmed Americans' greatest suspicions by claiming their reward for hard labor. Like blacks, these Chinese men ostensibly craved white women. Sexual power offered the immigrants' true equality and even manly superiority over native-born Americans. The repercussions of Chinese progress in America were thus frightening; they posed a threat to prevailing racial and sexual barriers.

FIGURE 13. *Pacific Railroad Complete, Harper's Weekly,* June 12, 1869. Illustration by W.L. Palin. Courtesy of the Bancroft Library, University of California, Berkeley, AP2.H3, 13:384.

Yet in the eyes of Americans, as suggested in a subsequent *Harper's Weekly* illustration by Thomas Nast, the achievement of the Chinese in building the railroad conferred neither manhood nor citizenship. Race had trumped labor, rendering the Chinese no more than "Asiatic slaves," indispensable enemies whom western American men subjugated to confirm their own masculine and racial superiority—a new *Pacific Chivalry* (see figure 14). If, as the illustration suggests, the lack of legal standing and "extra taxes" for "yellowjack" did not satisfy anti-Chinese Americans, perhaps racial violence would do the trick. Apparently, *Harper's* found no irony in violence against the workingmen who built America. The Central Pacific had tested these

PACIFIC CHIVALRY.
Encouragement to Chinese Immigration.

FIGURE 14. *Pacific Chivalry: Encouragement to Chinese Immigration, Harper's Weekly,* August 7, 1869. Illustration by Thomas Nast. Courtesy of the Bancroft Library, University of California, Berkeley, AP2.H3, 13:512.

immigrants in the masculine work of constructing a railroad and building a nation, yet regardless of their contribution, the Chinese imperiled the republic. Racial purity demanded that they be erased from American history and eventually denied access to the land of liberty.

Though it would take over a decade to enact federal legislation, calls for Chinese exclusion met a receptive audience following the completion of the transcontinental railroad. Conditions in California favored widespread fear, blame, and xenophobia, especially amid a bloated labor market and the fact that success in railroad building enabled the Chinese to expand into other industries seeking cheap labor. Consequently, native-born and Irish immigrant workers, labor organizations such as the (Irish-born) Denis Kearney–led Workingmen's Party of California, and members of both major political parties feared the Chinese and frequently blamed economic hardship on them. They argued that the Chinese had become a very real threat economically and culturally, and popular periodicals such as *Harper's* and San Francisco's *The Wasp* helped package this argument, in vivid illustrations, to the rest of the nation.[107]

In the post-Promontory period, popular travel writers, pictorial reporters, photographers, artists, and illustrators commemorated American progress

FIGURE 15. *Across the Continent: "Westward the Course of Empire Takes Its Way,"* 1868. Currier and Ives lithograph, drawn by Fanny Palmer. Courtesy of the Library of Congress, Prints and Photographs Division, LC-DIG-ppmsca-03213, Washington, DC.

and remembered those who created it. Historian Martha Sandweiss argues persuasively that photographers and artists, in particular, labored to produce work that could interest and appeal to an audience "hooked on dramatic narratives of western life." In effect, their craft became the storyteller's craft, and their images "became substitutes for firsthand experience." In addition to capturing visual evidence of the "divine blessings bestowed upon the American nation," these images presented Americans with evidence of "what they had, who they were, and what they could become."[108]

To be sure, Americans had been primed for celebrations of progress since the canal era, whether in speeches, parades, or printed narratives. Visuals of railroad progress only reinforced their sentiments. Pictorial journalism thus presented a new way to express an old yet influential tradition. The renowned Currier and Ives print *Across the Continent: "Westward the Course of Empire Takes Its Way"* anticipated this in 1868 when it reified the unfinished transcontinental railroad by juxtaposing tradition with the future and savagery with civilization and by linking railroad progress with empire (see figure 15). The Currier and Ives lithograph, drawn by Fanny Palmer, depicts a continental empire before the fact, imbuing it with meaning along the road's right-of-way. A steam locomotive carrying white passengers, perhaps including some tourists, both charts and quickens this "Course of Empire." To the left of the train, some passengers have joined a civilized American settlement characterized by education, industry, and agriculture, while others wave to passengers as the locomotive heads westward. Telegraph poles mark this new western town, well-dressed women signify its proper domestication, children frolic outside of a public school, and men clear trees to make way for expansion. Meanwhile, to the right of the train, a giant puff of smoke nearly engulfs two mounted Indian warriors, while in the distant background other Indians as well as buffalo retreat to the mountains. The iron horse overwhelms savage man and beast alike; a future Union Pacific president, Charles Francis Adams, echoed this when he wrote that "the Pacific railroads have settled the Indian question."[109] White Americans are active participants in this scene of progress, while Indians watch from the other side of the tracks as the locomotive pierces through their once-unspoiled land and steams into the seemingly empty West, the great wide open, its road extending forever.

Artists gave texture and meaning to the railroad progress about which proponents had waxed eloquently since midcentury. Isaac Guyer, who authored one of the first histories of Chicago, convinced his readers in 1862 that railroads "do wonders—they work miracles. They are . . . the pioneer, and van-guard of civilization." Adams, writing after the completion of the first transcontinental, described the railroad as "an enormous . . . incalculable force practically let loose suddenly upon mankind; exercising all sorts of influences, social, moral, and political; precipitating upon us novel problems which demand immediate solution; banishing the old before the new is half matured to replace it." Moreover, he credited it with "bringing the nations into close contact before yet the antipathies of race have begun to be eradicated," a claim worth charting in the work of America's leading pictorial periodicals following the completion of the East and West lines.[110] How did these sources incorporate work and race into their narratives of the railroad that supposedly bound the republic together?

To this end, the railroad stories and images in periodicals such as *Harper's Weekly* and *Frank Leslie's Illustrated Newspaper* offered far more than amusement for nineteenth-century Americans. With hundreds of thousands of subscribers and long shelf lives, these sources played on the hearts and minds, the fears and anxieties, of the nation's citizens.[111] Through the cultural medium of popular periodicals, Americans discovered and celebrated history just made. On the subject of the Pacific Railroad, Frank Leslie and his team of writers and illustrators carefully constructed a landscape of American progress. Chinese construction workers were drawn to fit national needs and attitudes.

Labor posed a particular problem for the writers and illustrators entrusted with the task of celebrating the landscape of progress. "Landscape," wrote Ralph Waldo Emerson, "has no owner," and the pure viewing of it is spoiled by economic factors, for "you cannot freely admire a noble landscape if laborers are digging in the field hard by." Moreover, Raymond Williams argued that "a working country is hardly ever a landscape," for "the very idea of landscape implies separation and observation." He claimed that the "real history" was much dirtier than the wonder, meaning, and pleasure of observed landscapes.[112] Whereas workers came to know nature through labor, day after day on the railroad, artists depicted it, in landscape form, in ways that suited other agendas.

In nineteenth-century America few transformations of the natural landscape evoked more wonder and pleasure than the completion of the transcontinental railroad. In crafting vivid images of the progress the railroad had generated, *Frank Leslie's Illustrated Newspaper* exacerbated the separation of physical production from cultural consumption that was a hallmark of industrializing America.[113] Through its images readers were encouraged to discover, remember, and celebrate the building of this unparalleled achievement as uniquely American. In doing so, they had to both reimagine history and forget it. The Central Pacific's Chinese construction workers were among the casualties of this process. Chinese immigrants were central to the portrayal of the road as an invention that physically transformed and "civilized" a wilderness and "annihilated space and time."[114] Yet landscapes of railroad progress functioned as a "dreamwork" of imperialism that distanced foreign, uncivilized, or unfortunate elements from the pageant of American history, much as the Currier and Ives print did with the Indians.[115] Sandweiss has documented how western images pictured indigenous peoples "largely to show that they would soon fade before the superior culture of the expanding United States."[116] Frank Leslie's team of illustrators depicted the Chinese in ways that evoke such an approach.

In late 1869 Frank Leslie asked his young illustrator Joseph Becker to make an unprecedented trip across the nation on a railway sketching tour. For the first time tourists could traverse the entire country on rails, and Becker had the privilege of being among the first in his profession to experience and convey this defining moment to the American public. It was history in the making. Yet, as Becker recalled in a 1905 interview for *Leslie's Weekly,* his real mission was to reach the Sierra Nevada and sketch the "celestials" as they worked on the Central Pacific Railroad:

> Mr. Leslie commissioned me to go to California to portray the Chinese who had come over in large numbers to build the Union Pacific Railway *[sic]*. These people were then a novel addition to our population, and Mr. Leslie planned a "scoop" on our competitors. My destination was kept a secret. I reached California in due time, [and] spent six weeks among the celestials, making many drawings.[117]

The illustrated Across the Continent series that resulted from Becker's 1869 trip was repeated in 1877 by Leslie himself and two other young "special artists," Harry Ogden and Walter Yeager, in *Across the Continent: The Frank Leslie Transcontinental Excursion.*[118] Both trips were celebrated media events and also produced some of the earliest illustrations of Chinese immigrants at work on the railroad. These illustrated transcontinental tours were self-conscious and patriotic productions that heralded the railroad as the paramount symbol of modernity and were remarkable for their quantity and diversity of illustrations and the breadth of territory covered.

In *Across the Continent: The Snow Sheds on the Central Pacific Railroad,* Becker crafts a scene in which the railroad's Chinese workers, most of whom are positioned a considerable distance from the tracks, appear stationary as they applaud the passing train as it rounds the Sierra mountainside (see figure 16). The Chinese-built snow sheds, crucial to the Central Pacific's ascent through the Sierra high country, were a remarkable achievement, as they guarded the railroad tracks from the heavy snow drifts that hampered both freight and passenger travel. While meticulously constructed, the snow sheds nevertheless required frequent maintenance from the Chinese workers when snowfall was so heavy that it caused the roof to settle at the crown of each shed. Becker trivializes their importance by angling the sheds away from the focal point of the illustration, the locomotive, which dominates the foreground and even appears too long for these hand-built structures, entering the second snow shed while the rail cars have not completely exited the previous shed.

Yet the most conspicuous feature of the illustration is the Chinese workers. As the train carves up the Sierras and emerges from the sheds, the Chinese, depicted in their baggy homespun garments with long queues dangling down their backs, offer their salutations. They look more like tour-

ACROSS THE CONTINENT.

FIGURE 16. *Across the Continent: The Snow Sheds on the Central Pacific Railroad, in the Sierra Nevada Mountains, Frank Leslie's Illustrated Newspaper,* February 5, 1870. Engraving from a sketch by Joseph Becker. Courtesy of the Bancroft Library, University of California, Berkeley, Robert B. Honeyman Jr. Collection of Early Californian and Western American Pictorial Material, BANC PIC 1963.002:0808-C.

ists than actual workers, though some carry tools. Several of the men lean on their shovels, while others doff their caps and wave in admiration. The nearest worker on the right appears stooped over, with his back bent; he and his colleagues are seemingly in awe of the locomotive that was, in reality, a common sight for them.

Another Becker illustration, *Railroad Pass with Chinese Workers,* is similarly indicative of how railroad progress distanced its immigrant workers and even rendered them invisible (see figure 17). The sketch incorporates a large group of Chinese construction workers, who resemble the swarming "army" to which company management and commentators often referred. To Central Pacific officials, the Chinese were movers of mountains, preparing the way for American progress. Becker's illustration challenges this notion. A couple of the laborers rush away from the coming train, while others at a more comfortable distance sit, stand, and gaze in the direction of the marvelous locomotive. Becker literally draws some of the Chinese workers

FIGURE 17. *Railroad Pass with Chinese Workers,* ca. 1869–70. Sketch by Joseph Becker. Courtesy of the Becker Collection, Boston, RR-JB-69–70–18.

into the bedrock of the mountain, as they vanish into—and become part of—the ancient wilderness landscape that the railroad has conquered. These immigrant workers are depicted as a static, archaic, and evocative reminder of the now-receding landscape, overwhelmed by the technological power and industrial velocity of railroad progress. In "annihilating space and time," the railroad annihilated its Chinese laborers.

True, the Chinese workers' presence in Becker's illustration suggests a role for them in the history of American progress, but the artist's careful positioning of these men—scurrying from the track, marveling at the locomotive, and symbolically engulfed by the ominous mountains—suggests their appropriate place in the pageant of American achievement. Becker transformed the Chinese workers from model agents of railroad progress to parts of the ancient landscape that the railroad had civilized. In this transformation of the landscape, the Chinese remain untamed, exotic relics of the past.

Following the second *Leslie* transcontinental excursion in 1877, artists Harry Ogden and Walter Yeager produced, among other illustrations and engravings, one depicting "the excursion train Rounding Cape Horn" (see

FIGURE 18. *Across the Continent: The Frank Leslie Transcontinental Excursion, Frank Leslie's Illustrated Newspaper,* April 27, 1878, 129. Engraving by Harry Ogden and Walter Yeager. Courtesy of the Bancroft Library, University of California, Berkeley, Robert B. Honeyman Jr. Collection of Early Californian and Western American Pictorial Material, BANC PIC 1963.002:0504-C.

figure 18). The engraving modifies, in interesting ways, an 1876 Carleton E. Watkins photograph of a similar title, *Rounding Cape Horn, CPRR* (see figure 19). Watkins's photograph looks southeast toward Kings Hill and captures this curve around the forbidding granite ridge, fifty-seven miles east of Sacramento, named to highlight the obstacle it presented to construction. Charles Crocker brought in several thousand Chinese workers to remove tons of rock through blasting that called for up to five hundred kegs of gunpowder per day.[119] Watkins captures the locomotive as it chugs around the ridge, from a platform overlooking the American River. The picture is no doubt staged, as travelers (perhaps dignitaries) on this excursion train pack the railroad cars, while employees stand atop three of the cars and to the side of the tracks in the distance.

Ogden and Yeager's engraving changed this scene considerably. Imbued with patriotic nostalgia, their caption notes that the scene is "at the head of the Great American Cañon, with a view of the South Fork of the American River, where gold was first discovered in 1848." Of course, both the American

FIGURE 19. *Rounding Cape Horn, CPRR, 1876*. Photograph by Carleton E. Watkins, n.s. 1112:13–1304u. Courtesy of the Phoebe A. Hearst Museum of Anthropology, University of California, Berkeley.

River and Cape Horn were of great significance to California's Chinese immigrants. They had long panned for gold on the river's south fork, and Cape Horn was the site of one of their most remarkable achievements in building the Central Pacific. In the Ogden and Yeager engraving, however, the railroad has transformed this old frontier into a new industrial and technological landscape, and the pioneering work of Chinese immigrants is but a dim memory.

The massive locomotive dominates this new—and uniquely American—landscape of progress in the Sierra Nevada, and although the Chinese were intimately linked to the history of this place, the engraving depicts them as inert observers. They built this railroad landscape with their own hands, but its past (and present) is not theirs to claim. As a group, the Chinese workers appear stationary as the train thunders by, while the laborer in the middle offers a welcoming salute. Closing in on the group, a stick-wielding white foreman and his barking dog approach the worker nearest him, in the foreground, whose back is characteristically bent. The underlying message is apparent: the Chinese know their place. Moreover, in a cloud of dust and a puff of smoke, their role in the building of American progress had passed. Like illustrations of Native Americans, the Chinese are reflections of the past, not of the present or future.

Though they had raced the Union Pacific's Irish tracklayers to complete the railroad, in these illustrations the Chinese workers are depicted as stagnant and miniature compared to the natural environment they had tamed. These and other popular sketches of the railroad often render the Chinese as part of the passing scenery, no different than the rocks, hills, and rivers traversed by the speeding train. Nearly always positioned at a distance from the rails and locomotives, Chinese workers are passive observers, seemingly in awe of Yankee ingenuity and the industrial progress they helped create. Celebratory observations of the railroad thus produced a landscape of progress that rendered its un-American workers invisible and relatively useless. Whether or not these images transformed Americans' "collective imaginings" of the West, they have, over time, shaped America's "master narrative" of western history and its peoples.[120]

Yet these nameless armies of Chinese immigrants built the Central Pacific Railroad, and in doing so often outperformed their American and European counterparts. The Chinese presence on the railroad frontier had in fact elevated the social and economic status of Irish immigrant workers, who once held a similar, lowly place in the American mind. In the decade following the completion of the transcontinental railroad, a son of Erin, Denis Kearney, would lead a workingmen's movement to remove the Chinese from the country.[121] Yet by sweat of brow and strain of muscle the Chinese helped create American progress, an accomplishment that their superiors on the Central Pacific frequently acknowledged. In the process these "Celestials" proved their worth as a tireless, disciplined, patient, and potent workforce—as model laborers on the railroad frontier.

Digging, climbing, hacking, drilling, and blasting their way through the rugged Sierra Nevada to Utah, these men proved their masculinity through their arduous labor on the transcontinental railroad. The Chinese demonstrated that they were not a homogenous mass of pack animals or pests, despite popular stereotypes. They competed for jobs with rivals from other Chinese labor companies and even fought one another on occasion. Not only did they sacrifice life and limb in the name of western development and American progress, but their actions on the railroad proved that they were neither submissive nor ignorant of democratic traditions. To this end, Chinese construction workers struck for higher pay, reduced hours, and better conditions. They also demanded dignified burials, when possible, for their countrymen who perished while building the railroad.

But during and after the completion of the transcontinental railroad in 1869, writers, politicians, and fellow workers aggressively distanced Chinese immigrant workers as strange, uncivilized, immoral, unmanly, and devious foreigners. Artists and illustrators went even further and portrayed them as static, archaic, and invisible. In an ultimate paradox of American progress, the Chinese were alienated from the railroad and nation they helped build. As men and bearers of progress, the Chinese were denied, moved off the tracks of civilization as the railroad carried true Americans to their golden mountains.

SIX

End-of-Track

REFLECTIONS ON THE HISTORY OF IMMIGRANT
LABOR AND AMERICAN PROGRESS

> The case is no longer that of a single community pressing for an avenue through vast tracts of uninhabited wildernesses, to a tenantless harbor upon the unpeopled coast, but that of the united longings of two great communities, composed of a people of the same blood, race and origin, bound together by a national tie and linked in a common destiny.
>
> *GOLDEN ERA* (San Francisco), January 29, 1860

> Our camp was made up of a far different class of workmen. The Utah work, east of Ogden, was done by Mormons, who were law-abiding, conscientious and peace-loving men. They rested from all labors on the Sabbath Day and heeded religious worship. And they also asked a blessing upon their food and closed ... with singing and prayer ... after a day of hard work.
>
> W. C. A. SMOOT, interview, 1923

IN HIS MEMOIRS GENERAL GRENVILLE M. DODGE, chief engineer of the Union Pacific Railroad, elaborated on two violent incidents that occurred between Ogden and Promontory Summit, Utah Territory, in April 1869, as the rival companies inched closer to the "wedding of the rails." The Union Pacific and Central Pacific, Dodge noted,

> Each ... graded a line, running side by side, and in some places one line was right above the other. The laborers upon the Central Pacific were Chinamen, while ours were Irishmen, and there was much ill feeling between them. Our Irishman were in the habit of firing their blasts in the cuts without giving warning to the Chinamen on the Central Pacific working right above them. From this cause several Chinamen were severely hurt. Complaint was made to me by the Central Pacific people, and I endeavored to have the contractors bring all hostilities to a close, but for some reason or other, they failed to do so.[1]

A few days later, in retaliation, Dodge stated that "the Chinamen, appreciating the situation, put in what is called a 'grave' on their work, and when the Irishmen right under them were all at work, let go their blast and buried several of our men."[2] Matter-of-factly reporting this outburst of racial violence, Dodge reinforced popular stereotypes of the unskilled immigrants to whom the title of his memoirs, *How We Built the Union Pacific Railway,* most certainly did not refer. Wielding his authority as chief engineer, Dodge confirmed bloodshed between these cultural inferiors as indicative of the perils of progress. Moreover, such violence was ostensibly inherent to the foreign workers, who were ruthless and uncivilized and, in the end, posed a danger to this noble American achievement. The Chinese workers, as he noted, appreciated the chance to inflict violence on their rivals.

The problem is that these skirmishes never occurred. The Central Pacific's Chinese immigrants never graded "side by side" with the Union Pacific's Irish laborers, and nearly all the parallel grading in the vicinity of Promontory was completed by Mormon crews that subcontracted for both companies and did not hire Chinese workers. Dodge, who was actually in Washington, DC, for most of 1869 (representing Iowa's Fifth Congressional District in Congress), helped perpetuate this notion of ethnic and labor warfare. Written forty years after the completion of the transcontinental railroad, his account is not corroborated by Union or Central Pacific correspondence, contractors' reports, telegraphs, telegrams, or any credible newspapers.[3]

Instead, Dodge found inspiration in a thrilling, sensationalist source, one of the most popular periodicals of the era: *Harper's Weekly.* In its May 29, 1869, edition, only weeks after the Golden Spike ceremony, *Harper's* published an illustration with the caption, "Work on the last mile of the Pacific Railroad—mingling of European with Asiatic laborers" (see figure 20). The illustration depicts a mindless scene of racial violence, including the very "blasts" and "graves" Dodge recounted in his memoirs.[4] It actually appears to be a gross exaggeration of an 1867 photograph, by Alfred A. Hart, of Chinese workers near the "Summit Tunnel," tunnel number 6, in the Sierra Nevada (see figure 21). The implication in the *Harper's* account is that even as the transcontinental railroad neared completion, it had not civilized its immigrant workers. They still despised one another to such an extent that they had engaged in reckless bloodshed and even delayed and endangered the "great national project." In the accompanying column, the *Harper's* writer referred to the crews as a "medley of Irishmen and Chinamen," who were busy constructing the "last line" of the transcontinental railroad. The scene, according

FIGURE 20. *Work on the Last Mile of the Pacific Railroad—Mingling of European with Asiatic Laborers, Harper's Weekly,* May 29, 1869. Sketch by A. R. Waud. Courtesy of the Bancroft Library, University of California, Berkeley, fF850.W18, 13: 348.

FIGURE 21. *Laborers and Rocks, Near Opening of Summit Tunnel,* 1867. Photograph by Alfred A. Hart. Courtesy of the Library of Congress, Prints and Photographs Division, LC DIG-stereo-1500510, Washington, DC.

to the writer, suggested that "the very laborers upon the road typify its significant result, bringing Europe and Asia face to face, grasping hands across the American Continent."[5] Yet, while "grasping hands," they apparently murdered one another.

Despite this sensationalism, the accounts from *Harper's* and Dodge served important purposes. While focusing national attention on the railroad, they distanced the immigrant laborers whose work completed it. Through the perceived violence of these "others," they claimed the railroad for civilized, white America. Thus, if the *Harper's Weekly* story was entirely invented, native-born Americans did not see it as a fabrication. Instead, it offered a history as recalled and reclaimed by its rightful beneficiaries. Through the negative stereotyping of immigrant railroad workers, Americans could imagine them as a temporary distraction—a sidelight—to the story of national progress. Interpreting the *Harper's* dramatization as a historical fact, Americans celebrated, remembered, and reimagined the railroad. The Chinese, the Irish, and the Mormons were the voiceless, invisible beasts of burden. If once necessary, they were easy to distance from the act of progress and the value of independent, white labor. But their critical role in building the American West made these "others" impossible to merely discard. The Chinese, in particular, elicited danger to an extent that demanded work on several fronts, including the press, to convince red-blooded Americans to take a stand. The following cartoon served as an object lesson (see figure 22).

As Charles Crocker and James Strobridge revealed, by 1869 the Central Pacific's labor force consisted of roughly ten thousand men, of whom 90 percent were Chinese and 10 percent were Irish or American foremen.[6] Najia Aarim-Heriot argues that in addition to the work performed, another noteworthy aspect of construction was that the hiring of Chinese workers *did not* displace white workers, who not only abhorred "dangerous and dirt-shoveling" work but were provided supervisory opportunities on the railroad largely because of the thousands of men willing to shovel. Similar to transportation frontiers in Indiana and Illinois, in the Far West, native-born whites denigrated labor that stripped citizens of manly honor and independence—work that compromised American personhood according to the nation's founding precepts. They preferred to give orders, not dig ditches, and they knew that American society honored those who commanded and led. However, in the previous chapter I underscore anti-Chinese arguments that played on fears that immigrants who accepted cheap wages monopolized America's labor market, taking white jobs. These arguments,

FIGURE 22. *The Great Fear of the Period, That Uncle Sam May Be Swallowed by Foreigners: The Problem Solved*, ca. 1860–69. In scene 1 an Irish immigrant has the head of Uncle Sam in his mouth and a Chinese immigrant has the feet in his mouth. They consume Uncle Sam in scene 2, and in the final scene the Chinese immigrant consumes the Irish immigrant. Railroads crisscross the nation on the landscape in the distant background. San Francisco: White and Bauer. Courtesy of the Library of Congress, Prints and Photographs Division, LC-DIG-pga-03047.

while influential, were as empty in the nineteenth-century American West as they are in today's nation.

The paucity of evidence on white workers' reactions to the Chinese strike on the Central Pacific Railroad in 1867 is surprising in some respects, but not if we consider that the Chinese didn't displace whites in the first place. Their bargaining efforts were confined to their own peer group and revealed organization, self-determination, and strength in numbers. Certainly, at that time as well, white workers who preferred mining to railroad labor had already moved on to Nevada's Comstock Lode. Readers will recall that Charles Crocker's decision to employ Chinese workers on the Central Pacific came on the heels of a labor crisis. As early as 1864, the railroad's white labor-ers had joined an exodus to the newly discovered quartz and silver mines in neighboring Nevada. Unskilled construction labor on the Central Pacific had become, in many respects, the preserve of Chinese immigrants. By 1870, when the "Chinese problem" had attracted a wider audience, events further accelerated in California to make race, immigration, and wage labor a cor-nerstone of a white workingmen's movement, which sought to expel the Chinese from the workplace and the country.[7]

Yet when we chart the movement of that same group of Chinese strikers, 1,100 of them, to be sure, to Virginia City, Nevada, after the completion of the transcontinental railroad in May 1869, white resistance reemerges.[8] That summer, William Sharon, a Nevada agent for the Bank of California with an interest in loaning money for silver mining operations, hired these Chinese workers to build a railroad into Virginia City. Their work on the Central Pacific had impressed Sharon, who would later represent Nevada as a U.S. senator, and he had failed to employ whites to perform the same. Members of the Virginia City and Gold Hill Miners' Unions bristled at Sharon's plan. In a July 7 notice in the *Gold Hill Daily News*, they condemned the Chinese workers and warned that "Capital has decreed that Chinese shall supplant and drive hence the present race of toilers," apparently predict-ing that the Chinese railroaders would soon seek mining work. The notice continued,

> Can we compete with a barbarous race, devoid of energy and careless of the State's weal? Sunk in their own debasement, having no voice in government, how long would it be ere ruin would swamp the capitalist and poor man together? ... We appeal to the working men to step to the front and hurl back the tide of barbarous invaders.[9]

The miners unions' condemnation of the Chinese as simultaneously "bar-barous" and "devoid of energy" was a contradiction in terms, yet thoroughly gendered and racialized. The timing was awful, as well, for earlier that month Chinese had just completed the nation's most remarkable feat of labor. The Chinese had proven themselves as capable workers and had also demonstrated their capacity for collective action during the 1867 railroad strike, when they put down their tools and demanded higher pay, an eight-hour day, and a choice over the selection of foremen. Yet when these men had nearly finished building the railroad to Virginia City in July 1869, three hundred white unionists marched, in military formation, to the end-of-track and ejected the

Chinese from their tents. The Comstock unions then demanded that Sharon sign an agreement that prohibited the employment of Chinese workers within the town limits of Virginia City and Gold Hill. Upon signing the agreement, Sharon reassured the protesters that "we want miners and not Chinamen. They have no interest in this country . . . and we can only employ them at menial service, inferior occupations, railroad grading, and that sort of thing."[10]

The national importance of internal improvements, and the notion that canals and railroads were the ultimate symbols of American progress, did not begin or end with the transcontinental railroad. The idea of an integrated transportation network was in fact older than the American republic. In 1770, George Washington of Virginia proposed a donation to improve the navigation of the Potomac River, the results of which, he promised, would create a "channel of commerce" for "the trade of a rising empire."[11] When John C. Calhoun, Henry Clay, and a new generation of nineteenth-century statesmen pushed for federal support for canals and railroads, they too envisioned vital and patriotic projects that would transform nature, civilize a wilderness, and, in Calhoun's words, "bind the Republic together . . . [and] conquer space."[12]

Historians have revealed the divisiveness, sectionalism, corporate and personal greed, political logrolling, and constitutional dilemmas that this quest for internal improvements produced.[13] Yet modern scholars, like nineteenth-century American statesmen, have ignored a deeper dilemma, a more troublesome paradox, which lay at the core of transportation projects: the un-American builders of progress and the communities of contestation that their work produced. When the voices clamoring for improvements quieted and the actual construction commenced, it was conflict, not community, that defined these projects.

The Americans who designed, promoted, managed, and helped finance internal improvements did so in a country built on the backs of the poor, both slave and free. Statesmen of this era, regardless of region, were accustomed to the existence of a permanent, dependent, and racially demarcated labor force that carried out the important project of nation building. The earliest artificial waterways, including George Washington's beloved Potomac Canal, were heavily reliant on forced immigrant and slave labor; throughout the antebellum period, slaves, free blacks, and convicts joined European immigrants in creating American progress.[14] Although the canals and railroads in this study did not utilize the labor of slaves or free blacks, the proximity of their armies of progress to labor that resembled slavery was not lost on contemporary observers. South Carolina senator James Henry Hammond argued that these transient "hirelings" were no different than slaves, for they too were "the very mud-sill of society":

> In all social systems there must be a class to do the menial duties, to perform the drudgery of life . . . [a] class requiring but a low order of intellect and but little skill. . . . Such a class you must have, or you would not have that other class[,] which leads to progress, civilization, and refinement. It constitutes the very mud-sill of society. . . . And you might as well attempt to build a house in the air, as to build either the one or the other, except on this mud-sill. Fortunately for the South, she found a race adapted to that purpose. . . . We . . . call them slaves. . . . I will not characterize that class [in] the North by that term; but you have it; it is there; it is everywhere; it is eternal.[15]

Canal and railroad companies, abdicating any moral responsibility, used contractors as middlemen on the frontiers of transportation labor, authorizing them with the power to hire and fire, set wages and hours, and institute disciplinary measures. This decentralization of labor-management relations made the daily work of building canals and railroads, though not slavery, particularly brutal and oppressive.

The hard work of non-American laborers spawned creative responses on the part of states undertaking massive transportation projects. How to celebrate a glorious American achievement built by men who, at best, were not considered fully American? This question lay at the heart of the paradox of progress. An early strategy was revealed at an 1825 celebration of the completion of New York's famous Lockport locks, where a capstone hailed "that these works of internal improvement were achieved by the spirit and perseverance of REPUBLICAN FREE MEN."[16] It mattered little that the Irish did not fit this vision. That, of course, was the point of the celebration.

Following the success of the Erie Canal, statesmen in Indiana and Illinois carried forward the banner of progress to the antebellum frontier. Overtaken by "canal mania" in the 1830s and 1840s, Hoosiers and Illinoisans trumpeted their canals as the nation's most superior. To build them, they enlisted a moving army of Irish immigrants. Canal officials searched far and wide for able-bodied construction workers, luring them from County Cork and County Longford in Ireland, from Canada, and from neighboring transportation projects in America. Thus, in addition to laying the groundwork for the development of American capitalism, canals and similar projects linked local demand with far-flung labor markets, often transatlantic in character—a trend that continues throughout today's economy. The results were impressive. Despite a national financial panic in 1837 and unending cycles of abysmal weather, fatal illnesses, injuries, death, and desertion, the Wabash & Erie Canal was the nation's longest, and the Illinois & Michigan Canal transformed Chicago from a muddy trading post into the "Gateway City" of the "Great West."[17]

Like New York, Indiana and Illinois found it more practical and worthwhile to imagine the canal as a product of native-born American labor. Celebrations were designed to produce such an effect, as were explanations of canal and railroad progress as simply inevitable. Chicago, more than any other western frontier, straddled American progress in its close connection to the canals and railroads, which were its ultimate symbols. It took twelve years to build the Illinois & Michigan Canal, yet in 1847, as the canal neared completion, dignitaries met in Chicago at the national River and Harbor Convention to salute the I&M management and, before a single rail was laid, celebrate the coming of the Iron Horse. Jesse B. Thomas, the former Illinois attorney general and state Supreme Court justice, noted that railroads would "at once, *and by magic*" revolutionize Chicago's "condition and prospects."[18] When the Illinois Central and other railroads had crisscrossed the state, Isaac Guyer memorialized them as "talismanic wands [with] a charming power." Moreover, he argued, "They do wonders—they work miracles. They are better than laws; they are essentially, politically, and religiously—the pioneer, and van-guard of civilization."[19] Neither of the men mentioned the immigrant builders of such progress because they were irrelevant. Joining like-minded colleagues in encouraging Congress to fund a national system of internal improvements, they pointed to the inevitability of such progress as part of America's manifest destiny. It was "by magic" that these canals and railroads transformed the country, and fittingly so. They were an American birthright.

At the same time, a distancing of Irish immigrant workers took place. As Irish construction laborers endured the daily hell that was canal and railroad building in the Midwest, native-born Americans clung to beliefs and narratives that justified the subordination of this "drinking, sweating, dying mass."[20] The Irish were a race apart, disease-carrying, immoral, drunken, clannish, violent, and "papist," legally eligible but wholly unfit for citizenship. Even their bodies were marked as strange and inhuman, as the immigrants appeared "brutish," "low-browed," and "simian."[21] Moreover, these workers were a homogenous mass of "Canal Irish," stuck in a "wretched" line of work because they "neglect[ed] the more useful cultivation of the soil, which would, at once, make them independent . . . respectable" and more American.[22]

Few Americans opposed this timely employment of Irish immigrants on the nation's waterways and roads. In fact, nearly every major transportation project of the nineteenth century suffered from the want of a more abundant labor force. The "Heroes of the Emerald Isle," as one Chicago editor labeled them, engaged in a system that, at times, seemed as harsh as slavery, though it was enhanced with the advent of monthly wages.[23] Still, according to native-born citizens, these were "savage" and "repulsive" Irishmen. Observers claimed that they were "drunken, dirty, indolent, and riotous" and "objects of dislike and fear" in every "neighborhood [where] they congregate in large numbers."[24]

In the face of such prejudices that characterized the midwestern transportation frontier, Irish workers turned arduous and dangerous labor, unpredictable wages, and oppressive conditions into badges of manly honor. Though not recognized—legally or culturally—as American citizens, this army of progress carved out an aggressive manhood from the depths of the muck in which they toiled. Indiana's Irish canallers used violence, grueling labor, protests, and drinking as outward signs of manhood, which they felt earned them the same respect as any native-born worker. Pressuring their bosses to provide or tolerate alcohol on the job, these immigrants sought and performed a self-identification as fearless and formidable Irish workingmen. Beyond beasts of burden, they saw themselves as rough yet worthy builders of progress.

Canallers' masculinity had an oppositional quality as well. When Chicago's luminaries staged a groundbreaking ceremony for the Illinois & Michigan Canal, a crew of Irish workers sabotaged it, hurling rocks as they protested their exclusion from a pageant made possible by their sweat and blood. Confronted with an unyielding labor arrangement, meager wages, denied payments, dishonest contractors, and the "closed fist" of frontier capitalism, Irish construction workers challenged this system head-on. Canallers abandoned work sites, wrecked projects for which they had not been paid, and threatened their coworkers in the hope of dominating the work. Demonstrating their knowledge of republican traditions, Irish workers made use of strikes, petitions, political favors, and information networks that singled out the contractors and canals that promised a decent living. When they squared off in violent outbursts against rival Irish crews, transferring their native feuds to a new environment, canallers belied the notion that they were a faceless mass. On the canal frontier these builders of American progress were nonetheless casualties of the nation's experiment in the expansion of free labor, often "delv[ing] . . . fourteen hours per day for the bare necessities of physical life."[25] Yet their tireless work in hand-carving an artificial waterway through clay, rock, and muck and enduring injuries, illness, and death had earned them a measure of self-respect—a small piece of this progress, of their own and the nation's history.

In the Mountain West, the Union Pacific and Central Pacific railroads became part of the pioneer narrative in Americans' conquest of nature, a nationalistic civilizing of the wilderness that was the trans-Mississippi frontier. Mormons, however, had a pioneer history of their own and rallied around it to contest the civilization promised by the railroad's most vehement supporters. As part of the only settled community to engage—en masse—in unskilled railroad construction, Mormons came closest to approximating the notion that internal improvements were the product of white men, of farmers—independent "republican free men"—working overtime to build the American dream. The problem, however, was that the Mormons were not considered Americans. Whether Mormons were native- or foreign-born, Americans believed them incapable of citizenship and without character. Like the Irish and Chinese, they were uncivilized "others," the antithesis of American progress.

As the tracks neared Utah, Mormon rhetoric suggested that they were indeed laboring for American citizenship. Faced with an onslaught of attacks on their religious beliefs and practices, Mormons interpreted railroad labor as an opportunity to surmount national prejudices and discredit accusations of defiant isolationism. Anti-Mormon commentators thought otherwise and argued that the Pacific Railroad would signal the end of "Mormondom" and cut the "loathsome ulcer" of polygamy out of American society.[26] Nonetheless, a closer examination reveals just how deeply Mormons contested both the goals and consequences of railroad progress. In working on the railroad, the Mormons were not merely groveling for scraps at the table of Americanness. Instead, they appropriated this opportunity to "bind the Republic together" into a contest to demonstrate the moral superiority of their men and to build and strengthen their holy community. A Mormon-American manhood, chiseled in the canyons of the Wasatch Mountains, emphasized hard work, faith, righteousness, and permanent settlement against the backdrop of the "hell on wheels" that allegedly permeated the construction camps of the Union Pacific and Central Pacific railroads.

On this wageworkers' frontier Mormons thus crafted an alternate iteration of western masculinity. Celebrating the temperance and morality of
their construction camps in Echo and Weber Canyons, Mormons attacked
alcohol use—a central prop of immigrant workers' masculinity—and transformed it into uncivilized and unmanly behavior. Not only were Mormon
"boys" superior railroad workers; they were the core of a virtuous people who
did not seek, nor require, "civilization" in the form of immoral, transient, and
heathen immigrant "company men." On the railroad, contact with the
"other" bolstered the resolve of Mormon communities and clarified their
ideas about proper manhood and productive progress.

Mormon construction work alone, however, failed to eradicate the negative attention on their religious practices, namely polygamy, which rendered
them uncivilized outcasts in the minds of countless Americans. On this
point the federal government would not budge. The Edmunds-Tucker Act of
1887 prohibited the practice of polygamy, punished offenders with a fine
of up to $800 and a five-year imprisonment, and disincorporated the Church
of Jesus Christ of Latter-day Saints and the Perpetual Emigration Fund on
the grounds that they fostered this reviled practice. Among other stipula-
tions, the act also replaced local judges with federally appointed ones, disen-
franchised women (who had been granted suffrage by the Territorial legislature in 1870), and authorized the federal government to confiscate all church
properties. In the 1890 Manifesto, church president Wilford Woodruff
advised Mormons against entering into any marriage prohibited by the federal government, which paved the way for statehood six years later. Tracing
ideas about whiteness and Americanism from the nineteenth century to
today's vantage point, the historical arc of Mormonism is nothing short of
remarkable. Historian W. Paul Reeve frames it quite well in the conclusion
of *Religion of a Different Color*: "from not white to too white."[27]

Numbering between twelve thousand and fifteen thousand, the Central
Pacific's Chinese workers were the most numerous group of railroad builders
and yet arguably the least visible. Their employment was a test to determine
whether race would prove as a barrier to achieving manhood on the railroad
and, by extension, in working-class society. Without them, the transcontinental railroad would have remained only a dream, but their hard work and
endurance paid the nation great dividends. As they conquered the Sierra
Nevada and guided the Central Pacific to the fame of a nation and the fortune of the world, company officials praised the "industry" and "fidelity" of
the Chinese as the single "greatest monument of human labor."[28]

Yet it was not enough. In the end, their "inferior" race proved the most difficult obstacle to overcome along the right-of-way of American progress. Opponents attacked them as enemy outsiders, or "sojourners," whose cheap, transient labor drove down white workingmen's wages.[29] Perceived as weak in constitution and feminine in appearance, the Chinese were reviled for smoking opium and bathing after a hard day's work, as such practices rejected the grime and drunkenness that the railroad's Irish laborers deemed essential to workers' camaraderie. On the Central Pacific, labor did not prove manhood, as race trumped even the most staggering of human accomplishments. Despite the courageous efforts of these Chinese immigrants, their unyielding determination and sacrifice, and their willingness to accept the patriotic duty of working for low wages to rush the tracks to Utah, Americans celebrated the transcontinental railroad but distanced them and rejected their contribution.

Events accelerated in California in the 1870s, but with an ironic twist: the Chinese faced an exclusion campaign led by the state's Irish workers. The Workingmen's Party of California, imbued with the rhetoric of white masculinity and republicanism and bolstered by angry wage-working communities, played on white fears of Chinese labor and anxieties caused by the decade's economic depression. According to one historian, the Irish members of the Party transplanted what was "to them, a normal and acceptable kind of political behavior" to the streets of San Francisco.[30] Mayhem, arson, riots, and violence proved effective in California, if only temporarily. In 1882 the federal government enacted the Chinese Exclusion Act, one of the most significant restrictions on immigration in United States history, which prohibited the immigration of all Chinese laborers.

If physically building American progress was an arduous and detailed process, so too was celebrating it. For native-born Americans, to commemorate a successful transportation project was to reimagine, redraw, and rewrite the present and past. In the very act of celebrating canals and railroads, citizens and statesmen contested history. Some simply ignored the labor of immigrants, Mormons, and unskilled transients, while others imagined that it was Anglo-Americans "derived from the proper origins" who were solely responsible for progress.[31] Still others denied immigrant workers, such as the Chinese, by erasing them visually from the scene of triumph.

Once the canals teemed with packets and the final railroad spikes were driven, transient and immigrant construction workers collected whatever remained of their meager pay and took their skills elsewhere, often to other transportation frontiers. Workers continued to transform physically the nation's landscape, build progress, usher in civilization, and fill in seemingly empty spaces on the map of the American West. For native-born Americans, the original mission of canals and railroads to bind the country together, despite its ironies, had triumphed—insofar as their completion (and celebrations) suggested. Yet, in reality, someone had to construct these dreams with hands and muscles and suffer the consequences. Slaves, convicts, Irish immigrants, Mormons, and the Chinese were best suited for the othering that this experiment entailed. In feting and remembering American progress, citizens looked through these men and rendered them invisible.

James Campbell, the Central Pacific Railroad's superintendent of rolling stock, echoed this fact when he gave the final speech at the 1869 Golden Spike ceremony in Utah. With the western landscape transformed and American civilization at hand, he noted that while "philosophers would dream away a lifetime contemplating this scene, the officers of the Pacific Railroad would look and exclaim: 'We are a great people and can accomplish great things.'"[32] In commemorating the railroad, Americans dared not acknowledge what, or who, lay on the other side of the tracks.

NOTES

CHAPTER 1. CANALS, RAILROADS, AND
THE PARADOX OF PROGRESS

1. While the term originally appeared as "internal improvement"—applied broadly in the 1780s to refer to various programs to foster enlightenment, prosperity, and security among the people of the infant United States—gradually the plural "internal improvements" came to symbolize means of improvement that demanded public attention, such as roads, bridges, canals, schools, and technological innovations. Americans hailed these instruments of progress as physical proof of the wisdom of independence and the virtue of republicanism. John Lauritz Larson writes, "eventually the concept narrowed still further until it became synonymous with public works for improved transportation, because in the sprawling continental Union nothing threatened the mutual interests of citizens and their states like geographical isolation." *Internal Improvement: National Public Works and the Promise of Popular Government in the Early United States* (Chapel Hill: University of North Carolina Press, 2001), 3. Chapter title quotes John C. Calhoun, in Annals of Cong., 14th Cong., 2d Sess. (February 4, 1817), 854.

2. The best overview of this process can be found in Larson, *Internal Improvement*, 1–38.

3. More broadly, see John Lauritz Larson, "'Bind the Republic Together': The National Union and the Struggle for a System of Internal Improvements," *Journal of American History* 74, no. 2 (1987): 363–87; Larson, "A Bridge, a Dam, a River: Liberty and Innovation in the Early Republic," *Journal of the Early Republic* 7, no. 4 (1987): 351–75; and Carol Sheriff, *The Artificial River: The Erie Canal and the Paradox of Progress, 1817–1862* (New York: Hill and Wang, 1996).

4. On the "general utility" debate over public works, see Larson, "Bind the Republic Together," 363–87. Although this labor process has received little treatment outside of the colonial era, a number of scholars have addressed it more broadly and at times indirectly. See Dana D. Nelson, *National Manhood: Capitalist Citizenship and the Imagined Fraternity of White Men* (Durham, NC: Duke University

Press, 1998); Alexander Saxton, *The Rise and Fall of the White Republic: Class Politics and Mass Culture in Nineteenth-Century America* (New York: Verso, 1990); Jonathan A. Glickstein, *Concepts of Free Labor in Antebellum America* (New Haven: Yale University Press, 1991); and Eric Foner, *Free Soil, Free Labor, Free Men: The Ideology of the Republican Party before the Civil War,* rev. ed. (New York: Oxford University Press, 1995), x–xxix, 11–18. On canal workers in the antebellum northeast, see Sheriff, *Artificial River;* Peter Way, *Common Labour: Workers and the Digging of North American Canals, 1780–1860* (New York: Cambridge University Press, 1993); and Ronald E. Shaw, *Erie Water West: A History of the Erie Canal, 1792–1854* (Lexington: University of Kentucky Press, 1966).

5. Rogers M. Smith, *Civic Ideals: Conflicting Visions of Citizenship in U.S. History* (New Haven: Yale University Press, 1997), 2–3; Noel Ignatiev, *How the Irish Became White* (New York: Routledge, 1995); Nell Irvin Painter, *The History of White People* (New York: Norton, 2010).

6. Sheriff, *Artificial River,* 39–40.

7. *Baltimore Patriot and Mercantile Advertiser,* March 1, 1826. For a recent analysis of free and unfree labor on the Chesapeake & Ohio Canal, see Seth Rockman, *Scraping By: Wage Labor, Slavery, and Survival in Early Baltimore* (Baltimore: Johns Hopkins University Press, 2009).

8. Quotes from Walter Licht, *Working for the Railroad: The Organization of Work in the Nineteenth Century* (Princeton, NJ: Princeton University Press, 1983). See also Way, *Common Labour;* and James H. Ducker, *Men of the Steel Rails: Workers on the Atchison, Topeka and Santa Fe Railroad, 1869–1900* (Lincoln: University of Nebraska Press, 1983).

9. See Terry Coleman, *The Railway Navvies: A History of the Men Who Made the Railways* (Harmondsworth, Middlesex: Penguin, 1968).

10. See Way, *Common Labour;* and Jeffrey Marcos Garcilazo, "'Traqueros': Mexican Railroad Workers in the United States, 1870 to 1930" (PhD diss., University of California, Santa Barbara, 1995), 4.

11. David Montgomery, *The Fall of the House of Labor: The Workplace, the State, and American Labor Activism, 1865–1925* (New York: Cambridge University Press, 1987), 65–66. See chapter 2, "The Common Laborer," in particular.

12. Leonard Dinnerstein and David M. Reimers, *Ethnic Americans: A History of Immigration,* 5th ed. (New York: Columbia University Press, 2009), 31–32. See chapter 2 in particular.

13. For discussions of early America's immigrant labor narratives, see Way, *Common Labour;* Sheriff, *Artificial River,* 27–51; Matthew E. Mason, "'The Hands Here Are Disposed to Be Turbulent': Unrest among the Irish Trackmen of the Baltimore and Ohio Railroad, 1829–1851," *Labor History* 39, no. 3 (1998): 253–72; Roger E. Carp, "The Limits of Reform: Labor and Discipline on the Erie Canal," *Journal of the Early Republic* 10, no. 2 (1990): 191–219; David Montgomery, *Citizen Worker: The Experience of Workers in the United States with Democracy and the Free Market during the Nineteenth Century* (New York: Cambridge University Press, 1993); Ignatiev, *Irish Became White;* David Roediger, *The Wages of Whiteness: Race and the*

Making of the American Working Class, rev. ed. (New York: Verso, 1999); and Rockman, *Scraping By.*

14. This statistic excludes, of course, Indian-white warfare and white-on-Indian massacres.

15. Barbara Young Welke, *Recasting American Liberty: Gender, Race, Law, and the Railroad Revolution, 1865–1920* (New York: Cambridge University Press, 2001), 126.

16. Benjamin Harrison, "First Annual Message to Congress," December 3, 1889, reel 120, series 8, Speeches, 1878–1901, Benjamin Harrison Papers, Manuscript Division, Library of Congress, Washington, DC. See also Mark Aldrich, *Death Rode the Rails: American Railroad Accidents and Safety, 1828–1965* (Baltimore: Johns Hopkins University Press, 2006).

17. I have benefited greatly from the insights of Ned Blackhawk on the centrality of violence to the building of the American empire as well as on the importance of the West to that empire. See his *Violence over the Land: Indians and Empires in the Early American West* (Cambridge, MA: Harvard University Press, 2006).

18. Frederick Jackson Turner and John Mack Faragher, eds., *Rereading Frederick Jackson Turner: The Significance of "The Frontier in American History," and Other Essays* (New York: Holt, 1994). Other notable reassessments of Frederick Jackson Turner's "frontier thesis" include Kerwin Lee Klein, *Frontiers of Historical Imagination: Narrating the European Conquest of Native America, 1890–1990* (Berkeley: University of California Press, 1997); Richard W. Etulian, ed., *Does the Frontier Experience Make America Exceptional?* (Boston: Bedford/St. Martin's, 1999); and Patricia Nelson Limerick, *The Legacy of Conquest: The Unbroken Past of the American West* (New York: Norton, 1987).

19. Carlos A. Schwantes, "The Concept of the Wageworkers' Frontier: A Framework for Future Research," *Western Historical Quarterly* 18, no. 1 (1987): 39–55.

20. While this book begins in what is today considered the Midwest, Indiana and Illinois were part of the Old Northwest in the first half of the nineteenth century, and canals and railroads in these states passed through regions then known as the antebellum frontier.

21. For generations canal and railroad historians have promoted a rather traditional narrative. Their accounts narrate the conquest of space and time in a manner that would surely have delighted the organizers of the 1869 Golden Spike ceremony. Even some recent studies of the transcontinental railroad tend to privilege the far-sighted engineering prowess of company officials and fail to integrate the experiences of construction workers into the larger pageantry of American progress. In fairness, very few book-length, scholarly studies have been devoted to transportation workers. Some historians of railroad labor have moved beyond the "romance of the rails" narratives to explore the daily lives of railroad workers. Nonetheless, much of their scholarship concentrates exclusively on union activity. Not only had thousands of miles of track been laid in the American West prior to union formation, but railroad unions in general were primarily composed of skilled workers, not the ditchdiggers, rock blasters, road graders, and tracklayers who are the basis of this

study. For traditional studies of canals and railroads, see George Rogers Taylor, *The Transportation Revolution, 1815–1860* (New York: Rinehart, 1951); Carter Goodrich, *Government Promotion of American Canals and Railroads, 1800–1890* (New York: Columbia University Press, 1960); Madeline Sadler Waggoner, *The Long Haul West: The Great Canal Era, 1817–1850* (New York: Putnam, 1958); Robert Fogel, *Railroads and American Economic Growth* (Baltimore: Johns Hopkins University Press, 1964); and Oscar Winther, *The Transportation Frontier, 1865–1890* (New York: Holt, Rinehart, and Winston, 1964). More recently, see Ronald E. Shaw, *Canals for a Nation: The Canal Era in the United States, 1790–1860* (Lexington: University Press of Kentucky, 1990); Licht, *Working for the Railroad;* Shelton Stromquist, *A Generation of Boomers: The Pattern of Railroad Labor Conflict in Nineteenth-Century America* (Urbana: University of Illinois Press, 1987); John Hoyt Williams, *A Great and Shining Road: The Epic Story of the Transcontinental Railroad* (New York: Times Books, 1988); and Stephen Ambrose, *Nothing Like It in the World: The Men Who Built the Transcontinental Railroad, 1863–1869* (New York: Simon and Schuster, 2000).

22. Given that railroads have generated more historical scholarship than canals, it is important to point out two recent exceptions to the trends described earlier. These works, in particular, stand out as the definitive studies of the transcontinental railroad, and yet this book departs quite dramatically from both. Most notable is David Haward Bain's *Empire Express: Building the First Transcontinental Railroad* (New York: Penguin, 2000), an exhaustively researched, encyclopedic history of the Union Pacific and Central Pacific railroads. Bain charts these massive projects from start to finish, with business and political history, rather than labor and cultural history, taking center stage. Richard White's *Railroaded: The Transcontinentals and the Making of Modern America* (New York: Norton, 2012) is the latest study of the multiple transcontinental railroad lines in the United States and is thus not limited to the Union and Central Pacific. White offers a scathing critique of these companies, their officials and investors, and capitalism in a study that concentrates mostly on the late nineteenth century—well beyond the original construction period—and on the economic consequences of the transcontinentals. While he presents a stunning reinterpretation of the Gilded Age through railroad (mis)management, he focuses primarily on business and economic history and not on labor. In addition to Bain and White, Mark Fiege has written a superb chapter on the environmental history of the transcontinental railroad in *The Republic of Nature: An Environmental History of the United States* (Seattle: University of Washington Press, 2012), chap. 6. Richard Orsi's *Sunset Limited: The Southern Pacific Railroad and the Development of the American West, 1850–1920* (Berkeley: University of California Press, 2007), while well beyond the scope of this book, is widely regarded as the definitive study of the Southern Pacific and its influence on western settlement, water policy, agriculture, preservation, and conservation.

23. See Way, *Common Labour,* and Sheriff, *Artificial River.* Sheriff's study of the Erie Canal does not focus exclusively on construction workers but is even more relevant to this book because it incorporates the "invisible" army into broader narratives of American progress and anxiety. Though she gives more attention to boatmen

and longshoreman than to the actual canal builders, Sheriff juxtaposes the workers' "rough" culture of taverns, violence, and irreverence with attempts by canal sponsors and moral reformers to define the progress that the canal produced. Speeches, memorials, and toasts associated with the Erie's construction always referred to the dignitaries who "built" the canal but ignored the literal builders. The immigrants and strangers who constituted this "unskilled" class of wageworkers fell outside the scope of the republican vision; thus the canal promoters "tried to convince themselves, and others, that the class of degraded workers they came to scorn was a necessary—but temporary—evil" (50). Sheriff's critique of progress on the Erie Canal has far less to do with construction workers than my study. She draws on the work of William Cronon, who, in *Nature's Metropolis: Chicago and the Great West* (New York: Norton, 1991) and elsewhere, juxtaposes the influence of "first nature," the geography and prehuman environment, with "second nature," the environment shaped by human intervention. Sheriff builds on Cronon's interpretation to argue that New Yorkers, in light of the Erie Canal's success, began to interpret the manmade "artificial river" as "natural." Americans expected an abundance of transportation networks to facilitate the creation of a new empire. In the process, they equated manmade progress with national destiny. While not discounting Sheriff's intriguing arguments, I depart in a significant way by juxtaposing the image and ideal of American progress with the reality of immigrant labor.

24. Way, *Common Labour,* 3.

25. Though written in a previous generation, new labor history scholarship, following the work of E. P. Thompson (*The Making of the English Working Class* [New York: Vintage, 1966]), documents the artisan-to-worker transformation and emphasizes—at times even idealizes—forms of workers' agency, collective action, and class consciousness. This literature includes several classic studies such as Herbert Gutman, *Work, Culture, and Society in Industrializing America: Essays in American Working-Class and Social History* (New York: Vintage, 1977); Alan Dawley, *Class and Community: The Industrial Revolution in Lynn* (Cambridge, MA: Harvard University Press, 1976); Sean Wilentz, *Chants Democratic: New York City and the Rise of the American Working Class, 1788–1850* (New York: Oxford University Press, 1984); Bruce Laurie, *Artisans into Workers: Labor in Nineteenth-Century America* (New York: Hill and Wang, 1989); Montgomery, *House of Labor;* and Montgomery, *Citizen Worker.* Montgomery, it should be noted, critiques the new labor history model of class formation, agency, and consciousness by highlighting workers' struggles for control of the point of production. Nonetheless, he still concentrates on skilled craftsmen.

26. Way, *Common Labour,* 286; see 3–17 in general. While an excellent study and remarkably ahead of its time, Way's book is rather limited in its singular focus on capitalism's permutations and flaws as they related to canal building during North America's earliest industrial revolution.

27. Two notable studies that examine multiple (and moving) Wests include David R. Wrobel and Michael C. Steiner, eds., *Many Wests: Place, Culture, and Regional Identity* (Lawrence: University Press of Kansas, 1997); and, more recently,

Anne Hyde, *Empires, Families, and Nations: A New History of the North American West, 1800–1860* (Lincoln: University of Nebraska Press, 2011).

28. Nonetheless, a rich historical literature exists on the challenges faced by Irish immigrants in nineteenth-century America. See Kerby A. Miller, *Emigrants and Exiles: Ireland and the Irish Exodus to North America* (New York: Oxford University Press, 1985); Hasia R. Diner, *Erin's Daughters in America: Irish Immigrant Women in the Nineteenth Century* (Baltimore: Johns Hopkins University Press, 1983); Dale T. Knobel, *Paddy and the Republic: Ethnicity and Nationality in Antebellum America* (Middletown, CT: Wesleyan University Press, 1986); David M. Emmons, *The Butte Irish: Class and Ethnicity in an American Mining Town, 1875–1925* (Urbana: University of Illinois Press, 1989); Saxton, *Rise and Fall;* Ignatiev, *Irish Became White;* Roediger, *Wages of Whiteness;* Kevin Kenny, ed., *New Directions in Irish-American History* (Madison: University of Wisconsin Press, 2003); J.J. Lee and Marion Casey, eds., *Making the Irish American: History and Heritage of the Irish in the United States* (New York: New York University Press, 2007); David M. Emmons, *Beyond the American Pale: The Irish in the West, 1845–1910* (Norman: University of Oklahoma Press, 2010); and James R. Barrett, *The Irish Way: Becoming American in the Multiethnic City* (New York: Penguin, 2012).

29. See, for example, Alexander Saxton, *The Indispensable Enemy: Labor and the Anti-Chinese Movement in California* (Berkeley: University of California Press, 1971); Tomás Almaguer, *Racial Fault Lines: The Historical Origins of White Supremacy in California* (Berkeley: University of California Press, 1994); Way, *Common Labour;* Gunther Peck, *Reinventing Free Labor: Padrones and Immigrant Workers in the North American West, 1880–1930* (New York: Cambridge University Press, 2000); Mae M. Ngai, *Impossible Subjects: Illegal Aliens and the Making of Modern America* (Princeton, NJ: Princeton University Press, 2005); Moon-Ho Jung, *Coolies and Cane: Race, Labor, and Sugar in the Age of Emancipation* (Baltimore: Johns Hopkins University Press, 2006); and Rockman, *Scraping By.*

30. For studies of masculine "crises" and American masculinities, see Judith A. Allen, "Men Interminably in Crisis? Historians on Masculinity, Sexual Boundaries, and Manhood," *Radical History Review* 82 (Winter 2002): 191–207; Mark C. Carnes, *Secret Ritual and Manhood in Victorian America* (New Haven: Yale University Press, 1989); Ava Baron, "Technology and the Crisis of Masculinity: The Gendering of Work and Skill in the U.S. Printing Industry, 1850–1920," in *Skill and Consent: Contemporary Studies in the Labour Process,* ed. Andrew Sturdy, David Knights, and Hugh Willmott (New York: Routledge, 1992), 67–96; Michael Kimmel, *Manhood in America: A Cultural History* (New York: Free Press, 1996); Calvin Thomas, *Male Matters: Masculinity, Anxiety, and the Male Body on the Line* (Urbana: University of Illinois Press, 1996); Ava Baron, ed., *Work Engendered: Toward a New History of American Labor* (Ithaca: Cornell University Press, 1991); Ava Baron, "Masculinity, the Embodied Male Worker, and the Historian's Gaze," *International Labor and Working-Class History* 69 (Spring 2006): 143–60; Gregory L. Kaster, "Labour's True Man: Organised Workingmen and the Language of Manliness in the U.S.A, 1827–1877," *Gender and History* 13, no. 1 (2001): 24–64; Steven

Maynard, "Rough Work and Rugged Men: The Social Construction of Masculinity in Working-Class History," *Labour/Le Travail* 23 (Spring 1989): 159–69; Gail Bederman, *Manliness and Civilization: A Cultural History of Gender and Race in the United States, 1880–1917* (Chicago: University of Chicago Press, 1995); Amy S. Greenberg, *Manifest Manhood and the Antebellum American Empire* (New York: Cambridge University Press, 2005); D. Nelson, *National Manhood*; Kristin L. Hoganson, *Fighting for American Manhood: How Gender Politics Provoked the Spanish-American and Philippine-American Wars* (New Haven: Yale University Press, 1998); Mark C. Carnes and Clyde Griffen, eds., *Meanings for Manhood: Constructions of Masculinity in Victorian America* (Chicago: University of Chicago Press, 1990); E. Anthony Rotundo, *American Manhood: Transformations in Masculinity from the Revolution to the Modern Era* (New York: Basic Books, 1993); and Joshua R. Greenberg, *Advocating the Man: Masculinity, Organized Labor, and the Household in New York, 1800–1840* (New York: Columbia University Press, 2009).

31. Maynard, "Rough Work."

32. Kaster, "Labour's True Man," 26. This study is unique in that it does not deal with organized, skilled, white workingmen but rather with unskilled workers (native-born and immigrant) on remote frontiers of the U.S. West.

33. Bederman, *Manliness and Civilization*, 6–7.

34. Dana Nelson argues that throughout the nineteenth century, American manhood was characterized by "anxiety-making at its foundation." It promised white middle-class men (and elites) a "rich emotional mutuality" through "fraternal sameness," which functioned as an escape from "competitive, hierarchically ordered relations." Of course, this imagined fraternity masked class and racial inequalities and was thus denied to black and white working-class men; see *National Manhood*, 16, 19. See note 36 (of this chapter) for Toby Ditz's critique.

35. Bederman, *Manliness and Civilization*, 6–8. The othering of African American men, in particular, was critical to this process, and it is yet another factor that differentiates my analysis from Bederman's. Moreover, railroad construction workers (whether native-born or immigrant) typically did not identify as, nor were they considered, middle class. Finally, when the terms "manhood," "manly," "manliness," "masculine," and "masculinity" appear in the following study, they do not refer to fixed traits or values but rather to culturally adaptable ones that immigrant and native-born men transformed and contested over time.

36. Toby L. Ditz has offered a thoughtful critique of the recurrent emphasis on crises and obsessions in men's history, challenging historians who compare men only to other men to consider the dynamics of the broader gender order lest they position men yet again at the center of the master historical narrative. See "The New Men's History and the Peculiar Absence of Gendered Power: Some Remedies from Early American Gender History," *Gender and History* 16, no. 1 (2004): 1–35.

37. See notes 13 and 25 (of this chapter).

38. Peck, *Reinventing Free Labor*, 129–45.

39. While Peck's *Reinventing Free Labor* covers a different period than this one, he illustrates the hollowness of visions of the West as a paradise of "free land" and

"free labor" in ways that have benefited my study. For earlier studies of immigration, migration, and labor, see John Bodnar, *The Transplanted: A History of Immigrants in Urban America* (Bloomington: Indiana University Press, 1987); James R. Barrett, *Work and Community in the Jungle: Chicago's Packinghouse Workers, 1894–1922* (Urbana: University of Illinois Press, 1987); and Lizabeth Cohen, *Making a New Deal: Industrial Workers in Chicago, 1919–1939* (New York: Cambridge University Press, 1991). Peck's work builds on that of Sarah Deutsch, *No Separate Refuge: Culture, Class, and Gender on an Anglo-Hispanic Frontier in the American Southwest, 1880–1940* (New York: Oxford University Press, 1989). More recently, see Matthew Frye Jacobson, *Whiteness of a Different Color: European Immigrants and the Alchemy of Race* (Cambridge, MA: Harvard University Press, 1998); Jung, *Coolies and Cane;* Ngai, *Impossible Subjects;* Erika Lee, *At America's Gates: Chinese Immigration during the Exclusion Era, 1882–1943* (Chapel Hill: University of North Carolina Press, 2007); and Emmons, *Beyond the American Pale.*

CHAPTER 2. IRISH CANAL DIGGERS IN THE HOOSIER STATE

1. Francis J. Grund, *The Americans in Their Moral, Social, and Political Relations* (1837; repr., New York: Johnson Reprint, 1968), 9–10, 61–62 (italics in the original), 220–21. See, in particular, chapters 3, 8, and 10.

2. Ibid., 321, 305.

3. For scholarship on the canal era, see Ronald E. Shaw, *Canals for a Nation: The Canal Era in the United States, 1790–1860* (Lexington: University Press of Kentucky, 1990); and Carol Sheriff, *The Artificial River: The Erie Canal and the Paradox of Progress, 1817–1862* (New York: Hill and Wang, 1996).

4. John Lauritz Larson, *Internal Improvement: National Public Works and the Promise of Popular Government in the Early United States* (Chapel Hill: University of North Carolina Press, 2001).

5. "An Act to Provide for a General System of Internal Improvements," *Indiana Laws,* chap. 2, Indiana General Assembly, 20th Sess. (1836), 5. The Mammoth Bill was signed on January 27, 1836, and included the Whitewater and Central Canals; an extension of the W&E Canal from the mouth of the Tippecanoe to Terre Haute (with a link to the Central Canal via the Eel River); a railroad from Madison to Lafayette through Columbus and Indianapolis; a macadamized road from New Albany to Vincennes; a resurvey of routes between Jeffersonville and Crawfordsville to determine the practicality of either a railroad or macadamized turnpike; removal of "obstructions" to navigation on the Wabash River (which undoubtedly concerned Indian lands); and a survey for a canal or railroad from the W&E Canal near Fort Wayne to Michigan City.

6. R. Shaw, *Canals for a Nation,* 134–35; Paul Fatout, *Indiana Canals* (West Lafayette, IN: Purdue University Studies, 1972), 76. In his seminal study of America's nineteenth-century transportation revolution, George Rogers Taylor argued

that "no state became more disastrously involved in the general enthusiasm for the canal building than Indiana." See *The Transportation Revolution, 1815–1860* (New York: Rinehart, 1951), 47–48.

7. For discussions and repercussions of the Mammoth Bill, see Fatout, *Indiana Canals,* chap. 5; Peter Way, *Common Labour: Workers and the Digging of North American Canals, 1780–1860* (New York: Cambridge University Press, 1993), 209–10; Larson, *Internal Improvement,* chap. 6; and John Joseph Wallis, "The Property Tax as a Coordinating Device: Financing Indiana's Mammoth Internal Improvement System, 1835–1842," *Explorations in Economic History* 40 (2003): 224–25. As Wallis notes, New York (in 1817) and Ohio (in 1826) created similar "special," or ad valorem, property taxes on land and personal property to shift taxes away from agricultural lands on a per-acre basis and toward a "more equitable [tax] base" on town lands, farm lands, and various personal property. The thought was to assuage sectional rivalries and help coordinate the financing of transportation projects.

8. *National Intelligencer* (Washington, DC), July 22, 1835.

9. McCulloch's speech was reprinted in the *Indiana Journal* (Indianapolis), September 18, 1835.

10. David Burr to Noah Noble, December 30, 1835, Noah Noble Collection, Rare Books and Manuscripts, Indiana State Library, Indianapolis. This letter is reprinted in Dorothy Riker and Gayle Thornbrough, eds., *Messages and Papers relating to the Administration of Noah Noble, Governor of Indiana, 1831–1837* (Indianapolis: Indiana Historical Bureau, 1958), 419–23.

11. *National Intelligencer* (copying the *Fort Wayne [IN] Sentinel*), August 26, 1835, repr., *Newspaper Clippings on the Wabash and Erie Canal*, vol. 2, *April 1835–January 1841* (Fort Wayne, IN: Allen County Public Library Genealogy Center, n.d.); Burr to Noble, December 30, 1835, Noah Noble Collection, Indiana State Library.

12. *National Intelligencer* (copying the *Fort Wayne Sentinel*), August 26, 1835.

13. Burr to Noble, December 30, 1835, Noah Noble Collection, Indiana State Library.

14. Henry S. Tanner, *A Description of the Canals and Rail Roads of the United States, Comprehending Notices of All the Works of Internal Improvement throughout the Several States* (New York: Tanner and Disturnell, 1840), 240–41; Way, *Common Labour,* 136–37; Indiana Historical Bureau, "Canal Construction in Indiana," *Indiana Historian,* September 1997, 12.

15. Indiana House of Representatives, *Report of the Commissioners of the Wabash and Erie Canal* (Indianapolis, 1833), 11–13.

16. "Rules to Be Observed in Constructing the Whitewater Canal," November 10, 1838, broadside printed at the Watchman Office in Connersville, Broadside Collection, Indiana Historical Society, Indianapolis.

17. *Indianapolis Star,* July 26, 1907, in John TenBrook Campbell, Scrapbook, Campbell Papers, Rare Books and Manuscripts, Indiana State Library.

18. "Song of the Canal," in Fatout, *Indiana Canals,* 58.

19. John R. Commons, David J. Saposs, Helen L. Sumner, E. B. Mittelman, H. E. Hoagland, John B. Andrews, and Selig Perlman, *History of Labour in the*

United States, 2 vols. (New York: Macmillan, 1936), 2:415; Matthew Carey, *Reflections on the Subject of Emigration from Europe* (Philadelphia: Carey and Lea, 1826), 22.

20. Charles E. Rosenberg, *The Cholera Years: The United States in 1832, 1849, and 1866* (Chicago: University of Chicago Press, 1962), 121, 137, 228; R. Shaw, *Canals for a Nation,* 192.

21. Drake's editorial was first printed in the *Cincinnati Chronicle,* October 12, 1832, and was reprinted in the *Indiana Republican* (Madison), October 18, 1832.

22. Fatout, *Indiana Canals,* 52–53.

23. For a description of canal agitation and celebrations, see Charles E. Poinsatte, *Fort Wayne during the Canal Era, 1828–1855: A Study of a Western Community in the Middle Period of American History* (Indianapolis: Indiana Historical Bureau, 1969), 38–67; and Fatout, *Indiana Canals,* 52–53, 74–75, and chaps. 4–5.

24. *Lawrenceburg (IN) Palladium,* January 25, 1834.

25. *Lafayette (IN) Journal and Free Press,* January 21, 1836; *Covington (IN) Western Constellation,* May 20, 1838.

26. Catherine Tobin, "The Lowly Muscular Digger: Irish Canal Workers in Nineteenth-Century America" (PhD diss., University of Notre Dame, 1987), 43; Sheriff, *Artificial River,* 36–37.

27. William Lalor to Patrick Lalor, May 12, 1843, quoted in Kerby A. Miller, *Emigrants and Exiles: Ireland and the Irish Exodus to North America* (New York: Oxford University Press, 1985), 269.

28. Jonathan A. Glickstein, *Concepts of Free Labor in Antebellum America* (New Haven: Yale University Press, 1991), 5–13. See Eric Foner, *Free Soil, Free Labor, Free Men: The Ideology of the Republican Party before the Civil War,* rev. ed. (New York: Oxford University Press, 1995) for a clearer understanding of the origins and implications of "free labor" ideology.

29. Poinsatte, *Fort Wayne,* 54–58; Fatout, *Indiana Canals,* 85.

30. "Notice to Contractors," *Indiana Journal,* April 27, 1833.

31. Tobin, "Lowly Muscular Digger," 43n22.

32. Walter Sanderlin, *The Great National Project: A History of the Chesapeake and Ohio Canal* (Baltimore: Johns Hopkins University Press, 1946), 72; *Boston Pilot,* August 6, 1836; *Niles' Weekly Register* (Baltimore), August 6, 1836; Alvin Fay Harlow, *Old Towpaths: The Story of the American Canal Era* (Port Washington, NY: Kennikat, 1964), 236–37. See Fatout, *Indiana Canals,* 57–58, for canal commissioner Samuel Lewis's labor recruiting tour.

33. This advertisement originally appeared in the *Cass County Times* (Logansport, IN), August 25, 1832 (italics in the original).

34. *Indiana Journal,* August 4, 1832.

35. For details on I&M's recruitment process, see Tobin, "Lowly Muscular Digger"; David L. Lightner, "Construction Labor on Illinois Central Railroad," *Journal of the Illinois State Historical Society* 66, no. 3 (1973): 285–86; Way, *Common Labour,* 102; and *Chicago American,* June 11, 1836.

36. *Bloomington (IL) Intelligencer,* September 8, 1852; *Chicago Tribune,* January 18, 1853.

37. The advertisement for laborers on the Central Canal was printed in the *Evansville (IN) Journal,* May 1, 1837; W. H. Bass Photo Company Collection, folder 4, box 47, P0130, Indiana Historical Society, Indianapolis. The image is also available at http://images.indianahistory.org/cdm/ref/collection/P0130 /id/1090.

38. *Evansville Daily Journal,* May 1, 1837.

39. *Report of the Board of Internal Improvement to the General Assembly of the State of Indiana* (Indianapolis, 1837), 237. See also Indiana Historical Bureau, "Canal Construction in Indiana," 9.

40. K. Miller, *Emigrants and Exiles,* 193–201, 291–92. See also R. Shaw, *Canals for a Nation,* 169n26, 169n27; and Sheriff, *Artificial River,* 40–41.

41. R. Shaw, *Canals for a Nation,* 168–69; Ernest Teagarden, "Builders of the Ohio Canal, 1825–1832," *Inland Seas* 19, no. 2 (1963): 95–96.

42. Robert J. Steinfeld, *The Invention of Free Labor: The Employment Relation in English and American Law and Culture, 1350–1870* (Chapel Hill: University of North Carolina Press, 1991), 179; Sanderlin, *Great National Project,* 73–78; petitioners quoted in Seth Rockman, *Scraping By: Wage Labor, Slavery, and Survival in Early Baltimore* (Baltimore: Johns Hopkins University Press, 2009), 242.

43. Sheriff, *Artificial River;* R. Shaw, *Canals for a Nation,* 168–69.

44. George Potter notes that the Union Emigrant Society "placed 1,162 idle in work, mostly on canals" during its tenure in 1829; see *To the Golden Door: The Story of the Irish in Ireland and America* (Boston: Little, Brown, 1960), 318.

45. R. Shaw, *Canals for a Nation,* 170–71; Potter, *To the Golden Door,* 336–37.

46. Elfrieda Lang, "Irishmen in Northern Indiana before 1850," *Mid-America: An Historical Review* 35, no. 3 (1954): 190–92; 194; Thomas T. McAvoy, *The Catholic Church in Indiana, 1789–1834* (New York: Columbia University Press, 1940), 189; Poinsatte, *Fort Wayne,* 63; J. Lawrence Richart, "A Narrative History of Saint Joseph Church, Terre Haute, Indiana, 1838–1872" (master's thesis, Indiana State University, 1969), 31; Harlow, *Old Towpaths,* 267; Robert M. Taylor Jr. and Connie A. McBirney, eds., *Peopling Indiana: The Ethnic Experience* (Indianapolis: Indiana Historical Society, 1996), 249.

47. Fatout, *Indiana Canals,* 85; Poinsatte, *Fort Wayne,* 54–58.

48. Charles Dickens, *American Notes for General Circulation* (1842; repr., London: Penguin, 2000), 99, 91; Orestes Brownson to James McMaster, March 14, 1849, James McMaster Papers, 1820–86, University of Notre Dame Archives, Indiana; James Silk Buckingham, *The Eastern and Western States of America,* 3 vols. (London: Fisher, Son, 1842), 3:222.

49. J. Gould, "Wanderings in the West, 1839," in *Travel Accounts of Indiana, 1679–1961: A Collection of Observations by Wayfaring Foreigners, Itinerants, and Peripatetic Hoosiers,* comp. Shirley S. McCord, Indiana Historical Collections 47 (Indianapolis: Indiana Historical Bureau, 1970), 179.

50. *Maumee City (OH) Express,* August 25, 1838.

51. The Western Seamen's Friend Society, a branch of the American Seamen's Friend Society, was organized in Cleveland in 1830 and chartered by the Ohio Senate in 1850, its purpose to "promote the Intellectual, Social, Moral, and Spiritual condition of Sailors and Boatmen employed on the Western Waters." In addition to sponsoring religious services, the society advocated temperance, provided poor relief, published magazines to spread its message, and, by the 1850s, operated an itinerant missionary service throughout the Midwest. See the *First Annual Report of the Western Seamen's Friend Society* (Sandusky City, OH: Moore, 1848), 13–14.

52. *Spirit of the Lakes and Boatmen's Magazine* (Cleveland) 1, no. 8 (1848): 116; no. 9 (1849): 141. See also Records of the American Seamen's Friend Society, coll. 158, G. W. Blunt White Library, Mystic Seaport Museum, Mystic, CT.

53. Quoted in K. Miller, *Emigrants and Exiles,* 322.

54. John O'Hanlon, *Reverend John O'Hanlon's "The Irish Emigrant Guide for the United States,"* ed. Edward J. Maguire (1851; repr., New York: Arno, 1976), 12. Citations are to the 1976 edition.

55. Emerson, quoted in Richard D. Borgeson, "Irish Canal Laborers in America, 1817–1846" (master's thesis, Pennsylvania State University, 1964), 24.

56. Parker, quoted in Carl Wittke, *The Irish in America* (Baton Rouge: Louisiana State University Press, 1956), 41; *Boston Pilot,* July 31, 1852.

57. McAvoy, *Catholic Church,* 169; R. Shaw, *Canals for a Nation,* 170–71; Potter, *To the Golden Door,* 336–37.

58. Stephen T. Badin to John Baptist Purcell, September 23, 1834, Stephen T. Badin Papers, 1768–1943, University of Notre Dame Archives, Indiana.

59. Ibid.

60. Father John McDermott to the Trustees of the Wabash and Erie Canal, December 13, 1849, Wabash and Erie Canal Correspondence, Internal Improvement Papers, Records of the Auditor of the State, Archives Division, Indiana Commission on Public Records, Land Department, Indiana State Archives, Indianapolis.

61. *Report of the Commissioners,* 163–64.

62. William Gooding to William H. Swift, July 6, 1846, William H. Swift Papers, Chicago Historical Society; Way, *Common Labour,* 102–3.

63. *Fort Wayne Sentinel,* August 27, 1842.

64. *New York Freeman's Journal,* June 25, 1842.

65. Frederick Marryat, *Diary in America* (1839; repr., Bloomington: Indiana University Press, 1960), 92–93.

66. Grund, *Americans,* 9–10, 220–21.

67. "Paddy on the Canal," in *Irish Emigrant Ballads and Songs,* ed. Robert L. Wright (Bowling Green, OH: Bowling Green University Popular Press, 1975), 533.

68. A. J. Mosely to Thomas H. Blake, August 15, 1849, Wabash and Erie Canal Correspondence, Internal Improvement Papers, Records of the Auditor of the State, Archives Division, Indiana Commission on Public Records, Indiana State Archives, Indianapolis.

69. On working-class notions of republicanism, see Sean Wilentz, *Chants Democratic: New York City and the Rise of the American Working Class, 1788–1850* (New York: Oxford University Press, 1984).

70. On what W. E. B. Du Bois coined the "psychological wage," see *Black Reconstruction in America, 1860–1880* (New York: Harcourt, Brace, 1935; repr., Atheneum, 1977), 700–701. For David Roediger's analysis, see *The Wages of Whiteness: Race and the Making of the American Working Class,* rev. ed. (New York: Verso, 1999), 12–15. The difference, in the case of Irish midwestern canallers, was the absence of the black population to solidify claims or notions of "whiteness."

71. Rogers M. Smith, *Civic Ideals: Conflicting Visions of Citizenship in U.S. History* (New Haven: Yale University Press, 1997), 214–15 and chap. 8 in particular.

72. On canallers and political participation, see Way, *Common Labour,* 180–81; and Peter A. Wallner, "Politics and Public Works: A Study of the Pennsylvania Canal System, 1825–1857" (PhD diss., Pennsylvania State University, 1973), 163–64, 175–79.

73. R. S. Ford to E. Lucas, February 9, 1844, Mary J. Aborn Collection, Rare Books and Manuscripts, Indiana State Library.

74. See Roy Rozenweig, *Eight Hours for What We Will: Workers and Leisure in an Industrializing City, 1870–1920* (New York: Cambridge University Press, 1983), 4, 61–64; Way, *Common Labour,* 181–83; W. J. Rorabaugh, *The Alcoholic Republic: An American Tradition* (New York: Oxford University Press, 1979), 8–11, 140; and David A. Gerber, *The Making of an American Pluralism: Buffalo, New York, 1825–1860* (Urbana: University of Illinois Press, 1989), 133–34.

75. James Chute to Absalom Peters, December 17, 1832, American Home Missionary Society Papers, 1816–94 (Glen Rock, NJ: Microfilming Corporation of America, 1975), Graduate Theological Union Library, Berkeley, CA; *Fort Wayne Sentinel,* April 17, 1905; Poinsatte, *Fort Wayne,* 60–62.

76. *Lafayette (IN) Journal,* September 23, 1899.

77. Anonymous traveler, quoted in Potter, *To the Golden Door,* 320.

78. Robert Ernst, *Immigrant Life in New York City, 1825–1863* (Syracuse: Syracuse University Press, 1994), 105; Way, *Common Labour,* 198.

79. *Fort Wayne Sentinel,* April 17, 1905.

80. Frances Trollope, *Domestic Manners of the Americans* (London: Whittaker, Treacher, 1832), 290–91.

81. Robert Stuart to William Gooding, March 3, 1847; William L. Perce and John Clifford to Board of Trustees of the Illinois and Michigan Canal, August 2, 1846, both in Illinois and Michigan Canal Archives, Chicago Historical Society.

82. Chute to Peters, December 17, 1832, American Home Missionary Society Papers; Poinsatte, *Fort Wayne,* 60–62.

83. Canal contract, signed by William Rockhill and Samuel Lewis, June 4, 1832, Miscellaneous Papers, Allen County–Fort Wayne Historical Society, Fort Wayne, IN; see also B. J. Griswold, *Pictorial History of Fort Wayne,* vol. 1 (Chicago: Law, 1917), 314.

84. Chute to Peters, July 8, 1835, American Home Missionary Society Papers.

85. "Paddy on the Canal," in Wright, *Irish Emigrant Ballads,* 533.

86. David Leavitt to Swift, December 8, 1845, Illinois and Michigan Canal Archives.

87. *New York Truth Teller,* August 31, 1839.

88. Samuel Clark and James S. Donnelly Jr., eds., *Irish Peasants: Violence and Political Unrest, 1780–1914* (Madison: University of Wisconsin Press, 1983), 64–101; Peter Way, "Shovel and Shamrock: Irish Workers and Labor Violence in the Digging of the Chesapeake and Ohio Canal," *Labor History* 30, no. 4 (1989): 490–506, 515–16.

89. David Grimsted, "Rioting in Its Jacksonian Setting," *American Historical Review* 77 (1972): 390.

90. Way, *Common Labour,* 196–97, 214–17, and chap. 7 in general; Richard B. Morris, "Andrew Jackson, Strikebreaker," *American Historical Review* 55, no. 1 (1949): 54–68. For a view of secret societies, strikes, and rioting as tied more to ethnic and regional loyalties than to job concerns, see David Grimsted, "Antebellum Labor: Violence, Strike, and Communal Arbitration," *Journal of Social History* 19, no. 1 (1985): 5–28.

91. *Indianapolis News,* February 26, 1902.

92. Trollope, *Domestic Manners,* 163, 233.

93. Wesley J. Whicker, "Historical Lore of the Wabash Valley," from *Waynetown (IN) Dispatch,* May 15, 1916, Wabash Valley File, Rare Books and Manuscripts, Indiana State Library.

94. M. J. Adams, letter reprinted in the *Cork Examiner* (County Cork, Ireland), August 10, 1860, courtesy of Arnold Schrier, Professor of History Emeritus, Schrier Collection, University of Cincinnati, quoted in K. Miller, *Emigrants and Exiles,* 323.

95. Quoted in K. Miller, *Emigrants and Exiles,* 326.

96. *Indianapolis Star,* July 26, 1907, in Campbell, Scrapbook, L258. Since heavy rains could threaten certain canal-building tasks, Burns required a "dry month," or four full weeks of work, before Campbell received his wages. Canal scrip refers to the colored-paper currency the state provided to the W&E Canal Company and its contractors for meeting expenses of supplies and labor following the panic of 1837 and during the state's period of bankruptcy. See Samuel Bigger, annual message, December 9, 1840, in Dorothy Riker and Gayle Thornbrough, eds., *Messages and Papers relating to the Administration of Samuel Bigger, Governor of Indiana, 1840–1843* (Indianapolis: Indiana Historical Bureau, 1964), 110–28; Larson, *Internal Improvement,* 213–14; *Harper's New Monthly Magazine* 51 (June–November 1875): 565; Way, *Common Labour,* 210; and R. Shaw, *Canals for a Nation,* 139.

97. *Indianapolis Star,* July 26, 1907, Campbell, Scrapbook, L258. See also Henry Lee, *History of the Campbell Family* (New York: Polk, 1920).

98. *Indianapolis Star,* July 26, 1907, in Campbell, Scrapbook, L258.

99. Reprinted from the *Attica (IN) Ledger,* 1916, in John Wesley Whicker, *Historical Sketches of the Wabash Valley* (Attica, IN: printed by author, 1916), 78, 79.

100. Ibid., 78, 79, 77.

101. Burr to Noble, December 30, 1835, Noah Noble Collection, Indiana State Library.

102. *Frederick (MD) Herald,* February 1, 1834; *Williamsport (MD) Banner,* January 25, 1834. For accounts of this conflict and subsequent conflicts on the C&O, see Way, *Common Labour,* 200–201; Way, "Shovel and Shamrock," 489–517; Morris, "Andrew Jackson, Strikebreaker"; W. David Baird, "Violence along the Chesapeake Canal: 1839," *Maryland Historical Magazine* 66 (Summer 1971): 121–34; and Noel Ignatiev, *How the Irish Became White* (New York: Routledge, 1995), 93–94.

103. *Williamsport Banner,* January 25, 1834; *Hagerstown (MD) Mail,* January 31, 1834.

104. Potter, *To the Golden* Door, 330. See also Morris, "Andrew Jackson, Strikebreaker," 57–61; and Way, *Common Labour,* 201.

105. The treaty as it appeared in the *Niles' Weekly Register* is quoted in Potter, *To the Golden Door,* 330.

106. *Hagerstown (MD) Herald,* February 1, 1834.

107. Burr to Noble, December 30, 1835, Noah Noble Collection, Indiana State Library; Noble to C. B. Smith, December 30, 1835, House of Representatives, Executive Department, Manuscript Division, Rare Books and Manuscripts, Indiana State Library.

108. Burr to Noble, December 30, 1835, Noah Noble Collection, Indiana State Library.

109. *National Intelligencer,* August 26, 1835, copying the *Fort Wayne Sentinel.*

110. Burr to Noble, December 30, 1835, Noah Noble Collection, Indiana State Library.

111. Ibid.

112. *National Intelligencer,* copying the *Fort Wayne Sentinel,* August 26, 1835.

113. Burr to Noble, December 30, 1835, Noah Noble Collection, Indiana State Library.

114. Elias Murray to John Tipton, March 31, 1836, in *The John Tipton Papers,* ed. Nellie Armstrong Robertson and Dorothy Riker, 3 vols. (Indianapolis: Indiana Historical Bureau, 1942), 3:250.

115. Burr to Noble, December 30, 1835, Noah Noble Collection, Indiana State Library.

116. V. Frederika Van Buskirk, *The Wabash-Erie Canal, 1832–1876, with Emphasis on the Lagro Locks* (Wabash, IN: Wabash Historical Society, 1965), 4–6.

117. Noble to Caleb Blood Smith, December 30, 1835, Noah Noble Collection, Indiana State Library.

118. Frederick Jackson Turner, *The Frontier in American History* (New York: Holt, 1935), in particular, chap. 9.

119. "Oration of General Lewis Cass," *Fort Wayne (IN) Weekly Sentinel,* July 15, 1843. Cass's oration has been reprinted in various publications, most recently in *Canal Celebrations in Old Fort Wayne* (Fort Wayne, IN: Public Library of Fort Wayne and Allen County, 1953), 54–79.

120. Ibid.

121. *Fort Wayne Weekly Sentinel,* July 15, 1843.

122. Ibid.

123. Ibid.

124. On "struggles for recognition," see Pierre Bordieu, *In Other Words: Essays towards a Reflexive Sociology* (Stanford, CA: Stanford University Press, 1990), 22. On "rites of nationhood" and celebrations of the early American republic, see David Waldstreicher, *In the Midst of Perpetual Fetes: The Making of American Nationalism, 1789–1820* (Chapel Hill: University of North Carolina Press, 1997), 1–14. On early American mob behavior and workers' public protests, see Paul Gilje, *The Road to Mobocracy: Popular Disorder in New York City, 1763–1834* (Chapel Hill: University of North Carolina Press, 1987).

125. See John Lauritz Larson, "'Bind the Republic Together': The National Union and the Struggle for a System of Internal Improvements," *Journal of American History* 74, no. 2 (1987): 365–66, 377–78, and Annals of Cong., 14th Cong., 2d Sess. (February 4, 1817).

126. *Reports of the Debates and Proceedings of the Convention for the Revision of the Constitution of the State of Indiana,* 2 vols. (Indianapolis, 1850–51), 1:645, 647; 677. See also John D. Barnhart and Donald Carmony, eds., *Indiana: From Frontier to Industrial Commonwealth,* 2 vols. (New York: Lewis Historical, 1954), 1:344.

CHAPTER 3. IRISH WORKERS, ILLINOIS TRANSPORTATION FRONTIER

1. *Chicago Weekly Journal,* April 17, 1848.

2. *Gem of the Prairie* (Chicago), April 18, 1848, quoted in George D. Berndt, "Celebrating the Illinois and Michigan Canal," *Cultural Resource Management* 21, no. 11 (1998): 18.

3. *Chicago American,* July 9, 1836.

4. See Reuben Gold Thwaites, ed., *Early Western Travels, 1748–1846,* vol. 26, pt. 1 of *The Far West, 1836–1837,* by Edmund Flagg (Cleveland: Clark, 1906), 81.

5. Ray Allen Billington, *Westward Expansion: A History of the American Frontier,* 4th ed. (New York: Macmillan, 1974), 320.

6. Writer David Henshaw, quoted in James E. Davis, *Frontier Illinois* (Bloomington: Indiana University Press, 1998), 5. Other observers argued that the canal's utility surpassed even that of New York's Erie Canal. Benjamin Wright, an engineer on the Erie, admitted that the I&M "may truly be considered as one of the greatest and most important in its consequences of any work of any age or nation." "Engineer's Report to the Board of Commissioners of the Illinois and Michigan Canal," reprinted in the *Illinois State Register* (Springfield), April 13, 1838.

7. The Illinois Central's management and organization would serve as a model for future land grant railroads. As generations of historians have also noted, the ICRR played a critical role during the Civil War, transporting Union troops and

supplies southward to open the Mississippi River to the Gulf of Mexico. For the definitive work on the ICRR, see Paul Wallace Gates, *The Illinois Central Railroad and Its Colonization Work* (Cambridge, MA: Harvard University Press, 1934).

8. Wayne A. Johnston, *The Illinois Central Heritage, 1851–1951: A Centenary Address* (New York: Newcomen Society, 1951), 11.

9. Minutes of the Meetings of the Board of Commissioners of the Illinois and Michigan Canal, April 13, 1839, Illinois State Archives, Springfield, G.22, p. 156.

10. See chapter 2 of this volume for a detailed discussion. Catherine Tobin, "The Lowly Muscular Digger: Irish Canal Workers in Nineteenth-Century America" (PhD diss., University of Notre Dame, 1987), 46–51. In the spring of 1853 ICRR chief engineer Roswell Mason complained that Illinois could not furnish one-fourth of the men necessary for construction. "My only hope," Mason wrote, "is in a large emigration from the East," and "I have arrangement . . . with an Irish Emigrant Society to send a large number." Mason to Schuyler, April 18, 1853, Mason, Out-Letters, IC 1 M3.1, Illinois Central Railroad Company Archives, Roger and Julie Baskes Department of Special Collections, Newberry Library, Chicago.

11. *Chicago Tribune,* January 18, 1853.

12. Archer Butler Hulbert, *The Paths of Inland Commerce: A Chronicle of Trail, Road, and Waterway,* Chronicles of America Series 21 (New Haven: Yale University Press, 1921), 74.

13. H. Jerome Cranmer, "Canal Investment, 1815–1860," in *Studies in Income and Wealth,* vol. 24, ed. National Bureau of Economic Research (Princeton, NJ: Princeton University Press, 1960), 557; Jim Redd, *The Illinois and Michigan Canal: A Contemporary Perspective in Essays and Photographs* (Carbondale: Southern Illinois University Press, 1993), 2; Berndt, "Celebrating," 18; Hulbert, *Paths of Inland Commerce,* 74.

14. See George Potter, *To the Golden Door: The Story of the Irish in Ireland and America* (Boston: Little, Brown, 1960), 302.

15. Jack Manning to M. Lyrell, "Letterbooks," December 15, 1836, record series 491.004, Illinois and Michigan Canal Records, Illinois State Archives, Springfield.

16. *Boston Pilot,* July 13, 1839.

17. *Chicago Daily Journal,* October 15, 1845.

18. Robert E. Bailey and Elaine Shemoney Evans, eds., *The Illinois and Michigan Canal, 1827–1911: A Selection of Documents from the Illinois State Archives* (Springfield: Office of the Secretary of State, 1998), doc. 11, p. 2; *Chicago Daily Journal,* October 15, 1845; "Time Books," 1847, record series 491.044, Illinois and Michigan Canal Records, Illinois State Archives, Springfield.

19. "Time Books," Illinois and Michigan Canal Records.

20. "Supplies Furnished to Workers," record series 491.046, Illinois and Michigan Canal Records, Illinois State Archives, Springfield.

21. James Silk Buckingham, *The Eastern and Western States of America,* 3 vols. (London: Fisher, Son, 1842), 3:222–24.

22. Ibid.

23. Ibid.

24. Quoted in Kerby A. Miller, *Emigrants and Exiles: Ireland and the Irish Exodus to North America* (New York: Oxford University Press, 1985), 270.

25. *Boston Pilot,* July 13, 1839, cited in Tobin, "Lowly Muscular Digger," 133.

26. *Report of the Board of Commissioners of the Illinois and Michigan Canal* (Vandalia, IL: Walters, 1838), 30; Richard D. Borgeson, "Irish Canal Laborers in America, 1817–1846" (master's thesis, Pennsylvania State University, 1964), 42–44; Peter Way, *Common Labour: Workers and the Digging of North American Canals, 1780–1860* (New York: Cambridge University Press, 1993), 106–8.

27. Monthly workforce numbers are based on the following sources: *Report of the Board,* 52; *Fourth Annual Report of the Canal Commissioners of the Illinois and Michigan Canal* (Springfield, IL: Waters, 1840), 24. The presence of livestock also varied correspondingly to the number of hands employed, with thirty-eight teams of horses and oxen per five hundred men on the I&M in 1838.

28. *Report of the Board,* 52, 37.

29. William F. Thornton to Thomas Carlin, May 31, 1839, "Letterbooks."

30. *Annual Report of the Commissioners of the Illinois and Michigan Canal, 1840* (Lockport, IL, 1840), 185; Way, *Common Labour,* 210–11.

31. *Annual Report,* 185.

32. Ibid.

33. Robert Stuart to William H. Swift, July 10, 1846; William Gooding to Swift, July 6, 1846, both in Illinois and Michigan Canal Archives, Chicago Historical Society.

34. Gooding to Swift, December 26, 1845, Illinois and Michigan Canal Archives.

35. In this company reorganization, one trustee (Charles Oakley) represented the state and two (William H. Swift, based in Washington, DC, and David Leavitt in New York) represented the bondholders.

36. Gooding to Swift, February 20, 1846; Stuart to David Leavitt, November 5, 1845, both in Illinois and Michigan Canal Archives.

37. Gooding to Swift, July 6, 1846, Illinois and Michigan Canal Archives.

38. Gooding to G. W. Green, February 9, 1848, "Letterbooks."

39. The Petition of the Undersigned Laborers to Honourable Col. Oakley, July 12, 1847, Illinois and Michigan Canal Archives.

40. See, for example, Gunther Peck, *Reinventing Free Labor;* Cindy Hahamovitch, *The Fruits of Their Labor: Atlantic Coast Farmworkers and the Making of Migrant Poverty, 1870–1945* (Chapel Hill: University of North Carolina Press, 1997); and Evelyn Glenn, *Unequal Freedom: How Race and Gender Shaped American Citizenship and Labor* (Cambridge, MA: Harvard University Press, 2002).

41. Mark Wyman, *Hoboes: Bindlestiffs, Fruit Tramps, and the Harvesting of the West* (New York: Hill and Wang, 2010).

42. Myron S. Webb to William Webb, September 22, 1838, Whitewater Canal Correspondence, Internal Improvement Papers, Land Department, Records of the Auditor of the State, Archives Division, Indiana Commission on Public Records, Indiana State Archives, Indianapolis.

43. *Report of the Board,* 52.

44. *Chicago Daily Journal,* October 15, 1845.

45. Quoted in Isaac D. Rawlings, *The Rise and Fall of Disease in Illinois,* 2 vols. (Springfield: Illinois Department of Public Health, 1927), 1:39.

46. Stuart to Thomas Ward, October 22, 1846, Indiana and Michigan Canal Archives, Chicago Historical Society.

47. Ward B. Burnett, "Report of Ward B. Burnett, Resident Engineer on the Western Division," December 1838, reprinted in *Report of the Canal Commissioners of Illinois to Governor John R. Tanner, 1900* (Springfield, IL: Phillips Brothers, 1901), 171.

48. In the nineteenth century the cause of cholera was unknown, and it proved fatal in over 50 percent of cases, often killing the affected person within a few days. This disease spread through Asia and Europe in 1817 and appeared in Great Britain in 1831 and in Canada in 1832. See Charles E. Rosenberg, *The Cholera Years: The United States in 1832, 1849, and 1866* (Chicago: University of Chicago Press, 1962); Geoffrey Bilson, *A Darkened House: Cholera in Nineteenth-Century Canada* (Toronto: University of Toronto Press, 1980), 2–4; and Walter Sanderlin, *The Great National Project: A History of the Chesapeake and Ohio Canal* (Baltimore: Johns Hopkins University Press, 1946), 93–96.

49. Mercer, quoted in Way, *Common Labour,* 157.

50. *Bloomington (IL) Intelligencer,* August 4, 1852; *Bloomington (IL) Weekly Pantagraph,* August 9, 1854, copying the *Galena (IL) Jeffersonian.*

51. *Alton (IL) Courier,* August 2, 21, 1852.

52. William P. Burrall to Jonathan Sturges, June 13, 1854, Burrall, Out-Letters, IC 1 B9.1, Illinois Central Railroad Company Archives; David L. Lightner, "Construction Labor on the Illinois Central Railroad," *Journal of the Illinois State Historical Society* 66, no. 3 (1973): 292.

53. Burrall to Sturges, June 13, 1854, Burrall, Out-Letters, Illinois Central Railroad Company Archives.

54. Lewis F. Ashley to Mason Brayman, January 25, 1853, Mason Brayman Papers, 1850–65, Chicago Historical Society; Mason to Sturges, November 12, 1854, Mason, Out-Letters, Illinois Central Railroad Company Archives.

55. *Bloomington Intelligencer,* August 4, 1852.

56. Rawlings, *Rise and Fall,* 1:188.

57. See Margaret Humphreys, *Malaria: Poverty, Race, and Public Health in the United States* (Baltimore: Johns Hopkins University Press, 2001). For Irish canallers whiskey was considered a remedy for malaria, and during severe outbreaks company policy permitted its use. Quinine was the proper medical remedy, but its rather high cost eliminated it as an option for most poor canallers. Prior to the widespread use of quinine, various treatments were practiced, including mixtures of molasses and ginger with water, bloodletting, and the cathartic use of calomel. See *New York Freeman's Journal,* August 28, 1841.

58. Elmer Baldwin, *History of LaSalle County, Illinois* (Chicago: Rand McNally, 1877), 159–60.

59. Tyrone Power, *Impressions of America, during the Years 1833, 1834, and 1835,* 2 vols. (London: Bentley, 1836), 2:241–42.

60. Francis J. Grund, *The Americans in Their Social, Moral, and Political Relations* (1837; repr., New York: Johnson Reprint, 1968), 221.

61. John Blasius Raho to Joseph Rosati, July 23, 1838, August 23, 1838, Rosati Correspondence, Charles Leon Souvay Collection, 1798–1922, University of Notre Dame Archives, Indiana.

62. Raho to John Timon, August 13, 1838, reprinted in Thomas A. Shaw, *Story of the LaSalle Mission: From 1838, Arrival of First Missioners, to 1857, Departure of Rev. J. O'Reilly, C. M.,* 2 vols. (Chicago: Donohue, n.d.), 1:52.

63. *Boston Pilot,* July 13, 1839.

64. Power, *Impressions of America,* 2:239.

65. Drake, quoted in Rawlings, *Rise and Fall,* 1:39.

66. Burrall to J. N. Perkins, September 6, 1854, Burrall, Out-Letters, Illinois Central Railroad Company Archives.

67. Thomas Low Nichols, *Forty Years of American Life,* 2 vols. (1864; repr., New York: Johnson Reprint, 1969), 1:120.

68. Gunther Peck, "Manly Gambles: The Politics of Risk on the Comstock Lode, 1860–1880," *Journal of Social History* 26, no. 4 (1993): 701–23.

69. Grund, *Americans,* 61.

70. Alfred T. Andreas, *History of Cook County, Illinois* (Chicago: printed by author, 1884), 290.

71. Contractors on the Illinois & Michigan risked a loss of their contracts if found guilty of selling or providing alcohol to their workers, because, according to the commissioners, labor riots on canals were "attributable in most cases to the use of ardent spirits." A contributing problem was that contractors who lacked cash wages or canal scrip sometimes resorted to paying workers in "grog and provisions." When the company prohibition tactic failed, I&M officials recommended following the lead of Indiana's canal board, which petitioned the state legislature to enact a law prohibiting the sale of alcohol within three miles of public works projects. Irish workers defied such rules regularly. See *Annual Report of the Board of Commissioners of the Illinois and Michigan Canal for 1836* (Vandalia, IL: Walters and Sawyer, 1837), 177; David Leavitt to Swift, December 8, 1845; Gooding to Gen. Jacob Fry, July 27, 1846; and Gooding to the Board of Trustees of the Illinois and Michigan Canal, August 30, 1847, in Illinois and Michigan Canal Archives; "Report of the State Board of Internal Improvements," in *Documentary Journal of Indiana Reports* (Indianapolis, 1836), 11.

72. George Woodruff, *History of Will County, Illinois* (Chicago: Le Baron, 1878), 301, quoted in Tobin, "Lowly Muscular Digger," 98.

73. *Ottawa (IL) Republican,* July 2, 1853; *Bloomington Intelligencer,* June 16, 1852. See also Lightner, "Construction Labor," 298.

74. John Lamb, "Drunken, Dirty Irish Build Canal," *Lockport (IL) Free Press,* June 15, 1978, in John M. Lamb Collection, Lewis University, Romeoville, IL.

75. Buckingham, quoted in Lamb, "Drunken, Dirty Irish."

76. William L. Perce and John Clifford to Board of Trustees of the Illinois and Michigan Canal, August 2, 1846, Illinois and Michigan Canal Archives.

77. Stuart to Gooding, March 3, 1847, Illinois and Michigan Canal Archives.

78. Anne Royall, *Mrs. Royall's Pennsylvania; or, Travels Continued in the United States,* 2 vols. (Washington, DC, 1829), 2:126.

79. See Earl Niehaus, *The Irish in New Orleans, 1800–1860* (Baton Rouge: Louisiana State University Press, 1965), 48.

80. *Maumee City Express,* August 25, 1838; *History of Grundy County, Illinois* (Chicago: Baskin, 1882), 158–59.

81. *DeWitt Courier* (Clinton, IL), June 15, 1855.

82. Henry Giles, "The New Exodus," *Christian Examiner* 52 (May 1852): 375.

83. Dale T. Knobel, *Paddy and the Republic: Ethnicity and Nationality in Antebellum America* (Middletown, CT: Wesleyan University Press, 1986), 80, 88, 90; Matthew Frye Jacobson, *Whiteness of a Different Color: European Immigrants and the Alchemy of Race* (Cambridge, MA: Harvard University Press, 1998), 48–50.

84. Knobel, *Paddy and the Republic,* 70.

85. Though his scope and subject differ considerably from mine, I have benefited a great deal from Thomas A. Guglielmo's unpacking of the literal and rhetorical differences between race and color in the late nineteenth and early twentieth century. Guglielmo argues that race and color were the primary "ways of categorizing people based on supposedly inborn physical, mental, moral, and cultural traits." Color, as a social category, "roughly coincides with today's census categories," and race owed more to one's location in the "racialized social system" and its consequences. *White on Arrival: Italians, Race, Color, and Power in Chicago, 1890–1945* (New York: Oxford University Press, 2003), 6–9.

86. Eduardo Bonilla-Silva, "Rethinking Racism: Toward a Structural Interpretation," *American Sociological Review* 62 (June 1996): 469–70; W. E. B. Du Bois, *Black Reconstruction in America, 1860–1880* (New York: Harcourt, Brace, 1935; repr., Atheneum, 1977), 700–701. For a critique, see David Roediger, *The Wages of Whiteness: Race and the Making of the American Working Class,* rev. ed. (New York: Verso, 1999).

87. Roediger, *Wages of Whiteness,* 12–13.

88. Knobel, *Paddy and the Republic,* 88, 90, 123; Jacobson, *Different Color,* 48.

89. Jacobson, *Different Color,* 48. In addition to Knobel, *Paddy and the Republic;* Jacobson, *Different Color;* and K. Miller, *Emigrants and Exiles,* see J. J. Lee and Marion Casey, eds., *Making the Irish American: History and Heritage of the Irish in the United States* (New York: New York University Press, 2007), and Noel Ignatiev, *How the Irish Became White* (New York: Routledge, 1995).

90. Way, in *Common Labour,* flirts with this idea, but his conclusions tend toward the relative powerlessness of canal workers amid oppressive employee-employer relations and against the emergence of industrial capitalism. See also Carol Sheriff, *The Artificial River: The Erie Canal and the Paradox of Progress, 1817–1862* (New York: Hill and Wang, 1996); Walter Licht, *Working for the Railroad: The Organization of Work in the Nineteenth Century* (Princeton, NJ: Princeton University Press, 1983); Shelton Stromquist, *A Generation of Boomers: The Pattern of Railroad Labor Conflict in*

Nineteenth-Century America (Urbana: University of Illinois Press, 1987); Matthew E. Mason, "'The Hands Here Are Disposed to Be Turbulent': Unrest among the Irish Trackmen of the Baltimore and Ohio Railroad, 1829–1851," *Labor History* 39, no. 3 (1998): 253–72; and Roger E. Carp, "The Limits of Reform: Labor and Discipline on the Erie Canal," *Journal of the Early Republic* 10, no. 2 (1990): 191–219. Such intelligence was ostensibly the preserve of working-class (and aspiring middle-class) craftsman, guild workers, and early labor union leaders, not poor, downtrodden, and drunken transients. For an overview of drinking in the antebellum period, see W.J. Rorabaugh, *The Alcoholic Republic: An American Tradition* (New York: Oxford University Press, 1979).

91. William Byrne to Rosati, December 19, 1837, Rosati Correspondence. The first official history of the LaSalle Vincentian mission described "Billy Byrne" as a "great Catholic." See T. Shaw, *Story,* 1:16.

92. Raho to Rosati, August 23, 1838, Rosati Correspondence.

93. Byrne to Rosati, January 29, 1838, ibid.

94. Ibid.

95. Ibid., December 19, 1837.

96. T. Shaw, *Story,* 1:22–23; Raho to Father Jean-Baptiste Nozo, 1840, in T. Shaw, *Story,* 1:24.

97. T. Shaw, *Story,* 1:34, 39.

98. Ibid., 35–37.

99. Ibid., 35

100. Raho to Rosati, July 23, 1838, Rosati Correspondence.

101. T. Shaw, *Story,* 1:43–44.

102. Raho to I. Timon, August 13, 1838, ibid., 48–49.

103. Raho to Rosati, August 23, 1838, Rosati Correspondence.

104. Unnamed AHMS missionary to Milton Badger, October 20, 1848, American Home Missionary Society Papers, 1816–94 (Glen Rock, NJ: Microfilming Corporation of America, 1975), Graduate Theological Union Library, Berkeley, CA.

105. Rev. Jeremiah Porter to Badger, November 5, 1840, American Home Missionary Society Papers.

106. Rev. Joel Grant to the Executive Committee of the American Home Missionary Society, July 14, 1846, American Home Missionary Society Papers.

107. "List of Names and Amount Paid by Men to Reverend Parodi" on the "Receipt of Mr. William L. Perce," November 11, 1839, Marseilles, Perce Correspondence, Illinois State Historical Society, Springfield.

108. Louis Aloysius Parodi to Rosati, June 13, 1838, Rosati Correspondence.

109. *Ottawa (IL) Free Trader,* July 2, 1841; *Catholic Telegraph* (Cincinnati), May 3, 1838.

110. Joseph Thompson, "The Irish in Early Illinois," *Illinois Catholic Historical Review* 2, no. 3 (1920): 18–19.

111. Buckingham, quoted in Andreas, *History of Cook County,* 238. See also "Catholic Almanac and Laity's Directory, 1839," in *American Catholic Directories, 1817–1879* (Washington, DC: Catholic University of America, 1952), 131.

112. Andreas, *History of Cook County,* 238.

113. See Potter, *To the Golden Door,* 336.

114. *Catholic Telegraph,* May 3, 1838.

115. Nichols, *Forty Years,* 1:70; *Catholic Telegraph,* May 3, 1838.

116. See Knobel, *Paddy and the Republic,* 80.

117. Way, *Common Labour,* 80–81; Tobin, "Lowly Muscular Digger," 216.

118. Gail Bederman, *Manliness and Civilization: A Cultural History of Gender and Race in the United States, 1880–1917* (Chicago: University of Chicago Press, 1995), 171.

119. Rev. Nahum Gould to the Secretary of the American Home Missionary Society, September 10, 1837, American Home Missionary Society Papers.

120. See John Higham, *Strangers in the Land: Patterns of American Nativism, 1860–1925* (New Brunswick, NJ: Rutgers University Press, 1955).

121. Quoted in Jacqueline H. Katz and William L. Katz, *Making Our Way: America at the Turn of the Century in the Words of the Poor and Powerless* (New York: Ethrac, 1975), 77.

122. John P. Sanderson, *Republic Landmarks: The Views and Opinions of American Statesmen on Foreign Immigration* (Philadelphia: Lippincott, 1856), 333. Historian Dale T. Knobel argues that tyranny and papism had produced a perceived "climate of ill-education" in Ireland. According to the editors of the *American Quarterly Review,* Catholic immigrants to America brought "deplorable ignorance," for "the whole ceremonial of the Romish church, the doctrine, the gorgeous ritual, are adapted precisely to meet the inclinations and circumstances of all the ignorant men . . . in our land." "Papacy in the United States," *American Quarterly Review* 7 (August 1835): 58–60, quoted in Knobel, *Paddy and the Republic,* 58–59.

123. *History of Grundy County,* 143.

124. *Chicago American,* July 31, 1839. On Illinois politics and the Irish canal vote, see George Fleming, "Canal at Chicago: A Study in Political and Social History" (PhD diss., Catholic University of America, 1951), 150–52.

125. *Chicago American,* November 27, 1840.

126. Lamb, "Drunken, Dirty Irish."

127. *Chicago American,* August 14, 1840. An irony of Irish canallers voting Democrat is, of course, the widespread support on the part of Whigs for federal funding for internal improvement projects—the livelihood of countless Irish wageworkers. Whigs, in fact, tempered their anti-immigrant and exclusionary policy goals in various regions where immigrant votes were the temporary path to power.

128. *Ottawa Free Trader,* July 31, 1840; August 7, 1840.

129. From a different angle, however, such evidence suggests that Irish canallers were exploiting politicians for access to whiskey. Nahum Gould to the Secretary of the American Home Missionary Society, October 25, 1838, American Home Missionary Society Papers.

130. *History of Grundy County,* 201–2, 143–44.

131. *Native American* (Philadelphia), November 29, 1844.

132. Knobel, *Paddy and the Republic,* 179–81. Arguably the best treatment of this conundrum is in Guglielmo, *White on Arrival.*

133. Knobel, *Paddy and the Republic,* 102–3; 88–89.

134. Nell Irvin Painter, *The History of White People* (New York: Norton, 2010), 132–33.

135. See Guglielmo, *White on Arrival,* on Chicago's Italians at the turn of the century, 3–10.

136. Patrick Donohue, *Boston Pilot,* November 25, 1848.

137. Ibid., February 4, 1860.

138. *New York Freeman's Journal,* January 30, 1842.

139. Bederman, *Manliness and Civilization,* 171–72; see, in general, 1–44, and chap. 5. See also Dana D. Nelson, *National Manhood: Capitalist Citizenship and the Imagined Fraternity of White Men* (Durham, NC: Duke University Press, 1998).

140. Jesse Chickering, *Immigration into the United States* (Boston: Little and Brown, 1848), 64–65.

141. *Native American,* September 17, 1844.

142. John C. Calhoun, quoted in Annals of Cong., 14th Cong., 2d Sess. (February 4, 1817), 854.

143. T. Shaw, *Story,* 1:45.

144. Raho to Rosati, June 20, 1838, August 23, 1838, Rosati Correspondence.

145. Baldwin, *History of LaSalle County,* 199–200; Henry Beebe, *History of Peru, Illinois* (Peru, IL: Linton, 1858), 136–40; George Woodruff, *Forty Years Ago: A Contribution to the Early History of Joliet and Will County, Illinois* (Joliet: Goodspeed, 1874), 70–72. The best historical work is in Tobin, "Lowly Muscular Digger," 186–88.

146. Quoted in T. Shaw, *Story,* 1:45–46.

147. Baldwin, *History of LaSalle County,* 199–200.

148. Quoted in T. Shaw, *Story,* 1:45–46.

149. Tobin, "Lowly Muscular Digger," 186.

150. Byrne was from Leinster Province.

151. Parodi to Rosati, June 13, 1838, Rosati Correspondence.

152. Raho to I. Timon, August 13, 1838, quoted in T. Shaw, *Story,* 1:48–49.

153. *Report of the Board;* "Reports," 1838, record series 491.006, Illinois and Michigan Canal, Illinois State Archives, Springfield.

154. The company's tacit support of the combined force of Woodruff's militia and Byrne's Fardowners indicated its loyalty to a local sheriff and well-known contractor and businessman (Byrne) against the violent Corkonians. Moreover, the lack of a company voice here suggests that internal violence among Irish workers threatened the popular image of canallers as a monolithic group.

155. See Sean Wilentz, *Chants Democratic: New York City and the Rise of the American Working Class, 1788–1850* (New York: Oxford University Press, 1984); Alan Dawley, *Class and Community: The Industrial Revolution in Lynn* (Cambridge, MA: Harvard University Press, 1976); and Bruce Laurie, *Artisans into Workers: Labor in Nineteenth-Century America* (New York: Hill and Wang, 1989).

156. Bederman, *Manliness and Civilization,* 172.

157. *Chicago American,* July 15, 1837; Andreas, *History of Cook County,* 384; Tobin, "Lowly Muscular Digger," 181. Tobin incorrectly notes that this riot occurred in the winter of 1838.

158. James Brooks, "James Brooks to the Commissioners of the Illinois and Michigan Canal, February 23, 1838," *The Illinois and Michigan Canal, 1827–1911: A Selection of Documents from the Illinois State Archives,* accessed May 15, 2015, www .cyberdriveillinois.com/departments/archives/teaching_packages/I_and_M_ canal/doc11.html.

159. *Ottawa Free Trader,* May 13, 1846.

160. Brownson, quoted in Isaac McDaniel, "Orestes A. Brownson on Irish Immigrants and American Nativism," *American Benedictine Review* 32, no. 2 (1981): 125.

161. Oakley, appointed in 1847 as the canal's state trustee, resented private trustees William Swift (Washington, DC) and David Leavitt (New York). He accused them of negligence and dishonesty and criticized their salaries of $5,000, twice that of his own, as evidence that they valued personal wealth over public service, despite Illinois's financial woes. Oakley was also infuriated with the canal office in Lockport, claiming that Secretary Stuart and Chief Engineer Gooding had withheld information and "banned together" against him. In these conflicts Oakley portrayed himself as an honorable public servant, champion of both the taxpaying citizens of Illinois and the struggling Irish canallers. His nemesis Gooding viewed Oakley's ascent as a devious "plan of certain wire pullers to get control of the canal and the Canal property, distribute the offices and make fortunes at the expense of the State and her creditors." Tobin, "Lowly Muscular Digger," 86; *Ottawa Free Trader,* July 23, 1847; Leavitt to William Smith, July 3, 1846; Isaac Hardy to Thomas Tileson, July 9, 1847, both in Illinois and Michigan Canal Archives; *Chicago Daily Journal,* June 17 and October 24, 1847; and Gooding to Swift, January 27, 1847, Illinois and Michigan Canal Archives.

162. Tobin argues that Irish canallers "played a negligible role" in the strike, merely providing Oakley "with a convenient excuse" to denounce his colleagues. She suggests that the strike was "contrived" by Oakley and contractor Daniel Lynch, leader of the Corkonian faction on the canal, and depicts the workers as mere pawns in a politically motivated quarrel on the part of management. In her view, Oakley had anticipated the hard stance Gooding would take against the striking workers, thus clarifying a letter he wrote to the New York bondholders that blamed Gooding for delaying progress on the canal by refusing to compromise with the Irish workers. Peter Way argues that the canallers timed their strike in hope of exploiting a rift in the canal management. Both scholars agree that the strike was a failure, demonstrating a lack of agency on the part of immigrant canallers in the face of an "obdurate" and unfair labor system. Tobin, "Lowly Muscular Digger," 93–94, 90; quote in Way, *Common Labour,* 255.

163. Petition, July 12, 1847, Illinois and Michigan Canal Archives.

164. Roediger, *Wages of Whiteness,* 13–15, 7–9.

165. Evidence of William Gooding, March 4, 1847, Illinois and Michigan Canal Archives, app. L, pp. 9–10,

166. Quoted in Lamb, "Drunken, Dirty Irish."

167. Tobin, "Lowly Muscular Digger," 195–97.

168. Stuart to Swift, July 17, 23, and August 16, 1847, Illinois and Michigan Canal Archives (emphasis in original).

169. Report of the Majority of the Board of Trustees of the Illinois and Michigan Canal, November 1847, Illinois and Michigan Canal Archives, app. E, p. 160,

170. *Chicago Tribune,* November 15, 1847; Evidence of Gooding, March 4, 1847, Illinois and Michigan Canal Archives, 10. As a result of further investigations, Chief Engineer Gooding was removed from the position he had held since construction opened.

171. David L. Lightner, "Labor on the Illinois Central Railroad, 1852–1900" (PhD diss., Cornell University, 1969), 40.

172. *Chicago Tribune,* June 16, 1854.

173. *Alton Courier,* June 17, 1853.

174. Lightner, "Illinois Central Railroad," 42–43.

175. The men involved worked for the contracting firm of Story, Talmadge, and Conklin. For various reports on this conflict, see *Chicago Tribune,* December 17, 19, 1853; *Ottawa Republican,* December 17, 1853; *Alton Courier,* December 19, 20, 21, 1853; and P. B. Wyman to Mason, December 16, 1853, In-Letters, New York Office, IC 11 N1.5, Illinois Central Railroad Company Archives. For a historical account, see Lightner, "Illinois Central Railroad," 48–49; Brayman to Burrall, December 17, 1853, Brayman, Out-Letters, IC 1 B7.1, Illinois Central Railroad Company Archives.

176. *Chicago Tribune,* December 17, 1853.

177. *Alton Courier,* December 21, 1853. See Manfred Berg, *Popular Justice: A History of Lynching in America* (Chicago: Dee, 2011).

178. Timothy Blackstone, Division Engineer, to Mason, December 22, 1853, New York Office, Illinois Central Railroad Company Archives.

179. *Chicago Tribune,* June 16, 1854, quoted in Lightner, "Illinois Central Railroad," 49n86.

180. Brayman to Matteson, July 4, 1854, Brayman Papers. Matteson had worked on railroads in the South prior to his arrival in Illinois, where he was a contractor for the I&M Canal.

181. Roswell B. Mason to Burrall, August 6, 1854, Mason, Out-Letters, Illinois Central Railroad Company Archives.

182. *Alton (IL) Telegraph,* July 21, August 4, 1854.

183. Ignatiev, *Irish Became White,* 2–3, 96.

184. *Eighth Annual Report of the Acting Commissioner of the Illinois and Michigan Canal to the General Assembly* (Springfield, IL: Walters and Weber, 1844), 51.

185. William Gooding, "Engineer's Report to the Board of Commissioners of the Illinois and Michigan Canal, 1842," reprinted in *Canal Commissioners of Illinois,* 202.

186. *Eighth Annual Report,* 51.

187. *Gem of the Prairie,* April 18, 1848, quoted in Berndt, "Celebrating," 18.

188. Buckingham wrote for the *Boston Courier.* Harry E. Pratt, ed., *Illinois as Lincoln Knew It: A Boston Reporter's Record of a Trip in 1847,* reprinted from Members of the Abraham Lincoln Association, *Papers in Illinois History and Transactions for the Year 1937* (Springfield, IL, 1938), 24, 27, 80.

189. Hulbert, *Paths of Inland Commerce,* 74.

190. Pratt, *Lincoln Knew It,* 49.

191. Culmann, quoted in John M. Lamb, "William Gooding, Chief Engineer, Illinois and Michigan Canal," *Illinois Canal Society* 5 (1982): 139 (italics added).

192. Raho to Rosati, August 23, 1838, Rosati Correspondence.

193. Chickering, *Immigration,* 64.

194. Johnston, *Illinois Central Heritage,* 10–17 (italics in the original).

195. Stuart to Swift, August 16, 1847, Illinois and Michigan Canal Archives.

CHAPTER 4. MORMONS, TRANSCONTINENTAL RAILROAD

1. Samuel Bowles, *Our New West: Records of Travel between the Mississippi River and the Pacific Ocean* (New York: Dennison, 1869), 73. Bowles was the publisher and editor of the *Springfield (MA) Republican* from 1844 until his death in 1878.

2. Ibid., 73–74.

3. Elliott West, *The Last Indian War: The Nez Perce Story* (New York: Oxford University Press, 2009), 319; and for an extended analysis, see E. West, "Reconstructing Race," *Western Historical Quarterly* 34 (Spring 2003): 7–26.

4. John Lauritz Larson, *The Market Revolution in America: Liberty, Ambition, and the Eclipse of the Common Good* (New York: Cambridge University Press, 2010), 50. See also Richard L. Bushman, *Joseph Smith, Rough Stone Rolling: A Cultural Biography of Mormonism's Founder* (New York: Knopf, 2005). On Rochester as a canal town, see Paul Johnson, *A Shopkeeper's Millennium: Society and Revivals in Rochester, New York, 1815–1837* (New York: Hill and Wang, 1978).

5. Gary Y. Okihiro, *Common Ground: Reimagining American History* (Princeton, NJ: Princeton University Press, 2001), see chap. 1 in particular. While many historians have examined the role of the transcontinental railroad in completing America's continental empire, few have attempted to connect it to endeavors and developments beyond the West and the nation, namely, the centuries-long quest to reach the Orient. America's transcontinental railroads achieved this by establishing ownership of (and operating) steamship companies that served Asia from ports on the West Coast. For a recent study that conceptualizes and situates the West transnationally, see Richard V. Francaviglia, *Go East, Young Man: Imagining the American West as the Orient* (Logan: Utah State University Press, 2011).

6. California's golden spike remains on display at Stanford University's Cantor Arts Center; see http://museum.stanford.edu/.

7. Quoted in John Hoyt Williams, *A Great and Shining Road: The Epic Story of the Transcontinental Railroad* (New York: Times Books, 1988), 264.

8. Mark Fiege, *The Republic of Nature: An Environmental History of the United States* (Seattle: University of Washington Press, 2012), 229.

9. As some scholars, most notably W. Paul Reeve, have explored, the apparent differences were not only religious, cultural, and ideological; they were physical. *Religion of a Different Color: Race and the Mormon Struggle for Whiteness* (New York: Oxford University Press, 2015); see note 14 (of this chapter).

10. Richard White, *Railroaded: The Transcontinentals and the Making of Modern America* (New York: Norton, 2012), 281–82.

11. Leonard J. Arrington, *Great Basin Kingdom: An Economic History of the Latter-day Saints, 1830–1900* (Cambridge, MA: Harvard University Press, 1958).

12. Following Arrington, historians have emphasized the Mormon Church's seemingly unwavering support for the transcontinental railroad in spite of national attention to the church's "isolationism." Robert G. Athearn focuses on the role that Mormon leaders and missionaries played in identifying both the threats and benefits that the railroad posed to the church's economic control over Utah and its people. See "Opening the Gates of Zion: Utah and the Coming of the Union Pacific Railroad," *Utah Historical Quarterly* 36, no. 4 (1968): 292–314. John J. Stewart devotes a chapter to Utah's contribution to the railroad in a study that otherwise describes the foremost role of Union and Central Pacific officials. His brief discussion of Utah's involvement highlights the scandal that prevented Union Pacific officials from adequately remunerating Mormon workers in Echo and Weber Canyon in 1868 and 1869. See *The Iron Trail to the Golden Spike* (Salt Lake City: Deseret Book, 1969). Clarence Reeder's dissertation maintains a territorial focus, describing Mormon labor on the Union and Central Pacific with emphasis on the various branch line railroads in Utah. Clarence Reeder, "The History of Utah's Railroads, 1869–1883" (PhD diss., University of Utah, 1970). See also Richard E. Kotter, "The Transcontinental Railroad and Ogden City Politics," *Utah Historical Quarterly* 42, no. 3 (1974): 278–84; Richard O. Cowan, "Steel Rails and the Utah Saints," *Journal of Mormon History* 27, no. 2 (2001): 177–84; and Craig L. Foster, "'That Canny Scotsman': John Sharp and the Union Pacific Negotiations, 1869–72," *Journal of Mormon History* 27 (2001): 197–214. Confirming, but not building on Arrington's work, these scholars see unanimity among Mormon leaders about the nature of progress and the Mormon contribution to it and describe the challenges the railroad presented in distinctly religious and economic terms.

13. New York representative Fernando Wood, quoted in Orson F. Whitney, *Popular History of Utah* (Salt Lake City: Deseret News, 1916), 194. Wood's use of the adjective "profligate" connoted not recklessness but cultural and religious depravity.

14. W. Paul Reeve, "The Wrong Side of White," *Sightings,* May 31, 2012, https://divinity.uchicago.edu/sightings/wrong-side-white-w-paul-reeve. As Reeve notes, "The historical arc of Mormonism's racial dance is richly ironic," for by today's standards Mormons are viewed "as too white."

15. Referred to as the Pacific Railway Act, its original title was "An Act to Aid in the Construction of a Railroad and Telegraph Line from the Missouri River to the

Pacific Ocean, and to Secure to the Government the Use of the Same for Postal, Military, and Other Purposes," Stat. 12 (1862): 489. An 1864 revision of this act ceded all natural resources on the line to the railroads and empowered each company to "enter . . . purchase, take, and hold any lands or premises," within one hundred feet of the main line, "that may be necessary and proper for the construction and working of said road." Stat. 13 (1864): 356.

16. See David Haward Bain, *Empire Express: Building the First Transcontinental Railroad* (New York: Penguin, 2000); and Maury Klein, *Union Pacific*, vol. 1, *Birth of a Railroad, 1862–1893* (New York: Doubleday, 1987).

17. Joint Resolution of April 10, 1869, Union Pacific Railroad Company, the Central Pacific Railroad Company . . . Stat. 16 (1869): 56.

18. Patricia Nelson Limerick, *The Legacy of Conquest: The Unbroken Past of the American West* (New York: Norton, 1987), 27–28.

19. Terryl L. Givens, *The Viper on the Hearth: Mormons, Myths, and the Construction of Heresy* (New York: Oxford University Press, 1997), 4–5. Peculiarities included ongoing revelation, contemporary prophets, and the doctrines of plural marriage and blood atonement. Though the concept of blood atonement was repudiated by the LDS Church in 1978, in traditional Mormon theology it refers to sins for which the atonement of Jesus does not apply. To achieve the highest degree of salvation, Mormons who have committed such sins must, in the words of Brigham Young, "have their blood spilt upon the ground, that the smoke thereof might ascend to heaven as an offering for their sins." Brigham Young, September 21, 1856; February 8, 1857, *Journal of Discourses,* 26 vols. (London: LDS Booksellers Depot, 1857), Church History Library, Church of Jesus Christ of Latter-day Saints, 4:51–63, 220–21.

20. Daniel P. Kidder, *Mormonism and the Mormons: A Historical View of the Rise and Progress of the Sect Self-Styled Latter-day Saints* (New York: Lane and Sandford, 1842); 7–8. See also Pomeroy Tucker, *Origin, Rise, and Progress of Mormonism: Biography of Its Founders and History of Its Church; Personal Remembrances and Historical Collections Hitherto Unwritten* (New York: Appleton, 1867).

21. Robert W. Beers, *The Mormon Puzzle and How to Solve It* (New York: Funk and Wagnalls, 1887), 17. Beers then lamented, "But thus far it has successfully withstood even the fiercest opposition."

22. Givens, *Viper on the Hearth,* 5; see also 3–13.

23. T. B. H. Stenhouse, *The Rocky Mountain Saints: A Full and Complete History of the Mormons, from the First Vision of Joseph Smith to the Last Courtship of Brigham Young* (London: Ward, Lock, and Tyler, 1874), 497–98.

24. See E. Anthony Rotundo, *American Manhood: Transformations in Masculinity from the Revolution to the Modern Era* (New York: Basic Books, 1993), chaps. 8–9.

25. See Michael Kimmel, *Manhood in America: A Cultural History* (New York: Free Press, 1996).

26. Megan Sanborn Jones, *Performing American Identity in Anti-Mormon Melodrama* (New York: Routledge, 2009), 53, 63–65. In an 1870 sermon Brigham Young

argued that, as a polygamous husband, his authority extended beyond his family to "my neighbors and people around me." He continued, "If I am thus controlled by the Spirit of the Most High I am a king, I am supreme so far as the control of self is concerned; and it also enables me to control my wives and children . . . [for] they will be perfectly submissive to my dictates." Young, July 24, 1870, *Journal of Discourses,* 13:272.

27. Quoted in Arrington, *Great Basin Kingdom,* 255.

28. Jones, *Performing American Identity,* 65.

29. Charles H. Brigham, "The Mormon Problem," *Old and New* 1 (May 1870): 638.

30. See Figures 1 and 2. Dan Moos, *Outside America: Race, Ethnicity, and the Role of the American West in National Belonging* (Hanover, NH: Dartmouth College Press, 2005), 108.

31. Alfred Henry Lewis, "The Viper on the Hearth," pt. 1, "Mormonism: Its Plots, Plans, and Intrigues against American Homes," *Cosmopolitan* 50, no. 4 (1911): 439.

32. Eric Foner, *Free Soil, Free Labor, Free Men: The Ideology of the Republican Party before the Civil War,* rev. ed. (New York: Oxford University Press, 1995), 130.

33. Douglas, quoted in Brigham Henry Roberts, *History of the Church of Jesus Christ of Latter-day Saints, Period I,* 5 vols. (Salt Lake City: Church of Jesus Christ of Latter-day Saints, 1909), 5:397. See also Whitney, *Popular History of Utah,* 158.

34. Roberts, *History of the Church,* 5:397.

35. Quoted in Edward Tullidge, *Life of Brigham Young; or, Utah and Her Founders* (New York: Tullidge and Crandall, 1877), 387.

36. Cong. Globe, 37th Cong., 2d Sess. (1862), pt. 2, 1581; pt. 3, 2507; app. 385. See also E. B. Long, *The Saints and the Union: Utah Territory during the Civil War* (Urbana: University of Illinois Press, 1981), 71–72; and W. Paul Reeve, *Making Space on the Western Frontier: Mormons, Miners, and Southern Paiutes* (Urbana: University of Illinois Press, 2006), 35.

37. Wood, quoted in Whitney, *Popular History of Utah,* 194.

38. For the House of Representatives debate over Ashley's 1866 bill, see Cong. Globe, 39th Cong., 1st Sess. (1866), pt. 3, 2368–70. The best discussion of James Ashley's 1866 bill is in Reeve, *Making Space,* 43–46. See also William P. MacKinnon, "'Like Splitting a Man Up His Backbone': The Territorial Dismemberment of Utah, 1850–1896," *Utah Historical Quarterly* 71 (Spring 2003): 100–124.

39. For Ashley's proposed 1869 bill to remap Utah, see Cong. Globe, 40th Cong., 3rd Sess. (1869), pt. 1, 363–64. See also Reeve, *Making Space,* 58–61.

40. "After the Mormons," *Salt Lake Daily Telegraph,* January 28, 1869, copying the *San Francisco Call.*

41. Both Grenville Dodge of the Union Pacific and Leland Stanford of the Central Pacific—each of whom benefited from Mormon grading and embankment work on the railroad—delayed informing Young of their decision to link the railroads north of the Great Salt Lake until early in 1868. Utah Territory, *A Memorial to Congress for the Construction of a Great National Central Railroad to the Pacific*

Coast, *Utah Session Laws,* 1st Sess. (1852), 225; Utah Territory, *A Memorial to Congress in relation to the Pacific Railway, Utah Session Laws,* 3rd Sess. (1854), 30–32; Arrington, *Great Basin Kingdom,* 234–37; *Deseret News* (Utah Territory), January 22, 1867.

42. Brigham Young to George Nebeker, November 4, 1868, Brigham Young Collection, Archives Division; Young to Franklin D. Richards, May 23, 1868, Journal History of the Church of Jesus Christ of Latter-day Saints, Church History Library, both in Church of Jesus Christ of Latter-day Saints, Salt Lake City.

43. *Omaha Republican,* November 15, 1865.

44. This editorial, titled "Higher Civilization," appeared in the *Providence (RI) Journal* in 1868 and was reprinted in the *Deseret News,* August 12, 1868.

45. The article, titled "Mormonism Doomed," first appeared in the *Chicago Republican* and was reprinted in the *Deseret News,* May 13, 1868.

46. *Deseret News,* May 13, 1868, copying the *Chicago Republican.* The punctuation (?) after "civilizing" is in the original.

47. *Deseret News,* June 3, 1868; Arrington, *Great Basin Kingdom,* 236–37.

48. *Deseret News,* June 3, 1868.

49. "The Great Railroad of the West," *Latter-day Saints' Millennial Star* (Liverpool, UK) 30 (June 27, 1868): 408–10.

50. Arrington, *Great Basin Kingdom,* 234–35; 245–51. Moreover, the School of Prophets raised money to facilitate the construction of branch railroads to serve the Utah hinterland; established the Zion's Cooperative Mercantile Institution to control the importation and purchase of outside goods; and raised monies for the Perpetual Emigration Fund. Additionally, the "Word of Wisdom," a revelation announced by Joseph Smith in 1833 that called for abstinence from tobacco and "strong drinks" such as hot tea, coffee, and liquor, was reinforced by Brigham Young prior to the arrival of the railroad. Church leaders felt that such abstinence would not only save money to devote to the emigration fund but demonstrate Mormon self-control in comparison to the habits of Gentile "outsiders." Arrington, *Great Basin Kingdom,* 249–50.

51. Journal History, May 22, 28, 29, 1868, quoted in Arrington, *Great Basin Kingdom,* 246. Arrington also notes that the school tried to "minimize the influx of undesirable 'outsiders' by deflating the reports of Utah's mineral wealth," thereby limiting a rush of miners to the territory.

52. Celestial Roberts Knight, "Interview," *Utah Pioneer Biographies* 17 (1936): 131–33, Family History Library, Church of Jesus Christ of Latter-day Saints.

53. George Reynolds to George F. Gibbs, June 4, 1868, reprinted in the *Millennial Star* 30 (1868): 443.

54. "The Coming Railroad," *Deseret News,* June 3, 1868.

55. Ibid.

56. *Ogden (UT) Junction,* January 29, 1879.

57. Book of Mormon, I Nephi 13:5, 14:16, quoted in Brigham D. Madsen, *Glory Hunter: A Biography of Patrick Edward Connor* (Salt Lake City: University of Utah Press, 1990), 66.

58. David M. Emmons, *Beyond the American Pale: The Irish in the West, 1845–1910* (Norman: University of Oklahoma Press, 2010), 226.

59. *Deseret News,* June 17, 1868. Speeches from the June 1868 Mass Meeting were also reprinted in the *Millennial Star* 30 (July 18, August 1, August 8, 1868): 449–53; 484–88; 499–501.

60. *Deseret News,* June 17, 1868.

61. Ibid.

62. Ibid.

63. *Millennial Star* 30 (July 18, 1868): 451, 499.

64. *Deseret News,* June 17, 1868.

65. Arrington, *Great Basin Kingdom,* 261–62; Stewart, *Iron Trail,* 188–99. Stewart lists the amount of the contract at "one million dollars," with 80 percent being paid monthly according to the progress of the work and the remaining 20 percent after the Mormons' project was completed (188).

66. Young to Franklin D. Richards, Journal History, May 23, 1868.

67. Wilford Woodruff to Franklin D. Richards, January 6, 1868, reprinted in the *Millennial Star* 30 (February 8, 1868): 90–91. Woodruff went on to serve as the LDS Church's fourth president, from 1887 to 1898.

68. The *New York Express* article (July 12, 1868), was reprinted in the *Millennial Star* 30 (September 12, 1868): 590. This emigration strategy, in some ways, mirrored the experience of antebellum Irish immigrants who arrived in New York and were immediately plugged into networks of transportation labor, often on remote frontiers.

69. British Mission Emigration Register, Family History Library, Church of Jesus Christ of Latter-day Saints, bk. 1048, pp. 333–72; "A Compilation of General Voyage Notes," *Millennial Star* 30 (July 4, 1868): 426.

70. Joseph Smith Horne, "Autobiography," *Utah Pioneer Biographies* 2 (1909): 60–61, Family History Library, Church of Jesus Christ of Latter-day Saints.

71. John Thomas Lazenby, Journal, MS 6043, Church History Library, Church of Jesus Christ of Latter-day Saints, 3–5.

72. Jens Iver Jensen, "Autobiography," in *Our Pioneer Heritage,* comp. Kate B. Carter (Salt Lake City: Daughters of Utah Pioneers, 1967), 10: 74–75.

73. British Mission Emigration Register, bk. 1041, pp. 1–20; "Compilation," 442–43; Emily Pickering Anderson, "Reminiscences," in *Denmark to Manti: The History of William Anderson and Family* (Salt Lake City: printed by author, n.d.), 66–69.

74. Zebulon Jacobs, "Reminiscences and Diaries," Church History Library, Church of Jesus Christ of Latter-day Saints, fol. 3, pp. 114–34.

75. "Great Railroad," 408–10.

76. *Deseret Evening News* (Utah Territory), May 26, 1868.

77. Arrington, *Great Basin Kingdom,* 261–62; Stewart, *Iron Trail,* 190–91.

78. *Deseret News,* September 23, 1868.

79. Besides Sharp and Young, Levi Stewart, Thomas E. Ricks, and John Taylor were prominent subcontractors, as were their counterparts Ezra T. Benson,

Chauncey W. West, and Ogden Mayor Lorin Farr on the Central Pacific. See Reeder, "History of Utah's Railroads." This study discusses Mormon labor on the UPRR and CPRR but focuses primarily on the Utah Central, the Utah Northern, the Utah Southern, the Denver and Rio Grande, and other branch lines in Utah.

80. The Union Pacific would later transfer unpaid wages in the form of capital and construction materials for the Utah Central Railroad. See M. Guy Bishop, "Building Railroads for the Kingdom: The Career of John W. Young, 1867–91," *Utah Historical Quarterly* 48, no. 1 (1980): 66–80; and Reeder, "History of Utah's Railroads," 73–75.

81. Mindi Sitterud-McCluskey, "'Saints in the Pit': Mormon Colliers in Britain and the Intermountain West," in *Immigrants in the Far West: Historical Identities and Experiences*, ed. Brian Q. Cannon and Jessie Embry (Salt Lake City: University of Utah Press, 2014), 355, 354.

82. *Deseret Evening News,* June 23, 1868; the letter was dated June 18.

83. Adolphus Noon, quoted in *Deseret News,* July 15, 1868; the letter was dated June 28; *Deseret News,* July 22, 1868; the letter was dated July 13.

84. *Deseret News,* September 8, 1868.

85. *Deseret News,* August 12, 1868.

86. *Deseret News,* July 15, 1868; Samuel W. Richards to Franklin D. Richards, May 24, 1868, reprinted in the *Millennial Star* 30 (June 27, 1868): 410–12; Brigham Young to Albert Carrington, February 4, 1869, reprinted in the *Millennial Star* 31 (1869): 164.

87. On the "rough" masculinity of transportation workers, see Peter Way, *Common Labour: Workers and the Digging of North American Canals, 1780–1860* (New York: Cambridge University Press, 1993); Carol Sheriff, *The Artificial River: The Erie Canal and the Paradox of Progress, 1817–1862* (New York: Hill and Wang, 1996); and Steven Maynard, "Rough Work and Rugged Men: The Social Construction of Masculinity in Working-Class History," *Labour/Le Travail* 23 (Spring 1989): 159–69.

88. Sitterud-McCluskey, "Saints in the Pit," 355.

89. Young to Franklin D. Richards, August 4, 1868, Journal History.

90. See John Casement to Frances Casement, March 3, 8, and 12, 1869, folder 15, box 1, John Stephen and Frances Jennings Casement Papers, 1837–1928, accession number 308, American Heritage Center, University of Wyoming, Laramie.

91. S. Richards to F. Richards, May 24, 1868, *Millennial Star,* 410–12; Young to Carrington, February 4, 1869, *Millennial Star,* 164.

92. S. Richards to F. Richards, May 24, 1868, *Millennial Star,* 410–12.

93. Ibid.

94. *Deseret News,* September 16, 1868.

95. Joseph A. West, "Construction of the Union and Central Pacific Railroads across Utah, Fifty-Five Years Ago," *Union Pacific Magazine,* October 6, 1922, 8; John H. Beadle, *The Undeveloped West; or, Five Years in the Territories* (Philadelphia: National, 1873), 140, 154.

96. George A. Smith to W. S. Elderkin, April 14, 1869, Journal History.

97. Athearn, "Opening the Gates," 309–10.

98. "Higher Civilization."

99. *Deseret News,* August 19, 1868. According to Clarence Reeder, Mormon railroaders "work[ed] together in harmony," and in their camps "order was the common preoccupation and cooperation the key word." "History of Utah's Railroads," 35–36.

100. *Deseret News,* August 19, 1868.

101. "How We Are Getting On in Echo," *Deseret News,* July 15, 1868. The letter was dated June 28, 1868.

102. *Deseret News,* September 16, 1868.

103. *Deseret News,* June 24, 1868.

104. The Horton D. Haight and Frederick Kesler party departed Florence, Nebraska, on June 6, 1859, and arrived in Salt Lake City on September 1, 1859. See James Crane, Journal, and related sources in *Mormon Pioneer Overland Travel, 1847–1868,* Overland Travel Database, accessed May 23, 2015, https://history.lds.org /overlandtravels/home, Church History Library, Church of Jesus Christ of Latter-day Saints; Alice Davis Crane, "History of Alice Davis Crane," in *A History of the Three Wives of James Crane: Alice Davis Crane, Elizabeth Stewart Crane, and Rachel Briggs Crane*, ed. Crane Family Genealogical Committee, Family History Library, Church of Jesus Christ of Latter-day Saints.

105. This song was reprinted in the *Deseret News,* August 12, 1868.

106. Thomas E. Cheney, ed., *Mormon Songs from the Rocky Mountains: A Compilation of Mormon Folksong* (Austin: University of Texas Press, 1968), 92–98. For a slightly different version of this song, see Duncan Emrich, ed., *Songs of the Mormons, and Songs of the West* (Washington, DC: Library of Congress, 1952), 6–7.

107. Athearn, "Opening the Gates," 300.

108. See Leonard J. Arrington, Feramorz Fox, and Dean L. May, *Building the City of God: Community and Cooperation among the Mormons* (Urbana: University of Illinois Press, 1992); and Dean L. May, *Three Frontiers: Family, Land, and Society in the American West, 1850–1900* (New York: Cambridge University Press, 1994).

109. "Work and Good Wages for All," *Deseret News,* September 16, 1868.

110. Reynolds to Gibbs, June 4, 1868, *Millennial Star.*

111. *Deseret News,* September 16, 1868.

112. *Union Vedette* (Camp Douglas, Utah Territory), March 12, 1867. Established in 1863, the *Vedette* had short life span of four years. In 1872 the *Corinne Daily Reporter* (Utah Territory) was established as a successful opposition newspaper. It too was rather short-lived. See Brigham D. Madsen, *Corinne: The Gentile Capital of Utah* (Salt Lake City: Utah State Historical Society, 1980).

113. "Chinese Labor in the West," *Deseret News,* May 26, 1869.

114. For a discussion of widespread democratic support for anti-Chinese legislation in the West, see Limerick, *Legacy of Conquest.*

115. "Chinese Labor."

116. Bain, *Empire Express,* 605–7.

117. Emmons, *Beyond the American Pale.*

118. See *The Statistics of the Population of the United States, Ninth Census*, vol. 1 (Washington, DC: U.S. Bureau of Census, 1870), 373.

119. A January 29, 1879, editorial in the *Ogden Junction* argued that "the wages of white men ... have dwindled to such an extent that there is ... but a trifling difference between the prices paid for work performed by the white man and that done by the copper-colored incubus.... There are unquestionably more workmen than there is work to be performed; and to divide what little work there is with the inferior and alien race, is not a good nor a just policy."

120. "The Railroad in the Cañons, No. IX," *Deseret News*, August 1, 1868.

121. *Deseret Evening News*, October 9, 1868; Athearn, "Opening the Gates," 304–6.

122. *Deseret Evening News*, October 9, 1868.

123. Young, quoted in the *Deseret News*, January 22, 1867. For the LDS Church's efforts at theologizing concepts of race, primarily in relation to their own "Israelite lineage," and in Mormon interactions with American Indians and African Americans, see Armand L. Mauss, "The Children of Ham and the Children of Abraham: The Construction and Deconstruction of Ethnic Identities in the Mormon Heartland," in *Race, Religion, Region: Landscapes of Encounter in the American West*, ed. Fay Botham and Sara M. Patterson (Tucson: University of Arizona Press, 2006), 115–24. See also Mauss, *All Abraham's Children: Changing Mormon Conceptions of Race and Lineage* (Urbana: University of Illinois Press, 2003).

124. Arrington, *Great Basin Kingdom*, 264.

125. "Tunnelville, 12 Miles below Mouth of Echo," *Deseret News*, January 1, 1869. This letter was dated December 27, 1868, and was written by a Mormon railroad worker who referred to himself as "ANON." See also Golden Spike Railroad Scrapbook, Special Collections, J. Willard Marriott Library, University of Utah, Salt Lake City.

126. On "horns" and a "cloven foot," see George Q. Cannon's speech at the 1868 Mass Meeting, *Deseret News*, June 17, 1868. See also W. Paul Reeve, "'Nits Make Lice': The Construction of a Mormon-Indian Body" (work-in-progress presentation, Tanner Humanities Center, University of Utah, November 2007), copy in the possession of the author.

127. The word *crayther*, sometimes used as a term of endearment in Ireland, was invariably utilized in a dehumanizing context during immigrant encounters. See Fiona Bateman, "Defining the Heathen in Ireland and Africa: Two Similar Discourses a Century Apart," *Social Sciences and Missions* 21, no. 1 (2008): 89.

128. Young to Carrington, February 4, 1869, *Millennial Star*, 164. When the Irish workers and their "Gentile" contractors were moved off of two Weber Canyon tunnels for Mormon blasters, a number of the workers immediately went on strike and were fired. Nitroglycerin's effectiveness saved the Union Pacific tens of thousands of dollars in the canyons, as contractors could fire workers and reduce the number of shifts. See John R. Gillis, "Tunnels of the Pacific Railroad" (paper delivered before the American Society of Civil Engineers, January 5, 1870), repr. in *Van Nostrand's Eclectic Engineering Magazine* 2 (January 1870): 418–23; and Bain, *Empire Express*, 606.

129. See George L. Mosse, *The Image of Man: The Creation of Modern Masculinity* (New York: Oxford University Press, 1996). On martial masculinity, see Kristin L. Hoganson, *Fighting for American Manhood: How Gender Politics Provoked the Spanish-American and Philippine-American Wars* (New Haven: Yale University Press, 1998).

130. Interestingly, in light of the achievement at Promontory just eight months before, Utah's Saints depicted the Utah Central Railroad from Salt Lake to Ogden as more honorable and influential. After the completion of this branch line in January 1870, John W. Young's loyal workers thanked and praised their boss, a rare occurrence in a field of labor as filthy and oppressive as railroad construction. Despite enduring the difficulties of construction and receiving little or no wages, the workers did not flee or protest but praised their boss in a joint letter to the *Deseret Evening News,* January 11, 1870: "We the brethren employed in laying track on the Utah Central Railroad, take this present occasion of congratulating you on the speedy and successful termination of the greatest enterprise of the age, which we feel is mainly due to the energy and spirit displayed by you."

131. Charles R. Savage, Journals, May 7, 1869, L. Tom Perry Special Collections, Harold B. Lee Library, Brigham Young University, Provo, UT.

132. Martha A. Sandweiss, *Print the Legend: Photography and the American West* (New Haven: Yale University Press, 2002), 160–61.

133. *Salt Lake Daily Telegraph,* May 11, 1869.

CHAPTER 5. CHINESE IMMIGRANTS,
TRANSCONTINENTAL RAILROAD

1. Albert D. Richardson, *Beyond the Mississippi: From the Great Rim to the Great Ocean* (Hartford, CT: American, 1867), 438–40.

2. Stanford would immediately rename the camp "Colfax" in honor of the Speaker.

3. Richardson, *Beyond the Mississippi,* 438–40.

4. Samuel Bowles, *Our New West: Records of Travel between the Mississippi River and the Pacific Ocean* (New York: Dennison, 1869), 410–13; See also David Haward Bain, *Empire Express: Building the First Transcontinental Railroad* (New York: Penguin, 2000), 234–35.

5. Bowles, *Our New West,* 397.

6. Bain, *Empire Express,* 205–6; Mae M. Ngai, *The Lucky Ones: One Family and the Extraordinary Invention of Chinese America* (Boston: Houghton Mifflin, 2010), 3–5.

7. John Hoyt Williams, *A Great and Shining Road: The Epic Story of the Transcontinental Railroad* (New York: Times Books, 1988), 75; Scott Reynolds Nelson, "After Slavery: Forced Drafts of Irish and Chinese Labor in the American Civil War, or the Search for Liquid Labor," in *Many Middle Passages: Forced Migrations and*

the *Making of the Modern World,* ed. Emma Christopher, Cassandra Pybus, and Marcus Rediker (Berkeley: University of California Press, 2007), 157.

8. S. Nelson, "After Slavery," in Christopher, Pybus, and Rediker, *Many Middle Passages,* 156–61; Thomas W. Chinn, ed., *A History of the Chinese in California: A Syllabus* (San Francisco: Chinese Historical Society of America, 1969), 11–15.

9. Lucy M. Cohen, *Chinese in the Post–Civil War South: A People without History* (Baton Rouge: Louisiana State University Press, 1984), 174–75; Yong Chen, *Chinese San Francisco, 1850–1943: A Trans-Pacific Community* (Stanford, CA: Stanford University Press, 2000), 21.

10. S. Nelson, "After Slavery," in Christopher, Pybus, and Rediker, *Many Middle Passages,* 150–65; Him Mark Lai, *Becoming Chinese American: A History of Communities and Institutions* (Walnut Creek: Alta Mira, 2004), 39–76; Richard White, *Railroaded: The Transcontinentals and the Making of Modern America* (New York: Norton, 2012), 294–95; Manu Vimalassery, "Skew Tracks: Racial Capitalism and the First Transcontinental Railroad" (PhD diss., New York University, 2011), 56–66. The Anglicized spelling of *Huiguan* is *Huikuan.*

11. William L. Tung, *The Chinese in America, 1820–1973* (Dobbs Ferry, NY: Oceana, 1974), 7–11. Although the 1850 Foreign Miners' License Tax was written as a racially neutral law, its focus became Chinese miners, who were required to pay twenty dollars a month for mining licenses; this law also applied to the white miners and mining companies that hired Chinese workers. It was revised in 1852, 1853, 1855, 1856, and 1861. See Andrew Gyory, *Closing the Gate: Race, Politics, and the Chinese Exclusion Act* (Chapel Hill: University of North Carolina Press, 1998), 266n8. For a colorful account of this law, see Mark Twain, *Roughing It* (Hartford, CT: American, 1871), 393.

12. Rossiter W. Raymond, *Statistics of Mines and Mining in the States and Territories West of the Rocky Mountains,* 42nd Cong., 1st Sess., House Ex. Doc. 10, serial 1470 (Washington, DC: Government Printing Office, 1871), 4.

13. *Report of the Joint Special Committee to Investigate Chinese Immigration,* Sen. Rept. 689, 44th Cong., 2d Sess. (1877), 667. See also Bain, *Empire Express,* 207.

14. Quoted in Gyory, *Closing the Gate,* 18.

15. *Cincinnati Chronicle,* July 11, 1870; *New York Star,* September 24, 1870.

16. *Harper's Weekly,* August 14, 1869, 514–15.

17. Cong. Globe, 41st Cong., 3rd Sess. (January 7, 1871), 351–60.

18. Richardson, *Beyond the Mississippi,* 438–40; *Cincinnati Chronicle,* July 11, 1870; *Workingman's Advocate* (Chicago), February 6, 1869.

19. *New York Herald,* October 30, 1870.

20. Arthur B. Stout, *Chinese Immigration and the Physiological Causes of the Decay of a Nation* (San Francisco: Agnew and Deffebach, 1862), 1–26.

21. Quoted in Stuart Creighton Miller, *The Unwelcome Immigrant: The American Image of the Chinese, 1785–1882* (Berkeley: University of California Press, 1969), 165. On Chinese immigrants in California, and in the United States in general, see Elmer Clarence Sandmeyer, *The Anti-Chinese Movement in California* (Urbana:

University of Illinois Press, 1939); Ping Chiu, *Chinese Labor in California, 1850–1880* (Madison: University of Wisconsin Press, 1963); Gunther Barth, *Bitter Strength: A History of the Chinese in the United States, 1850–1870* (Cambridge, MA: Harvard University Press, 1964); Alexander Saxton, *The Indispensable Enemy: Labor and the Anti-Chinese Movement in California* (Berkeley: University of California Press, 1971); Ronald Takaki, *Strangers from a Different Shore: A History of Asian Americans,* rev. ed. (Boston: Little, Brown, 1998); and Gyory, *Closing the Gate.* For comparative studies of Chinese immigration, labor, and exclusion, see Robert E. Wynne, *Reaction to the Chinese in the Pacific Northwest and British Columbia, 1850–1910* (New York: Arno, 1978); Arif Dirlik, ed., *Chinese on the American Frontier* (Lanham, MD: Rowman and Littlefield, 2001); Najia Aarim-Heriot, *Chinese Immigrants, African Americans, and Racial Anxiety in the United States, 1848–82* (Urbana: University of Illinois Press, 2003); David Gouter, "Drawing Different Lines of Color: The Mainstream English Canadian Labour Movement's Approach to Blacks and Chinese, 1880–1914," *Labor: Studies in Working-Class History of the Americas* 2, no. 1 (2005): 55–76; and Lisa Yun, *The Coolie Speaks: Chinese Indentured Laborers and African Slaves in Cuba* (Philadelphia: Temple University Press, 2008).

22. The closest sources to Chinese workers, such as the Crocker brothers and James Strobridge, indicate that Chinese workers were first employed in early 1865. Nonetheless, the valuable (but woefully incomplete) Central Pacific payroll records at the California State Railroad Museum and Library reveal that Chinese crews were hired the previous year, in 1864. Payrolls, 1864–67, Personnel Records, series 4, MS 79, Central Pacific Railroad Collection, Sacramento. See also William Chew, *Nameless Builders of the Transcontinental* (Victoria, BC: Trafford, 2004).

23. *Sacramento Union*, January 5, 1865.

24. *Shasta Courier* (Redding, CA), January 2, 1865; *Sacramento Union*, January 5, 1865. Strobridge was awarded subcontracts by Crocker in late 1863 and early 1864, first for grading along the Sacramento waterfront and then for tracklaying past Roseville, California. See Bain, *Empire Express,* 207.

25. Crocker testimony, *Joint Special Committee,* 666–69.

26. Wesley S. Griswold, *A Work of Giants: Building the First Transcontinental Railroad* (New York: McGraw-Hill, 1962), 109; Bain, *Empire Express,* 208. Others found their way to the mines in Idaho's Owyhee District and even into southwestern and northeastern Oregon. See Randall E. Rohe, "After the Gold Rush: Chinese Mining in the Far West, 1850–1890," in Dirlik, *American Frontier,* 3–26.

27. Stanford, quoted in Erle Heath, "From Trail to Rail," *Southern Pacific Bulletin* 15, chap. 15 (1927): 12.

28. On mining as the "new" American dream, see H. W. Brands, *The Age of Gold: The California Gold Rush and the New American Dream* (New York: Doubleday, 2002).

29. Frederick F. Low testimony, Sen. Rept. 689, 44th Cong., 2d Sess. (1877), 77–78, quoted in W. Griswold, *Work of Giants,* 91; and Bain, *Empire Express,* 207.

30. Robert Lardin Fulton, *The Epic of the Overland* (San Francisco: Robertson, 1925), 31–33. Fulton was a telegraph operator for the Union Pacific Railroad in the 1860s and, in the preparation for his study, engaged in frequent correspondence with Strobridge.

31. Charles Crocker, "Reminiscences," Bancroft Library, University of California, Berkeley, 14. Alternatively, see Charles Crocker et al., "Facts Obtained from the Lips of Charles Crocker, Regarding His Identification with the Central Pacific Railroad, and Other Roads Growing of It: Dictation and Related Material Assembled in Preparing His Biography for H. H. Bancroft's 'Chronicles of the Builders of the Commonwealth, 1865–1890,'" Bancroft Library.

32. Crocker, "Reminiscences," 49–51.

33. Crocker and Strobridge were widely known for their repugnance of workers' drinking habits. Both were teetotalers. See Bain, *Empire Express,* 207; and W. Griswold, *Work of Giants,* 120–21.

34. Victor Clark, "Mexican Labor in the United States," *U.S. Labor Bulletin* 78 (September 1908): 478–81; Jeffrey Marcos Garcilazo, "'Traqueros': Mexican Railroad Workers in the United States, 1870 to 1930" (PhD diss., University of California, Santa Barbara, 1995).

35. Clark, *Mexican Labor,* 478–81.

36. Crocker testimony, *Joint Special Committee,* 666–69.

37. Strobridge testimony, ibid., 723–24, 727.

38. Crocker and Strobridge, in *Joint Special Committee,* 6, 23–24; J. Williams, *Great and Shining Road,* 96–97. David Roediger and Elizabeth Esch contribute an excellent, if brief, essay on this subject in *The Production of Difference: Race and the Management of Labor in U.S. History* (New York: Oxford University Press, 2012), 70–81.

39. Alexander Saxton, "The Army of Canton in the High Sierra," *Pacific Historical Review* 35, no. 2 (1966): 144.

40. See Bain, *Empire Express,* 208.

41. E. B. Crocker to Cornelius Cole, April 12, 1865, box 2, coll. no. 217, Cornelius Cole Family Papers, Department of Special Collections, University of California Library, Los Angeles. This letter is also quoted in an early Cole biography; see Catherine Coffin Phillips, *Cornelius Cole, California Pioneer and United States Senator: A Study in Personality and Achievements Bearing upon the Growth of a Commonwealth* (San Francisco: Nash, 1929), 138.

42. Crocker to Cole, April 12, 1865, Cole Family Papers.

43. John Debo Galloway, *The First Transcontinental Railroad* (New York: Arno, 1981), 86, 89; George Kraus, *High Road to Promontory: Building the Central Pacific across the High Sierra* (Palo Alto: American West, 1969), 134; J. Williams, *Great and Shining Road,* 94; Saxton, *Indispensable Enemy,* 61; Roediger and Esch, *Production of Difference,* 76.

44. Quoted in Galloway, *First Transcontinental Railroad,* 144.

45. Chiu, *Chinese Labor in California,* 89.

46. *Sacramento Union,* June 16, 1865, copying the *Auburn (CA) Stars and Stripes; Joint Special Committee,* 667.

47. *Report of the Chief Engineer upon Recent Surveys and Progress of Construction of the Central Pacific Railroad of California* (Sacramento: Central Pacific Railroad Company, 1865).

48. *Central Pacific Railroad Statement Made to the President of the United States, and Secretary of the Interior, of the Progress of the Work* (Sacramento: Crocker, 1865), 7; Bain, *Empire Express,* 226. Stanford's statement was reprinted in the *Sacramento Daily Union,* January 1, 1866.

49. *Central Pacific Railroad Statement,* 8.

50. The credit-ticket system had long been used by indentured migrants from southern China who left to work in what the Chinese called Nanyang ("Southern Ocean"), a region that included the Philippines, the former Dutch East Indies, the Malay Peninsula, Borneo, Indochina, Thailand, and Burma. The system sparked considerable controversy in the United States. See Cohen, *Post-Civil War South,* 41–44; and Estelle T. Lau, *Paper Families: Identity, Immigration Administration, and Chinese Exclusion* (Durham, NC: Duke University Press, 2007), 63–65.

51. *Central Pacific Railroad Statement.*

52. Vimalassery, "Skew Tracks," 72–73; Combined Asian American Resources Project: Oral History Transcripts of Tape-Recorded Interviews Conducted 1974–1976, Bancroft Library.

53. Crocker testimony, *Joint Special Committee,* 667.

54. *Report and Testimony Taken by the United States Pacific Railway Commission,* 8 vols., Sen. Exec. Doc 51, 50th Cong., 1st Sess. (1888), 3660.

55. Robert L. Harris, "The Pacific Railroad—Unopen," *Overland Monthly* 3, no. 3 (1869): 248.

56. Bain, *Empire Express,* 238–39.

57. Harris, "Pacific Railroad," 245, 248, 245.

58. There were thirteen major tunnels in the vicinity of the Sierras.

59. See George Kraus, "Chinese Laborers and the Construction of the Central Pacific," *Utah Historical Quarterly* 37, no. 1 (1969): 47. This label was invented by historians, and it seems that the earliest usage was in Edwin L. Sabin, *Building the Pacific Railway* (Philadelphia: Lippincott, 1919), 111. See also Saxton, "Army of Canton," 145.

60. On January 26, 1867, the editor of the *Dutch Flat (NV) Enquirer* noted that "we are now in the midst of one of the most severe winters we have experienced.... The fills, we hear, are so completely washed out that nothing but the rails are to be seen suspended in the air resembling telegraph wires."

61. John R. Gillis, "Tunnels of the Pacific Railroad" (paper delivered before the American Society of Civil Engineers, January 5, 1870), repr. in *Van Nostrand's Eclectic Engineering Magazine* 2 (January 1870): 418–23. See also Kraus, "Chinese Laborers," 44–60.

62. J.O. Wilder, interviewed by Erle Heath for the *Southern Pacific Bulletin,* quoted in Kraus, "Chinese Laborers," 49.

63. Ibid.

64. *Sacramento Union,* August 14, 1866.

65. Gillis, "Pacific Railroad," 421.

66. William Cronon has produced some of definitive studies in this field, including *Changes in the Land: Indians, Colonists, and the Ecology of New England* (New York: Hill and Wang, 1983); *Nature's Metropolis: Chicago and the Great West* (New York: Norton, 1991); and his edited volume, *Uncommon Ground: Rethinking the Human Place in Nature* (New York: Norton, 1995). See also Richard White, "Are You an Environmentalist or Do You Work for a Living? Work and Nature," in Cronon, *Uncommon Ground*, 171–85; White, *The Organic Machine: The Remaking of the Columbia River* (New York: Hill and Wang, 1995); and Thomas G. Andrews, *Killing for Coal: America's Deadliest Labor War* (Cambridge, MA: Harvard University Press, 2008).

67. Gillis, "Pacific Railroad," 418–23.

68. A. P. Partridge, interview, CPRR Biographical Notes, Lynn D. Farrar Collection, http://cprr.org/Museum/Farrar/index.html#2005–03–09–01–02, Central Pacific Railroad Photographic History Museum, 7–10.

69. *Sacramento Daily Union,* December 28, 1866, copying the *Dutch Flat Enquirer.*

70. Strobridge testimony, in *Report and Testimony,* 5:2580–81.

71. Charles Crocker to Collis P. Huntington, January 20, 1868, Collis P. Huntington Papers, reel 1, series 4, Bancroft Library.

72. Crocker testimony, *Joint Special Committee,* 666–88.

73. *Elko (NV) Independent,* January 5, 1870.

74. "Bones in Transit," *Sacramento Reporter,* June 30, 1870.

75. *Sacramento Union,* June 30, 1870.

76. A. W. Loomis, "How Our Chinamen Are Employed," *Overland Monthly* 2, no. 3 (1869): 232.

77. Leland Stanford to Huntington, September 9, 1867, Huntington Papers.

78. Huntington to Edwin B. Crocker, October 3, 1867, Huntington Papers.

79. Twain, *Roughing It,* 391.

80. Ibid., 394; *Sacramento Daily Union,* July 9, 1866. This would put the number of Chinese workers on the CPRR somewhere between 10,000 and 14,575. Historians' calculations have typically fallen between 10,000 and 12,000, but the (incomplete) CPRR payroll records at the California State Railroad Museum and Library in Sacramento suggest a number closer to 15,000 and perhaps even higher. Payrolls, 1864–67. William F. Chew has made a calculation, based on these payroll records and the July 9, 1866, article in the *Sacramento Daily Union,* which puts the number of Chinese workers on the CPRR between 14,575 and 23,004. See *Nameless Builders,* 7, 42–45.

81. Twain, *Roughing It,* 394; *Sacramento Daily Union,* July 9, 1866. On the Chinese Six Companies, see Otis Gibson, *The Chinese in America* (Cincinnati: Hitchcock and Walden, 1877), 308. See also William Hoy, *The Chinese Six Companies: A Short, General Historical Résumé of Its Origin, Function, and Importance in the Life of the California Chinese* (San Francisco: Chinese Consolidated Benevolent Association, 1942); and "Documents of the Chinese Six Companies Pertaining to

Immigration," in *Chinese American Voices: From the Gold Rush to the Present,* ed. Judy Yung, Gordon H. Chang, and Him Mark Lai (Berkeley: University of California Press, 2006), 17–25.

82. See R. Scott Baxter, "The Response of California's Chinese Populations to the Anti-Chinese Movement," *Historical Archaeology* 42, no. 3 (2008): 29–36; Moon-Ho Jung, *Coolies and Cane: Race, Labor, and Sugar in the Age of Emancipation* (Baltimore: Johns Hopkins University Press, 2006), 181–220; and Aarim-Heriot, *Chinese Immigrants.*

83. Bain, *Empire Express,* 360.

84. E.B. Crocker to Huntington, June 4, 1867, Huntington Papers (italics added).

85. Quoted in W. Griswold, *Work of Giants,* 111.

86. E.B. Crocker to Huntington, June 27, 28, 1867; Mark Hopkins to Huntington, June 26, 1867; E.B. Crocker to Huntington, June 28, 1867, all in Huntington Papers.

87. E.B. Crocker to Huntington, July 2, 1867; June 27, 1867; Hopkins to Huntington, June 27, 1867, all in Huntington Papers.

88. H.W. Brands, *American Colossus: The Triumph of Capitalism, 1865–1900* (New York: Knopf Doubleday, 2010), 56.

89. Ibid.

90. *Sacramento Union,* July 6, 1867.

91. *San Francisco Examiner,* June 5, 1867.

92. Saxton, *Indispensable Enemy,* 1–2, 35–36.

93. See Barth, *Bitter Strength.* On Americans bringing ideas about race to the West, see Patricia Nelson Limerick, *The Legacy of Conquest: The Unbroken Past of the American West* (New York: Norton, 1987).

94. *San Francisco Real Estate Circular,* September, 1874.

95. White, *Railroaded,* 297. For an in-depth discussion of coolie labor versus the credit-ticket system, see Vimalassery, "Skew Tracks," 53–64.

96. Cong. Globe, 41st Cong., 2d Sess. (June 9, 1870), 4275–79.

97. *Workingman's Advocate,* February 6, 1869.

98. Crocker testimony, *Joint Special Committee,* 668.

99. John Miller, "Certain Phrases of the Chinese Question," *Overland Monthly* 7, no. 10 (1886): 431.

100. Galloway, *First Transcontinental Railroad,* 143–44; J. Williams, *Great and Shining Road,* 98.

101. Quoted in Stan Steiner, *Fusang: The Chinese Who Built America* (New York: Harper and Row, 1979), 130.

102. *San Francisco Bulletin,* May 6, 1869.

103. *Sacramento Daily Union,* May 8, 1869.

104. *San Francisco Bulletin,* May 8, 1869.

105. Ibid.

106. *San Francisco Newsletter,* May 15, 1869. See also J.N. Bowman, "Driving the Last Spike at Promontory, 1869," *Utah Historical Quarterly* 37, no. 1 (1969): 100. For

an excellent recent account of the Golden Spike ceremony, see Michael W. Johnson, "Rendezvous at Promontory: A New Look at the Golden Spike Ceremony," *Utah Historical Quarterly* 74, no. 1 (2004): 47–68.

107. To view another illustration as the Chinese Exclusion Act neared, see "What Shall We Do with Our Boys?" *The Wasp* (San Francisco) 8 (January–June 1882), courtesy of Bancroft Library, no. 292, 136–37, www.oac.cdlib.org/ark:/13030 /hb938nb337/?brand = oac4. Anti-Chinese cartoons such as this one were common during the years leading up to the Chinese Exclusion Act of 1882. The seated Chinese worker conjures up images of multiple "hands," a term often used to describe unskilled railroad construction workers.

108. Martha A. Sandweiss, *Print the Legend: Photography and the American West* (New Haven: Yale University Press, 2002), 2–3.

109. Charles F. Adams to Moorfield Story, February 2, 1885, quoted in White, *Railroaded,* xxiii.

110. Isaac D. Guyer, *History of Chicago: Its Commercial and Manufacturing Interests and Industry, Together with Sketches of Manufacturers and Men Who Have Most Contributed to Its Prosperity and Advancement* (Chicago: Church, Goodman and Cushing, 1862), 153; Charles Francis Adams, "The Era of Change," in *Chapters of Erie, and Other Essays,* by Charles F. Adams and Henry Adams (Boston: Osgood, 1871), 335.

111. In 1861 both publications reached a circulation of two hundred thousand. And while subscriptions for *Harper's Weekly* would eventually outpace those for *Frank Leslie's Illustrated Newspaper* by the end of the decade, both publications maintained their popularity. See M. Paul Holsinger, ed., *War and American Popular Culture: An Historical Encyclopedia* (Westport, CT: Greenwood, 1999), 99; and Leslie Butler, *Critical Americans: Victorian Intellectuals and Transatlantic Liberal Reform* (Chapel Hill: University of North Carolina Press, 2007), 179.

112. Ralph Waldo Emerson, "Nature" (1836), in *Nature, Addresses, and Lectures: The Collected Works of Ralph Waldo Emerson,* ed. Robert E. Spiller and Alfred R. Ferguson (Cambridge, MA: Harvard University Press, 1971), 1:39; Raymond Williams, *The Country and the City* (New York: Oxford University Press, 1973), 120.

113. Thomas G. Andrews's treatment of this topic as it relates to Colorado history and his creative handling of the writings of Denver and Rio Grande railroad worker John Watt provides a model for future studies. See "'Made by Toile'? Tourism, Labor, and the Construction of the Colorado Landscape, 1858–1917," *Journal of American History* 92, no. 3 (2005): 837–63. On landscape studies and theory, see Rachael Ziady DeLue and James Elkins, eds., *Landscape Theory,* Art Seminar 6 (New York: Routledge, 2008); W. J. T. Mitchell, ed., *Landscape and Power* (Chicago: University of Chicago Press, 1994); R. Williams, *Country and the City;* David E. Nye, ed., *Technologies of Landscape: From Reaping to Recycling* (Amherst: University of Massachusetts Press, 1999); and Martin A. Berger, *Sight Unseen: Whiteness and American Visual Culture* (Berkeley: University of California Press, 2005).

114. That railroads "annihilated space and time" was a common refrain of nineteenth-century Americans and foreign visitors to America. See Wolfgang

Schivelbusch, *The Railway Journey: The Industrialization of Time and Space in the 19th Century* (Berkeley: University of California Press, 1977), 37; and Leo Marx, *The Machine in the Garden: Technology and the Pastoral Ideal in America* (New York: Oxford University Press, 1964), 194, quoting Alexis de Tocqueville.

115. On observed landscapes as "dreamworks" of imperialism, see Mitchell, "Imperial Landscape," in Mitchell, *Landscape and Power,* 10. As Mitchell suggests, "Landscape might be seen ... [as] the 'dreamwork' of Imperialism, unfolding its own movement in time and space from a central point of origin and folding back on itself to disclose both utopian fantasies of the perfected imperial prospect and fractured images of unresolved ambivalence and unsuppressed resistance."

116. Sandweiss, *Print the Legend,* 2.

117. Joseph Becker, "An Artist's Interesting Recollections of Leslie's Weekly," *Leslie's Weekly,* December 14, 1905, 570.

118. On this and *Leslie's* other excursions and endeavors, see Robert Taft, *Artists and Illustrators of the Old West, 1850–1900* (Princeton, NJ: Princeton University Press, 1982), 149–61; Andrea Pearson, "*Frank Leslie's Illustrated Newspaper* and *Harper's Weekly:* Innovation and Imitation in Nineteenth-Century American Pictorial Reporting," *Journal of Popular Culture* 23, no. 4 (1990): 81–111; Joshua Brown, *Beyond the Lines: Pictorial Reporting, Everyday Life, and the Crisis of Gilded Age America* (Berkeley: University of California Press, 2001); and Deirdre Murphy, "The Look of a Citizen: Representations of Immigration in Gilded Age Painting and Popular Press Illustration" (PhD diss., University of Minnesota, 2007), chap. 2.

119. Weston Naef and Christine Hult-Lewis, *Carleton Watkins: The Complete Mammoth Photographs,* no. 948 (Los Angeles: Getty Museum, 2011), 402.

120. Sandweiss, *Print the Legend,* 343.

121. On Kearney and the workingmen's movement in California, see Neil Larry Shumsky, *The Evolution of Political Protest and the Workingmen's Party of California* (Columbus: Ohio State University Press, 1991); Saxton, *Indispensable Enemy;* Jean Pfaelzer, *Driven Out: The Forgotten War against Chinese Americans* (New York: Random House, 2007); and Sandmeyer, *Anti-Chinese Movement.*

CHAPTER 6. END-OF-TRACK

1. W. C. A. Smoot, "Tales from Old Timers—No. 9," *Union Pacific Magazine,* December 1923; Grenville M. Dodge, *How We Built the Union Pacific Railway, and Other Railway Papers and Addresses* (1911; repr., Denver: Sage Books, 1965), 17, 28, 29. Dodge, who resigned his military position and was named chief engineer of the Union Pacific in 1866, served simultaneously in the House of Representatives.

2. Dodge, *Union Pacific Railway,* 29.

3. See Wallace D. Farnum, "Grenville Dodge and the Union Pacific: A Study of Historical Legends," *Journal of American History* 51, no. 4 (1965): 632–50. Farnum notes that Dodge "had no direct connection with the physical construction of the Union Pacific," including graders, tie cutters, bridge builders, or John and Dan

Casement's tracklayers. According to Dodge himself, "My duties commenced and ended with the development of the Country and determining the Line across the Continent. I disbursed no Contractors funds, and I had no control, directly or indirectly, over Contracts or Contractors" (642).

4. In addition to Farnum, other sources refute Dodge's claims, including the personal papers of John Casement, the Union Pacific's construction supervisor. John Casement to Frances Casement, October 31, 1868, folder 13, box 1; John to Frances, February 8, 11, 1869, folder 15, box 1; John to Frances, April 4, 13, 1869, and W. Snyder to Oliver Ames, October 2, 1869, folder 16, box 1, John Stephen and Frances Jennings Casement Papers, 1837–1928, accession number 308, American Heritage Center, University of Wyoming, Laramie. See also Central Pacific Railroad Photographic History Museum, "Fiction or Fact: Did the Chinese and Irish Railroad Workers Really Try to Blow Each Other Up?," with comments from David Bain, Edson T. Strobridge, and Chris Graves, http://cprr.org/Game/Interactive_Railroad_Project/Fiction_or_Fact.html.

5. "The Pacific Railroad," *Harper's Weekly*, May 29, 1869, 342.

6. See Charles Crocker's testimony, as well as that of his superintendent James H. Strobridge, in the *Report of the Joint Special Committee to Investigate Chinese Immigration*, Sen. Rept. 689, 44th Cong., 2d Sess. (1877), 666–68 (Crocker); 723–28 (Strobridge). See also Tzu-Kuei Yen, "Chinese Workers and the First Transcontinental Railroad of the United States of America" (PhD diss., St. John's University, 1976), 28–29, 96–146.

7. See, among other studies, Najia Aarim-Heriot, *Chinese Immigrants, African Americans, and Racial Anxiety in the United States, 1848–82* (Urbana: University of Illinois Press, 2003); Andrew Gyory, *Closing the Gate: Race, Politics, and the Chinese Exclusion Act* (Chapel Hill: University of North Carolina Press, 1998); and Jean Pfaelzer, *Driven Out: The Forgotten War against Chinese Americans* (New York: Random House, 2007). For an excellent comparative history of Chinese labor that stretches from California to Louisiana to the Caribbean, see Moon-Ho Jung, *Coolies and Cane: Race, Labor, and Sugar in the Age of Emancipation* (Baltimore: Johns Hopkins University Press, 2006).

8. See Gunther Peck, "Manly Gambles: The Politics of Risk on the Comstock Lode, 1860–1880," *Journal of Social History* 26, no. 4 (1993): 701–23.

9. *Gold Hill (NV) Daily News*, July 7, 1869.

10. Ibid., October 7, 1869.

11. George Washington to Thomas Johnson, July 20, 1770, in Corra Bacon-Foster, *Early Chapters in the Development of the Potomac Route to the West* (Washington, DC: Columbia Historical Society, 1912), 18–21; see also John Lauritz Larson, "'Bind the Republic Together': The National Union and the Struggle for a System of Internal Improvements," *Journal of American History* 74, no. 2 (1987): 366–67.

12. Annals of Cong., 14th Cong., 2d Sess. (February 4, 1817), 854.

13. John Lauritz Larson, *Internal Improvement: National Public Works and the Promise of Popular Government in the Early United States* (Chapel Hill: University of North Carolina Press, 2001); C. Edward Skeen, *1816: America Rising* (Lexington:

University Press of Kentucky, 2003); David R. Meyer, *The Roots of American Industrialization* (Baltimore: Johns Hopkins University Press, 2003); Steven Usselmann, *Regulating Railroad Innovation: Business, Technology, and Politics in America, 1840–1920* (New York: Cambridge University Press, 2002); Richard White, *Railroaded: The Transcontinentals and the Making of Modern America* (New York: Norton, 2012). For traditional studies, see Carter Goodrich, *Government Promotion of American Canals and Railroads, 1800–1890* (New York: Columbia University Press, 1960); Goodrich, "Internal Improvements Reconsidered," *Journal of Economic History* 30 (June 1970): 289–311; and Robert A. Lively, "The American System, a Review Article," *Business History Review* 29 (Spring 1955): 81–95.

14. Robert J. Kapsch, *The Potomac Canal: George Washington and the Waterway West* (Morgantown: West Virginia University Press, 2007), 213; Peter Way, *Common Labour: Workers and the Digging of North American Canals, 1780–1860* (New York: Cambridge University Press, 1993), 6–7.

15. James Henry Hammond, *Selections from the Letters and Speeches of the Honorable James Henry Hammond* (New York: Trow, 1866), 318–19.

16. Quoted in Carol Sheriff, *The Artificial River: The Erie Canal and the Paradox of Progress, 1817–1862* (New York: Hill and Wang, 1996), 35.

17. William Archer, *America To-day: Observations and Reflections* (New York: Scribner's Sons, 1899), 91; Glen E. Holt, "The Birth of Chicago: An Examination of Economic Parentage," *Journal of the Illinois State Historical Society* 76 (Summer 1983): 87; William Cronon, *Nature's Metropolis: Chicago and the Great West* (New York: Norton, 1991), 23–24, 63–74, and chaps. 1–2 in general. Archer (and later Cronon) noted that, prior to the canals and railroads that "created" Chicago, it was a gathering place known only for its abundance of garlic plants, which gave it the name *Chigagou,* the "wild-garlic place."

18. Jesse B. Thomas, *Report of Jesse B. Thomas as a Member of the Executive Committee Appointed by the Chicago Harbor and River Convention, of the Statistics concerning the City of Chicago* (Chicago: Wilson, 1847), 25 (emphasis added).

19. Isaac D. Guyer, *History of Chicago: Its Commercial and Manufacturing Interests and Industry, Together with Sketches of Manufacturers and Men Who Have Most Contributed to Its Prosperity and Advancement* (Chicago: Church, Goodman and Cushing, 1862), 153.

20. Way, *Common Labour,* 161.

21. Dale T. Knobel, *Paddy and the Republic: Ethnicity and Nationality in Antebellum America* (Middletown, CT: Wesleyan University Press, 1986), 88, 90, 123; Matthew Frye Jacobson, *Whiteness of a Different Color: European Immigrants and the Alchemy of Race* (Cambridge, MA: Harvard University Press, 1998), 48.

22. Francis J. Grund, *The Americans in Their Social, Moral, and Political Relations* (1837; repr., New York: Johnson Reprint, 1968), 221.

23. *Chicago American,* July 9, 1836.

24. James Silk Buckingham, *The Eastern and Western States of America,* 3 vols. (London: Fisher, Son, 1842), 3:222–24.

25. Ohio governor William Bebb, quoted in Horace Greeley, "The Great River-and-Harbor Convention at Chicago—Railroad to the Pacific—Internal Improvements and Party Politics," reprinted in the *New York Tribune,* July 17, 1847.

26. Quoted in Edward Tullidge, *Life of Brigham Young; or, Utah and Her Founders* (New York: Tullidge and Crandall, 1877), 387.

27. See W. Paul Reeve, *Religion of a Different Color: Race and the Mormon Struggle for Whiteness* (New York: Oxford University Press, 2015), 247–73.

28. *Sacramento Daily Union,* May 8, 1869.

29. On white perceptions of Chinese immigrants as "sojourners," see Gunther Barth, *Bitter Strength: A History of the Chinese in the United States, 1850–1870* (Cambridge, MA: Harvard University Press, 1964); and Gyory, *Closing the Gate,* for a critique.

30. See Neil Larry Shumsky, *The Evolution of Political Protest and the Workingmen's Party of California* (Columbus: Ohio State University Press, 1991).

31. Among other references, see Judge Nathaniel Bennett's speech on the completion of the transcontinental railroad in the *San Francisco Bulletin,* May 8, 1869.

32. Campbell's speech was reprinted two days later in the *Chicago Tribune,* May 12, 1869.

BIBLIOGRAPHY

ARCHIVES AND MANUSCRIPTS

Allen County–Fort Wayne Historical Society, Fort Wayne, Indiana
Canal contract, signed by William Rockhill and Samuel Lewis, June 4, 1832. Miscellaneous Papers.

American Heritage Center, University of Wyoming, Laramie
Stephen, John, and Frances Jennings Casement. Papers, 1837–1928.

Bancroft Library, University of California, Berkeley
Combined Asian American Resources Project: Oral History Transcripts of Tape-Recorded Interviews Conducted 1974–76.
Crocker, Charles. "Reminiscences."
Crocker, Charles, Mary A. Deming Crocker, Guysbert Bogart Vroom DeLamater, Joseph A. Benton, Lester Ludyah Robinson, Aaron Augustus Sargent, Ira Packard Rankin, et al. "Facts Obtained from the Lips of Charles Crocker, Regarding His Identification with the Central Pacific Railroad, and Other Roads Growing of It: Dictation and Related Material Assembled in Preparing His Biography for H. H. Bancroft's 'Chronicles of the Builders of the Commonwealth, 1865–1890.'"
Griswold, Wesley S., Papers, 1955–90.
Hopkins, Mark. Biographical manuscript.

California State Railroad Museum and Library, Sacramento
Payrolls, 1864–67. Personnel Records. Series 4. MS 79. Central Pacific Railroad Collection.

Central Pacific Railroad Photographic History Museum
Partridge, A. P., Interview. CPRR Biographical Notes. Lynn D. Farrar Collection. http://cprr.org/Museum/Farrar/index.html#2005-03-09-01-02.

Chicago Historical Society
Brayman, Mason. Papers, 1850–65.
Illinois and Michigan Canal Archives (formerly the William Swift Collection).
Swift, William H., Papers, 1843–65.

Church of Jesus Christ of Latter-day Saints, Salt Lake City
ARCHIVES DIVISION
Young, Brigham. Collection.
Young, John W., Papers. Outgoing Correspondence.

CHURCH HISTORY LIBRARY
Crane, James. Journal. *Mormon Pioneer Overland Travel, 1847–1868.* Overland Travel
    Database. Accessed May 23, 2015. https://history.lds.org/overlandtravels/home.
Jacobs, Zebulon. "Reminiscences and Diaries."
Journal History of the Church of Jesus Christ of Latter-day Saints.
Journal of Discourses. 26 vols. London: LDS Booksellers Depot, 1855–86.
Lazenby, John Thomas. Journal. MS 6043.

FAMILY HISTORY LIBRARY
British Mission Emigration Register.
Crane, Alice Davis. "History of Alice Davis Crane." In *A History of the Three Wives
    of James Crane: Alice Davis Crane, Elizabeth Stewart Crane, and Rachel Briggs
    Crane,* edited by the Crane Family Genealogical Committee.
Horne, Joseph Smith. "Autobiography." *Utah Pioneer Biographies* 2 (1909): 60–61.
Knight, Celestial Roberts. "Interview." *Utah Pioneer Biographies* 17 (1936): 131–33.

Department of Special Collections, Stanford University Library, California
Hopkins, Mark. Correspondence.
Hopkins, Timothy. Transportation Collection, 1816–1942.
Stanford, Leland. Papers, 1841–97.

Department of Special Collections, University of California Library, Los Angeles
Cole, Cornelius. Family Papers, 1833–1943.

Graduate Theological Union Library, Berkeley, California
American Home Missionary Society Papers, 1816–94. Glen Rock, NJ: Microfilming
    Corporation of America, 1975.

Illinois and Michigan Canal Records
ILLINOIS STATE ARCHIVES, SPRINGFIELD
"Letterbooks." 1836–1915. Record series 491.004.
Minutes of the Meetings of the Board of Commissioners of the Illinois and
    Michigan Canal. April 13, 1839, G.22.

"Reports." 1838. Record series 491.006.
"Supplies Furnished to Workers." Record series 491.046.
"Time Books." 1847. Record series 491.044.

Illinois Central Railroad Company Archives
ROGER AND JULIE BASKES DEPARTMENT OF SPECIAL COLLECTIONS,
NEWBERRY LIBRARY, CHICAGO
Brayman, Mason. Out-Letters, IC 1 B7.1.
Burrall, William P., Out-Letters, IC 1 B9.1.
Mason, Roswell B., Out-Letters, IC 1 M3.1.
New York Office. In-Letters, IC 11 N1.5.

Illinois State Historical Society, Springfield
Perce, William L., Correspondence.

Indiana Historical Society, Indianapolis
Bass, W. H., Photo Company Collection.
Broadside Collection.

Indiana State Archives, Indianapolis
Indiana Commission on Public Records.
    Wabash and Erie Canal Correspondence. Internal Improvement Papers. Land
        Department. Records of the Auditor of the State. Archives Division.
    Whitewater Canal Correspondence. Internal Improvement Papers. Land Depart-
        ment. Records of the Auditor of the State. Archives Division.

Lewis University, Romeoville, Illinois
Lamb, John M., Collection.

Library of Congress, Washington, DC
Harrison, Benjamin. "First Annual Message to Congress." December 3, 1889.
    Reel 120. Series 8. Speeches, 1878–1901. Benjamin Harrison Papers. Manuscript
    Division.
Huntington, Collis P., Papers. Series 4. Reel 1.
———. "Reminiscences." 1856–1901.

L. Tom Perry Special Collections, Harold B. Lee Library, Brigham Young University,
Provo, Utah
Savage, Charles R., Journals.

Mystic Seaport Museum, Mystic, Connecticut
Blunt White, G. W., Library. Records of the American Seamen's Friend Society.

Rare Books and Manuscripts, Indiana State Library, Indianapolis
Aborn, Mary J., Collection.
Campbell, John TenBrook. Scrapbook. Campbell Papers.
Cottman, George A., Scrapbook.
House of Representatives. Executive Department. Manuscript Division.
Noble, Noah. Collection.
Wabash Valley File.
Worden, Charles James. Family Papers.

Special Collections, J. Willard Marriott Library, University of Utah, Salt Lake City
Golden Spike Railroad Scrapbook.

University of Notre Dame Archives, Indiana
Badin, Stephen T., Papers, 1768–1943.
McMaster, James. Papers, 1820–86.
Souvay, Charles Leon. Collection, 1798–1922.
Rosati, Joseph. Correspondence.

HISTORICAL PERIODICALS

Alton (IL) Courier
Alton (IL) Telegraph
Attica (IN) Ledger
Auburn (CA) Stars and Stripes
Baltimore Patriot and Mercantile Advertiser
Bloomington (IL) Intelligencer
Bloomington (IL) Weekly Pantagraph
Boston Pilot
Cass County Times (Logansport, IN)
Catholic Telegraph (Cincinnati)
Cheyenne (WY) Daily Leader
Chicago American
Chicago Daily Journal
Chicago Republican
Chicago Tribune
Chicago Weekly Journal
Cincinnati Chronicle
Corinne Daily Reporter (Utah Territory)
Cork Examiner (County Cork, Ireland)
Covington (IN) Western Constellation
Deseret Evening News (Utah Territory)
Deseret News (Utah Territory)

DeWitt Courier (Clinton, IL)
Dutch Flat (NV) Enquirer
Elko (NV) Independent
Evansville (IN) Daily Journal
Fort Wayne (IN) Sentinel
Fort Wayne (IN) Weekly Sentinel
Frank Leslie's Illustrated Newspaper
Frederick (MD) Herald
Galena (IL) Jeffersonian
Gem of the Prairie (Chicago)
Golden Era (San Francisco)
Gold Hill (NV) Daily News
Hagerstown (MD) Herald
Hagerstown (MD) Mail
Harper's New Monthly Magazine (New York)
Harper's Weekly (New York)
Illinois State Register (Springfield)
Indiana Journal (Indianapolis)
Indianapolis News
Indianapolis Star
Indiana Republican (Madison)
Lafayette (IN) Journal
Lafayette (IN) Journal and Free Press
Latter-day Saints' Millennial Star (Liverpool, UK)
Lawrenceburg (IN) Palladium
Lockport (IL) Free Press
Maumee City (OH) Express
National Intelligencer (Washington, DC)
Native American (Philadelphia)
New York Express
New York Freeman's Journal
New York Herald
New York Star
New York Tribune
New York Truth Teller
Niles' Weekly Register (Baltimore)
Ogden (UT) Junction
Omaha Republican
Ottawa (IL) Free Trader
Ottawa (IL) Republican
Providence (RI) Journal
Sacramento Daily Union
Sacramento Reporter
Sacramento Union

Salt Lake Daily Telegraph
San Francisco Bulletin
San Francisco Call
San Francisco Examiner
San Francisco Newsletter
San Francisco Real Estate Circular
Shasta Courier (Redding, CA)
Spirit of the Lakes and Boatmen's Magazine (Cleveland)
Springfield (MA) Republican
Union Vedette (Camp Douglas, Utah Territory)
The Wasp (San Francisco)
Waynetown (IN) Dispatch
Williamsport (MD) Banner
Workingman's Advocate (Chicago)

GOVERNMENT DOCUMENTS: FEDERAL

Act of July 2, 1864, to Amend [Pacific Railway Act], Stat. 13 (1864): 356.

Annals of Cong., 14th Cong., 2d Sess. (February 4, 1817).

Cong. Globe, 37th Cong., 2d Sess. (1862).

Cong. Globe, 39th Cong., 1st Sess. (1866).

Cong. Globe, 40th Cong., 3rd Sess. (1869).

Cong. Globe, 41st Cong., 2d Sess. (June 9, 1870).

Cong. Globe, 41st Cong., 3rd Sess. (January 7, 1871).

Joint Resolution of April 10, 1869, Union Pacific Railroad Company, the Central Pacific Railroad Company . . . Stat. 16 (1869): 56.

Pacific Railway Act of 1862, Stat. 12 (1862): 489.

Raymond, Rossiter W. *Statistics of Mines and Mining in the States and Territories West of the Rocky Mountains,* 42nd Cong., 1st Sess., House Ex. Doc. 10. Serial 1470. Washington, DC: Government Printing Office, 1871.

Report and Testimony Taken by the United States Pacific Railway Commission. 8 vols. Sen. Exec. Doc 51, 50th Cong., 1st Sess. (1888).

Report of the Joint Special Committee to Investigate Chinese Immigration, Sen. Rept. 689, 44th Cong., 2d Sess. (1877).

The Statistics of the Population of the United States, Ninth Census. Vol. 1. Washington, DC: U.S. Bureau of Census, 1870.

GOVERNMENT DOCUMENTS: STATE AND TERRITORY

An Act to Provide for a General System of Internal Improvements, *Indiana Laws,* chap. 2, Indiana General Assembly, 20th Sess. (1836).

General Laws of the State of Indiana. Indianapolis, 1841.

General Laws of the State of Indiana. Indianapolis, 1842.

General Laws of the State of Indiana. Indianapolis, 1843.

Report of the Board of Internal Improvement to the General Assembly of the State of Indiana. Indianapolis, 1837.

"Report of the State Board of Internal Improvements." In Documentary Journal of Indiana Reports. Indianapolis, 1836.

Reports of the Debates and Proceedings of the Convention for the Revision of the Constitution of the State of Indiana. 2 vols. Indianapolis, 1850–51.

Utah Territory. A Memorial to Congress for the Construction of a Great National Central Railroad to the Pacific Coast. Utah Session Laws, 1st Sess. (1852).

———. A Memorial to Congress in Relation to the Pacific Railway. Utah Session Laws, 3rd Sess. (1854).

CANAL AND RAILROAD COMPANY DOCUMENTS

Annual Report of the Board of Commissioners of the Illinois and Michigan Canal for 1836. Vandalia, IL: Walters and Sawyer, 1837.

Annual Report of the Commissioners of the Illinois and Michigan Canal, 1840. Lockport, IL, 1840.

Bailey, Robert E., and Elaine Shemoney Evans, eds. The Illinois and Michigan Canal, 1827–1911: A Selection of Documents from the Illinois State Archives. Springfield: Office of the Secretary of State, 1998.

Burnett, Ward B. "Report of Ward B. Burnett, Resident Engineer on the Western Division." December, 1838. Reprinted in Report of the Canal Commissioners of Illinois to Governor John R. Tanner, 1900. Springfield, IL: Phillips Brothers, 1901.

Central Pacific Railroad Statement Made to the President of the United States, and Secretary of the Interior, of the Progress of the Work. Sacramento: Crocker, 1865.

Eighth Annual Report of the Acting Commissioner of the Illinois and Michigan Canal to the General Assembly. Springfield, IL: Walters and Weber, 1844.

Fifth Annual Report of the Commissioners of the Illinois and Michigan Canal. Springfield, IL: Waters, 1840.

Fourth Annual Report of the Canal Commissioners of the Illinois and Michigan Canal. Springfield, IL: Waters, 1840.

Gooding, William. "Engineer's Report to the Board of Commissioners of the Illinois and Michigan Canal, 1842." In Report of the Canal Commissioners of Illinois to Governor John R. Tanner, 1900. Springfield, IL: Phillips Brothers, 1901.

Indiana House of Representatives. Report of the Commissioners of the Wabash and Erie Canal. Indianapolis, 1833.

Report of the Board of Commissioners of the Illinois and Michigan Canal. Vandalia, IL: Walters, 1838.

Report of the Chief Engineer upon Recent Surveys and Progress of Construction of the Central Pacific Railroad of California. Sacramento: Central Pacific Railroad Company, 1865.

Wright, Benjamin. *Engineer's Report to the Board of Commissioners of the Illinois and Michigan Canal.* N.p., 1838.

ADDITIONAL NINETEENTH-CENTURY PRINTED SOURCES

Adams, Charles Francis. "The Era of Change." In *Chapters of Erie, and Other Essays.* By Charles F. Adams and Henry Adams. Boston: Osgood, 1871.

Avery, B. P. "The Building of the Iron Road." *Overland Monthly* 2, no. 5 (1869): 469–78.

Beadle, John H. *The Undeveloped West; or, Five Years in the Territories.* Philadelphia: National, 1873.

Beers, Robert W. *The Mormon Puzzle and How to Solve It.* New York: Funk and Wagnalls, 1887.

Bowles, Samuel. *Our New West: Records of Travel between the Mississippi River and the Pacific Ocean.* New York: Dennison, 1869.

Brigham, Charles H. "The Mormon Problem." *Old and New* 1 (May 1870): 628–41.

Brooks, Charles Wolcott. "The Chinese Labor Problem." *Overland Monthly* 3, no. 5 (1869): 407–19.

Buckingham, James Silk. *The Eastern and Western States of America.* 3 vols. London: Fisher, Son, 1842.

Carey, Matthew. *Reflections on the Subject of Emigration from Europe.* Philadelphia: Carey and Lea, 1826.

Chickering, Jesse. *Immigration into the United States.* Boston: Little and Brown, 1848.

Crofutt, George A. *Crofutt's Trans-continental Tourist's Guide.* Vol. 3. 2nd annual revise. New York: Printed by author, 1871.

First Annual Report of the Western Seamen's Friend Society. Sandusky City, OH: Moore, 1848.

Gibson, Otis. *The Chinese in America.* Cincinnati: Hitchcock and Walden, 1877.

Giles, Henry. "The New Exodus." *Christian Examiner* 52 (May 1852): 361–84.

Gillis, John R. "Tunnels of the Pacific Railroad." Paper delivered before the American Society of Civil Engineers, January 5, 1870. Reprinted in *Van Nostrand's Eclectic Engineering Magazine* 2 (January 1870): 418–23.

"The Great Railroad of the West." *Latter-day Saints' Millennial Star* (Liverpool, UK) 30 (June 27, 1868): 408–10.

Grund, Francis J. *The Americans in Their Social, Moral, and Political Relations.* 1837. Reprint, New York: Johnson Reprint, 1968.

Hammond, James Henry. *Selections from the Letters and Speeches of the Honorable James Henry Hammond.* New York: Trow, 1866.

Harris, Robert L. "The Pacific Railroad—Unopen," *Overland Monthly* 3, no. 3 (1869): 244–52.

Hill, Thomas. *The Last Spike, a Painting by Thomas Hill: Illustrating the Last Scene in the Building of the Overland Railroad, with a History of Enterprise.* San Francisco: Bosqui, 1881.

Loomis, A. W. "Holiday in the Chinese Quarter." *Overland Monthly* 2, no. 2 (1869): 144–53.

———. "How Our Chinamen Are Employed." *Overland Monthly* 2, no. 3 (1869): 231–39.

———. "Occult Science in the Chinese Quarter." *Overland Monthly* 3, no. 2 (1869): 160–69.

———. "What Our Chinamen Read." *Overland Monthly* 1, no. 6 (1868): 525–30.

Marryat, Frederick. *Diary in America.* 1839. Reprint, Bloomington: Indiana University Press, 1960.

Miller, John. "Certain Phrases of the Chinese Question." *Overland Monthly* 7, no. 10 (1886): 428–35.

"The Pacific Railroad." *Harper's Weekly,* May 29, 1869.

"Papacy in the United States." *American Quarterly Review* 7 (August 1835): 58–60.

Power, Tyrone. *Impressions of America, during the Years 1833, 1834, and 1835.* 2 vols. London: Bentley, 1836.

Richardson, Albert D. *Beyond the Mississippi: From the Great Rim to the Great Ocean.* Hartford, CT: American, 1867.

Royall, Anne. *Mrs. Royall's Pennsylvania; or, Travels Continued in the United States.* 2 vols. Washington, DC, 1829.

Sanderson, John P. *Republic Landmarks: The Views and Opinions of American Statesmen on Foreign Immigration.* Philadelphia: Lippincott, 1856.

Stillman, J. D. B. "The Last Tie." *Overland Monthly* 3, no. 1 (1869): 77–84.

Stout, Arthur B. *Chinese Immigration and the Physiological Causes of the Decay of a Nation.* San Francisco: Agnew and Deffebach, 1862.

Thomas, Jesse B. *Report of Jesse B. Thomas as a Member of the Executive Committee Appointed by the Chicago Harbor and River Convention, of the Statistics concerning the City of Chicago.* Chicago: Wilson, 1847.

Trollope, Frances. *Domestic Manners of the Americans.* London: Whittaker, Treacher, 1832.

Tucker, Pomeroy. *Origin, Rise, and Progress of Mormonism: Biography of Its Founders and History of Its Church; Personal Remembrances and Historical Collections Hitherto Unwritten.* New York: Appleton, 1867.

Tullidge, Edward. *Life of Brigham Young; or, Utah and Her Founders.* New York: Tullidge and Crandall, 1877.

BOOKS AND ARTICLES

Aarim-Heriot, Najia. *Chinese Immigrants, African Americans, and Racial Anxiety in the United States, 1848–82.* Urbana: University of Illinois Press, 2003.

Aldrich, Mark. *Death Rode the Rails: American Railroad Accidents and Safety, 1828–1965*. Baltimore: Johns Hopkins University Press, 2006.

Allen, Judith A. "Men Interminably in Crisis? Historians on Masculinity, Sexual Boundaries, and Manhood." *Radical History Review* 82 (Winter 2002): 191–207.

Almaguer, Tomás. *Racial Fault Lines: The Historical Origins of White Supremacy in California*. Berkeley: University of California Press, 1994.

Ambrose, Stephen. *Nothing Like It in the World: The Men Who Built the Transcontinental Railroad, 1863–1869*. New York: Simon and Schuster, 2000.

Anderson, Emily Pickering. "Reminiscences." In *Denmark to Manti: The History of William Anderson and Family*. Salt Lake City: Printed by author, n.d.

Andreas, Alfred T. *History of Cook County, Illinois*. Chicago: Printed by author, 1884.

Andrews, Thomas G. *Killing for Coal: America's Deadliest Labor War*. Cambridge, MA: Harvard University Press, 2008.

———. "'Made by Toile'? Tourism, Labor, and the Construction of the Colorado Landscape, 1858–1917." *Journal of American History* 92, no. 3 (2005): 837–63.

Angle, Paul M., ed. *Prairie State: Impressions of Illinois, 1673–1967, by Travelers and Other Observers*. Chicago: University of Chicago Press, 1968.

Archer, William. *America To-day: Observations and Reflections*. New York: Scribner's Sons, 1899.

Arrington, Leonard J. *Brigham Young: American Moses*. Urbana: University of Illinois Press, 1985.

———. *Great Basin Kingdom: An Economic History of the Latter-day Saints, 1830–1900*. Cambridge, MA: Harvard University Press, 1958.

Arrington, Leonard J., Feramorz Fox, and Dean L. May. *Building the City of God: Community and Cooperation among the Mormons*. Urbana: University of Illinois Press, 1992.

Athearn, Robert G. "Opening the Gates of Zion: Utah and the Coming of the Union Pacific Railroad." *Utah Historical Quarterly* 36, no. 4 (1968): 292–314.

———. *Union Pacific Country*. Lincoln: University of Nebraska Press, 1976.

Bacon-Foster, Corra. *Early Chapters in the Development of the Potomac Route to the West*. Washington, DC: Columbia Historical Society, 1912.

Bain, David Haward. *Empire Express: Building the First Transcontinental Railroad*. New York: Penguin, 2000.

Baird, W. David. "Violence along the Chesapeake Canal: 1839." *Maryland Historical Magazine* 66 (Summer 1971): 121–34.

Baldwin, Elmer. *History of LaSalle County, Illinois*. Chicago: Rand McNally, 1877.

Barnhart, John D., and Donald Carmony, eds. *Indiana: From Frontier to Industrial Commonwealth*. 2 vols. New York: Lewis Historical, 1954.

Baron, Ava. "Masculinity, the Embodied Male Worker, and the Historian's Gaze." *International Labor and Working-Class History* 69 (Spring 2006): 143–60.

———. "Technology and the Crisis of Masculinity: The Gendering of Work and Skill in the U.S. Printing Industry, 1850–1920." In *Skill and Consent: Contempo-*

rary Studies in the Labour Process, edited by Andrew Sturdy, David Knights, and Hugh Willmott, 67–96. New York: Routledge, 1992.

———, ed. *Work Engendered: Toward a New History of American Labor.* Ithaca: Cornell University Press, 1991.

Barrett, James R. *The Irish Way: Becoming American in the Multiethnic City.* New York: Penguin, 2012.

———. *Work and Community in the Jungle: Chicago's Packinghouse Workers, 1894–1922.* Urbana: University of Illinois Press, 1987.

Barth, Gunther. *Bitter Strength: A History of the Chinese in the United States, 1850–1870.* Cambridge, MA: Harvard University Press, 1964.

Bateman, Fiona. "Defining the Heathen in Ireland and Africa: Two Similar Discourses a Century Apart." *Social Sciences and Missions* 21, no. 1 (2008): 73–96.

Baxter, R. Scott. "The Response of California's Chinese Populations to the Anti-Chinese Movement," *Historical Archaeology* 42, no. 3 (2008): 29–36.

Becker, Joseph. "An Artist's Interesting Recollections of Leslie's Weekly." *Leslie's Weekly,* December 14, 1905, 570.

Bederman, Gail. *Manliness and Civilization: A Cultural History of Gender and Race in the United States, 1880–1917.* Chicago: University of Chicago Press, 1995.

Beebe, Henry. *History of Peru, Illinois.* Peru, IL: Linton, 1858.

Berg, Manfred. *Popular Justice: A History of Lynching in America.* Chicago: Dee, 2011.

Berger, Martin A. *Sight Unseen: Whiteness and American Visual Culture.* Berkeley: University of California Press, 2005.

Berndt, George D. "Celebrating the Illinois and Michigan Canal." *Cultural Resource Management* 21, no. 11 (1998): 18–19.

Billington, Ray Allen. *Westward Expansion: A History of the American Frontier.* 4th ed. New York: Macmillan, 1974.

Bilson, Geoffrey. *A Darkened House: Cholera in Nineteenth-Century Canada.* Toronto: University of Toronto Press, 1980.

Bishop, M. Guy. "Building Railroads for the Kingdom: The Career of John W. Young, 1867–91." *Utah Historical Quarterly* 48, no. 1 (1980): 66–80.

Blackhawk, Ned. *Violence over the Land: Indians and Empires in the Early American West.* Cambridge, MA: Harvard University Press, 2006.

Bodnar, John. *The Transplanted: A History of Immigrants in Urban America.* Bloomington: Indiana University Press, 1987.

Bonilla-Silva, Eduardo. "Rethinking Racism: Toward a Structural Interpretation." *American Sociological Review* 62 (June 1996): 469–70.

Bordieu, Pierre. *In Other Words: Essays towards a Reflexive Sociology.* Stanford, CA: Stanford University Press, 1990.

Bowman, J. N. "Driving the Last Spike at Promontory, 1869." *Utah Historical Quarterly* 37, no. 1 (1969): 76–101.

Brands, H. W. *The Age of Gold: The California Gold Rush and the New American Dream.* New York: Doubleday, 2002.

————. *American Colossus: The Triumph of Capitalism, 1865–1900*. New York: Knopf Doubleday, 2010.

Brooks, James. "James Brooks to the Commissioners of the Illinois and Michigan Canal, February 23, 1838." *The Illinois and Michigan Canal, 1827–1911: A Selection of Documents from the Illinois State Archives*. Accessed May 15, 2015. www .cyberdriveillinois.com/departments/archives/teaching_packages/I_and_M _canal/doc11.html.

Brown, Joshua. *Beyond the Lines: Pictorial Reporting, Everyday Life, and the Crisis of Gilded Age America*. Berkeley: University of California Press, 2001.

Brownson, Howard Gray. *History of the Illinois Central Railroad to 1870*. Urbana: University of Illinois Press, 1915.

Bushman, Richard L. *Joseph Smith, Rough Stone Rolling: A Cultural Biography of Mormonism's Founder*. New York: Knopf, 2005.

Butler, Leslie. *Critical Americans: Victorian Intellectuals and Transatlantic Liberal Reform*. Chapel Hill: University of North Carolina Press, 2007.

Canal Celebrations in Old Fort Wayne. Fort Wayne, IN: Public Library of Fort Wayne and Allen County, 1953.

Carnes, Mark C. *Secret Ritual and Manhood in Victorian America*. New Haven: Yale University Press, 1989.

Carnes, Mark C., and Clyde Griffen, eds. *Meanings for Manhood: Constructions of Masculinity in Victorian America*. Chicago: University of Chicago Press, 1990.

Carp, Roger E. "The Limits of Reform: Labor and Discipline on the Erie Canal." *Journal of the Early Republic* 10, no. 2 (1990): 191–219.

Carter, Kate B. "The Utah Central and Other Railroads." In *Treasures of Pioneer History*, vol. 1, edited by Kate B. Carter, 1–36. Salt Lake City: Daughters of Utah Pioneers, 1952.

"Catholic Almanac and Laity's Directory, 1839." In *American Catholic Directories, 1817–1879*. Washington, DC: Catholic University of America, 1952.

Central Pacific Railroad Photographic History Museum. "Fiction or Fact: Did the Chinese and Irish Railroad Workers Really Try to Blow Each Other Up?" With comments from David Bain, Edson T. Strobridge, and Chris Graves. Accessed June 22, 2009. http://cprr.org/Game/Interactive_Railroad_Project/Fiction_or_ Fact.html.

Chen, Yong. *Chinese San Francisco, 1850–1943: A Trans-Pacific Community*. Stanford, CA: Stanford University Press, 2000.

Cheney, Thomas E., ed. *Mormon Songs from the Rocky Mountains: A Compilation of Mormon Folksong*. Austin: University of Texas Press, 1968.

Chew, William. *Nameless Builders of the Transcontinental*. Victoria, BC: Trafford, 2004.

Chinn, Thomas W., ed. *A History of the Chinese in California: A Syllabus*. San Francisco: Chinese Historical Society of America, 1969.

Chiu, Ping. *Chinese Labor in California, 1850–1880*. Madison: University of Wisconsin Press, 1963.

Christopher, Emma, Cassandra Pybus, and Marcus Rediker, eds. *Many Middle Passages: Forced Migrations and the Making of the Modern World*. Berkeley: University of California Press, 2007.

Chua, Amy, and Jed Rubenfeld. *The Triple Package: How Three Unlikely Traits Explain the Rise and Fall of Cultural Groups in America*. New York: Penguin, 2014.

Clark, Samuel, and James S. Donnelly Jr., eds. *Irish Peasants: Violence and Political Unrest, 1780–1914*. Madison: University of Wisconsin Press, 1983.

Clark, Victor. "Mexican Labor in the United States." *U.S. Labor Bulletin* 78 (September 1908): 466–522.

Cohen, Lizabeth. *Making a New Deal: Industrial Workers in Chicago, 1919–1939*. New York: Cambridge University Press, 1991.

Cohen, Lucy M. *Chinese in the Post–Civil War South: A People without History*. Baton Rouge: Louisiana State University Press, 1984.

Coleman, Terry. *The Railway Navvies: A History of the Men Who Made the Railways*. Harmondsworth, Middlesex: Penguin, 1968.

Commons, John R., David J. Saposs, Helen L. Sumner, E.B. Mittelman, H.E. Hoagland, John B. Andrews, and Selig Perlman. *History of Labour in the United States*. 2 vols. New York: Macmillan, 1936.

Cowan, Richard O. "Steel Rails and the Utah Saints." *Journal of Mormon History* 27, no. 2 (2001): 177–84.

Cranmer, H. Jerome. "Canal Investment, 1815–1860." In *Studies in Income and Wealth*, vol. 24, edited by National Bureau of Economic Research, 547–70. Princeton, NJ: Princeton University Press, 1960.

Cronon, William. *Changes in the Land: Indians, Colonists, and the Ecology of New England*. New York: Hill and Wang, 1983.

———. *Nature's Metropolis: Chicago and the Great West*. New York: Norton, 1991.

———. *Uncommon Ground: Rethinking the Human Place in Nature*. New York: Norton, 1995.

Davis, James E. *Frontier Illinois*. Bloomington: Indiana University Press, 1998.

Dawley, Alan. *Class and Community: The Industrial Revolution in Lynn*. Cambridge, MA: Harvard University Press, 1976.

DeLue, Rachael Ziady, and James Elkins, eds. *Landscape Theory*. Art Seminar 6. New York: Routledge, 2008.

Deutsch, Sarah. *No Separate Refuge: Culture, Class, and Gender on an Anglo-Hispanic Frontier in the American Southwest, 1880–1940*. New York: Oxford University Press, 1989.

Dickens, Charles. *American Notes for General Circulation*. 1842. Reprint, London: Penguin, 2000.

Diner, Hasia R. *Erin's Daughters in America: Irish Immigrant Women in the Nineteenth Century*. Baltimore: Johns Hopkins University Press, 1983.

Dinnerstein, Leonard, and David M. Reimers. *Ethnic Americans: A History of Immigration*. 5th ed. New York: Columbia University Press, 2009.

Dirlik, Arif, ed. *Chinese on the American Frontier*. Lanham, MD: Rowman and Littlefield, 2001.

Ditz, Toby L. "The New Men's History and the Peculiar Absence of Gendered Power: Some Remedies from Early American Gender History." *Gender and History* 16, no. 1 (2004): 1–35.

"Documents of the Chinese Six Companies Pertaining to Immigration." In *Chinese American Voices: From the Gold Rush to the Present*, edited by Judy Yung, Gordon H. Chang, and Him Mark Lai, 17–25. Berkeley: University of California Press, 2006.

Dodge, Grenville M. *How We Built the Union Pacific Railway, and Other Railway Papers and Addresses*. 1911. Reprint, Denver: Sage Books, 1965.

Doyle, Don H. *The Social Order of a Frontier Community: Jacksonville, Illinois, 1825–70*. Urbana: University of Illinois Press, 1978.

Du Bois, W. E. B. *Black Reconstruction in America, 1860–1880*. New York: Harcourt, Brace, 1935. Reprint, Atheneum, 1977.

Ducker, James H. *Men of the Steel Rails: Workers on the Atchison, Topeka and Santa Fe Railroad, 1869–1900*. Lincoln: University of Nebraska Press, 1983.

Dykstra, Robert R. *The Cattle Towns*. New York: Knopf, 1968.

Emerson, Ralph Waldo. "Nature." 1836. In *Nature, Addresses, and Lectures: The Collected Works of Ralph Waldo Emerson*, edited by Robert E. Spiller and Alfred R. Ferguson, 1:3–45. Cambridge, MA: Harvard University Press, 1971.

Emmons, David M. *Beyond the American Pale: The Irish in the West, 1845–1910*. Norman: University of Oklahoma Press, 2010.

———. *The Butte Irish: Class and Ethnicity in an American Mining Town, 1875–1925*. Urbana: University of Illinois Press, 1989.

Emrich, Duncan, ed. *Songs of the Mormons, and Songs of the West*. Washington, DC: Library of Congress, 1952.

Ernst, Robert. *Immigrant Life in New York City, 1825–1863*. Syracuse: Syracuse University Press, 1994.

Etulian, Richard W., ed. *Does the Frontier Experience Make America Exceptional?* Boston: Bedford/St. Martin's, 1999.

Farnum, Wallace D. "Grenville Dodge and the Union Pacific: A Study of Historical Legends." *Journal of American History* 51, no. 4 (1965): 632–50.

Fatout, Paul. *Indiana Canals*. West Lafayette, IN: Purdue University Studies, 1972.

Fiege, Mark. *The Republic of Nature: An Environmental History of the United States*. Seattle: University of Washington Press, 2012.

Fogel, Robert. *Railroads and American Economic Growth*. Baltimore: Johns Hopkins University Press, 1964.

Foner, Eric. *Free Soil, Free Labor, Free Men: The Ideology of the Republican Party before the Civil War*. Rev. ed. New York: Oxford University Press, 1995.

Foster, Craig L. "'That Canny Scotsman': John Sharp and the Union Pacific Negotiations, 1869–72." *Journal of Mormon History* 27 (2001): 197–214.

Foster, Thomas A., ed. *New Men: Manliness in Early America*. New York: New York University Press, 2011.

Francaviglia, Richard V. *Go East, Young Man: Imagining the American West as the Orient*. Logan: Utah State University Press, 2011.

Frost, Linda. *Never One Nation: Freaks, Savages, and Whiteness in U.S. Popular Culture, 1850–1877*. Minneapolis: University of Minnesota Press, 2005.

Fulton, Robert Lardin. *The Epic of the Overland*. San Francisco: Robertson, 1925.

Galloway, John Debo. *The First Transcontinental Railroad*. New York: Arno, 1981.

Garman, Harry O. "Whitewater Canal, Cambridge City to the Ohio River." In *Yearbook of the Society of Indiana Pioneers*. Indianapolis: Society of Indiana Pioneers, 1944.

Gates, Paul Wallace. *The Illinois Central Railroad and Its Colonization Work*. Cambridge, MA: Harvard University Press, 1934.

Gerber, David A. *The Making of an American Pluralism: Buffalo, New York, 1825–1860*. Urbana: University of Illinois Press, 1989.

Gilje, Paul A. *Rioting in America*. Bloomington: Indiana University Press, 1999.

———. *The Road to Mobocracy: Popular Disorder in New York City, 1763–1834*. Chapel Hill: University of North Carolina Press, 1987.

Givens, Terryl L. *The Viper on the Hearth: Mormons, Myths, and the Construction of Heresy*. New York: Oxford University Press, 1997.

Glenn, Evelyn. *Unequal Freedom: How Race and Gender Shaped American Citizenship and Labor*. Cambridge, MA: Harvard University Press, 2002.

Glickstein, Jonathan A. *Concepts of Free Labor in Antebellum America*. New Haven: Yale University Press, 1991.

Goodrich, Carter. *Government Promotion of American Canals and Railroads, 1800–1890*. New York: Columbia University Press, 1960.

———. "Internal Improvements Reconsidered." *Journal of Economic History* 30 (June 1970): 289–311.

Gordon, Sarah Barringer. *The Mormon Question: Polygamy and Constitutional Conflict in Nineteenth-Century America*. Chapel Hill: University of North Carolina Press, 2001.

Gould, J. "Wanderings in the West, 1839." In *Travel Accounts of Indiana, 1679–1961: A Collection of Observations by Wayfaring Foreigners, Itinerants, and Peripatetic Hoosiers*, comp. Shirley S. McCord. Indiana Historical Collections 47. Indianapolis: Indiana Historical Bureau, 1970.

Gouter, David. "Drawing Different Lines of Color: The Mainstream English Canadian Labour Movement's Approach to Blacks and Chinese, 1880–1914." *Labor: Studies in Working-Class History of the Americas* 2, no. 1 (2005): 55–76.

Greenberg, Amy S. *Manifest Manhood and the Antebellum American Empire*. New York: Cambridge University Press, 2005.

Greenberg, Joshua R. *Advocating the Man: Masculinity, Organized Labor, and the Household in New York, 1800–1840*. New York: Columbia University Press, 2009.

Greene, Julie. *The Canal Builders: Making America's Empire at the Panama Canal*. New York: Penguin, 2009.

Grimsted, David. "Ante-bellum Labor: Violence, Strike, and Communal Arbitration." *Journal of Social History* 19, no. 1 (1985): 5–28.

———. "Rioting in Its Jacksonian Setting." *American Historical Review* 77, no. 2 (1972): 361–97.

Griswold, B. J. *Pictorial History of Fort Wayne.* Vol. 1. Chicago: Law, 1917.

Griswold, Wesley S. *A Work of Giants: Building the First Transcontinental Railroad.* New York: McGraw-Hill, 1962.

Guglielmo, Thomas A. *White on Arrival: Italians, Race, Color, and Power in Chicago, 1890–1945.* New York: Oxford University Press, 2003.

Gutman, Herbert. *Work, Culture, and Society in Industrializing America: Essays in American Working-Class and Social History.* New York: Vintage, 1977.

Guyer, Isaac D. *History of Chicago: Its Commercial and Manufacturing Interests and Industry, Together with Sketches of Manufacturers and Men Who Have Most Contributed to Its Prosperity and Advancement.* Chicago: Church, Goodman and Cushing, 1862.

Gyory, Andrew. *Closing the Gate: Race, Politics, and the Chinese Exclusion Act.* Chapel Hill: University of North Carolina Press, 1998.

Hahamovitch, Cindy. *The Fruits of Their Labor: Atlantic Coast Farmworkers and the Making of Migrant Poverty, 1870–1945.* Chapel Hill: University of North Carolina Press, 1997.

Harlow, Alvin Fay. *Old Towpaths: The Story of the American Canal Era.* Port Washington, NY: Kennikat, 1964.

Heath, Erle. "From Trail to Rail." *Southern Pacific Bulletin* 15, chap. 15 (1927): 9–12.

Higham, John. *Strangers in the Land: Patterns of American Nativism, 1860–1925.* New Brunswick, NJ: Rutgers University Press, 1955.

History of Grundy County, Illinois. Chicago: Baskin, 1882.

Hoganson, Kristin L. *Fighting for American Manhood: How Gender Politics Provoked the Spanish-American and Philippine-American Wars.* New Haven: Yale University Press, 1998.

Holsinger, M. Paul, ed. *War and American Popular Culture: An Historical Encyclopedia.* Westport, CT: Greenwood, 1999.

Holt, Glen E. "The Birth of Chicago: An Examination of Economic Parentage." *Journal of the Illinois State Historical Society* 76 (Summer 1983): 83–94.

Howard, Robert P. *Illinois: A History of the Prairie State.* Grand Rapids: Eerdmans, 1972.

Hoy, William. *The Chinese Six Companies: A Short, General Historical Résumé of Its Origin, Function, and Importance in the Life of the California Chinese.* San Francisco: Chinese Consolidated Benevolent Association, 1942.

Hoyt, Amy, and Sara M. Patterson. "Mormon Masculinity: Changing Gender Expectations in the Era of Transition from Polygamy to Monogamy, 1890–1920." *Gender and History* 23, no. 1 (2011): 72–91.

Hulbert, Archer Butler. *The Paths of Inland Commerce: A Chronicle of Trail, Road, and Waterway.* Chronicles of America Series 21. New Haven: Yale University Press, 1921.

Humphreys, Margaret. *Malaria: Poverty, Race, and Public Health in the United States.* Baltimore: Johns Hopkins University Press, 2001.

Hyde, Anne. *Empires, Families, and Nations: A New History of the North American West, 1800–1860.* Lincoln: University of Nebraska Press, 2011.

Ignatiev, Noel. *How the Irish Became White.* New York: Routledge, 1995.

Indiana Historical Bureau. "Canal Construction in Indiana." *Indiana Historian,* September 1997, 1–15.

Jacobson, Matthew Frye. *Whiteness of a Different Color: European Immigrants and the Alchemy of Race.* Cambridge, MA: Harvard University Press, 1998.

Jensen, Jens Iver. "Autobiography." In *Our Pioneer Heritage,* comp. Kate B. Carter. Salt Lake City: Daughters of Utah Pioneers, 1967.

Johnson, Michael W. "Rendezvous at Promontory: A New Look at the Golden Spike Ceremony." *Utah Historical Quarterly* 74, no. 1 (2004): 47–68.

Johnson, Paul. *A Shopkeeper's Millennium: Society and Revivals in Rochester, New York, 1815–1837.* New York: Hill and Wang, 1978.

Johnston, Wayne A. *The Illinois Central Heritage, 1851–1951: A Centenary Address.* New York: Newcomen Society, 1951.

Jones, Megan Sanborn. *Performing American Identity in Anti-Mormon Melodrama.* New York: Routledge, 2009.

Jung, Moon-Ho. *Coolies and Cane: Race, Labor, and Sugar in the Age of Emancipation.* Baltimore: Johns Hopkins University Press, 2006.

Kapsch, Robert J. *The Potomac Canal: George Washington and the Waterway West.* Morgantown: West Virginia University Press, 2007.

Kasson, John F. *Civilizing the Machine: Technology and Republican Values in America, 1776–1900.* New York: Hill and Wang, 1999.

Kaster, Gregory L. "Labour's True Man: Organised Workingmen and the Language of Manliness in the U.S.A, 1827–1877." *Gender and History* 13, no. 1 (2001): 24–64.

Katz, Jacqueline H., and William L. Katz. *Making Our Way: America at the Turn of the Century in the Words of the Poor and Powerless.* New York: Ethrac, 1975.

Kenny, Kevin, ed. *New Directions in Irish-American History.* Madison: University of Wisconsin Press, 2003.

Keyssar, Alexander. *The Right to Vote: The Contested History of Democracy in the United States.* Rev. ed. New York: Basic Books, 2009.

Kidder, Daniel P. *Mormonism and the Mormons: A Historical View of the Rise and Progress of the Sect Self-Styled Latter-day Saints.* New York: Lane and Sandford, 1842.

Kimmel, Michael. *Manhood in America: A Cultural History.* New York: Free Press, 1996.

Klein, Kerwin Lee. *Frontiers of Historical Imagination: Narrating the European Conquest of Native America, 1890–1990.* Berkeley: University of California Press, 1997.

Klein, Maury. *Union Pacific.* Vol. 1, *Birth of a Railroad, 1862–1893.* New York: Doubleday, 1987.

Knobel, Dale T. *Paddy and the Republic: Ethnicity and Nationality in Antebellum America.* Middletown, CT: Wesleyan University Press, 1986.

Kotter, Richard E. "The Transcontinental Railroad and Ogden City Politics." *Utah Historical Quarterly* 42, no. 3 (1974): 278–84.

Kraus, George. "Chinese Laborers and the Construction of the Central Pacific." *Utah Historical Quarterly* 37, no. 1 (1969): 41–57.

———. *High Road to Promontory: Building the Central Pacific across the High Sierra.* Palo Alto: American West, 1969.

Lai, Him Mark. *Becoming Chinese American: A History of Communities and Institutions.* Walnut Creek, CA: Alta Mira, 2004.

Lamb, John M. "William Gooding, Chief Engineer, Illinois and Michigan Canal." *Illinois Canal Society* 5 (1982): 132–43.

Lang, Elfrieda. "Irishmen in Northern Indiana before 1850." *Mid-America: An Historical Review* 35, no. 3 (1954): 190–98.

Larson, John Lauritz. "'Bind the Republic Together': The National Union and the Struggle for a System of Internal Improvements." *Journal of American History* 74, no. 2 (1987): 363–87.

———. "A Bridge, a Dam, a River: Liberty and Innovation in the Early Republic." *Journal of the Early Republic* 7, no. 4 (1987): 351–75.

———. *Internal Improvement: National Public Works and the Promise of Popular Government in the Early United States.* Chapel Hill: University of North Carolina Press, 2001.

———. *The Market Revolution in America: Liberty, Ambition, and the Eclipse of the Common Good.* New York: Cambridge University Press, 2010.

Lau, Estelle T. *Paper Families: Identity, Immigration Administration, and Chinese Exclusion.* Durham, NC: Duke University Press, 2007.

Laurie, Bruce. *Artisans into Workers: Labor in Nineteenth-Century America.* New York: Hill and Wang, 1989.

Lee, Catherine. "'Where the Danger Lies': Race, Gender, and Chinese and Japanese Exclusion in the United States, 1870–1924." *Sociological Forum* 25, no. 2 (2010): 248–71.

Lee, Erika. *At America's Gates: Chinese Immigration during the Exclusion Era, 1882–1943.* Chapel Hill: University of North Carolina Press, 2007.

Lee, Henry. *History of the Campbell Family.* New York: Polk, 1920.

Lee, J.J., and Marion Casey, eds. *Making the Irish American: History and Heritage of the Irish in the United States.* New York: New York University Press, 2007.

Levy, Jonathan. *Freaks of Fortune: The Emerging World of Capitalism and Risk in America.* Cambridge, MA: Harvard University Press, 2012.

Lewis, Alfred Henry. "The Viper on the Hearth." Pt. 1, "Mormonism: Its Plots, Plans, and Intrigues against American Homes." *Cosmopolitan* 50, no. 4 (1911): 439–52.

Licht, Walter. *Working for the Railroad: The Organization of Work in the Nineteenth Century.* Princeton, NJ: Princeton University Press, 1983.

Lightner, David L. "Construction Labor on the Illinois Central Railroad." *Journal of the Illinois State Historical Society* 66, no. 3 (1973): 285–301.

Limerick, Patricia Nelson. *The Legacy of Conquest: The Unbroken Past of the American West*. New York: Norton, 1987.

Lively, Robert A. "The American System, a Review Article." *Business History Review* 29 (Spring 1955): 81–95.

Long, E. B. *The Saints and the Union: Utah Territory during the Civil War*. Urbana: University of Illinois Press, 1981.

MacKinnon, William P. "'Like Splitting a Man Up His Backbone': The Territorial Dismemberment of Utah, 1850–1896." *Utah Historical Quarterly* 71 (Spring 2003): 100–124.

Madsen, Brigham D. *Corinne: The Gentile Capital of Utah*. Salt Lake City: Utah State Historical Society, 1980.

———. *Glory Hunter: A Biography of Patrick Edward Connor*. Salt Lake City: University of Utah Press, 1990.

Marx, Leo. *The Machine in the Garden: Technology and the Pastoral Ideal in America*. New York: Oxford University Press, 1964.

Mason, Matthew E. "'The Hands Here Are Disposed to Be Turbulent': Unrest among the Irish Trackmen of the Baltimore and Ohio Railroad, 1829–1851." *Labor History* 39, no. 3 (1998): 253–72.

Mauss, Armand L. *All Abraham's Children: Changing Mormon Conceptions of Race and Lineage*. Urbana: University of Illinois Press, 2003.

———. "The Children of Ham and the Children of Abraham: The Construction and Deconstruction of Ethnic Identities in the Mormon Heartland." In *Race, Religion, Region: Landscapes of Encounter in the American West,* edited Fay Botham and Sara M. Patterson, 115–24. Tucson: University of Arizona Press, 2006.

May, Dean L. *Three Frontiers: Family, Land, and Society in the American West, 1850–1900*. New York: Cambridge University Press, 1994.

Maynard, Steven. "Rough Work and Rugged Men: The Social Construction of Masculinity in Working-Class History." *Labour/Le Travail* 23 (Spring 1989): 159–69.

McAvoy, Thomas T. *The Catholic Church in Indiana, 1789–1834*. New York: Columbia University Press, 1940.

McCaffrey, Lawrence J. *The Irish Catholic Diaspora in America*. Washington, DC: Catholic University of America Press, 1997.

McDaniel, Isaac. "Orestes A. Brownson on Irish Immigrants and American Nativism." *American Benedictine Review* 32, no. 2 (1981): 122–39.

Meyer, David R. *The Roots of American Industrialization*. Baltimore: Johns Hopkins University Press, 2003.

Miller, Kerby A. *Emigrants and Exiles: Ireland and the Irish Exodus to North America*. New York: Oxford University Press, 1985.

———. *Ireland and Irish America: Culture, Class, and Transatlantic Migration*. Dublin: Field Day, 2008.

Miller, Stuart Creighton. *The Unwelcome Immigrant: The American Image of the Chinese, 1785–1882*. Berkeley: University of California Press, 1969.

Mitchell, W. J. T. "Imperial Landscape." In Mitchell, *Landscape and Power*, 5–34.

———, ed. *Landscape and Power*. Chicago: University of Chicago Press, 1994.

Molina, Natalia. *How Race Is Made in America: Immigration, Citizenship, and the Historical Power of Racial Scripts*. Berkeley: University of California Press, 2014.

Montgomery, David. *Citizen Worker: The Experience of Workers in the United States with Democracy and the Free Market during the Nineteenth Century*. New York: Cambridge University Press, 1993.

———. *The Fall of the House of Labor: The Workplace, the State, and American Labor Activism, 1865–1925*. New York: Cambridge University Press, 1987.

Moos, Dan. *Outside America: Race, Ethnicity, and the Role of the American West in National Belonging*. Hanover, NH: Dartmouth College Press, 2005.

Morris, Richard B. "Andrew Jackson, Strikebreaker." *American Historical Review* 55, no. 1 (1949): 54–68.

Mosse, George L. *The Image of Man: The Creation of Modern Masculinity*. New York: Oxford University Press, 1996.

Naef, Weston, and Christine Hult-Lewis. *Carleton Watkins: The Complete Mammoth Photographs*. Los Angeles: Getty Museum, 2011.

Nelson, Dana D. *National Manhood: Capitalist Citizenship and the Imagined Fraternity of White Men*. Durham, NC: Duke University Press, 1998.

Nelson, Scott Reynolds. "After Slavery: Forced Drafts of Irish and Chinese Labor in the American Civil War, or the Search for Liquid Labor." In Christopher, Pybus, and Rediker, *Many Middle Passages*, 150–65.

Newspaper Clippings on the Wabash and Erie Canal. Vol. 2, *April 1835–January 1841*. Fort Wayne, IN: Allen County Public Library Genealogy Center, n.d.

Ngai, Mae M. *Impossible Subjects: Illegal Aliens and the Making of Modern America*. Princeton, NJ: Princeton University Press, 2005.

———. *The Lucky Ones: One Family and the Extraordinary Invention of Chinese America*. Boston: Houghton Mifflin, 2010.

Nichols, Thomas Low. *Forty Years of American Life*. 2 vols. 1864. Reprint, New York: Johnson Reprint, 1969.

Niehaus, Earl. *The Irish in New Orleans, 1800–1860*. Baton Rouge: Louisiana State University Press, 1965.

Nye, David E., ed. *Technologies of Landscape: From Reaping to Recycling*. Amherst: University of Massachusetts Press, 1999.

O'Hanlon, John. *Reverend John O'Hanlon's "The Irish Emigrant's Guide for the United States."* Edited by Edward J. Maguire. 1851. Reprint, New York: Arno, 1976.

Okihiro, Gary Y. *Common Ground: Reimagining American History*. Princeton, NJ: Princeton University Press, 2001.

Orsi, Richard. *Sunset Limited: The Southern Pacific Railroad and the Development of the American West, 1850–1920*. Berkeley: University of California Press, 2007.

"Paddy on the Canal." In *Irish Emigrant Ballads and Songs*. Edited by Robert L. Wright. Bowling Green, OH: Bowling Green University Popular Press, 1975.

Painter, Nell Irvin. *The History of White People*. New York: Norton, 2010.

Pearson, Andrea. *"Frank Leslie's Illustrated Newspaper* and *Harper's Weekly:* Innovation and Imitation in Nineteenth-Century American Pictorial Reporting." *Journal of Popular Culture* 23, no. 4 (1990): 81–111.

Peck, Gunther. "Manly Gambles: The Politics of Risk on the Comstock Lode, 1860–1880," *Journal of Social History* 26, no. 4 (1993): 701–23.

———. *Reinventing Free Labor: Padrones and Immigrant Workers in the North American West, 1880–1930.* New York: Cambridge University Press, 2000.

Pegler-Gordon, Anna. "Chinese Exclusion, Photography, and the Development of U.S. Immigration Policy." *American Quarterly* 58, no. 1 (2006): 51–77.

Pfaelzer, Jean. *Driven Out: The Forgotten War against Chinese Americans.* New York: Random House, 2007.

Phillips, Catherine Coffin. *Cornelius Cole, California Pioneer and United States Senator: A Study in Personality and Achievements Bearing upon the Growth of a Commonwealth.* San Francisco: Nash, 1929.

Poinsatte, Charles E. *Fort Wayne during the Canal Era, 1828–1855: A Study of a Western Community in the Middle Period of American History.* Indianapolis: Indiana Historical Bureau, 1969.

Potter, George. *To the Golden Door: The Story of the Irish in Ireland and America.* Boston: Little, Brown, 1960.

Pratt, Harry E., ed. *Illinois as Lincoln Knew It: A Boston Reporter's Record of a Trip in 1847.* Reprinted from Members of the Abraham Lincoln Association, *Papers in Illinois History and Transactions for the Year 1937.* Springfield, IL, 1938.

Rawlings, Isaac D. *The Rise and Fall of Disease in Illinois.* 2 vols. Springfield: Illinois Department of Public Health, 1927.

Redd, Jim. *The Illinois and Michigan Canal: A Contemporary Perspective in Essays and Photographs.* Carbondale: Southern Illinois University Press, 1993.

Reeve, W. Paul. *Making Space on the Western Frontier: Mormons, Miners, and Southern Paiutes.* Urbana: University of Illinois Press, 2006.

———. "'Nits Make Lice': The Construction of a Mormon-Indian Body." Work-in-progress presentation, Tanner Humanities Center, University of Utah, November 2007. Copy in the possession of the author.

———. *Religion of a Different Color: Race and the Mormon Struggle for Whiteness.* New York: Oxford University Press, 2015.

———. "The Wrong Side of White." *Sightings,* May 31, 2012. https://divinity.uchicago.edu/sightings/wrong-side-white-w-paul-reeve.

Riker, Dorothy, and Gayle Thornbrough, eds. *Messages and Papers relating to the Administration of Noah Noble, Governor of Indiana, 1831–1837* (Indianapolis: Indiana Historical Bureau, 1958).

———, eds. *Messages and Papers relating to the Administration of Samuel Bigger, Governor of Indiana, 1840–1843.* Indianapolis: Indiana Historical Bureau, 1964.

Roberts, Brigham Henry. *History of the Church of Jesus Christ of Latter-day Saints, Period I.* 5 vols. Salt Lake City: Church of Jesus Christ of Latter-day Saints, 1909.

Robertson, Nellie Armstrong, and Dorothy Riker, eds. *The John Tipton Papers.* 3 vols. Indianapolis: Indiana Historical Bureau, 1942.

Rockman, Seth. *Scraping By: Wage Labor, Slavery, and Survival in Early Baltimore.* Baltimore: Johns Hopkins University Press, 2009.

Roediger, David. *The Wages of Whiteness: Race and the Making of the American Working Class.* Rev. ed. New York: Verso, 1999.

Roediger, David, and Elizabeth Esch. *The Production of Difference: Race and the Management of Labor in U.S. History.* New York: Oxford University Press, 2012.

Rohe, Randall E. "After the Gold Rush: Chinese Mining in the Far West, 1850–1890." In Dirlik, *American Frontier,* 3–26.

Rorabaugh, W. J. *The Alcoholic Republic: An American Tradition.* New York: Oxford University Press, 1979.

Rosenberg, Charles E. *The Cholera Years: The United States in 1832, 1849, and 1866.* Chicago: University of Chicago Press, 1962.

Rotundo, E. Anthony. *American Manhood: Transformations in Masculinity from the Revolution to the Modern Era.* New York: Basic Books, 1993.

Rozenweig, Roy. *Eight Hours for What We Will: Workers and Leisure in an Industrializing City, 1870–1920.* New York: Cambridge University Press, 1983.

Sabin, Edwin L. *Building the Pacific Railway.* Philadelphia: Lippincott, 1919.

Sanderlin, Walter. *The Great National Project: A History of the Chesapeake and Ohio Canal.* Baltimore: Johns Hopkins University Press, 1946.

Sandmeyer, Elmer Clarence. *The Anti-Chinese Movement in California.* Urbana: University of Illinois Press, 1939.

Sandweiss, Martha A. *Print the Legend: Photography and the American West.* New Haven: Yale University Press, 2002.

Saxton, Alexander. "The Army of Canton in the High Sierra." *Pacific Historical Review* 35, no. 2 (1966): 141–52.

———. *The Indispensable Enemy: Labor and the Anti-Chinese Movement in California.* Berkeley: University of California Press, 1971.

———. *The Rise and Fall of the White Republic: Class Politics and Mass Culture in Nineteenth-Century America.* New York: Verso, 1990.

Schivelbusch, Wolfgang. *The Railway Journey: The Industrialization of Time and Space in the 19th Century.* Berkeley: University of California Press, 1977.

Schwantes, Carlos A. "The Concept of the Wageworkers' Frontier: A Framework for Future Research." *Western Historical Quarterly* 18, no. 1 (1987): 39–55.

Shaw, Ronald E. *Canals for a Nation: The Canal Era in the United States, 1790–1860.* Lexington: University Press of Kentucky, 1990.

———. *Erie Water West: A History of the Erie Canal, 1792–1854.* Lexington: University of Kentucky Press, 1966.

Shaw, Thomas A. *Story of the LaSalle Mission: From 1838, Arrival of First Missioners, to 1857, Departure of Rev. J. O'Reilly, C. M.* 2 vols. Chicago: Donohue, n.d.

Sheriff, Carol. *The Artificial River: The Erie Canal and the Paradox of Progress, 1817–1862.* New York: Hill and Wang, 1996.

Shumsky, Neil Larry. *The Evolution of Political Protest and the Workingmen's Party of California.* Columbus: Ohio State University Press, 1991.

Sitterud-McCluskey, Mindi. "'Saints in the Pit': Mormon Colliers in Britain and the Intermountain West." In *Immigrants in the Far West: Historical Identities and Experiences*, edited by Brian Q. Cannon and Jessie Embry, 324–62. Salt Lake City: University of Utah Press, 2014.

Skeen, C. Edward. *1816: America Rising*. Lexington: University Press of Kentucky, 2003.

Smith, Rogers M. *Civic Ideals: Conflicting Visions of Citizenship in U.S. History*. New Haven: Yale University Press, 1997.

———. *Stories of Peoplehood: The Politics and Morals of Political Membership*. New York: Cambridge University Press, 2003.

Smoot, W. C. A. "Tales from Old Timers—No. 9." *Union Pacific Magazine*, December 1923.

Steinfeld, Robert J. *The Invention of Free Labor: The Employment Relation in English and American Law and Culture, 1350–1870*. Chapel Hill: University of North Carolina Press, 1991.

Steiner, Stan. *Fusang: The Chinese Who Built America*. New York: Harper and Row, 1979.

Stenhouse, T. B. H. *The Rocky Mountain Saints: A Full and Complete History of the Mormons, from the First Vision of Joseph Smith to the Last Courtship of Brigham Young*. London: Ward, Lock, and Tyler, 1874.

Stewart, John J. *The Iron Trail to the Golden Spike*. Salt Lake City: Deseret Book, 1969.

Stromquist, Shelton. *A Generation of Boomers: The Pattern of Railroad Labor Conflict in Nineteenth-Century America*. Urbana: University of Illinois Press, 1987.

Taft, Robert. *Artists and Illustrators of the Old West, 1850–1900*. Princeton, NJ: Princeton University Press, 1982.

Takaki, Ronald. *Strangers from a Different Shore: A History of Asian Americans*. Rev. ed. Boston: Little, Brown, 1998.

Tanner, Henry S. *A Description of the Canals and Rail Roads of the United States, Comprehending Notices of All the Works of Internal Improvement throughout the Several States*. New York: Tanner and Disturnell, 1840.

Taylor, George Rogers. *The Transportation Revolution, 1815–1860*. New York: Rinehart, 1951.

Taylor, Robert M., Jr., and Connie A. McBirney, eds. *Peopling Indiana: The Ethnic Experience*. Indianapolis: Indiana Historical Society, 1996.

Taysom, Stephen C. "'There Is Always a Way of Escape': Continuity and Reconstitution in Nineteenth-Century Mormon Boundary Maintenance Strategies." *Western Historical Quarterly* 37, no. 2 (Summer 2006): 183–206.

Teagarden, Ernest. "Builders of the Ohio Canal, 1825–1832." *Inland Seas* 19, no. 2 (1963): 94–103.

Thomas, Calvin. *Male Matters: Masculinity, Anxiety, and the Male Body on the Line*. Urbana: University of Illinois Press, 1996.

Thompson, E. P. *The Making of the English Working Class*. New York: Vintage, 1966.

Thompson, Joseph. "The Irish in Early Illinois." *Illinois Catholic Historical Review* 2, no. 3 (1920): 18–19.

Thwaites, Reuben Gold, ed. *Early Western Travels, 1748–1846*. Vol. 26, pt. 1 of *The Far West, 1836–1837*, by Edmund Flagg. Cleveland: Clark, 1906.

Tung, William L. *The Chinese in America, 1820–1973*. Dobbs Ferry, NY: Oceana, 1974.

Turner, Frederick Jackson. *The Frontier in American History*. New York: Holt, 1935.

Turner, Frederick Jackson, and John Mack Faragher, eds. *Rereading Frederick Jackson Turner: The Significance of "The Frontier in American History," and Other Essays*. New York: Holt, 1994.

Twain, Mark. *Roughing It*. Hartford, CT: American, 1871.

Umbach, Greg. "Learning to Shop in Zion: The Consumer Revolution in Great Basin Mormon Culture, 1847–1910." *Journal of Social History* 38, no. 1 (2004): 29–61.

Usselmann, Steven. *Regulating Railroad Innovation: Business, Technology, and Politics in America, 1840–1920*. New York: Cambridge University Press, 2002.

Van Buskirk, V. Frederika. *The Wabash-Erie Canal, 1832–1876, with Emphasis on the Lagro Locks*. Wabash, IN: Wabash Historical Society, 1965.

Waggoner, Madeline Sadler. *The Long Haul West: The Great Canal Era, 1817–1850*. New York: Putnam, 1958.

Waldstreicher, David. *In the Midst of Perpetual Fetes: The Making of American Nationalism, 1789–1820*. Chapel Hill: University of North Carolina Press, 1997.

Wallis, John Joseph. "The Property Tax as a Coordinating Device: Financing Indiana's Mammoth Internal Improvement System, 1835–1842." *Explorations in Economic History* 40, no. 3 (2003): 223–50.

Way, Peter. *Common Labour: Workers and the Digging of North American Canals, 1780–1860*. New York: Cambridge University Press, 1993.

———. "Labor's Love Lost: Observations on the Historiography of Class and Ethnicity in the Nineteenth Century." *Journal of American Studies* 28, no. 1 (1994): 1–22.

———. "Shovel and Shamrock: Irish Workers and Labor Violence in the Digging of the Chesapeake and Ohio Canal." *Labor History* 30, no. 4 (1989): 489–517.

Welke, Barbara Young. *Recasting American Liberty: Gender, Race, Law, and the Railroad Revolution, 1865–1920*. New York: Cambridge University Press, 2001.

West, Elliott. *The Last Indian War: The Nez Perce Story*. New York: Oxford University Press, 2009.

———. "Reconstructing Race." *Western Historical Quarterly* 34 (Spring 2003): 7–26.

West, Joseph A. "Construction of the Union and Central Pacific Railroads across Utah, Fifty-Five Years Ago." *Union Pacific Magazine*, October 6, 1922, 8–10.

"What Shall We Do with Our Boys?" *The Wasp* (San Francisco) 8 (January–June 1882). Courtesy of Bancroft Library, no. 292, 136–37. www.oac.cdlib.org/ark:/13030/hb938nb337/?brand = oac4.

Whicker, John Wesley. *Historical Sketches of the Wabash Valley*. Attica, IN: Printed by author, 1916.

White, Richard. "Are You an Environmentalist or Do You Work for a Living? Work and Nature." In Cronon, *Uncommon Ground*, 171–85.

———. *The Organic Machine: The Remaking of the Columbia River.* New York: Hill and Wang, 1995.

———. *Railroaded: The Transcontinentals and the Making of Modern America.* New York: Norton, 2012.

Whitney, Orson F. *Popular History of Utah.* Salt Lake City: Deseret News, 1916.

Wilentz, Sean. *Chants Democratic: New York City and the Rise of the American Working Class, 1788–1850.* New York: Oxford University Press, 1984.

Williams, John Hoyt. *A Great and Shining Road: The Epic Story of the Transcontinental Railroad.* New York: Times Books, 1988.

Williams, Raymond. *The Country and the City.* New York: Oxford University Press, 1973.

Willumson, Glenn. *Iron Muse: Photographing the Transcontinental Railroad.* Berkeley: University of California Press, 2013.

Winther, Oscar. *The Transportation Frontier, 1865–1890.* New York: Holt, Rinehart, and Winston, 1964.

Wittke, Carl. *The Irish in America.* Baton Rouge: Louisiana State University Press, 1956.

Wood, Gordon S. *The Radicalism of the American Revolution.* New York: Vintage, 1993.

Woodruff, George. *Forty Years Ago: A Contribution to the Early History of Joliet and Will County, Illinois.* Joliet: Goodspeed, 1874.

———. *History of Will County, Illinois.* Chicago: Le Baron, 1878.

Wrobel, David R., and Michael C. Steiner, eds. *Many Wests: Place, Culture, and Regional Identity.* Lawrence: University Press of Kansas, 1997.

Wyman, Mark. *Hoboes: Bindlestiffs, Fruit Tramps, and the Harvesting of the West.* New York: Hill and Wang, 2010.

Wynne, Robert E. *Reaction to the Chinese in the Pacific Northwest and British Columbia, 1850–1910.* New York: Arno, 1978.

Young, David M. *The Iron Horse and the Windy City: How Railroads Shaped Chicago.* Dekalb: Northern Illinois University Press, 2005.

Yun, Lisa. *The Coolie Speaks: Chinese Indentured Laborers and African Slaves in Cuba.* Philadelphia: Temple University Press, 2008.

THESES AND DISSERTATIONS

Borgeson, Richard D. "Irish Canal Laborers in America, 1817–1846." Master's thesis, Pennsylvania State University, 1964.

Buss, James J. "The Winning of the West with Words: Clearing the Middle Ground for American Pioneers." PhD diss., Purdue University, 2007.

Fleming, George. "Canal at Chicago: A Study in Political and Social History." PhD diss., Catholic University of America, 1951.

Garcilazo, Jeffrey Marcos. "'Traqueros': Mexican Railroad Workers in the United States, 1870 to 1930." PhD diss., University of California, Santa Barbara, 1995.

Lightner, David L. "Labor on the Illinois Central Railroad, 1852–1900." PhD diss., Cornell University, 1969.

Murphy, Deirdre. "The Look of a Citizen: Representations of Immigration in Gilded Age Painting and Popular Press Illustration." PhD diss., University of Minnesota, 2007.

Reeder, Clarence. "The History of Utah's Railroads, 1869–1883." PhD diss., University of Utah, 1970.

Richart, J. Lawrence. "A Narrative History of Saint Joseph Church, Terre Haute, Indiana, 1838–1872." Master's thesis, Indiana State University, 1969.

Stevens, Thomas M. "The Union Pacific Railroad and the Mormon Church, 1868–1871: An In-Depth Study of the Financial Aspects of Brigham Young's Grading Contract and Its Ultimate Settlement." Master's thesis, Brigham Young University, 1972.

Tobin, Catherine. "The Lowly Muscular Digger: Irish Canal Workers in Nineteenth-Century America." PhD diss., University of Notre Dame, 1987.

Vimalassery, Manu. "Skew Tracks: Racial Capitalism and the First Transcontinental Railroad." PhD diss., New York University, 2011.

Wallner, Peter A. "Politics and Public Works: A Study of the Pennsylvania Canal System, 1825–1857." PhD diss., Pennsylvania State University, 1973.

Yen, Tzu-Kuei. "Chinese Workers and the First Transcontinental Railroad of the United States of America." PhD diss., St. John's University, 1976.

INDEX

Aarim-Heriot, Najia, 191

accidents. *See also* injuries; fatal, 47, 68, 73–74, 151, 165, 166

Adams, Charles Francis, 179

ad valorem property tax, 21, 211n7

African Americans, 3–4, 88, 116, 169, 175, 209n34, n35, 215n70; enslaved (*see* slavery); free, 3, 194

agency, 79, 153, 207n25, 227n162. *See also* resistance strategies; political, 84–86; through violence and protests, 45, 90, 93, 105–106

Alabama, 59

alcohol use, 35, 40–44, 66, 80–81, 84, 105, 157, 221n57, 222n71, 224n90; Chinese abstention from, 167, 200; disease attributed to, 24, 70–71; ineffective company policies against, 74–75; masculinity and, 13, 40–41, 75, 77, 104, 171–72; Mormon attitudes toward, 121, 141, 146–47; in stereotypes of Irish immigrants, 33, 34, 62, 75–76, 103, 116, 196–97; violence and, 50–51, 99

Alton Courier, 100

American Home Missionary Society, 81, 84

American Revolution, 2, 52

American Seamen's Friend Society, 214n51

American Society of Civil Engineers, 164

Ames, Oliver, 107

Andreas, Alfred T., 73

Andrews, Thomas G., 164, 245n113

Anglo-Americans, 3, 77, 87, 109, 124, 142, 172, 200

Archer, William, 248n17

Archibald, Mary Ann, 31

Arrington, Leonard, 123, 230n12, 233n51

Ashley, James M., 118–19

Athearn, Robert G., 140

Attica (Indiana), 47–48

Auburn (California), 158, 159, 171

Auburn Stars and Stripes, 160

Badin, Stephen, 35, 80

Bain, David Haward, 206n22

Baldwin, Elmer, 69–70, 91–92

Bangs, A. H., 80

Bank of Indiana, 21

Bavaria, 126

Bear River City (Wyoming), 144–45

Becker, Joseph, 180–83, *182, 183*

Bederman, Gail, 12, 110, 209n35

Beers, Robert W., 115

Bennett, Nathaniel, 173–75

Benson, Ezra T., 234n79

bigotry. *See* prejudice, racialization

Billington, Ray Allen, 59

blasting, 7, 24, 72, 88, 145, 157, 159, 162, 186, 205n21; and fictitious reports of racial violence, 188–89; types of explosives used for, 160, 163, 184

Bloomer Cut, 157

Bloomington Intelligencer, 69

Book of Mormon, 108, 123

Boston Pilot, 34, 61–63, 88

Bouck, William C., 53

Crane, James, 138–39

Crawfordsville (Indiana), 210n5

Crocker, Charles, 107, 165, 167–69, 173,
241n33; Strobridge as labor boss for,
156–59, 168, 191, 240n24; Chinese
immigrants hired by, 161–62, 192,
240n22

Crocker, Edwin, 159, 168, 169, 173, 240n22

Crofutt's Trans-continental Tourist's Guide,
147, *149*

Cronon, William, 164, 248n17; *Nature's
Metropolis,* 207n23

Culmann, C. W., 103

Currier and Ives,, *178,* 178–80

Davis, Alice, 138–39

Davis, Joseph, 138–39

deaths of workmen, 2, 7, 54, 75, 104, 105,
162, 168, 170, 196, 198; in accidents, 47,
68, 73–74, 151, 165, 166; from disease,
47, 67–72, 80, 166; from freezing, 151,
165; violent, 45–48, 68, 92, 94

Declaration of Independence, 54

Democratic Party, 39–40, 85–87, 101, 155,
225n127

Denver and Rio Grande Railroad, 235n79,
245n113

Deseret News, 120, 122, 123, 128, 131, 136, 137,
139, 141, 143–44, 238n130

Dickens, Charles, *American Notes for
General Circulation,* 32

Dinnerstein, Leonard, 5

discrimination. *See* prejudice, racialization

diseases. *See* illnesses

ditchdiggers, 3–6, 17, 23–24, 26, 29, 205n21;
bigotry against, 62; masculinity of, 94

Ditz, Toby L., 209n36

Dodge, Gen. Grenville M., 104, 107, 147,
188, 191, 232n41, 246n1, 246–47n3,
247n4

Donner Pass, 163

Donohue, Patrick, 88

Douglas, Stephen, 117–18

Drake, Daniel, 24–25, 67, 212n21

drinking/drunkenness. *See* alcohol use and
abuse

Du Bois, W.E.B., 76

Durant, Thomas, 107

Dutch Flat (NV) Enquirer, 242n60

dysentery, 74

Echo Canyon (Utah), 126–31, 136, 139,
144–45, 199, 230n12

Edmunds-Tucker Act (1887), 199

Elko (Nevada), 166

Elko Independent, 166

Emerson, Ralph Waldo, 34, 180

Emmons, David M., 123, 143

English immigrants, 30–31, 126

Erie Canal, 1–3, 30, 53, 102, 206–207n23,
218n6; completion of, 1, 108; Irish
immigrant workers on, 11, 31, 37, 43, 78;
through Montezuma marshes, 24; route
from New York City to, 26; success of,
canal-building mania following, 18, 195

Evansville (Indiana), 18, 213n37

excavation, 23–25, 163

exceptionalism, American, 10, 26

expansionism, 6–9, 108, 147, 179, 198. *See
also* westward expansion

exploitation, 5, 7, 76, 96–98; of canal
workers, 10, 17, 34–35, 39–40, 43, 45, 55,
70; political, 86, 225n129; of railroad
workers, 129, 133, 161, 168

Fardowns, 22–23, 31, 48–51, 70, 83, 91–92,
226n154

farmers, 17, 28, 29, 66–67, 69, 70, 87, 211n7;
as canal and railroad workers, 3, 25–29,
64; Chinese, 153; German, 26–27, 170;
Irish, 44; Mormon, 128, 135, 140–41,
198; politics of, 86

Farm Ridge (Illinois), 69

Farnsworth, John F., 100

Farnum, Wallace D., 246n3, 247n4

Farr, Lorin, 146, 234n79

fatalities. *See* deaths of workmen

Fiege, Mark, *The Republic of Nature,*
206n22

Fitzhugh, George, 5

Florence (Nebraska), 139, 236n104

Foner, Eric, 26

Foreign Miners' License Tax, 239n11

Fort Wayne (Indiana), 21–22, 25–29, 32, 35,
42, 51–53, 210n5

Fort Wayne Sentinel, 37, 52

Illinois & Michigan (I&M) Canal, 14,
57–98, 102, 103, 196, 218n6, 220n27;
alcohol use on, 74–77; celebration of
opening of, 57–58; contractors on, 28,
42, 66, 75, 222n71, 228n180; disease
outbreaks on, 63, 67–72; economic and
population growth resulting from,
60–61; financing of, 59, 60, 63–65;
ground-breaking for, 58, 197; injuries
on, 72–74; political participation by
workers on, 84–87; recruitment of
workers for, 59–60, 64, 90; religious
observances of workers on, 78–83;
resistance strategies on, 65–67, 95–98;
shanty towns on, 61–62; violence on,
43, 58, 65, 82, 90–95
Illinois River, 60
Illinoistown (California), 151, 156
illnesses, 6, 74, 49, 55, 63, 70–74, 196, 198.
See also cholera, malaria; of Chinese
workers, 156, 166; of Irish workers, 77,
82, 105, 171, 196
immigrants, 3, 5, 6, 8–9, 11–15, 18–19, 67,
207n23, 209n35. *See also* Chinese
immigrants, German immigrants, Irish
immigrants, Mormons, immigrant;
antipathy toward (*see* nativism); exclusion from celebrations of, 53–54, 191;
forced labor of, 194; from Great Britain,
30–31, 41, 126, 139; Italian, 113; Mexican,
4, 109, 158; Mormon attitudes toward,
109–10, 121, 122, 124, 128, 130, 135,
141–42, 146, 150, 199
indentured servitude, 30–31, 242n50
Independence (Missouri), 109
Indiana, 14, 16–56, 80, 132, 191, 195, 197,
205n20. *See also names of municipalities;*
Bank of, 21; canal building in, 18, *20,*
28–29, 61, 67, 132, 211n6 (*see also*
Wabash & Erie Canal); Catholics in, 35,
80; disease outbreaks in, 38–39, 67–68;
General Assembly, 29; impact of 1837
economic panic on, 63, 64; Mammoth
Internal Improvement Act (1836), 21,
54, 59, 210n5; missionaries in, 33; railroad construction in, 21, 34, 101–102;
violence in, 44–45, 47, 77
Indiana Journal, 28

Indianapolis (Indiana), 28, 50, 210
Indianapolis News, 44
Indiana Republican, 212n21
Indians, 16, 52, 93, 109, 117, 164, 186,
205n14; fictional representations in
pictorial journalism of, 147, *148, 178,*
179, 180; Irish immigrants compared to,
33, 80; Wabash & Erie Canal built on
lands of, 18, 21, 210n5
industrialization, 4, 9, 11, 28, 130, 186. *See*
also capitalism, industrial; separation of
physical production from cultural
consumption in, 180; technology and,
183, 185; voting with one's feet in
response to, 66–67
injuries, 72–73, 158, 167, 196, 198. *See also*
accidents
internal improvements, 1, 2, 8, 17, 73, 105,
106, 203n1. *See also* canals, railroads;
financing of, 21, 54, 59, 194, 196, 210n5;
Mormon attitudes toward, 110, 123, 198;
politics of, 85, 225n127
Iowa, 59
Irish Emigrant Association, 60, 219n10
Irish immigrants, 2, 8–9, 22–51, 62–106,
108, 132, 152, 186, 227n161, 237n127;
alcohol use and abuse by, 33–35, 40–44,
66, 74–78, 80–81, 84, 105, 171–72,
221n57, 222n71; allies of, 33–34, 88–89,
105; antagonism between Chinese and,
168, 188–89, *192;* Catholicism of, 30–32,
34, 60, 77–85, 88, 91–93, 225n122;
Chinese laborers as alternative to,
158–59, 162, 163, 168–71, 177; on
Erie Canal construction crews, 11, 31;
exploitation of, 35–38, 62; illnesses and
injuries of, 24–25, 35, 67–74, 221n57;
ignored in story of American progress,
17, 54–56, 58, 104, 114, 191, 195; living
conditions of, 25, 34–35, 37–38, 62–63;
masculine identity of, 14, 34, 39; Mormons and, 111, 120, 122–25, 127, 131,
133–34, 142–45, 147, 237n128; othering
of, 114; as perpetrators and victims of
violence, 22, 34, 41, 44–47, 51, 58, 60,
76–77, 81–82, 94–95, 105–106 (*see*
also Corkonians; Fardowns); politics
of, 39–40, 85–87, 101, 225n127, n129;

prejudice against, 16, 33–35, 40, 46–48, 88–90, 102–103, 106, 116, 156, 157, 197; racialization of, 3–4, 6, 76–77, 87–88, 101, 196–98, 215n70; recruitment for canal and railroad construction of, 27–34, 36–37, 59–60, 64, 90; resistance strategies of, 54–55, 65–67, 82–83, 88–101, 197–98, 227n162

Jacksonian democracy, 39, 86
Jacobs, Zebulon, 127, 128
Jeffersonville (Indiana), 210n5
Jensen, Jens Iver, 127
Jersey City (New Jersey), 33
John Bright (ship), 121, 126
Johnson, Andrew, 157, 160
Johnson, James, 40
Johnston, John, 53
Johnston, Wayne A., 103–104
Joliet (Illinois), 94, 101

Kaskaskia Indians, 80
Kearney, Denis, 177, 186
Kelley, Patrick, 87
Kentucky, 59
Kesler, Frederick, 139, 236n104
Kidder, Daniel P., 115
Kilgore, David, 54
Kirtland (Ohio), 109
Knight, Celestial Roberts, 121–22
Knobel, Dale T., 87, 225n122

labor agents, 27, 32, 33, 159, 166, 169
labor markets, 10, 44, 55, 76, 196; impact of Chinese in, 177, 191; uncertain, 39, 64 (*see also* labor shortages)
labor shortages in, 25, 30, 59, 74, 96–97, 158, 168
Lafayette (Indiana), 37, 40, 52, 210n5
Lagro (Indiana), 35, 41; Irish War in, 22–23, 47, 49–51, 77, 91
Lalor, William, 26
land grants, 21, 53, 59, 113, 218n7
Laramie (Wyoming), 122, 125, 127, 136
Larson, John Lauritz, 203n1
LaSalle (Illinois), 59, 70, 80, 91–93, 99–101
Lawrenceburg Palladium, 25
Lazenby, John, 127

Leavitt, David, 97, 220n35, 227n161
Leslie, Frank. See *Frank Leslie's Illustrated Newspaper*
Lewis, Samuel, 27
Lewis, Zimri, 92
liberalism, classical, 3
Limerick, Patricia Nelson, 115
Lincoln, Abraham, 104, 118
Lindley, Philo, 74
living conditions, 32, 60–62, 70, 104–105. *See also* construction camps, shanty towns; workers' efforts to control working conditions and. *See* agency, resistance stragies
Lockport (Illinois), 58, 73, 81, 85, 227n161
Lockport (New York), 31, 195
Logansport (Indiana), 35
Longfords. *See* Fardowns
Loomis, A. W., 166–67
Louisiana, 59
Lynch, Daniel, 97–98, 227n162
lynching, 100

Madison (Indiana), 210n5
malaria, 24, 67–71, 74, 221n57
Manhattan (ship), 127
manhood/manliness. *See* masculinity
Marryat, Frederick, 37–38
Marseilles (Illinois), 91
Marshall, Thomas, 123
Marxism, 10
masculinity, 9, 11–14, 54, 73, 88, 197, 209; alcohol use and, 40–42, 75, 77, 104, 172; American images and rhetoric of, 5, 17, 29, 39, 54–55, 89, 94, 96–97, 116, 191; based on danger and risk, 72–73; of Chinese immigrants, 168, 173, 175–77, 186–87, 199, 200; in Irish construction of identity, 34, 38–41, 46, 72–75, 77, 82, 84, 101; Mormon, 110–12, 125, 134, 136–39, 146–47, 149, 150, 199; violence and, 46, 82, 83, 90, 94–95, 101, 105
Mason, Roswell B., 69, 100–101, 104, 219n10
Matteson, Joel, 100–101, 228n180
Maumee City Express, 33
Maumee River, 18
McCafferty, Josiah, 44

slavery, 3, 56, 63, 120, 160, 194, 210; apologists for, 5; Chinese, 170, 176; contract labor compared to, 26, 90, 96–97, 106, 140, 155, 195, 197; prohibition in Western territories of, 117

smallpox, 165

Smith, Joseph, 108–109, 233n50

Smoot, W. C. A., 188

South Dakota, 59

Springfield Republican, 151, 229n1

Stanford, Leland, 107, 133, 151, 157, 160, 161, 167, 169, 232n41, 238n130

Stanford University, 229n6

State Bank of Illinois, 64

Stenhouse, T. B. H., 115

stereotypes, 11, 47, 106, 150, 186, 189; gender, 10

Stewart, Levi, 234n79

Story, Albert, 99–100

Story, Talmadge, and Conklin contracting firm, 228n175

Stout, Arthur B., 156

strikes, 14, 74, 94, 136; of Chinese immigrants, 168–69, 192–93; of Irish immigrants, 60, 66, 90, 95–98, 144, 155, 159, 162, 197, 227n162, 237n128

Strobridge, James Harvey, 156–59, 161, 165, 168, 175, 191, 240n22, n24, 241n30, n33

Stuart, Robert, 65, 68, 97, 98, 227n161

subcontractors, Mormon, 111, 130–31, 133, 234n79

suffrage, 3, 39, 85, 87, 199

Supreme Court, U.S., 53

Sweeney, Edward, 92

Swift, William H., 65, 102, 220n35, 227n161

Switzerland, 126

Taiping Rebellion, 153

taxes, 21, 25, 176, 211n7, 239n11

Taylor, George Rogers, 210–11n6

Taylor, John, 123, 124

Teng Wo Company, 173

Tennessee, 59

Terre Haute (Indiana), 210n5

Thomas, Jesse B., 196

Thompson, E. P., 207n25

Thornton, Jacob, 64

Toano (Nevada), 166

Tobin, Catherine, 97, 227n157, n162

Tocqueville, Alexis de, 16

Toledo (Ohio), 18

Tong Wars, 172–73

tourists, 15, 58, 179, 180; guides for, *112, 114, 147, 149*

tracklayers, 3, 131, 133, *134,* 140, 158, 205n21, 240n24, 245n3; Chinese, 142, 186; hostility of western residents to, 5; Irish, Mormon attitudes toward, 112, 130, 135, 144

transcontinental railroad, 2, 9, 121, 194, 229n5. *See also* Central Pacific Railroad, Union Pacific Railroad; ceremony and celebrations for completion of, 1, 108–109, 146–47, *148, 149,* 173, 175, 205–206n21; Mormon labor on, 125, 128, 140, 150; national media stories on and images of, 177–78, 183, *184*

transient laborers, 10, 13, 26, 29–31, 101, 224n90; census data lacking on, 31, 143; disease outbreaks among, 24–25, 67, 70; exclusion from celebrations of, 53, 200; immigrant, 15, 30 (*see also* Chinese immigrants; Irish immigrants); living conditions for, 61–62; masculinity of, 5, 9, 77, 131, 136; Mormons and, 110, 124, 129, 135–36, 140, 199; religion and, 15, 35, 78; slaves compared to, 195; violence of, 50, 91; working conditions of, 23–24, 50

Trollope, Frances, 16, 41, 44–45

Trott, Douglas, 46–47

Troy (New York), 37

Truckee (California), 167

tunnels, 23, 163–65, 189, *110,* 237n128, 242n58; in Echo and Weber canyons, 126, 129, 131, 144–45

Turner, Frederick Jackson, 8, 15, 51

Twain, Mark, 167–68

Tyler, John, 53

typhus, 74

Union Emigrant Society, 60, 213n44

Union Pacific Railroad, 14, 110, 120–50, *134, 137, 138,* 179, 198, 206n22, 241n30; Dodge as chief engineer of, 107, 147, 188, 232n41, 246n1, 246–47n3, 247n4; federal land grants and bonds for, 112,

Woodruff, Alson, 92, 226n154
Woodruff, Wilford, 126, 199
Woodworth, James H., 57–58
work camps. *See* construction camps,
 shanty towns
working conditions, 34–37, 40, 60; diseases
 associated with, 24, 63, 67, 69, 81;
 oppressive, 3, 17, 44, 50, 65, 72, 104;
 protests of (*see* protests; strikes); violent
 conflicts over, 99–100, 105–106; workers' efforts to control living conditions
 and (*see* agency; resistance stragies)
Workingman's Advocate, 171
Workingmen's Party of California, 177,
 200
Wright, Benjamin, 218n6
Württemberg, 126
Wyman, Mark, 67
Wyoming, 7, 121, 125, 127, 141

Yeager, Walter, 181, 183–85, *184*
Young, Brigham, 109, 119, 120, 133–34,
 144–45, 232n41; invitation to Promontory Point celebration declined
 by, 146; at mass meeting on railroad,
 123–25; polygamy practiced by, 116,
 231–32n16; theocratic leadership of
 Mormons by, 115, 117, 121, 231n19,
 233n50; Union Pacific Railroad's
 contracts with, 111, 123, 126, 128, 133,
 139
Young, Brigham, Jr., 128
Young, John W., 127, 128, 238n130
Young, Joseph A., 128–29, 131, *132*, 145,
 234n79

Zion. *See* Mormons
Zion's Cooperative Mercantile Institution,
 233n50

9 780520 284609